Descending on Humanity and Intervening in History

Descending on Humanity and Intervening in History

Notes from the Pulpit Ministry of P. T. Forsyth

Edited and introduced by
Jason A. Goroncy

Foreword by
David Fergusson

◆PICKWICK *Publications* • Eugene, Oregon

DESCENDING ON HUMANITY AND INTERVENING IN HISTORY
Notes from the Pulpit Ministry of P. T. Forsyth

Copyright © 2013 Jason A. Goroncy. All rights reserved. Except for brief quotations in critical publications or reviews, no part of this book may be reproduced in any manner without prior written permission from the publisher. Write: Permissions, Wipf and Stock Publishers, 199 W. 8th Ave., Suite 3, Eugene, OR 97401.

Pickwick Publications
An Imprint of Wipf and Stock Publishers
199 W. 8th Ave., Suite 3
Eugene, OR 97401

www.wipfandstock.com

ISBN 13: 978-1-60899-070-2

Cataloguing-in-Publication data:

Forsyth, Peter Taylor, 1848–1921.

Descending on humanity and intervening in history : notes from the pulpit ministry of P. T. Forsyth / edited and introduced by Jason A. Goroncy ; foreword by David Fergusson.

xx + 374 pp. ; 23 cm. Includes bibliographical references and index.

ISBN 13: 978-1-60899-070-2

1. Forsyth, Peter Taylor, 1848–1921. 2. Preaching. 3. Theology. I. Goroncy, Jason A. II. Fergusson, David. III. Title.

BX7260 F583 2013

Manufactured in the U.S.A.

Excerpt from "Out of the Blue" from *Poems 1975–1995: Hail! Madam Jazz and a Fragile City*, copyright 1999 by Micheal O'Siadhail, reprinted by permission of Bloodaxe Books. All rights reserved.

Excerpt from "Little Gidding" from *Four Quartets*, copyright 1942 by T. S. Eliot and renewed 1970 by Esme Valerie Eliot, reprinted by permission of Houghton Mifflin Harcourt Publishing Company. All rights reserved.

Excerpt from "I Sleep a Lot" from *The Collected Poems, 1931–1987*, copyright 1988 by Czesław Miłosz, reprinted by permission of HarperCollins Publishers. All rights reserved.

To Samuel Jamieson and Ambrie Jordyn,
witnesses to God's surprising joy.

Lord, how can man preach thy eternall word?
He is a brittle crazie glass:
Yet in thy temple thou dost him afford
This glorious and transcendent place,
To be a window, through thy grace.

GEORGE HERBERT

Contents

Foreword by David Fergusson | xi
Preface | xiii
Acknowledgments | xix

I. Preaching *Sub Specie Crucis* | 1

II. Published Sermons | 67

   1 The Turkish Atrocities, 1876 | 69
   2 Mercy the True and Only Justice, 1877 | 75
   3 The Strength of Weakness, 1878 | 86
   4 The Bible Doctrine of Hell and the Unseen, 1879 | 94
   5 Egypt: A Sermon for Young Men, 1882 | 102
   6 Pessimism, 1884 | 109
   7 The Argument for Immortality Drawn from the Nature of Love: A Lecture on Lord Tennyson's "Vastness," 1885 | 119
   8 The Pulpit and the Age, 1885 | 131
   9 Sunday-Schools and Modern Theology, 1887 | 145
  10 Preaching and Poetry, 1890 | 157
  11 Mystics and Saints, 1894 | 164
  12 The Way of Life, 1897 | 169
  13 The Empire for Christ, 1900 | 178
  14 The Slowness of God, 1900 | 197
  15 An Allegory of the Resurrection, 1902 | 204

16 Dumb Creatures and Christmas: A Little Sermon to Little Folk, 1903 | 224

17 The Problem of Forgiveness in the Lord's Prayer, 1903 | 227

18 Christ at the Gate, 1908 | 239

19 Christ Our Sanctification, 1911 | 255

20 Things New and Old, 1913 | 259

21 Music and Worship, 1914 | 270

22 Our Experience of a Triune God, 1914 | 277

23 The Meaning of a Sinless Christ, 1923 | 283

Sources for Published Sermons | 299

III. Unpublished Sermons | 301

1 Sermon on Philippians 4:4 | 303

2 Sermon on Matthew 7:21 | 305

3 Sermon on Hebrews 11:17–19 | 307

4 Sermon on 1 Peter 4:19 | 309

5 Sermon on Psalm 55:6 and Jeremiah 9:2 | 311

6 Sermon on Luke 11:9 | 313

7 Sermon on Psalm 130:1 | 315

8 Sermon on 1 Timothy 4:7 | 317

9 Sermon on 2 Corinthians 4:17–18 | 319

10 Sermon on Luke 17:10 | 321

11 Sermon on Acts 22:11 | 323

12 Sermon on 2 Timothy 4:7 | 325

13 Sermon on Psalm 32:8 | 327

14 Sermon on 1 Timothy 3:15 | 329

15 Sermon on Psalm 146:3 | 330

16 Sermon on Ecclesiasticus 2:18 | 332

17 Sermon on Romans 8:28 | 334

18 Sermon on Philippians 3:12 | 336

19 Sermon on Mark 14:3 | 338
20 Sermon on Revelation 2:28 | 340
21 Sermon on John 3:4 | 342
22 Sermon on Mark 12:43–44 | 344
23 Sermon on Luke 10:41–42 | 346
24 Sermon (Valedictory Address) on 1 Corinthians 4:1 | 349
25 Sermon (Ordination Address) on John 17:6 | 352

Bibliography | 357
Name Index | 365
Scripture Index | 371

Foreword

Peter Taylor Forsyth is a theologian whose work resists easy categorisation. Born and educated in the northeast of Scotland, he ministered and taught for the remainder of his life in England. A leading scholar of his day, he worked outside the established churches and universities of Britain. Although an exponent of the fashionable kenotic Christology of his day, he was impatient with many of the theological trends of the late nineteenth and early twentieth centuries, choosing to stand apart from these. Working independently of the German dialectical theologians, he reached conclusions that were strikingly similar in important respects. Versed in the traditions of European systematic theology, his writings were often unsystematic, occasional, and epigrammatic. Possessed of a rigorous scholarly intellect, he could write in ways that were expansive and elusive. For many years a pastor and preacher, his theological work was embedded in the life of the churches he served. That context for constructive theology is not shared by many in the guild today.

Yet it was those just same tensions that proved adequate to the tasks of theology in his day. The social and political upheavals of Europe during and after the Great War disturbed the convictions of many Christian intellectuals. A more critical theology was required that both displayed a greater degree of political suspicion but also had the confidence to return to the Bible and the theological tradition in the expectation that these would continue to assail the Church. In particular, the person and work of Christ could only be attested with fresh conviction especially when informed by a sense of divine holiness and transcendence. In this context, Forsyth's theology had a jarring effect. Intended to discompose, it could neither be ignored nor lightly dismissed. Once likened to a fireworks display in the fog, his thought is both complex and arresting.

Over a century later, we can recognise that his preaching and writing in the late Victorian period had a prescient effect, these coming into their own with the traumas of the twentieth century. Such qualities may explain the enduring value of his work and why he continues to be read with profit.

Foreword

Perhaps we should not be surprised that he speaks forcefully to Christians in different parts of the world today.

This collection of sermons, assembled and expertly introduced by Jason Goroncy, reveals the blending of theologian, pastor, and preacher in P. T. Forsyth. At a time of fragmentation, when theological study has become too much removed from the task of the preacher, Forsyth's work can remind us of the invigorating power of Christian doctrine interpreted and expounded in situations of pastoral and political exigency. Its capacity for the renewal of the Church is evident again from this rich collection.

How do we confront and challenge our congregations without losing their pastoral loyalty? That difficult question should not be evaded. Forsyth faced it, perhaps at some personal cost to his health, as he laboured at preaching to his congregations "in season and out of season." His sermons continue to repay study for those who regard the theological content of preaching as belonging to the *esse* of the Church in every day and generation.

—David Fergusson

Preface

In a 1972 review of Marvin Anderson's edited volume, *The Gospel and Authority: A P. T. Forsyth Reader*, Clifford McKay noted that "the journals for which [Forsyth] wrote are not readily available to the pastor and theologian who would like to read Forsyth; therefore, this volume is invaluable in making this material accessible."[1] An analogous agenda has birthed the motivation for this volume, too. The previously published sermons and preaching-related essays amassed herein were gathered mostly from newspapers by-and-large long out of production—*The Christian World Pulpit*, *Shipley and Saltaire Times*, *Wesleyan Methodist Magazine*, *Christian World*, *Congregational Quarterly*, *Cambridge Christian Life*, and *The Expositor*. Others, such as *The Expository Times*, continue, albeit in a somewhat different form from that established by James Hastings in 1889. Some of the previously published material, and all of the previously unpublished material, was ferreted out of abandoned filing cabinets and neglected cardboard boxes in church storerooms and home basements in Shipley, Leicester, Cambridge, and Adelaide, and from archives housed in local libraries in Bradford and Manchester. Woe to those who would shut down such invaluable public depositories!

Perhaps some explanation is warranted here regarding the decision to include certain sermons and so to exclude others. Of the previously published material, I have sought to include some of what the modest researcher or Forsyth reader may find difficult to source and which communicates most readily to our day. Keeping within some reasonable space limits for a single volume, I have also tried to offer a sample of sermons across a range of topics, and which span the full calendar of Forsyth's public life. Some may wish to question whether Forsyth's sermon, "Mercy the true and only Justice," ought to be included in such a collection because in some respects it represents, perhaps more than any other single piece of Forsyth's published writing, an example of the very "gospel" that the bulk of his literary output was concerned to debunk: those features of

1. McKay, Review of *The Gospel and Authority*, 409.

Ritschlianism of which his more mature work represents the most radical departure.[2] But this in itself, it seems to me, is precisely among the reasons that it ought to be included—to underscore the real-time journey that Forsyth made, and the transformation that grace effected in him along the way. But there is at least one further reason: this collection attempts, albeit in a most subtle way, to trace something of a story, and of the way that certain themes—those central and those less so—in Forsyth's mind would be chewed over, ingested, honed, matured, and, in some cases, inverted, as was the case with the relationship in his mind between mercy and justice. In addition to the sermons, the inclusion of several essays seems appropriate, given ongoing conversations around these subjects in our day, and the proximity of the subjects to preaching in the life of the gathered community. The latter is not surprising given that each of these essays were penned very much with preachers in mind, a fact underscored as each found a home in ministry-related journals. Three essays—"Preaching and Poetry," "Mystics and Saints," and "The Slowness of God"—appeared in *The Expository Times*. "Christ our Sanctification" was published in *Wesleyan Methodist Magazine*, and "Music and Worship" in the American journal *Homiletic Review*. "The Problem of Forgiveness in the Lord's Prayer" appeared in a collection of essays concerned with "practical exposition of the Lord's Prayer." The decision to include the posthumously published essay, "The Meaning of a Sinless Christ," was not only because therein Forsyth engages with some specific challenges faced by contemporary proclamation, but also to make available to a wider public the final essay in a series of essays that Forsyth penned on "The Preaching of Jesus and the Gospel of Christ" (a series which began in the *Expositor* in 1915), the first six of which were readily available from New Creation Publications in a volume published in 1987 and which includes a fine Foreword, Biographical Sketch, and Theological Introduction by Noel Due.

A note about the title of this volume is also in order. The phrase "descending on men and intervening in history" appears in Forsyth's Yale lectures.[3] In the section wherein the phrase appears, Forsyth was concerned about religious liberalism's tendency towards vagueness and detachment from a more intellectually and morally rigorous or "positive" religion that speaks to the deep crises of human history and experience. The former understands

---

2. To be sure, those familiar with Forsyth's later work will find in this sermon from 1877 numerous traces of the beginning of what he would later articulate more fully as a basic conviction of his soteriology—that God's "infinite purity is not the source of infinite indignation, but of infinite, insatiable redemption." Forsyth, *Mercy the true and only Justice*, 12. Reprinted in this volume, 75–85.

3. Forsyth, *Positive Preaching and the Modern Mind*, 165.

Christ to be the product rather than the creator of the Church, reduces the history of redemption to "the ascending history of the race developed with God's aid,"[4] and begins from ideas and ends in the theological suicide of positive belief and distinctive experience.[5] The so-called "positive" theology of the New Testament, however, is, he argues, chiefly concerned with God's action of overcoming human sin and, relatedly, with the hallowing of God's own name in the creation in order that God might hear an echo of himself therefrom. Whereas the former merely proposes prerequisites for and conditions of reconciliation, the latter bears witness to the reconciliation that has already taken place in Jesus Christ, trumpeting that we are already in a healed situation and "not merely in a world in process of empirical reconciliation."[6] Also, the gospel descends on, rather than arises from, us:

> It is not a projection of [our] innate spirituality. It is revealed, not discovered, not invented. It is of grace, not works. It is conferred, not attained. It is a gift to our poverty, not a triumph of our resource. It is something which holds us, it is not something that we hold. It is something that saves us, and nothing that we have to save. Its Christ is a Christ sent to us and not developed from us, bestowed on our need and not produced from our strength, and He is given for our sin more than for our weakness.[7]

So Forsyth could describe the experience of faith as that which rests on God's finished work and then "takes a line," appealing to "our moral mettle" and calling us not to mere consideration and pondering but to "moral verve and vigilance," to stake the entirety of our being and eternity on selection, decision, and committal.[8] This choice, Forsyth averred, depicts a gulf faced by preachers, a gulf that Forsyth believed is as wide and as irreconcilable as that between being a herald of the gospel and an advocate of culture. The former, Forsyth said, "will make you strangers and sojourners in the world, the other citizens of the world . . . One will make you apostles of Christ, and one will make you champions of humanity. One will make you severe with yourself, one will make you tender with yourself. One will commend you to the naughty people, and one will commend you to the nice." He continues:

> Now of these two tendencies one means the destruction of preaching. If it cease to be God's word, descending on men and

---

4. Forsyth, *The Principle of Authority*, 222.
5. Forsyth, *Positive Preaching and the Modern Mind*, 142.
6. Forsyth, *The Work of Christ*, 182.
7. Forsyth, *Positive Preaching and the Modern Mind*, 144.
8. Ibid., 165.

Preface

intervening in history, then it will cease as an institution in due time. It may become lecturing, or it may become oratory, but as preaching it must die out with a positive Gospel. People cannot be expected to treat a message of insight from man to man as they do a message of revelation from God to man. An age cannot be expected to treat a message from another age as they treat a message from Eternal God to every age. Men with the passion of the present cannot be expected to listen even to a message from humanity as they would to one from God. And if humanity redeem itself you will not be able to prevent each member of it from feeling that he is his own redeemer.[9]

In other words, Forsyth sees at stake here nothing less than the nature of the gospel *as grace*, as that foreign word that descends and intrudes and makes alive, rather than that which arises from our own situation and in the end merely coddles a *frondeur* race in its blindness and recalcitrance. The latter promises to raise the dead while having nothing but death's machinery with which to do so—machinery reluctant, moreover, either to name the corpse *as corpse* or even to attend to the right grave. But not so the preacher of grace, the preacher who, with words given, names a thing for what it is and by such naming participates in grace's continuing event by which all things are being made new. To so recall Forsyth's plea here is to recall that he was, of course, ministering at a time when the theology of the day was radically out of joint with the situation confronting the human community in Europe, when the easy optimism heralded as the new orthodoxy was about to be crushed under the press of catastrophic historical events. In response, Forsyth attacked the amorality of established theology and raised a too-lonely voice in plea for a staurocentric theology of redemption.

Those familiar with Forsyth's work will know that he (and/or his editors!) was grammatically inconsistent throughout his writings. For example, while he mostly capitalizes references to the Cross, there is no shortage of places where the lower case is used. Conversely, often the upper case is used for a common noun. In most cases, I have decided to leave such inconsistencies unchanged from the original. Inconsistencies also abound in matters of grammar and spelling (both British and American English are used, for example). Again, I have retained (with few exeptions) the grammar and spelling used in the original publications. Also left unaltered from the original is the somewhat awkward Bible referencing that appears at various times. This is the most odd in the sermon, "The Bible Doctrine of Hell and the Unseen." Where noticed, words and names obviously misspelled have been corrected, though

---

9. Ibid., 165–66.

many words and spellings now archaic have been left unchanged. If nothing else, they are a reminder that we are reading outside our own century.

I have also sought, where possible, to include in footnotes some basic information about titles, quotations, or peculiar phrases cited by Forsyth. Unless otherwise attributed, all the footnotes throughout this volume are mine. I hope that this will assist readers to make further connections with and between Forsyth's ideas, and researchers to trace fruitful trajectories in Forsyth's thought.

Finally, a confession: this book represents something of the overflow of my own joy in discovering in P. T. Forsyth a pastor to pastors and a sojourner set free to roam in all those places where the radiance of the crucified, resurrected, and ascended God burns away the dross and makes all things new. As C. S. Lewis also supposed, such joy simply must be shared lest the enjoyment be cut off ahead of its "appointed consummation":

> I think we delight to praise what we enjoy because the praise not merely expresses but completes the enjoyment; it is its appointed consummation. It is not out of compliment that lovers keep on telling one another how beautiful they are; the delight is incomplete till it is expressed. It is frustrating to have discovered a new author and not to be able to tell anyone how good he is; to come suddenly, at the turn of the road, upon some mountain valley of unexpected grandeur and then to have to keep silent because the people with you care for it no more than for a tin can in the ditch; to hear a good joke and find no one to share it with.[10]

Dear reader, in such a spirit I offer this volume to you.

---

10. Lewis, *Reflections on the Psalms*, 81.

Acknowledgments

I AM GRATEFUL TO Geoffrey Bingham, Dean Carter, and Noel Due for first introducing me to the work of P. T. Forsyth; to Willy Carter-Golin, Rindy Hogger, Theng Huat Leow, Steve Holmes, Janet Smith, and Michael Jensen for their assistance in sourcing some of the material included in this volume; to Alan Sell and Rick Floyd for casting constructive eyes over the Introduction; and to Lol Bettany, Catherine van Dorp, and Jill Pope for their editorial assistance with its various parts. Many thanks too to David Fergusson for contributing the Foreword, and to the team at Wipf and Stock for the flexible manner with which they have related to this book's editor, especially when the "stuff of life" has necessitated repeated postponement of deadlines. Finally, my deepest thanks to my partner Judy and to our ambrosial progeny—Sinead, Samuel, and Ambrie—for the patience with which they have lived with this book's editor, particularly when "the book" has meant some postponement of lunch.

—Jason A. Goroncy
Dunedin

1

Preaching *Sub Specie Crucis*

An Introduction to the Preaching Ministry of P. T. Forsyth

JASON A. GORONCY

It was not always so, but even fewer sermons than poems today find a home in published form. This is not altogether to be lamented, for while the sermon manuscript may still speak, as it were, and while sermons continue to find extended voice via other media, the sermon itself remains an unrepeatable *event*. Such an avowal may appear a strange way to introduce a collection of "old" sermons, but the author of the forty-eight creations gathered in this volume would have insisted on no less a claim being made at the outset. He who once described preaching as "the Gospel prolonging and declaring itself" and as "a creative sacrament by the medium of a consecrated personality," and the preacher as "a hierophant from the holiest place" and "a living oracle of God,"[1] knew well that the Word of God is ever a dynamic and free personality who, in the proclamation of the apostolic message, "makes and unmakes us," who creates and "does not simply elicit" the power to answer him.[2] Clearly, the *event* of which I speak here is not an

---

1. Forsyth, *Positive Preaching and the Modern Mind*, 1, 3; Forsyth, *The Church and the Sacraments*, 142.

2. Forsyth, *The Preaching of Jesus and the Gospel of Christ*, 80.

I: Preaching Sub Specie Crucis

event owned by history. Rather, it is the action of the living God upon and in history who, in the sheer freedom of his holy benediction and felicity, unveils to and for human persons. This is to give history its proper due, to take it seriously, to receive its offerings with thanksgiving, and to resist the temptation to make an idol out of its parts or personalities. Of course, a volume like the one in your hands seeks to bespeak something else about history too, and about God; namely, that societies or persons which ignore or abandon their heritage are societies or persons which have abandoned any soteriology that involves time. This is a particular problem for those who wish to claim any interest in God. "A people without history," wrote T. S. Eliot in *Little Gidding*, "is not redeemed from time."[3] Eliot might properly be read here as saying, "To lose one's history is to be condemned to an 'unredeemed' condition, to absolute bondage to the temporal process."[4] This is not to encourage a kind of gross nostalgia or veneration of persons. On the contrary, it is to confess that our ability or otherwise to be liberated from the ways in which the present and the imagined future might serve to ensnare us requires that we engage in an ongoing work of historical awareness. It is in part towards this end, to the end of not losing one's history and so one's self, that this book is directed. But only in part.

In his essay "On the Reading of Old Books," C. S. Lewis gave voice to "a strange idea abroad that in every subject the ancient books should be read only by the professionals, and that the amateur should content himself with the modern books." "This mistaken preference for the modern books and this shyness of the old ones," he continued, "is nowhere more rampant than in theology."[5] Here Lewis encouraged his readers to maintain a balanced diet in their reading habits. We 'moderns' would do well to heed Lewis' advice not only in overcoming our shyness for classic texts but also in reading contemporary work in light of and alongside those words which have stood the test of time, which help us to see and hear again—as if for the first time—the eternal truths upon which rest the heavens and the earths. I suspect that few, if any, readers of P. T. Forsyth (1848–1921) will require convincing of Lewis' observation that the only palliative to the "characteristic blindness of the twentieth century . . . is to keep the clean sea breeze of the centuries blowing through our minds, and this can be done only by reading old books. Not, of course, that there is any magic about the past. People were no cleverer then than they are now; they made as many mistakes as we. But not the same

---

3. Eliot, *Four Quartets*, 58.

4. I am indebted to Rowan Williams for this point; see Williams, *Resurrection*, 30.

5. Lewis, "Introduction," 3. Lewis' essay, first published in 1944, was republished in Lewis, *God in The Dock*.

I: Preaching Sub Specie Crucis

mistakes . . . To be sure, the books of the future would be just as good a corrective as the books of the past, but unfortunately we cannot get at them."[6]

To return to Forsyth, there can be little doubt that one of the real gifts that this great Congregationalist and Edwardian theologian bequeathed to the Church is the encouragement of her ministers to forego the "affable bustle"[7] that would see them running errands for the culture motivated in no small part by an attempt to convince the world—and the Church!—of the use, value and worthiness of their vocation, and to instead give themselves wholly to echo and bear witness to divinely-ordained foolishness—what Forsyth calls "the Folly of the Cross"[8]—and to trust the outcome to God. Those who carry the burden—a joyous burden to be sure, but a burden nonetheless—of preaching week after week will no doubt be familiar with that anxiety that attends the sweat marks staining the manuscript, the fruit of one's wrestling with the very impossible possibility of the preacher's task[9]—which is nothing less than witness to and confession of God's self-disclosure—of addressing those not only desperate to hear the Word of life but also those long deafened by the drums of seemingly endless counter-words, that feeling that despite all one's best efforts the fire that burns so freshly in the heart of the biblical witness has all but been snuffed out by the time the sermon is made public. Such an experience is not uncommon among ministers; nor is the quest for some trustworthy guides. The pulpit is a demanding mistress!

A generation after Douglas Horton discovered Karl Barth's *Das Wort Gottes und die Theologie* in the library of the Harvard Divinity School and in Barth's "strange new world" a potent alternative to the dehydrated humanism in which he had been trained, Browne Barr, who later taught homiletics at Yale, made a similar discovery in 1944 when, as a green minister in a recently-vacated parsonage he found himself among old-looking and left behind books which lined the study walls where the "practice pulpit set up by his predecessor . . . faced the street."[10] He reasoned:

> The church was in such poor shape—no worship center, no 16mm projector, no personality games in the youth society or new signs

---

6. Ibid., 5.

7. Forsyth, *The Preaching of Jesus and the Gospel of Christ*, 119.

8. Forsyth, *Missions in State and Church*, 338; see also Forsyth, "The Foolishness of Preaching," 153–54.

9. As articulated so powerfully by Karl Barth in "The Need and Promise of Christian Preaching," and "The Word of God and the Task of the Ministry"; and by Dietrich Bonhoeffer in *Spiritual Care*, 85–86.

10. Barr, "P. T. Forsyth: The Preachers' Theologian," 37.

I: Preaching Sub Specie Crucis

on the front lawn—because the old minister, the stricken one, was a Britisher who simply was not up-to-date, modern. It was obvious he did not understand American needs nor use contemporary methods. There wasn't a single flannel cloth board in the whole church or parsonage, but he certainly had a lot of books! The young man glanced at the titles and his eye fell on one about "preaching" and the "modern mind." He picked it up and flipped a few pages into it . . . He remained there transfixed for a long time . . . He read until darkness and cold woke him to the hours' passing. He tucked that single volume under his arm and went down out of the attic and through the cold house and into the street. He had found the place where he was to study and practice to be a preacher for the next years of his life. He had also found the man, then dead 23 years, who was to be his instructor.[11]

The cause of the hypnosis was Forsyth's *Positive Preaching and [the] Modern Mind*. In many ways the origin of the book in your hands lies in a similar experience (or, more accurately, in a series of such experiences) in myself half a century and more since Barr's encounter with "the homiletician's theologian."[12] While sitting at a Melbourne bus stop some years before I entered pastoral ministry, the last bus for the evening had long departed before I looked up from my first reading of Forsyth's *The Justification of God*. During those late hours, I was given to see myself as one having been carried into the very crisis where God and the world meet. There was something arresting, too, about Forsyth's style. It seemed to simultaneously bear witness to the elusive nature of divine truth and to open up that space which had been cleared and invite—nay, command—me to enter, or, better still, to find myself already in, the new landscape created by the crisis, the view of and from which was entirely unexpected. Moreover, as I came to learn, this landscape, satiated as it is with the occupation of holy love, rendered hollow and disenchanting much of what my reading of theology had taught me, and what my own arrogance had assured me, and underlined the impotence of all creaturely aspirations, including and perhaps especially religion, to speak to the real issues facing human persons, their consciences and their communities. Here, I was confronted with a Word that one could live by with the honesty and integrity that being human demands, a Word which faced the world and not only a select minority within it living, as it were, in an ark, a Word destined to be made public to those living in the cynicism and despondency of the time, and of all times.

11. Ibid., 36–37.
12. Ibid., 38.

I: Preaching Sub Specie Crucis

Words from Czesław Miłosz come readily to mind: "I have read many books but I don't believe them/When it hurts we return to the banks of certain rivers."[13] One of those banks is called "reading P. T. Forsyth." On that bank, I experienced not only a dying but also a resurrection, a resurrection into a new and still largely-unsurveyed world wherein everything and every one—including God—is viewed *sub specie crucis*; that is, under the vista or form of the cross. Forsyth's thought, drenched as it is in the cruciality of God, came as a lifeline, even as something like a sacrament or as medicine which charged life itself with the Spirit who makes life life, with the Son who is the living content of God's own good news and who experienced in a divine life our death "unsustained by any sense of the grandeur and sublimity of the situation,"[14] and with the Father who in all the jealousy and joy of holy love transforms "bold and bitter"[15] mutineers into the delighted and forgiven children of God who "in their living centre and chronic movement of the soul experience sonship as the very tune of their heart, the fashion and livery of their will,"[16] and which cleared for me a way which bespoke of realities I can do little more than point to regarding the task of Christian ministry into which I was being called. Reading Forsyth, I also came to believe in preaching, and to keep on preaching when the content of my speech finds so little echo in the shape of my own living, or when my spirit is as dry as the Simpson Desert, or when it is soaking wet but off course and perilously close to the rocks, or when in darkness so overwhelming that escape seems impossible, and when, like Maurice Gee's Reverend George Plumb, I make "loud noises to persuade back my memories."[17]

To be sure, to believe in preaching is to believe in miracles; or, more properly, it is to believe in One who not only already longs to speak but who also "gives life to the dead and calls into existence things that do not exist" (Romans 4:17). Moreover, to believe in preaching is to believe that such calling into existence occurs via the irresponsible method of liberally sowing seeds whether in places where there is no soil, or on rocky ground, or among thorns, or in fertile and productive soil. Of course, to believe in preaching is not the same thing as to believe in preachers. Forsyth too taught me that, and enabled me to hear what I later learnt and heard again in Barth and in others—that "the Church does not live by its

---

13. Miłosz, "I Sleep a Lot," 178.
14. Forsyth, *God the Holy Father*, 57.
15. Ibid., 9.
16. Ibid., 6.
17. Gee, *Plumb*, 218.

preachers, but by its Word."[18] To those who so believe—or who wish to believe in such things in spite of all appearances—I hope that the words of Forsyth contained in this volume might come as an encouragement. As John Huxtable describes the testimony of not a few preachers, "a few pages of [Forsyth's] work recharges that battery as little else."[19]

In this introductory chapter, I consider some of the background to the material presented in this volume, and offer some comment on Forsyth's somewhat-enigmatic style. But first, it would be helpful, I think, to briefly introduce Forsyth, to ask what place preaching occupied in his tradition and theology, to enquire as to what Forsyth understood by preaching, its *raison d'être* and its relationship to more conventional forms of systematic theology, and also to express something of how, for Forsyth, the pulpit belongs to the Church in a way that the platform never can.

Peter Taylor Forsyth, the first of five children, was born on 12 May 1848 at 100 Chapel Street, Aberdeen, and was baptised the same year by the Rev. W. Grant at the Blackfriars Street Congregational Church. Peter's father, Isaac, was a merchant, church deacon, book courier, bibliophile, and postman who earned eleven shillings a week, and his mother, Elspet McPherson, was a Gaelic-speaking crofter's daughter who was born and raised on the foothills of the Cairngorm and Monadhliath ranges in Kingussie, the capital of the Highland district of Bàideanach, a region better known today for its Speyside waters of life. After a nine-year engagement, Isaac and Elspet were married in June 1847 in Old Machar, a coastal parish some four miles north of Aberdeen, by the minister of Blackfriars Church, the Rev. George Thompson. Elspet was employed as a housekeeper to Peter Taylor, a well-to-do retired shoemaker, a devout and public-spirited citizen of Aberdeen, and one of the founding members of the old Blackfriars Church. In 1851, the Forsyth family moved to Marischal Street, Aberdeen (near the docks), and they began to take in boarders to help make ends meet.

---

18. Forsyth, *Positive Preaching and the Modern Mind*, 41.

19. Huxtable, "Forsyth," 77. Such an assessment is echoed by, for example, Edgar DeWitt Jones who, in 1951, set about surveying the first eighty years of Yale's Beecher Lectures on Preaching (a series which by then had occupied such renowned names as Phillips Brooks, R. W. Dale, George A. Buttrick, H. H. Farmer, and W. H. Auden), and noted of Forsyth's lectures—which were "one of the fattest, physically, in the Series"—the following: "In talking with scores of ministers about the Lyman Beecher Lectures, I found without exception that those whose opinions are most highly valued, rated Forsyth's series at Yale as unrivaled of their kind, and a 'must' book for alert, studious preachers everywhere. This is superlative praise, for these distinguished preacher-scholars also rated highly the Lectures [sic] of Andrew M. Fairbairn, George Adam Smith, and Reinhold Niebuhr, in the same series." Jones, *The Royalty of the Pulpit*, 128, 134.

I: Preaching Sub Specie Crucis

In 1853, Peter began his formal education at the local parish school, and in 1859 he entered Aberdeen Grammar School where he was dux in 1864. In October that same year, Forsyth entered the annual Bursary Competition at Aberdeen University and was placed twenty-first in a class of 204, thereby winning a Cargill Bursary (£20 per year for four years). Between 1864 and 1869, Forsyth excelled in his undergraduate studies (in Latin, Greek, English, Mathematics, Natural History, Natural Philosophy, Logic, Chemistry, Natural Philosophy, and Moral Philosophy), and took prizes in Greek, Humanities, English and the "Special Prize for Excellence in Latin Composition, Prose and Verse." It was during this time that illness began to affect his plans; he was unable to complete his third year, for example. It was probably also during this period that he was first introduced to the work of Georg Wilhelm Friedrich Hegel and Immanuel Kant, two of the thunderous voices with which he would tussle for the remainder of his life.

After his graduation with an MA with first-class honours in Classical Literature in 1869, Forsyth came under the influence of John Hunter (b. 1848) with whom, probably during 1870 or 1871, he sought to resuscitate the recently-closed Congregational Chapel in Dee Street, Aberdeen. During these years, he first tried his hand at teaching, as a private tutor to the family of Patrick Davidson of Inchmarlo, and, during the 1871–72 academic year, as Assistant to Professor John Black, the teacher of Latin at Aberdeen University. He may well have continued along this path were it not for a call to ordination. And so, at the close of the academic session in 1872, and at the urging of W. Robertson Smith, Forsyth spent a semester with Albrecht Ritschl and Carl Stumpf in Göttingen (a familiar destination for young Nonconformist theological students at the time). Ritschl's impact on Forsyth's thought was brobdingnagian and abiding, and in not a few ways survived the departure with "Ritschlianism" which escorted Forsyth's famed theological turn in the late 1880s "from a Christian to a believer, from a lover of love to an object of grace,"[20] a turn which was perhaps most public in the publication, in 1891, of Forsyth's *The Old Faith and the New*.

In September 1872, upon Forsyth's return from Göttingen, he was accepted (on probation; he was fully admitted in 1873) at New College (London) to study theology. While his health continually restricted his attendance at classes, and he seems to have felt a "misfit" who was increasingly "wasting his time" there (which led to his resignation in 1874, before completion and in circumstances difficult to square with sound order[21]), there are two lasting results of his time at New College. First, he met Maria Hester

---

20. Forsyth, *Positive Preaching and the Modern Mind*, 193.
21. See Council of New College, "Extract from 386 Council Meeting," n.p.

I: Preaching Sub Specie Crucis

(Minna) Magness (1850/51–1894), the intellectual, cultured and devout Anglican whom he married in 1877. Second, he came under the influence of James Baldwin Brown, Congregationalism's mediator of F. D. Maurice.[22] In fact, it may have been Brown who first drew Forsyth to London, Forsyth travelling the six and a half miles out to Brixton every Sunday to hear the devout Maurician who he later described as "the greatest Independent of our times," indeed, the greatest since the seventeenth century.[23]

Forsyth's first pastoral charge, which began in November 1876, was at the Congregational Church in Springwood, Shipley (near Bradford, Yorkshire), where he was ordained by his mentor and former pastor J. Baldwin Brown, and by the Principal of New College, the Rev. Dr Samuel Newth. History records that the latter "preached an excellent sermon, full of good counsel to the congregation and in the evening the pastor [P. T. Forsyth] delivered an able discourse from the following text: 'But I am among you as he that serveth.' Luke xxii. 27. The congregation was very large."[24] Whilst at Shipley, Forsyth became a father—Jessie, whom he once called "a little candle of the Lord,"[25] was born in 1877 and baptised at Shipley in 1879; she was his only child. He also began to make a name for himself as a "challenging and unconventional preacher," attracting such eccentric characters that his church was nicknamed "The Cave of Adullam."[26] It was here too that his ministry was rejected by the Yorkshire Congregational Union and he experienced an increasingly awkward relationship with the denomination's more "orthodox" seniors, a parting which came to something of a head at the Leicester Conference in mid-October 1877.[27] Indeed, Forsyth's name appeared in no official denominational handbook for the best part of a decade, and even though his ordination, or "recognition" (as it was referred to), was reported by the local press and some key denominational leaders (including his own college principal, and J. Robertson Campbell) played prominent parts in it, the ordination was unrecorded in the national Congregational Year Book.[28] The first four sermons in this volume—"The Turkish Atrocities," "Mercy the true and only

---

22. Maurice was arguably the greatest of English preachers of the day and, at the recommendation of W. Robertson Smith, Forsyth studied Maurice's work closely.

23. Forsyth, "Baldwin Brown," 139, 142.

24. Forsyth, "Ordination Statement," 4.

25. Forsyth and Hamilton, *Pulpit Parables*, 50–51.

26. Andrews, "Memoir," xii–xiii.

27. On the Leicester Conference see Johnson, *The Dissolution of Dissent*, 63–114.

28. It is possible, of course, that the ordination took place too late in the year to be included in 1877 edition of the Year Book. Still, Forsyth's first mention in the Congregational Year Book is 1885, and the Shipley Church is steadily listed as "vacant."

I: Preaching Sub Specie Crucis

Justice," "The Strength of Weakness," and "The Bible Doctrine of Hell and the Unseen"—were preached during this period.

From a Bradford hinterland, Forsyth moved to a historic though equally marginalised church at St Thomas's Square in the established and middle-class London suburb of Hackney where, between 1879 and 1885, he filled the pulpit once occupied by the author of the famous "'Protestant Dissenters' Catechism" Samuel Palmer (1741–1813), the early nineteenth century pulpit prince Henry Forster Burder (1783–1864), and James Allanson Picton, and a local tradition whose theological capital included William Bates and Matthew Henry. In 1879, however, St Thomas's Square was a difficult pulpit to fill. Having severed its affiliation with both the London and national Congregational Unions, its minister, who would be Picton's successor, would unavoidably be branded for life as one carrying a dubious theological pedigree. As C. E. Larter recalled some forty years later in a letter to *The British Weekly* (a Nonconformist newspaper founded by William Robertson Nicoll), "it has seemed probable that the young minister might follow his predecessor along lines that led the latter ultimately to sever his connection with the churches, and to devote his noble powers rather to the exposition of Spinoza than any faith distinctly Christian."[29]

Forsyth's call to Hackney, like that to Shipley, was orchestrated by J. Baldwin Brown, and was to a church which was, like the Shipley Church, unaffiliated with any Congregational Union.[30] His daughter recalls:

> Here again he collected a congregation of heretics and suspects; and here, too, he was rejected by the London Congregational Union. When I look at contemporary portraits of orthodox nonconformist ministers I am not surprised, for in appearance he did not even conform to nonconformity. My baby memories begin during this period, and I see him in the pulpit, wearing a short black coat, shepherd's-plaid trousers, turndown collar and a brilliant tie. (He first began to preach in an academic gown to hide a sling, after breaking his collar-bone in a collision when he was figure-skating on the Serpentine.) London was like wine to him. He was in touch with so many sides of its life—politics, literature, art, music, and even the theatre, taboo to so many Victorian

---

29. Larter, "Letter, St. Mary Church. 18 November 1921," 196. The reference to Spinoza recalls Picton's *Spinoza: A Handbook to the Ethics* (1907).

30. The Hackney Church's affiliation with the London Congregational Union took place in 1884, the same year that Forsyth joined the same Union and Board, and a year before he left London for Manchester. Evident here is something of the young Forsyth's denominational looseness, a looseness which often signified some extreme positions and which, among Congregationalists during the 1870s and 1880s, were likely to be those of a "liberal" rather than "conservative" sapidity.

I: Preaching Sub Specie Crucis

saints. A rich friend took him to Bayreuth, and he was there at the crown of Wagner's career, the first performance of *Parsifal* in 1882; and henceforth it always seemed to my father a sacrament rather than an opera. All his enthusiasms he put into his preaching, and people of all denominations and of none came from everywhere in London to hear his Sunday evening lectures.[31]

He was, it seems, something like how John Updike described William Blake—"a triumph of eccentricity, the Englishman's cherished privilege and informal purchase on freedom."[32] His congregations at Hackney were small. But Forsyth was well known in the city, and his evening sermonic lectures, such as the one on Alfred Tennyson's "Vastness" (republished in this volume) drew large audiences. On 1 December 1921, just a few weeks after Forsyth's death, *The British Weekly* published a letter by "F.R.C.S" recalling memories of student life in London some thirty-seven years earlier, in 1884. F.R.C.S, then "a medical student, unsettled in matters of belief by the scientific teaching of the materialistic school," recalled being attracted to St. Thomas's Square by a course of lectures which were being offered by Forsyth on "the origin of the Gospels." F.R.C.S spoke enthusiastically of their content, and even republished some notes of the lectures which he had taken and kept, including this sentence: "The Word of God was not the Bible; it was left for us to get as low as that. The Bible contains the Word of God—Jesus Christ." And he ardently recalled Forsyth's style—a summary of the lecture chalked beforehand on the blackboard; questions and discussion afterwards; and a collect to preface each lecture: "Prevent us, O Lord, in all our doings . . ." So moved was he by Forsyth's lectures that he resolved to stay on and become part of the congregation at St. Thomas's Square. Forsyth's lectures on literary themes were "a great treat," he said, and if on Sundays the congregations "were comparatively scanty . . . to students like myself, unsettled in their religious thinking by the current materialism of the day, it was a godsend to find a preacher of outstanding intellectual power, who had fairly faced our modern difficulties for himself, and yet preached Christ with all the fire and earnestness of a prophet." He especially recalled a phrase Forsyth used in one of his prayers, "thanking God for the 'dark dis-peace' which besets us when we stray from Him." And he evoked memory of Forsyth's farewell sermon to the Hackney congregation—a "dramatic denunciation of the men who had applauded him for preaching a more liberal religion because it seemed to them to permit the moral laxity which they preferred to a higher life. Looking up from his manuscript, he

---

31. Andrews, "Memoir," xiii.
32. Updike, *Higher Gossip*, 241.

peered round the congregation. 'I hope I have offended such men' he said. 'I think I see some of them here tonight.'"[33]

While at Hackney, Forsyth instigated the monthly children's service—the sermons during which "were delightful, and were enjoyed by the adults in his congregation as much as any"[34]—and he was finally admitted to the Congregational Union. His sermons on "Egypt" and "Pessimism" (also republished in this volume) were preached from the pulpit at St Thomas's Square.

From Hackney, Forsyth moved to Cheetham Hill, Manchester, where he served until 1888. It was while at Cheetham Hill that his interest and involvement in political debate expanded. This is evident in the increase of political and social essays he penned for the *Manchester Examiner* as well as other forums (such as his 1888 lecture on "The Relation of the Church to the Poor" given before the Lancashire Congregational Union), and in letters which were published in that same newspaper between 1885 and 1889 under the pseudonym "Publicola." While he was at Manchester, Forsyth also saw the publication of his first book, *Pulpit Parables for Young Hearers* (1886), a collection of sermons primarily the product of his ministry at Hackney and co-authored with his closest local ministerial friend, John Arthur Hamilton (1845–1924),[35] and preached his sermon on "Sunday-Schools and Modern Theology" (included in this volume). Both the book and the sermon betray an acute awareness of the key role that Sunday schools played in Victorian religion, and of the influential and strategic relationship that they shared with social spheres and cultural formation far detached from usual chapel life. As one historian remarked of the period: "Sunday school earthed the culture and politics of Evangelical Dissent in the complexities of contemporary industrial society. It was radical acculturation."[36] These two publications of Forsyth's also

33. F.R.C.S, "A Medical Man's Tribute to Dr Forsyth," 203.

34. Ibid.

35. Hamilton held three pastorates spanning fifty-four years: Crowle (Lincolnshire), Saltaire (Yorskshire), and Penzance (Cornwall). He died three days after the latter made him its Pastor Emeritus. He wrote *The Life of John Milton* (1870), and assisted in the preparation for publication of Forsyth's *Religion in Recent Art* and R. J. Campbell's *The New Theology*. The *Congregational Yearbook* of 1925 obituarizes of him: "One of the old Independents, he was a fearless seeker after truth, and a man of wide culture" (147).

36. Binfield, "The Significance of Baby Babble: P. T. Forsyth's *Pulpit Parables* and their Context," 4. Binfield cites a passage from J. Allanson Picton's biography of his father who described the formative influence of the Leeds Street Sunday School thus: "The Sunday School was to me a new world of activity and energy: the republican form of government; its teachers' meetings; its library; the connexions and friendships to which it led; and the constant current of healthy excitement which it generated, in addition to the usefulness of the main objects at which it aimed, were, to me, sources of the keenest enjoyment and, I think, of improvement." Picton, *Sir James A. Picton*, 67–68.

I: Preaching Sub Specie Crucis

signify a genuine commitment to, and love and keen sense for, children and young people which was never to leave him. Indeed, one of Forsyth's first published sermons, "'Maid, Arise': A Sermon to School Girls," was preached during his first charge in Shipley on Sunday 18 July 1878, and one of his final addresses as a minister in pastoral charge was a contribution in late-1900 to "The School at the End of the Century: A Symposium on the Alleged Decline in Sunday School Attendance: Some Opinions and Suggestions."[37] In May 1913, *The British Weekly* published his piece on "The Church and the Children,"[38] and a year later, on 17 June 1914, on the eve of the Great War, Forsyth was at Stockwell College's valedictory day serving as the meeting's chairman. He had come, he said, "to say words to those girls who were going out of the College," and to enlist them into what to our sensitive ears might be easily dismissed as rank utopian liberalism but which for this Victorian college principal was both judiciously subversive and filled with evangelical realism—namely, a Christian commonwealth, "the growing up of each individual member of society into a holy temple of the Lord; an ideal society, a true brotherhood of mankind, the kingdom of the new humanity, which is the Kingdom of God."[39]

The year 1888 saw the beginning of Forsyth's fruitful and vibrant ministry at Clarendon Park, Leicester, a charge which included a regularly filled church lecture room for monthly lectures where, as was the case at Hackney, he drew large audiences on topics such as art, politics and popular literature, and which included his lecture on "Handel, with Musical Illustrations." His acceptance letter[40] to the Clarendon Park Church is worth citing here in full for it expresses not only how Forsyth articulated his faith but also something of the Congregational notion (in the late-nineteenth century) of the relation between the minister and the local congregation, as well as something of the nature and responsibility of preaching itself.

Binfield's reference to Picton is not without significance. Picton, as we have noted, was an ex-Congregational minister who, after twenty-three years in pastoral ministry (at Cheetham Hill, Manchester; Gallowtree Gate, Leicester, some people from which later became core members at Clarendon Park during Forsyth's time there; and St Thomas's Square, Hackney, where Forsyth was his successor), turned, in 1879, to politics and who in 1891 was Radical MP for Leicester during Forsyth's time in that city. Picton's younger brother married Mary Helen Stafford who came from a prominent family in Forsyth's Leicester congregation, and Picton's first wife, Margaret Beaumont of Cheetham Hill and Wilmslow, came from a family of active Congregationalists in Manchester, several members of which played a prominent role in Forsyth's Cheetham Hill Church.

37. Forsyth, "As to the Causes of Decline," 850.
38. Forsyth, "The Church and the Children," 169.
39. See Anonymous, *The Educational Record*, 106–12.
40. Published as "Appendix I," in Waddington, *The First Ninety Years*.

I: Preaching Sub Specie Crucis

Cheetham Hill,
Manchester,
12 May 1888

To the Church and Congregation,
Clarendon Park,
Leicester

My dear friends,

I have the honour of your Christian call; and you are aware of the special reasons for my delay in reply. I cannot longer defer my decision. I am your servant in Jesus Christ, if, when you hear the whole of this letter, you still will have it so. And let us trust that our interpretation of the Lord's will is right, and that we unite because *He* will have it so. In coming to you I come on a twofold footing which it is important to understand.

First, I come, not, in the main, to make a certain congregation a prosperous concern, but as a minister of Christ and of the Church Universal, to declare and to apply the gospel of the Cross. I believe in the Incarnation of the Eternal Son of God in the sinless person of Jesus Christ; in the Redemption of Mankind through His death; and in His risen life as the unseen personal power which guides both the world and the Church to fulfil the Kingdom of God—especially through personal union with the Saviour. You have a right to know thus clearly my position on such central points.

But secondly, I view these great truths not as a mere seal of orthodoxy, not as confining the action of the human mind, nor as hedging it up, so to speak, against mistake. But I view them as a *Gospel*, as the charter and impulse of the Soul's liberty and the guide to heights and ranges of freedom both in heart and head, which without Christ's gospel we should never have won. While therefore I should think it my duty if ever I departed from these truths to release you from any obligation to retain me among you, yet it is of the greatest importance that I should make clear this spirit in which they are held. In my present congregation I have the completest freedom in this respect. And I should not sustain the idea of a change to any sphere where my freedom should be less. This applies both to the specific ways of applying these truths to modern conditions and to my own personal style of phrase and speech. I always feel that my freedom is a responsibility, that the feelings of others are entitled to respect, and that it is cowardly to use the privilege of the pulpit to the disadvantage of those who have both to listen and perhaps to differ. I ask for

I: Preaching Sub Specie Crucis

no agreement with me except in such great principles as I have specified. And outside the region of thought and teaching, in the practical affairs of the congregation, I am as any other member who must either persuade the majority or go with it. But in the matter of teaching[,] the concession of the liberty aforesaid is paramount, and no other possible advantages I might gain in coming to you would atone for the loss of it as I have it here. The deacons quite understand this, but I am anxious there should be no mistake about it on the part of the church and congregation; I may farther add that I have neither time nor energy to waste on such contentions as sometimes arise in churches on doctrinal points. And if you receive me, and if you should desire in course to be rid of me, an ordinary vote of the church with a decided majority to that effect will be quite sufficient for the purpose.

I did not think it would be so hard for me to reach this decision as I have found it to be. I need not trouble you with any reference to the considerations which make parting more than difficult—painful, here. And I am far from absolutely certain that I have done the right thing. But I have used such effort as I could to attain a right judgment. I must go forward like so many greater ones, in a faith which is content not to see everything perfectly clear. I cast myself upon the help of the Spirit we serve and upon your Christian hearts. No man surely can make a fatal mistake who does that. May God help us to bend all our personal hopes, fears and ambitions to His great glory and the obedience of His Son. And may you be found to have no more made a mistake in me than I in you.

I am Yours for Jesus Christ,
P. T. Forsyth

Forsyth's interest in politics and art, which took a more mature turn while at Cheetham Hill, continued to find expression while at Clarendon Park. This is evident, for example, in his public support for the dock workers in the London Dock Strike of 1889, in his lectures on Dante Gabriel Rossetti, Edward Burne-Jones, George Frederic Watts, William Holman Hunt, and Richard Wagner, given in January that same year to a mostly "promiscuous audience"[41] in Leicester (though largely the product of his ministry at Cheetham Hill, and published as *Religion in Recent Art*), and in his appointment, in 1893, as a member of the borough's Museum and Art Gallery Committee. Some of these commitments also informed his ministry at Leicester, as is evident in some of the sermons from that period which are included in this

41. Forsyth, *Religion in Recent Art*, vii.

I: Preaching Sub Specie Crucis

collection, such as "Preaching and Poetry," and in his concern for a recently unemployed and distressed local woman whose situation Forsyth raised at a deacons' meeting where it was agreed that a representative from the congregation would visit her and "take her £1 to pay off her arrears to her landlady."[42] An appeal from the pulpit the following Sunday found work for her.

A snapshot of Forsyth's first few months at Clarendon Park describes the kind of activities which occupied his energies:

> On August 1 1888 the Rev. P. T. Forsyth presided over his first church meeting, at which he was obviously getting to know the Church members, but at the next Church meeting, held on October 31, he showed that he had already gone into action. He announced that he had arranged for "a course of Sunday Evening Lectures to Young Men and Women" on the first Sunday morning in each month—also that he intended on the second Sunday morning in each month to have a Children's Service and Sermon. The 2nd Anniversary of the Opening of the Organ would be held on November 18 and in the evening Mr. Forsyth would preach upon the "Song of Miriam." After the service Schubert's "Song of Miriam" would be performed. The week night service was to begin at 7 o'clock in order that the Bible Class might commence at 8 o'clock.
>
> For an infant of 2 years old, Clarendon Park Congregational Church was not only alive and kicking but filled with an adult sense of purpose and determination.[43]

In the following year, during which the church was embroiled in debate over whether or not to hold a bazaar to raise money to purchase land for the Sunday School, Forsyth announced the formation of a Bible Class which would be open to all, and which would be held on Tuesdays at 3 pm. They would begin by studying Mark's Gospel. Certainly, there is no evidence that Forsyth here neglected his pastoral and wider ecclesial responsibilities, responsibilities which included his being appointed Chairman of the Leicestershire and Rutland Congregational Union in 1891, and then, in March 1893, his appointment as College Pastor at Mansfield College, that prestigious Nonconformist institution previously located in Birmingham (where it was named Spring Hill College) and which opened in Oxford in 1886, a fruit of the Oxford University Act of 1854 which granted Independents and Dissenters legal admission to the University. Forsyth's time at Clarendon Park ended sadly, however, due to illness. So Waddington: "In 1893 Mr.

---

42. Waddington, *The First Ninety Years*, 7.
43. Ibid., 4.

I: Preaching Sub Specie Crucis

Forsyth's health was proving unsatisfactory with consequent depression and he appealed for the sympathy of the congregation in these circumstances. A resolution was unanimously passed sympathising with Mr. Forsyth, heartily approving his efforts in the work of the Church and pledging the Church to support him in his work."[44] Following doctor's advice, Forsyth took three months off for complete rest. Forsyth's wife, Minna, too, was gravely unwell and, sometime in early 1894, suddenly became infirm.

In February 1894, Forsyth received a call to Emmanuel Church, Cambridge, a significant church not only in terms of the denomination's life, but also because it was the chief Congregational Church in Cambridge, the university from which so many Nonconformist students graduated. "In May, to everyone's regret, he left [Leicester] and the Church was faced with the problem of finding a suitable successor to its first Minister, who had done so much to help it to start and to continue on its way."[45]

Minna died of paralysis during Forsyth's first week at Emmanuel Church. When, in October, the news regarding her death reached Clarendon Park the congregation resolved to send a "letter of deep regret at the death of (their) friend Mrs. Forsyth," and in which the church recalled how their former minister had "in the past shared their griefs and troubles and they would pray that the same Healer and Consoler he set forth to them may be his consolation."[46] Forsyth's reply was delayed because he himself was ill in bed for a fortnight, but in due course he penned the following words: "Your letter came to me like a warm air from the circle of those who knew her and esteemed her so well . . . But she is free and at rest, and crowned with glory and honour, having tasted of death in Him who tasted it for us all. Her life was a long death to herself. Her new life is a new living to God—and I must believe also, living for us whom He has visibly left but not spiritually forgotten."[47] This letter was accompanied by a copy of a poem that he had written in Minna's memory, and which was later published in *The British Weekly* under the title "The Healing of the Paralytic":

> 'Relaxed in death'! From death released also;
> Blest double sense of Faith—loosed, and let go.
>
> I've seen her drag herself to meet
> Me home from foreign stay;
> And lumber down the perilous stair
> Her poor pathetic way.

44. Ibid., 8.
45. Ibid.
46. Cited in ibid.
47. Cited in ibid., 8–9.

I: Preaching Sub Specie Crucis

> I've seen her, in the house unseen,
> Devoted, tireless, free,
> Smiling on her transfigured grief
> Seen through the crystal sea.
>
> And down the golden stair I'll see
> Her run with stately life,
> When from earth's foreign inn I turn
> And go home to my wife.[48]

Minna's death precipitated, for her widower, a period marked by deep depression, physical and nervous weakness, and with descents into hypochondriasis. During the period of his charge at Emmanuel Church, a period that spanned the years 1894 to 1901, Forsyth lived with his schoolgirl daughter Jessie, who later wrote of this period, "There can never have been a happier or more harmonious church than Emmanuel, Cambridge."[49] Forsyth's health, however, continued to deteriorate and he was forced to severely curtail his pastoral work. Throughout this period, he received loyal support from the church. Regarding his preaching at Cambridge, we might recall the diary testimony of Neville Keynes, who was "a trustee though never a member of Emmanuel."[50] On 24 January 1892, Keynes writes of Forsyth for the first time, and notes of his preaching: "his matter was excellent, but his delivery too rapid . . . Personally we liked him very much."[51] Then on 29 October the following year, Keynes referred to a "fine sermon from Forsyth of Leicester."[52] Keynes believed that Forsyth's preaching took a "very severe line," but was remarkably well received and often drew crowded congregations.[53] T. R. Glover, a Cambridge undergraduate student and the son of a Baptist minister, Dr Richard Glover of Bristol, also found himself drawn, along with a considerable number of undergraduates, to Emmanuel Church, and that largely through the preaching ministry of W. S. Houghton, from 1879, and Forsyth, from 1894.[54] In his diary entry on 21 October 1894,

---

48. Forsyth, "Paralytic," 4.

49. Andrews, "Memoir," xviii.

50. Thompson, *Cambridge Theology in the Nineteenth Century*, 150. The following citations from Keynes' and Glover's diaries are taken from ibid., 154–55.

51. Neville Keynes, Diary, 24 January 1892, Cambridge University Library Add Mss 7842.

52. Neville Keynes, Diary, 29 October 1893, Cambridge University Library Add Mss 7843.

53. Neville Keynes, Diary, 23 June 1895, 20 October 1895, 27 October 1895, Cambridge University Library Add Mss 7845.

54. On Keynes and Glover, see Thompson, "Nonconformists at Cambridge," 180–84.

I: Preaching Sub Specie Crucis

Glover wrote: "Mr Forsyth at last on Acts xii 19 . . . A splendid sermon on the obstructed power of a great enthusiasm, full of many serious points."[55] And just a fortnight later, he penned: "Mr Forsyth on the Sacrament—a striking sermon though I don't follow it all."[56] And a week later still, this time after hearing Forsyth preach on Romans 8: "He is out of one's reach a great deal. But it is stimulating and good."[57]

In 1895, Forsyth was made a doctor of divinity (in absentia) by Aberdeen University,[58] and the following year saw him take up the invitation to be the Congregational Union preacher for the Autumnal Assembly at Leicester where he preached what is among his greatest sermons, "The Holy Father."[59] Certainly this period was marked by a growing public role for Forsyth. In September 1899, he accepted the invitation to serve as the English delegate and to speak at the Decennial International Congregational Council in Boston. His address was entitled "The Evangelical Principle of Authority," a lecture so stirring that at its conclusion the audience uncharacteristically rose to their feet and started singing John Bowring's rousing hymn, "In the Cross of Christ I glory." From this time onwards, Forsyth enjoyed international repute as a theologian and preacher. In December of that same year, Forsyth was also invited by Professor William Sanday (who was, from 1895 until 1919, the Lady Margaret Professor of Divinity and Canon of Christ Church at Oxford) to speak at a two-day conference at Oxford on the theme of Priesthood, Sacrifice and Apostolic Succession. In addition to Professor Sanday, an august assemblage of the nation's leading theologians was present to hear Forsyth, including Robert Campbell Moberly, Charles Gore, Henry Scott Holland, Cosmo Gordon Lang, Andrew Fairbairn, Stewart D. F. Salmond and William Theophilus Davison. In May the following year, Forsyth preached the annual sermon of the Colonial Missionary Society; the sermon, "The Empire for Christ," is included in this volume. This period was also marked by the advance of what was to become a significant writing ministry, evidenced in the publication of a number of titles, including *The*

---

55. T. R. Glover, Diary 21 October 1894, St John's College Archives.

56. T. R. Glover, Diary 4 November 1894, St John's College Archives.

57. T. R. Glover, Diary 11 November 1894, St John's College Archives.

58. Honorary doctorates could wield enormous cultural capital for Dissenting ministers (having been prohibited from earning them until the middle of the nineteenth century). On the other hand, doctorates dishonorably sought or given by disreputable institutions could also bring ridicule and scorn to those who pursued them.

59. The sermon was subsequently published the same year in *Independent and Nonconformist, Christian World Pulpit, British Weekly* and abstracted in *Homiletic Review*, before appearing in *The Holy Father and the Living Christ* (1897) and *God the Holy Father* (1957, 1987).

I: Preaching Sub Specie Crucis

Charter of the Church (1896), *Intercessory Services for Aid in Public Worship* (1897), *The Holy Father and the Living Christ* (1897), *Christian Perfection* (1899), *Rome, Reform and Reaction* (1899), and *The Taste of Death and the Life of Grace* (1901), as well as a very considerable essay on the atonement published in *The Atonement in Modern Religious Thought* (1899).

Concerning things closer to home, it was a period which welcomed, from their marriage in 1897, Bertha Ison ("a much younger woman of great wit, charm and vivacity"[60]) into the Forsyth residence. Reflecting on this period some years later, Forsyth's daughter, Mrs Jessie Andrews, considered her step-mother to be "the real turning point of Forsyth's life": "This charming and devoted woman," she said, "was a true helpmate and unfailing inspiration, helping her husband to focus on the future rather than the past. There followed for him a great upsurge of physical and intellectual vigour."[61] And in her *Memoir* on her father, Mrs Andrews suggested that her stepmother "rescued" her father from the hypochondriasis that threatened to engulf his life during his first three years at Cambridge:

> [Bertha Ison] was many years younger than he, possessing great charm, and even fascination, of looks and manner, incredible vitality, much wit, and a born gift as a hostess. It was typical of her courage to take over a delicate man who was minister of a large congregation; and she carried her enterprise through more than triumphantly. For she gave him a new hold on life, she renewed the zest he had lost; and though he never could become a strong man, her devoted care of him, and perhaps still more, simply her charm and personality, made possible for him the twenty-four years in which his greatest work was done. It was a happy thing to see his face light up when she came into the room.[62]

Forsyth's affection for Bertha, and his deep gratitude for the new lease on life which came to him through her, is apparent in his dedication of his 1917 lectures on *The Church and the Sacraments*: "To My Wife, who contributes more than she knows, or I can tell her, to all I try to do."[63]

His ministry at Cambridge was relatively short and was marked by grief and ill-health, as well as by new energy and significant adjustments on the personal front. His seven years there also witnessed his signature on a number of significant shifts for English Congregationalism. I will highlight just two.

---

60. Carter, "Foreword," xv.

61. Jones, "The Christological Thought of Peter Taylor Forsyth and Emil Brunner," 10. The interview with Mrs. Andrews was conducted on 7 December 1968.

62. Andrews, "Memoir," xvii–xviii.

63. Forsyth, *The Church and the Sacraments*, v.

I: Preaching Sub Specie Crucis

First, as B. L. Manning has noted, it was while Forsyth was in this university town that he "made dogmatic theology attractive even to undergraduates"[64]—overcoming an impediment as exigent in Forsyth's day as in our own. Second, Forsyth procured his reputation as a laudable nonconformist leader on a national scale. From the summer of 1901, though Forsyth continued to preach on occasion at Emmanuel, and though he remained on the membership role of that church until 1917, his service to Congregationalism took him to London and from there, to an emergent global audience.

By far the majority of Forsyth's time in London—twenty of the twenty-four years of which Mrs Andrews spoke—was given to his work as Principal of Hackney College. And apart from the years 1905 and 1907 when Forsyth was ill for most of the year, and 1920 when he suffered an illness that gradually reduced his strength, this time between the spring of 1901 until his death on the fourth Armistice Day (11 November 1921) was to be the most prolific period of his public ministry. Not only was he elected Chairman of the Congregational Union of England and Wales in 1905, but he also increased his already substantial lecture load (the two are not unrelated),[65] addressing, in July 1908, the Third International Congregational Council in Edinburgh, and presenting in April and May the following year, the Congregational Lectures on "The Person and Place of Jesus Christ" and, also that year, a series of lectures at Campbell Morgan's annual summer conference for young ministers—lectures which were later prepared for publication in *The Work of Christ*. As an example of both his vigour and the costliness of such, we might recall that in the same year that he experienced significant ill health he also gave, in March 1907, his Lyman Beecher Lectures at Yale (subsequently published under the title *Positive Preaching and [the] Modern Mind*), and, in August, he lectured at the Cambridge Summer School of Theology. The years of his principalship were also marked, between 1907 and 1910, with The New Theology controversy associated with R. J. Campbell,[66] and by an extraordinarily fertility in terms of his maturing theology, his growing repute both at home[67] and abroad, and his published work, made palpable, for example, by the publication of the following titles which cover

---

64. Manning, *This Latter House*, 28.

65. So, for example, in 1905, Forsyth gave two public addresses in his capacity as chair: "A Holy Church the Moral Guide of Society," on May 9 at the City Temple, and "The Grace of the Gospel as the Moral Authority in the Church," on October 10 at the Coliseum, Leeds.

66. On which, see Goroncy, *Hallowed Be Thy Name*, 35–41.

67. Evident, for example, in his being made Dean of the Faculty of Theology in the University of London in 1910, and, during the following year, his appointment as Dean of the London Theological Colleges.

I: Preaching Sub Specie Crucis

a diverse number of themes: "The New Congregationalism and the New Testament Congregationalism" (1903), "The Evangelical Churches and the Higher Criticism" (1905), "Some Christian Aspects of Evolution" (1905), *Positive Preaching and the Modern Mind* (1907), *Missions in State and Church* (1908), *Socialism, the Church and the Poor* (1908), *The Cruciality of the Cross* (1909), *The Power of Prayer* (1910), *The Work of Christ* (1910), *Christ on Parnassus* (1911), *Faith Freedom and the Future* (1912), *Marriage: Its Ethic and Religion* (1912), *The Principal of Authority* (1912), *Theology in Church and State* (1915), *The Christian Ethic of War* (1916), *The Justification of God* (1916), *The Soul of Prayer* (1916), *Reunion and Recognition* (1917), *The Roots of a World Commonwealth* (1918), and *This Life and the Next* (1918), a book which, as William Bradley reminds us, is "unmatched for spiritual depth and beauty."[68]

What I hope has already been evident in this brief sketch of Forsyth's public ministry is that whereas most traditions of the Church are marked by the production of countless hefty theological tomes, this has largely not been the case within Congregationalism. This is not to say, of course, that Congregationalism has not produced some sturdy theologians but only to register that, by and large, Congregationalist theologians have gone about their task in other ways. This was well noted when A. J. Grieve, Principal of the Lancashire Independent College, Whalley Range, prepared, in 1931, a bibliography of Congregational theology wherein he inserted the following footnote:

> While one is naturally expected and obliged to keep to literary contributions, it is imperative to remember that these, so far from exhausting the subject, are probably but a small part of it. The teachers in our Academies and Colleges have not always reduced their instruction to the printed page; our preachers for 350 years have delivered more sermons than they have published; and perhaps as effective contributions to theology as any, if theology is a knowledge of God, have been those made one to another by members of the household of faith, the fellowship of the saints, in one generation after another.[69]

---

68. Bradley, *P. T. Forsyth*, 60.

69. Grieve, "Congregationalism's Contribution to Theology," 359n1. Grieve's use here of the word "always" is important for at least three reasons: (1) few knew better than Grieve that Congregationalists such as John Owen and Thomas Goodwin had been more than a little prone to publish on theological themes; (2) in the eighteenth century, much of the theology came in the form of published sermons (not least funeral discourses) and in the hymns of Isaac Watts, Philip Doddridge, and others; and (3) from 1890 until around 1950 there was a flowering of Congregational theology such as had not been seen for some time (see Sell, *Christ and Controversy*, 121–72). By the time Grieve wrote in 1931, Robert S. Franks, Alfred E. Garvie, Robert Mackintosh, and

I: Preaching Sub Specie Crucis

The sermons included in this volume bear witness to that tradition, for it would certainly not be going too far to say that the greatest portion of the public life of one of Congregationalism's favorite sons was given over to preaching. By any standard, Forsyth's literary output was significant, and included an impressive number of pamphlets, reviews and letters to editors, but by far the majority of the words in his more than 340 published articles and twenty-five books are sermons, or were ideas developed from sermons and public addresses. And even those relatively few that are not betray the rhetorical form of one shaped by the pulpit and the tasks that attend such space. As one commentator of an earlier generation noted, "Forsyth was no theorist in Christian theology, working out a system *in vacuo*, out of relation to [human beings] and their actual needs. He was essentially a *preacher*; his books were really printed *sermons*; and his message is, therefore, always living and warm, in close relation to the needs of his audience and the problems of his age."[70]

Three things might be noted about this assessment: The first concerns this matter of "working out a system," the second concerns Forsyth's determination to speak to real human needs, and the third concerns Forsyth's belief in preaching itself. Regarding the first of these, Forsyth held with some suspicion those forms of systematics "whose clear edges are apt to reduce the impressiveness of the vast spiritual contours."[71] The fairly unanimous documentation and denigration of the unsystematic tenor of Forsyth's writing would probably not have disturbed him insofar as he was suspicious of "systems" and there is something about his heterogeneous approach that makes his work less dated than most. He most certainly would have been concerned, however, if his readers deduced from his aversion to "systems" that his thought is not governed by, and around, certain crucial ideas at the heart of Christian truth. At the very least, Forsyth invited a reconsideration of what the adjective "systematic" in "systematic theology" might mean. Not only did he believe that the reduction of religion to a system eviscerates it but he also deemed that no system is fit for the task of stinging "the mind and conscience of the evangelicals out of their Hegelian day-dreams into a sense of theological reality and crisis."[72] Frederick Maurice's words regarding his famed father, F. D. Maurice, might well apply to Forsyth too: "His thoughts and character were not . . . built up like rows of neatly ordered bricks. Rather, as each new thread of thought was caught by the shuttle of his ever-working mind, it was dashed

---

Forsyth himself had made numerous substantial published contributions, and there had also been solid theology published from the likes of George Payne, David Worthington Simon, Andrew M. Fairbairn, and others.

70. Escott, *Director of Souls*, 21.
71. Forsyth, "The Meaning of a Sinless Christ," 308; reprinted in this volume, 283–98.
72. Griffith, "Peter Taylor Forsyth," 1; cf. Forsyth, "Intellectualism and Faith," 328.

I: Preaching Sub Specie Crucis

in and out through all the warp and woof of what had been laid on before, and one sees it disappearing and reappearing continually affecting all else, having its colour modified by successive juxtapositions, and taking its own place in the ever growing pattern."[73]

Evident here is something germane to the English tradition itself—a tendency to rest its laurels on historical, exegetical, homiletical and rhetorical skills rather than on those of systematics. And while Forsyth did not share the English tradition's "nationalist fear of continental thought,"[74] he was suspicious of "systems" that aim at a certain level of watertightness, not least because such systematizations tend to overlook the limits set by the nature of the subject itself—namely God. He was also aware that the theologian's task is far from complete when the historian and exegete has set down her pen. Carved out *against* his rejection of Hegel's monism, Schleiermacher's pessimism, Lessing's historiographical skepticism, and *from* which he developed his principle of authority, moral reality, and a proper distinction between creation and God, Forsyth's ministry represents not a *via media* but a third way: the interpretation of all history, thought and action in light of God's self-disclosure in Christ, the "continuous evangelical centre"[75] from which all *dogma*, *doctrine* and *theology* are developed, and to which the preacher, like the underside image of Martin Luther in Lucas Cranach's 1547 altarpiece in Stadtkirche St. Marien in Wittenberg, bears witness.[76] Standing undeliberately in the tradition of Augustine of Hippo

---

73. Maurice, *Life 1*, 147. Of F. D. Maurice, Forsyth once said: "I owe a great deal to Maurice; in some respects I owe him everything." Forsyth, "Ministerial Libraries," 268.

74. Gunton, "The Nature of Systematic Theology," 14.

75. Forsyth, "Newest Theology," 581.

76. The distinction Forsyth proposes between *Dogma*, *Doctrine*, and *Theology* is critical to understanding his presentation, and it is most clearly outlined in *Theology in Church and State* (1915). Briefly put, *Dogma*, for Forsyth, nearly always refers to the one compressed statement of the gospel. Forsyth suggests that this could be John 3:16, 2 Corinthians 5:18–19 or Romans 1:16–17. It should be brief, but the important thing is its finality. It forms the basis for doctrine and theology. *Dogma* is that which "holds the Church rather than is held by it." Forsyth, *Theology in Church and State*, vi. To employ an imperfect analogy from the world of botany, *Dogma*, if you like, is the tree's root system and trunk. It is *Dogma* that (1) makes the Church the Church; (2) secures the Church's freedom and rights from State interference; (3) forms the basis of ecumenical union and survival; and (4) provides the only basis by which churches might serve together in ministry and mission. *Doctrine* refers to the expansion, clarification and development of *Dogma*. It is indispensable for the Church's practical unity and for protection against other "gospels." To continue with the analogy, *Doctrine* refers to the tree's branches. It has a relationship integral to the trunk, but no one branch is indispensable to the life of the tree and can (indeed must) be pruned or lopped if the life of the tree is at stake. It has no finality (as *Dogma* does) and requires editing and revision in new circumstances. *Theology* is the prime necessity for *Doctrine*, for "it is theology which prepares the material for

I: Preaching Sub Specie Crucis

and of Gregory of Nyssa, Forsyth takes seriously what Rowan Williams refers to as "the oddity of the world, its irreducibility to the tidy patterns of logic,"[77] and "premature harmonies,"[78] and, like Saint John of the Cross, "the Christian suspicion of conceptual neatness, of private revelation and religious experience uncontrolled by the reference to the givenness of Christ's cross."[79] By seeing things whole, rather than in isolated clumps waiting to be ordered, Forsyth avoided the Enlightenment's traps of losing the "macro" through the dissection of the "micro." And by not succumbing to the provisionality of any "system" but rooting theology in the blood-satiated divine economy, Forsyth remained at once deeply and "thoroughly systematic,"[80] evangelical, trinitarian, ecclesial, ecumenical and catholic. Few have voiced it more exactly than J. K. Mozley:

> The student of this remarkable thinker [Forsyth] feels that language is taken by force, and strained to its utmost capacity for the expression of the conceptions which raise themselves from the great deeps of a mind wherein the Christian has triumphed over the philosopher, and then served himself of his adversary's weapons. Systematic is not a word that one would naturally apply to Dr. Forsyth; yet I know of no theologian of the day who has fewer loose ends to his thought. To adopt a phrase of his own he never attempts to set up in his theology a subsidiary centre, but at every point which he reaches in the

---

the doctrine by which the Church preaches its dogma." Pitt, *Church, Ministry and Sacraments*, 85. Forsyth also distinguishes between primary and secondary theology. Primary theology is that which is verifiable by experience. Secondary theology is that which is a scientific exposition of primary theology. Secondary theology is verified by thought. Moreover, secondary theology is necessary for the Church, its life and witness, but not for the individual. Primary theology is personal, experiential. It forms part of the very act of revelation upon which secondary theology reflects. Primary theology is sacramental itself. Secondary theology describes the sacrament given in primary theology. Primary theology is a theology of experience. Secondary theology is the experience of theology, what Forsyth calls "faith thinking." Theology, therefore, is something like the tree's leaves. Departure from the Church's *Doctrine* or *Theology* ought not to be considered as heresy. The Church's *Dogma*, its positive faith, is the only criteria for truth. Forsyth averred that we ought to be free to modify, re-evaluate and/or disregard our doctrines and theology against the Church's *Dogma*. When such modification, re-evaluation and/or disregard actually reduces or extinguishes the *Dogma* and replaces it with a new dogma (even under the banner of "freedom") then this is heresy (rather than freedom). Thus heresy, for Forsyth, is not an abandonment of the creeds but abandonment of the positive faith to which the creeds point.

77. Williams, *The Wound of Knowledge*, 79.
78. Williams, *Christian Theology*, 50.
79. Williams, *The Wound of Knowledge*, 180.
80. Sell, *Testimony and Tradition*, 179.

I: Preaching Sub Specie Crucis

gradual development of a position, or by some bold *coup de main* [vigorous attack], one knows that there is a straight line back, as from any point on the circle's circumference to its centre, to that which is the moral and therefore the only possible centre of the world—the Cross of Christ.[81]

On this matter, Karl Barth too offers words which we might employ to describe Forsyth's thought:

> Let us remember first an old hermeneutical rule which says that there is no law concerning the sequence of theological topics. You can begin theology anywhere, however you like. We are allowed to begin here, or there. Let us hope that we do not do it arbitrarily, but it can be done! Each specific doctrine or topic in theology is to be understood, let us say, as a point on the periphery of a circle, a point which points to the focus and common center. So, you can begin here, or here, or here, and you always have the same subject-matter with which to deal. Each doctrine or topic can be treated and explained adequately if it is clearly such a finger pointing towards the center. The criterion is that a point must point! If we look here, and here, and here but not at the same center, then all is wrong everywhere . . . Systematization is always the enemy of true theology.[82]

Insofar as it is possible, Forsyth directed much of his effort towards resisting the temptation to build a theology on the "foundations of the present"—on those systems which he suggested "do not last," are built "but to house a generation or a couple," and so are "all revisable, all on lease." Instead, Forsyth posited that we ought be building as did our forebears, citing the Latin phrase *In aeternum pinxerunt*, "They built/made to last forever." They built towards finality and universality—specifically, the finality and universality of God's action in the man Jesus of Nazareth. Herein, moreover, is soteriology not as a matter of scientific curiosity but of existential relation to the gospel. As he would put it in his lectures on preaching, "A few mighty cohesive truths which capture, fire, and mould the whole soul are worth much more than a correct conspectus of the total area of divine knowledge."[83] By so undertaking theology, Forsyth encourages an opening up rather than a shutting down of exploratory space and so promotes situations wherein the deepest of theological truths might mesh with "the texture of reality as we experience it, which is open-ended,

---

81. Mozley, *The Doctrine of the Atonement*, 182.
82. Barth, "A Theological Dialogue," 173–74.
83. Forsyth, *Positive Preaching and the Modern Mind*, 85–86.

complex and often elusive, resisting our efforts to pin it down."[84] The sermons contained in this volume bear witness to this deliberate habit. So this is the first observation that the reader of Forsyth's sermons would do well to keep in mind; namely, his suspicion of theological "systems" and his ardor for having his mind and speech governed by and around the gospel's primary dogma or "continuous evangelical centre"—that God was in Christ reconciling the world to himself.

The second observation concerns Forsyth's resolve to address real human needs. Forsyth reminded us that the often-made distinction between "practical" and "speculative" theology is unhelpful. A queen of the sciences, theology remains ever a "practical" science—that is, it exists not for its own sake but for the sake of the Christian community, and for that community's living witness to the Word of Life. Indeed, Forsyth, like those English Puritans that he appreciated so much, was an intensely practical theologian. Alan Gaunt named Forsyth "the preacher's theologian,"[85] and so he was, not least for his conviction that responsible theology doesn't come to birth in a vacuum, and so "we must pay attention to the world God has placed us in," taking it as we find it. For, as Forsyth averred, "it is this age that we are set to serve, change, and raise. It is not another in which we do not live. We must deal with our own conditions."[86] Such a conviction is evidenced in the fact that Forsyth penned what is not only one of the most profound books ever written on prayer[87] and one of the most compelling short studies on Christian perfection,[88] but also numerous articles, letters, poems and sermons on subjects as diverse as corruption,[89] politics,[90] slave labour, education,[91]

---

84. Hart, "Systematic—In What Sense?," 342.

85. Gaunt, "Preacher's Theologian," 41–66.

86. Forsyth, "Gain and Godliness," 357. Denney suggested that perhaps Forsyth's most powerful words are spared for diagnoses of the moral condition of both Church and society at large, diagnoses which Forsyth offers in light of humanity's neglect of God's holiness, the inexorability of God's love and the transforming judgement in God's forgiving grace. Forsyth, Denney avers, "takes care not to be personal, nor to say what implies censure of individuals, but he feels free to be scornful of much on which a whole generation has nursed its self-complacency." Denney, "Principal Forsyth on Preaching," 57.

87. Forsyth, *The Soul of Prayer*.

88. Forsyth, *Christian Perfection*. This essay was later included in *God the Holy Father*.

89. Forsyth, *Corruption and Bribery*.

90. See Forsyth, "Why Am I a Liberal," 4.

91. See Forsyth, "Church, State, Dogma, and Education," 827–36.

I: Preaching Sub Specie Crucis

faith and experience,[92] "cheap and scrappy" journalism,[93] motherhood,[94] divorce,[95] children,[96] Bible reading,[97] fundraising,[98] and weariness.[99] He also sounded significantly more loudly than most how the cross is not only the locus of God's self-justification and self-discovery but that its action is that which gifts our confidence in God's efficacy and determination to fully sanctify the creation of which we are a part, realities which are confirmed in the evangelical experience of forgiveness and whose goal is the transformation of the human conscience, will, relationships and society. These are all immensely "practical" themes, and each is firmly grounded in the most mature theological convictions within the Church's tradition.

In an article on Forsyth, Markus Barth described Forsyth as "the theologian the practical [person] needs!" He continued:

> I cannot understand why his works are not much more widely read, why such a man of interdenominational importance is not installed as a teacher and herald in thousands of hearts. Is he forgotten because tied down to his era? Is he too hard to be read? Is he too theoretical? He [or she] must be a very narrow minded and above all unpractical [person] who by such pretexts would cut himself [or herself] off from so rich a source of good theology. Biblical theology is practical by its very being; it helps us to preach and to pray, and may keep us from going too much astray in faith and life. We desire good Christian instruction for individual life, religious experience, and the problems of the modern world? If so, the books of modern philosophers, psychologists, and moralists may be more safely neglected than those of P. T. Forsyth. It is worth while spending time on his works, for they give us a standard by which our own preaching and teaching may be judged.[100]

And what Andrew Fairbairn has written of R. W. Dale might fittingly be applied to our subject too:

---

92. See Forsyth, "Faith and Experience," 415–17; Forsyth, "Faith, Timidity, and Superstition," 111–16.
93. Forsyth, "The Decay of Brain Power," 41–43.
94. Forsyth, "Motherhood," 255–56.
95. See Forsyth, "The Church and Divorce," 885.
96. See Forsyth, "The Church and the Children," 169.
97. See Forsyth, "A Few Hints about Reading the Bible," 530–44.
98. Forsyth, "The Fund and the Faith," 219; Forsyth, "Gain and Godliness, 356–58.
99. Forsyth, *The Weariness in Modern Life*.
100. M. Barth, "P. T. Forsyth," 437.

I: Preaching Sub Specie Crucis

> His theological work had the rare note of integrity and reality. It was his own; won by the sweat of his own brain; interpreted for him by the experiences of his own life. His manhood was rooted in it; and in it he had articulated the convictions by which he lived. He was a theologian by intellectual necessity, for his was a nature to which thought was native. No man ever had less of the mere rationalist in him; yet his faith, however penetrated by emotion and transfigured by imagination, had been passed through the fire of an intellect that was not so much critical as synthetic.[101]

Or, as another has written of Forsyth himself: "He does not indulge in theological abstractions for the joy of exercising his mental machinery. He wrestles with life and death, and then shows what they mean to the pastor, the church and the [person] on the street."[102] Certainly, Forsyth's theology was carved out at the coalface with people in their doubt and hope, their grief and joy, their disgrace and virtue, and their recalcitrance and repentance. Unlike those über-leaders who carry the title "Pastor" but whose principal attention is the conference tour or the promotion of their own merchandise, Forsyth was first and foremost a local chapel minister who, for twenty-five years and in five distinctive churches, knew and loved his people, and who took seriously his responsibilities to them.

Even when he, in the spring of 1901, was called to the Principalship of Hackney College, or when, just four years later, he assumed the role of Chairman of the Congregational Union of England and Wales, Forsyth did not use these callings to wider service as excuses to retreat into the havens of a cloistered cleric or to sail into those harbors which can so easily attend an institutional office. Rather, he was in touch with the wider community and church—publicly opposing in 1904 and again in 1906, for example, the importation of Chinese labour into the Transvaal on the grounds that it was a disguised form of slavery,[103] and occupying various pulpits until near the end of his days, and hammering out on the anvil of life the implications of the reality that "God was in Christ reconciling the world to himself," the Pauline text to which Forsyth drew frequent attention.[104]

That said, we must also underscore the fact that while Forsyth took his context seriously—one here recalls Barth's oft-quoted line about "the Bible and

---

101. Fairbairn, "Dale as a Theologian," 695.

102. Wiersbe, "Theologian for Pastors," 98.

103. From 18 to 29 January 1906, Forsyth penned at least five letters to the London newspaper *The Times* raising concern about the policy of slave labour in the Transvaal.

104. On the soteriological implications of this verse in Forsyth's theology, see Goroncy, "The Final Sanity Is Complete Sanctity," 249–79.

I: Preaching Sub Specie Crucis

the Newspaper"[105] made in a 1966 interview—he theologized and preached as one who believed that Scripture proves the world, *scriptura probat mundum*, rather than the other way around. He who believed that the Bible's expositor is "the organ of the only real and final authority for mankind"[106] would almost certainly have agreed with Herman Melville who, in *Moby Dick*, equated the world with a ship's rear, and the pulpit with its prow: "The pulpit is ever this earth's foremost part; all the rest comes in its rear; the pulpit leads the world. From thence it is the storm of God's quick wrath is first descried, and the bow must bear the earliest brunt. From thence it is the God of breezes fair or foul is first invoked for favorable winds. Yes, the world's a ship on its passage out, and not a voyage complete; and the pulpit is its prow."[107]

And this brings us to the third matter that will, hopefully, be apparent to readers of Forsyth's sermons and which we have already had reason to mention—Forsyth believed in preaching. Or, put more exactly, he believed that God is committed to self-disclosure and to human transformation through the ministry of the Church's pulpit work. He would even boldly announce, as he did in the opening words of his Lyman Beecher Lectures, that "with its preaching Christianity stands or falls."[108] In those same Yale lectures, Forsyth proceeded to articulate this conviction that the Church suffers from three things: (1) from *triviality* (with externality); (2) from *uncertainty* (of its foundation); and (3) from *satisfaction* (with itself). And to cure these, he averred, the gospel we have to preach prescribes three remedies. For the first, *triviality*, the gospel sounds a new note of greatness in our creed, the note that sounds in a theology more than in a sentiment. For the second, *uncertainty*, the gospel sounds a new note of wrestling and reality in our prayer. And for the third, *satisfaction* (or *complacency*), the gospel sounds a new note of judgment in our salvation. "These three remedies," he insisted, "cannot be taken by way of mere outward enterprise (which will,

---

105. "Der Pfarrer und die Gläubigen sollten sich nicht einbilden, dass sie eine religiöse Gesellschaft sind, die sich um bestimmte Themen herum dreht, sondern sie leben in der Welt. Wir brauchen doch—nach meiner alten Formulierung—die Bibel und die Zeitung." See also Barth and Thurneysen, *Revolutionary Theology in the Making*, 45. Perhaps the clearest published statement from Barth concerning his conviction that theology doesn't "stand on the air" but "must touch the earth somewhere, if only with one foot" (K. Barth, "The Need and Promise of Christian Preaching," 99), comes from a *Time Magazine* piece published on Friday 31 May 1963: "[Barth] recalls that 40 years ago he advised young theologians 'to take your Bible and take your newspaper, and read both. But interpret newspapers from your Bible.'" K. Barth, "Theologians: Barth in Retirement," cited in K. Barth, *Gespräche: 1963*, 356.

106. Forsyth, *Positive Preaching and the Modern Mind*, 27.

107. Melville, *Moby Dick*, 35.

108. Forsyth, *Positive Preaching and the Modern Mind*, 1.

I: Preaching Sub Specie Crucis

indeed, collapse for want of them). They can only be taken inwardly, by means of more religion, more positive religion, and more personal religion." He continued: "I believe that a Church really sanctified would develop more power, light, and machinery for dealing with the tremendous realities of the world than is possible while we are groping in the dark, picking our timid path in economics, or flogging up the energies of a flagging faith."[109]

Later on in those same lectures, Forsyth took a seldom-taken opportunity to reflect quite personally on his ministry in order to encourage those young men—and, in those days, they were all men and statistically younger than contemporary crops—who were preparing to enter pastoral ministry:

> Might I venture here to speak of myself, and of more than thirty years given to progressive thought in connection, for the most part, with a pulpit and the care of souls? Will you forgive me? I am addressing young men who have the ministry before them, as most of mine is behind, strewn indeed with mistakes, yet led up of the Spirit.
>
> There was a time when I was interested in the first degree with purely scientific criticism. Bred among academic scholarship of the classics and philosophy, I carried these habits to the Bible, and I found in the subject a new fascination, in proportion as the stakes were so much higher. But, fortunately for me, I was not condemned to the mere scholar's cloistered life. I could not treat the matter as an academic quest. I was kept close to practical conditions. I was in a relation of life, duty, and responsibility for others. I could not contemplate conclusions without asking how they would affect these people, and my word to them, in doubt, death, grief, or repentance. I could not call on them to accept my verdict on points that came so near their souls. That is not our conception of the ministry. And they were people in the press and care of life. They could not give their minds to such critical questions. If they had had the time, they had not the training. I saw amateurs making the attempt either in the pew or in the pulpit. And the result was a warning. Yet there were Christian matters which men must decide for themselves, trained or not. Therefore, these matters could not be the things which were at issue in historic criticism taken alone. Moreover, I looked beyond my immediate charge, and viewed the state of mind and faith in the Church at large—especially in those sections of it nearest myself. And I became convinced that they were in no spiritual condition to have forced on them those questions on which scholars so delighted

---

109. Ibid., 115–16.

and differed. They were not entrenched in that reality of experience and that certainty of salvation which is the position of safety and command in all critical matters. It also pleased God by the revelation of His holiness and grace, which the great theologians taught me to find in the Bible, to bring home to me my sin in a way that submerged all the school questions in weight, urgency, and poignancy. I was turned from a Christian to a believer, from a lover of love to an object of grace. And so, whereas I first thought that what the Churches needed was enlightened instruction and liberal theology, I came to be sure that what they needed was evangelization, in something more than the conventional sense of that word. "What we need is not the dechurching of Christianity, but the Christianizing of the Church." For the sake of critical freedom, in the long run that is so. Religion without an experimental foundation in grace, readily feels panic in the presence of criticism, and is apt to do wild and unjust things in its terror. The Churches are not, in the main, in the spiritual condition of certainty which enables them to be composed and fair to critical methods. They either expect too much from them, and then round upon them in disappointed anger when it is not forthcoming. Or they expect so little from them that they despise them as only ignorance can. They run either to rationalism or to obscurantism. There was something to be done, I felt, before they could freely handle the work of the scholars on the central positions.

And that something was to revive the faith of the Churches in what made them Churches; to turn them from the ill-found sentiment which had sapped faith; to re-open their eyes to the meaning of their own salvation; to rectify their Christian charity by more concern for Christian truth; to banish the amiable religiosity which had taken possession of them in the name of Christian love; and to restore some sense not only of love's severity, but of the unsparing moral mordancy in the Cross and its judgment, which means salvation to the uttermost; to recreate an experience of redemption, both profound and poignant, which should enable them to deal reasonably, without extravagance and without panic, with the scholars' results as these came in. What was needed before we discussed the evidence for the resurrection, was a revival of the sense of God's judgment grace in the Cross, a renewal of the sense of holiness, and so of sin, as the Cross set forth the one, and exposed the other in its light. We needed to restore their Christian footing to many in the Churches who were far within the zone which criticism occupies. In a word, it seemed to me that what the critical movement called for was not a mere palliation of orthodoxy, in the shape of liberal views, but a new positivity of Gospel. It was not a new comprehensiveness, but a new concentration, a new evangelization, that was demanded by the situation.[110]

In a moving memoir of her father, Jessie Andrews recorded the impressions offered by one of her father's friends and disciples:

> What a mental energy he had! There was something demonic in it. He never approached his themes with the studied grace of the academic. His mind flung itself on them, tearing away everything that was insensible, and pursuing until he got to the heart. His work will remain a puzzle to everyone who imagines that it was deliberate, that it was an affectation. It was just that energy of mind that flung him upon his themes, that kept him catching glimpse after glimpse of the truth, that kept him endeavouring with words to keep abreast with the pursuit of his mind. And just because words can never keep pace with mind, his style is difficult. It was the man himself and his passion speaking in it.[111]

But above all else, it was always the cross that drove him on, the cross that provided the content of his ministry, and the cruciality of which was given in his preaching like a perpetual offering. The Moderator of the General Assembly of the Presbyterian Church of Wales, T. Charles Williams, spoke for not a few when, in his moving tribute upon Forsyth's death in 1921, he articulated: "No one have ever made preaching a bigger thing, nor the Cross more real and central to me than he did."[112] And as Forsyth's "closest friend and colleague in the later years," his own son-in-law and Professor of New Testament Exegesis at New College and Hackney College, Herbert Tom Andrews, would write of Forsyth:

> He might have been a burning and a shining light in almost any intellectual firmament, but like St. Paul, he imposed upon himself the limitation, 'I determined to know nothing among you save Jesus Christ and Him crucified'... He was a theologian, but as a theologian he was *sui generis*, and totally unlike the other theologians with whom I was acquainted. As I came to know him more intimately there gradually grew up in my mind the conviction that he was a prophet—the greatest prophet of our times—a second Amos, an Amos with the vision of the Cross. And it is as the prophet of the Cross that I have regarded him

---

110. Ibid., 192–94.
111. Andrews, "Memoir," xxvii.
112. Williams, "A Tribute from Wales," 154.

I: Preaching Sub Specie Crucis

ever since ... For him the Cross was everything—'his rock, his reality, his eternal life.' Apart from the historic act of redemption, there was nothing in Christianity that counted for very much with him. He used all the weapons in the prophet's armour to confound his opponents. People thought sometimes that some of his blows were too hard, but he felt that he was fighting for the very life of the Faith, and that he had no option but to contend to the uttermost for his soul's convictions.[113]

In May 1918, at the invitation of the Congregational Union of England and Wales, Forsyth addressed the Assembly on the topic of "Congregationalism and Reunion," subjects that had occupied considerable energy of his for some decades. In that lecture, Forsyth suggested that those who would lay the blame for the Church's contemporary challenges at the feet of clericalism or materialism might more accurately and appropriately lay such at the feet of a number of other "isms," among which he named naturalism, humanism, and idealism, and also "spirituality of the æsthetic sort, which treats faith as but human nature at its best, knows nothing of a new birth, writes off sin as but a moral neuralgia, and regards atonement as but an anodyne."[114] It was against precisely such powers—such "isms"—that Forsyth would persuade fellow preachers to aim their pulpits. But not only there, for there was enough of John Calvin and of the English puritans in him—indeed, there was enough of St Paul in him!—to know that preaching must speak not only to the broad movements and ideas that give rise to human history but also, as we have seen, to living souls. Indeed, in a universe unified by the one moral reality, Jesus Christ, one ought not speak of one apart from the other. If Christianity is about "the absolute kingship of God in Christ," then its corollary involves putting to death that counter-word or "creed that preaches the humanities, the amenities, the urbanites, the sentimentalisms, and even the adventure and research

---

113. Andrews, "Memoir," xxvii–xxviii. In fact, not a few considered Forsyth to be something of a prophet, and J. K. Mozley was certainly correct when he wrote just a few years after Forsyth's death: "The fact is that Forsyth was eminently what the mind of his time, not least the Christian mind, needed, but not what it wanted." Mozley, *The Heart of the Gospel*, 69. On the notion of Forsyth as prophet see, for example, Anderson, "P. T. Forsyth: Prophet of the Cross," 146–61; Brown, *P. T. Forsyth: Prophet for Today*; Cunliffe-Jones, "P. T. Forsyth: Reactionary or Prophet?," 344–56; Escott, *Director of Souls*, 10–11; Higginson, "Peter Taylor Forsyth: Prophet and Pastor," 309, 315; Hunter, "P. T. Forsyth Neutestamentler," 100; Miller, Barr and Paul, *P. T. Forsyth: The Man, the Preachers' Theologian, Prophet for the 20th Century*; Pitt, *Church, Ministry and Sacraments*, 176–87; Simpson, "P. T. Forsyth: The Prophet of Judgment," 148–56.

114. Forsyth, *Congregationalism and Reunion*, 69.

I: Preaching Sub Specie Crucis

in life, at the cost of the moral realities, divinities, powers, and dominants of the historic Kingdom of God." Forsyth continues:

> The subtle danger is when mere impressions from the Unseen, pietist, aesthetic, or occult, take the place of moral regeneration by the Spirit. It is the construing of Christianity by the social affections instead of reading these by the affections of grace. It is the domination of religion by the homely instead of by the holy, by the hearty instead of by the heavenly. It is pre-occupation with a love that loves much instead of the love that is forgiven much, with love passionate in its intensity, instead of love moral in its quality. It is the type of religion that treats the supernatural as superior to nature only in degree and not in kind.[115]

It is at this point that Forsyth insisted that there is all the difference in the world between lecturing and preaching. Forsyth was certainly engaged in both activities, but he was clear that whereas the former plays with themes, the latter handles powers. And when he was preaching, he understood that to undertake the former only is fatal, both to the hearers and to the Church's witness to the living Word of God. To take up the mantle of the latter, however—that is, to be a preacher—was to work "in the wake of the prophet and the succession of the apostle."[116] And because preaching is nothing less than the cross—which is itself "God's 'preachment'"—declaring and prolonging itself, preaching, Forsyth insisted, is sacramental in a way that the lecture can never be.[117] It is the act, therefore, of the missionary church which understands that its power lies in Christ, not as an ideal but as the Redeemer, and whose "saving sacrament is the sacrament of the Word and of the living faith it stirs."[118] Or, as Forsyth would put it in his Yale lectures, "The gift of God's grace was, and is, His work of Gospel. And it is this act that is prolonged in the word of the preacher, and not merely proclaimed. The great, the fundamental, sacrament is the Sacrament of the Word."[119] We shall say more about this below. All we need note at this point is that here, as in other key places, Forsyth's position on preaching bore some resemblance to Rome's notion of the perpetual sacrifice of the cross in

---

115. Ibid., 70.

116. Ibid.

117. Forsyth, *The Preaching of Jesus and the Gospel of Christ*, 55. Indeed, Forsyth understood the pastoral office in both prophetic and sacramental terms. See Forsyth, *The Church and the Sacraments*, 133, 142, 144; Forsyth, *Revelation Old and New*, 121; Forsyth, *The Soul of Prayer*, 72–73. Unless stated otherwise all references to *The Soul of Prayer* in this volume are to the 1951 edition.

118. Forsyth, *Missions in State and Church*, 25–26.

119. Forsyth, *Positive Preaching and the Modern Mind*, 3.

the Eucharist, and anticipated some of Barth's best insights about the struggle that takes place in the confrontation between the gospel and the "false, mendacious thoughts about the world and life," when the "despotic rule" of the latter is "being overthrown" and "the new truth set up in its place."[120] For Forsyth, as for Barth, the preaching of the gospel (as with the reading of Holy Scripture) is not about the transference of data but is always an *event*, always a *becoming* of God afresh, and always, in the gracious economy of Holy Love, a *dynamic* possibility. So, in a volume of sermons by Barth and Eduard Thurneysen, we read:

> Preaching the gospel, the coming to the fore of God's truth, is always an occurrence, an event. The truth of God, no doubt, is true, too, irrespective of us; it wants to become true among us, by gaining entrance here and there with some person who surrenders to truth. In order that this may come about we must go to a particular place. As the fiery heat in the earth's interior breaks forth here and there, as a mountain smokes and a crater forms where we can come upon this heat, thus also the glowing fire of God's truth has broken forth at some place. This place, this breaking forth on the part of God's truth in this world, that is the place of the Saviour, that is Jesus Christ Himself.[121]

Or, as Forsyth himself had earlier articulated: "The greatest thing you can give any man is your God and your Saviour. The reason why some Ministers are valuable for other things than preaching, even valuable in spite of their preaching, is that they preach about God, and about Christ; they do not preach Christ. They are only messengers, not Sacraments."[122] To so recall this dynamic nature of revelation is to remember that Forsyth was, in the theological sense, a "positive" preacher. His Yale lectures published on North American soil are a vigorous articulation of the recent modern-positive theo-biblical program so dominant in Germany and championed through the likes of Theodor Kaftan, Karl Beth, Richard Grützmacher, Richard Rothe, Martin Kähler, Reinhold Seeberg, and others. In those lectures, Forsyth offered a two-pronged protest against both a scholastic and sterile orthodoxy—"canned theology gone stale,"[123] he called it—and the "negative" word proposed by the program associated with theological liberalism. In their place, he proposed a "positive" theology the task of which concerns expounding the saving facts (*Heilstatsachen*) given graciously and

---

120. Barth and Thurneysen, *God's Search for Man*, 71, 72.
121. Ibid., 72. See also Barth, *The Word of God and the Word of Man*.
122. Forsyth, "Ordination Address," np. Republished in this volume, 352–55.
123. Forsyth, *Positive Preaching and the Modern Mind*, 138.

I: Preaching Sub Specie Crucis

fully before we begin. This places us in a situation in which the Church is spared from beginning the theological task all over again, and which, while related to and thankful for the genius of the past, is unafraid of the currents of contemporary thought. Forsyth's is far removed from the mediating theology of the mid-nineteenth century, and expresses no interest in mediating between positions. Indeed, his concern was neither to preserve the truths of a "stiff old orthodoxy"[124] nor to dismantle liberalism *per se*, but rather to unleash the reserve of evangelical faith to promote not a new system of theology but a new pronunciation, a theology with different dialect, what Grützmacher, Seeberg and Beth termed "the modern positive theology" and Kaftan named a "modern theology of the old faith."[125] If not in the academy, then certainly a number of his twenty-seven years in the pastorate taught Forsyth that the "sunny liberalism"[126] he had once embraced with such naïve enthusiasm acquired dysphonia when faced with the actual moral situation wherein human existence happens. Written off by the sterile orthodox for espousing the value of biblical criticism, and by theological progressives for promoting an "out-of-date" gospel, Forsyth carved his own path and refused to be pigeonholed. His own name for his position was "heterodox"—the preservation of "a positive core and a flexible casing"[127]—and he regarded himself as a "large and generous *evangelical*"[128] while longing that the Church might too become such again, as she once was with Athanasius, convinced as he was that the very survival of the Church catholic was at stake. He wrote: "For no Church unity can be welded merely by the pressure of its environment, by the utilitarian need of cohesion in the face of social and moral ills. Such is the nature of the Church that its unity is possible only by the internal energy of the creative redemption that gave it birth; in a word, by the Holy Ghost."[129]

Forsyth considered himself advancing not a "theology" *per se* but an actuality earthed in the economy of the supreme holiness of God's love.[130] He championed a return to the personalism and evangelical authority which made the Reformation truly reforming: "new life and not a new creed, a new

---

124. Forsyth, "The Attitude of the Church to the Present Unrest," 214.
125. See Häring, *The Christian Faith*, 122–23.
126. Forsyth, *Positive Preaching and the Modern Mind*, 106.
127. Forsyth, "Orthodoxy, Heterodoxy, Heresy and Freedom," 322.
128. Ibid., 325.
129. Ibid.
130. See Goroncy, "The Elusiveness, Loss, and Cruciality of Recovered Holiness," 195–209.

I: Preaching Sub Specie Crucis

power and not a new institution."[131] British theology, at the time, recovering from a stiff and hackneyed orthodoxy, tended to misconceive vagueness for breadth and maudlinism for love. And so accusing his age of being "unreal, sentimental and impressionist," Forsyth sought to "go to the bottom of things"[132] and re-ground Christian dogmatics in the positive authority of the great eternities announced in the apostolic word—the triumph of holiness over that sin which would see God murdered. It is to here that we must "continually return," Forsyth insisted, "to adjust our compass and take our course."[133] This, it might be suggested, is part of Forsyth's enduring allure. While some of his ideas deserve more attention, and some others are distracting, his theocentric vision resists being contained or defined by passing fads or scaled down to capitulate to human systems, especially those which make a light thing of sin, and so a cheap and easy thing of its overcoming.

In his presentation of "The Meaning of a Sinless Christ,"[134] Forsyth insisted that we could neither respect nor honor nor worship a God who "smothered our conscience" in uncostly love, a God who thought so little of his "eternal and universal Righteousness" that he owed nothing to himself. Such a kindly God, Forsyth averred, would demand even less than our own consciences and would be incapable of that forgiveness which regenerates and creates anew. Indeed, such a God would be incapable of anything "beyond amnesty and benevolence." The God who has, in the crucified Christ, laid bare the very face of holiness and has thrown his all against sin "with the whole passion of His eternal energy" is the sole content of the gospel that the Church is called—nay, commanded—to proclaim, even at the threat of her own extinction. So Forsyth's apprehension at so much of what passed for preaching in his day, preaching which, he claimed, was concerned with notions of God fundamentally other than the God unveiled in Jesus Christ: "With such a cordial God as has taken the place of Christ's God need we ask why the moral influence of the pulpit decays in the very midst of its popularity; why preaching, as it grows interesting, and delightful, and humane, grows ineffective also upon moral life wherever the conflict is severe; why, especially, it is without effect on the ethic of international life, of public life, and of business life, where energy is tense and serious?"[135]

And Forsyth's response to such a situation? He told his students:

---

131. Forsyth, *Positive Preaching and the Modern Mind*, 210.
132. Forsyth, *The Church, the Gospel, and Society*, 100.
133. Forsyth, *Faith, Freedom, and the Future*, 119, 120.
134. Reprinted in this volume, 283–98.
135. Forsyth, "The Meaning of a Sinless Christ," 302.

I: Preaching Sub Specie Crucis

It is not a new theology we need so much as a renovated theology, in which orthodoxy is deepened against itself, and not pared away. It is a new touch with our mind and, conscience on the moral nerve of the old faith. We have had many new theologies in the last hundred years. Theological enterprise has been turning them out freely. But the vein of liberalism, which thus followed on the old Orthodoxy, has been worked out for the preacher's purpose. It is now exhausted of religious ore. The spring has given out (to change the image), and the stream runs thin, and whispers softly among little pebbles, though once it roared among great boulders now left behind in the hills. It is not sermons we need, but a Gospel, which sermons are killing. We need to go behind and beneath all our common thought and talk. Liberal theology is a standing necessity and a rich growth; but theological liberalism, abroad and at home, thins down into Unitarianism infallibly. What we require is not a race of more powerful preachers, but that which makes their capital—a new Gospel which is yet the old, the old moralised, and replaced in the conscience, and in the public conscience, from which it has been removed. We need that the Gospel we offer be moralised at the centre from the Cross, and not rationalised at the surface by thin science. We need that more people should be asking "What must I do to be saved?" rather than "What should I rationally believe?" We need power more than truth. We need a new sense of the living God as the God whose eternal Redemption is as relevant and needful to this age's conscience as to the first. It is not a ministry we need but a Gospel, which makes both ministry and Church. The Church will not furnish the ministers the age requires unless it provide them with a Gospel which they will never get from the age, but only from the Bible for the age. But it is from a Bible searched by regenerate men for a Gospel, and not exploited for sermons by preachers anxious to succeed with the public. It may be best to preach to the sinners and to the saints and never mind at present the public, who feel neither. If we do that well the public will respect us. If we think of the world, let us think chiefly of the world as the arena of an eternal Redemption, and not of a professional success, or of a social revolution.[136]

At this point, we might profitably recall the words of W. B. Selbie (who, in 1886, enrolled as Mansfield College's first student and who, from 1909, served as its second principal) that were contained in his tribute to Forsyth in the week following Forsyth's death. After noting that his "greatest debt" to

---

136. Forsyth, *The Church and the Sacraments*, 20–21.

I: Preaching Sub Specie Crucis

Forsyth was that the latter enabled him to remain a Congregationalist and so resist the Protestant scourge of denominational ship-jumping to which so many of us have succumbed, he wrote:

> But this, though the greatest debt, was not the only debt I owe him. To me, from the time I first heard him, he has been the most valued of all preachers of the Gospel, and that for two reasons. In the first place, I never heard him without going away enlightened, without receiving a new point of view. Of no other preacher can I say this. In the second place, he was conspicuous among the preachers that I have known, in the fact that his Gospel was such as a man could accept without surrendering his manliness. Too often in our age have we been offered milk-and-water doctrine which may be fit for babes and the shallower type of women, but Forsyth was always conscious of the reality, the deadly reality of sin, on the one hand, and the awful holiness of God on the other. A listener felt ready to bare his back for the punishment he served. All idea of a namby-pamby, foolishly indulgent God was banished for ever from our minds.[137]

Forsyth's confidence in the ever-present good news of God meant that he was not content to let the grammar employed in the past be redeployed to speak on his behalf in a time of crisis that came to its head with the loss of poise in liberal Protestantism's failure to speak to a world whose confidence in progress had been buried in the "chaotic, crater-ridden, uninhabitable, awful . . . abode of madness"[138]—the No Man's Lands of Flanders and France.

> The changeless Gospel must speak with equal facility the language of each new time, as well as of each far land. If it be missionary to every soul it is also missionary to the whole soul of history. There is an ironic, socratic docility in the everlasting Gospel. It must be flexible if it is to search and permeate. It must be tractable and reasonable because it is so supreme and sure. It must have the power to vary, and to meet the forms of thought and life which it does so much to produce. We could never preach to the time if our Gospel had but a lapidary and monumental eternity.[139]

But Forsyth was not only a preacher who was "positive" in the sense of avoiding extremes and staying off hobby-horses. He was also deeply positive in his encouragement of preachers to do so as well—not only to those who find

---

137. Selbie, "Tributes to the Late Rev. Principal Forsyth," 153.

138. Letter of Wilfred Owen to Susan Owen, 4 February 1917, in Owen, *The Collected Letters of Wilfred Owen*, 431.

139. Forsyth, *Positive Preaching and the Modern Mind*, 140–41.

I: Preaching Sub Specie Crucis

themselves contending for the faith at the very battle lines where those ideas which shape and disrail the world, at least for a time, are marching against the gospel and its Christ, but also to those who find themselves cast into despair by the "spiritual skeletons" about them, and within them. "What preacher," he asked, addressing with words animated with the hope of divine determination those who know all too well the sense of failure which overwhelms and the hopelessness which broods at the door, "has not many a time to answer with Ezekiel that they can only live by some miracle of God." Here, one preaches, perhaps, "out of duty more than inspiration ... prophesies in obedience rather than in hope." To such, Forsyth would say: "Well, preach hope till you have hope; then preach it because you have it. 'Prophesy over these bones; call out to the Spirit,' says the Lord. At the Lord's call, if not at your own impulse, call; call with a faith of life when the sense of life is low; speak the word you are bidden, and wait for the word you feel; and then the matter is the Lord's, and you win a new confidence in the midst of self-despair."[140]

And because it is neither bones nor mummies who is the object of the preacher's word, but flesh and blood, and flesh and blood often neither inspired nor kindled by the Spirit of life, the preacher, Forsyth averred, must also woo and wait upon the Spirit of life, and preach to the Spirit of life, invoking the very energy of God "to enter these easy forms" and blow new life on and in them that their feet might be set in the kingdom of God.[141] Such is the forbearing breath of love—love whose patient quests are finally inexplicable, whose gracious self-giving is never to be presumed upon, whose eucatastrophic nature never finally fails (in the words of Micheal O'Siadhail) to birth "a freak twist to the theme, subtle jazz of the new familiar, [a] trip of surprises." "Gratuitous, beyond our fathom, both binding and freeing, this love re-invades us, shifts the boundaries of our being."[142]

In June 1909, Forsyth addressed a number "about to go into the active ministry, and to become stewards of the mysteries of God," a reference to his chosen text (1 Cor 4:1) for that particular gathering. In that "Valedictory Address,"[143] Principal Forsyth was quick to tell those valedictorians present that they were "first of all stewards, not owners," that they were those "with a trust" rather than "with a property." He continued:

---

140. Forsyth, "An Allegory of the Resurrection," 315; reprinted in this volume, 204–23.

141. Ibid.

142. O'Siadhail, "Out of the Blue," 124.

143. Reprinted in this volume under the title, "Stewards of the Mysteries of God," 349–55.

I: Preaching Sub Specie Crucis

You have to carry what many others have tried to carry, a Gospel, a Truth many times uttered. And so I would warn you not to strive to win notice by originality but only by the Gospel you preach. The truest things you will have to say are those that have been said many times, but they are still the most original. Grace is the most original thing in the world. However original sin may be, Grace is more original still. The Grace of God is so original as to be unexplainable. It is great to have gifts to bring home to your hearers, truths, great truths, in a clever way, but remember always that the essential thing for a Minister is not gifts but faithfulness. Faithfulness not to your people but to God . . . [Y]our duty as preachers is not to preach sermons, but to preach a Gospel. What you have to dispense to the people is not anything of yours but a revelation of God's mystery. The great storehouse of this mystery is the Bible. The Bible is your source.

"The Bible is your source." Here one recalls that while Forsyth's writings are not bruised with the exegetical work of a Calvin or a Barth, they nevertheless betray a profound wrestling with Scripture and a mind irrigated with its words, images and themes. That said, his exegesis was sometimes less assiduous than it could have been. So, for example, his comments on Revelation 2:28 from his previously unpublished sermon which appears in this volume: "The peculiarity of this verse is that nobody knows exactly what it means, and we are therefore at liberty to let it suggest what it will."[144] One might well suppose that Forsyth's advice here is not the best posture to adopt when confronted with an obscure or ambiguous text, and, thankfully, this does not represent the default setting for how Forsyth viewed and practiced the expository task generally.

Forsyth wrestled with the implications of his own claim that "the Bible is the supreme preacher to the preacher," asking questions such as how then is the preacher to preach the Bible? And, is the preacher's relationship with the Bible merely suggestive or expository? What is the most fitting association between eisegesis and exegesis? Does the preacher preach whatever might tantalise his or her mind as if the Bible were "a jewelled mass of facets of trembling lights," or is the preacher's task to lead people "into the Bible's own great renewing heart?"[145] Forsyth was convinced of the latter, and he was persuaded that this meant cultivating the practice of preaching through large sections of Scripture and resisting (as certainly the mature Forsyth did) the widespread practice of reducing the Bible to a "religious

---

144. Reprinted in this volume, 340–41.
145. Forsyth, *Positive Preaching and the Modern Mind*, 18.

I: Preaching Sub Specie Crucis

scrap book,"[146] or of leading people "out of the Bible into subjectivities, fancies, quips, or queries."[147] The Bible, he insisted, has a world, a context, an ethos and even a cosmos of its own, and the preacher must lead people into that world—that is, into "the eternal of holy love, grace and redemption, the eternal and immutable morality of saving grace for our indelible sin."[148] Or again, "We must all preach to our age, but woe to us if it is our age we preach, and only hold up the mirror to the time."[149] Those who do the latter will feed up a word which is ever antiquated. There is, no doubt, a challenge here to our age for, as Forsyth was fully aware, the Bible has ceased to be "the text book"[150] of the preacher's audience. He confesses: "Our people, as a rule, do not read the Bible, in any sense which makes its language more familiar and dear to them than the language of the novel or the press. And I will go so far as to confess that one of the chief miscalculations I have made in the course of my own ministerial career has been to speak to congregations as if they did know and use the Bible."[151]

He was equally adamant that preaching is concerned with both instruction and edification: "We cannot do without either. On the one hand instruction with no idea of edification at all becomes mere academical discourse. It may begin anywhere and it may end anywhere. On the other hand, edification without instruction very soon becomes a feeble and ineffective thing."[152] But his foremost concern was to answer what he believed was "the great need of the religious world today"; namely, "a return to the Bible."[153] Encouraging a group of mainly young ministers at an annual conference at Mundesley, Norfolk, in July 1909, he declared:

> I have always done much in my ministry in the way of expounding the Bible, and I would say to the younger ministers particularly who are here, Do not be afraid of that manner of preaching . . . Do not be afraid of long texts, long passages. Preach less from verses and more from paragraphs. If I had my time over again I would do a great deal more in that way than I have done . . . You have to work your way through the chapter with the aid of the best commentary that you can get; and you have to

---

146. Ibid., 19.
147. Ibid., 20.
148. Ibid., 22.
149. Ibid., 5.
150. Ibid., 23.
151. Ibid.
152. Forsyth, *The Work of Christ*, 3.
153. Ibid., 33.

exercise continual judgment in doing so lest you be dragged away into little mallets of detail instead of keeping to the larger lines of thought in the passage in hand.[154]

While rejecting the temptation of dragging people back to the dogmas of scholastic Protestantism, and while embracing, with some caution, the insights of modern biblical criticism,[155] here he re-sounded the note he trumpeted two years earlier and some two-and-a-half thousand miles away in New Haven, Connecticut:

> We must meet criticism of the Bible with a hospitable face. We have learned much from it, and we have much to learn. We preachers, especially, must realize how it has rediscovered the Bible, as Luther rediscovered the Gospel. We must use all wise and tender means to give our people the results of that rediscovery, and to make the Bible for them the real historic and living book which it has so widely ceased to be. We must avoid irritating them with discoveries of what it is not, and statements of what is upset; and we must kindle them with the positive exposition of what it is now found to be for heart, history, faith and grace. We must get rid, as we wisely can, of the amateur and fantastic habit of laying out the Bible in diagrams and schemes, which treat it like a public park, and which ignore historic and critical study. We must give up the allegorical interpretations by which some attempt to save its verbal inspiration, now hopelessly gone. And we must restrain ourselves in the fanciful use of texts at the cost of the historic revelation which the whole context gives. These practices have a show of honouring the Bible, but they really treat it with the disrespect that is always there when we presume people to mean another thing than they say. If you treat a text mystically make it clear that you take a liberty in doing so. Preach more expository sermons. Take long

---

154. Ibid., 34–35, 36.

155. Forsyth believed that even if some of the critics had lost their way, biblical criticism itself exists to witness to faith's historicity, and to assist the Church to hear more clearly "the contingent reality of the early Church's witness to the *kerygmatic* Christ." Rodgers, *The Theology of P. T. Forsyth*, 169. Forsyth would agree with David Yeago's claim that "historical research is propaedeutic to the real theological-exegetical task . . . and it will not fare well if it is not pursued by the means proper to theological reflection." Yeago, "The New Testament and the Nicene Dogma," 97. Or, in Forsythian parlance, the biblical exegete helps the Church and its preachers to "disengage the kernel from the husk, to save the time so often lost in the defence of outposts, and to discard obsolete weapons and superfluous baggage." Forsyth, *Positive Preaching and the Modern Mind*, 280; cf. Forsyth, *The Church, the Gospel, and Society*, 67–70; Forsyth, "The Evangelical Churches and the Higher Criticism," 24, 34–35.

I: Preaching Sub Specie Crucis

passages for texts. Perhaps you have no idea how eager people are to have the Bible expounded, and how much they prefer you to unriddle what the Bible says, with its large utterance, than to confuse them with what you can make it say by some ingenuity. It is thus you will get real preaching in the sense of preaching from the real situation of the Bible to the real situation of the time. It is thus you make history preach to history, the past to the present, and not merely a text to a soul.[156]

And again:

Even if you leap from book to book, finish one book before you take up another. Spend days or weeks at a time in the spiritual climate of one writer and one work. If you go to Switzerland for strength you do not go for a day. You make as many weeks as you can of it. So with the bracing air of Scripture. Live in one district long enough to rest there, to get its benefit, and to feel its spell. Then you come to know it, you possess it, you are built up upon it, and it is amply worth your while. And within each book ministers might preach more on long passages, and unfold their spiritual dialectic, with some care not to import their own or that of the seventeenth century.[157]

Forsyth's response to what he perceived to be "a growing desire for expository preaching—for a long text, and the elucidation of a passage"[158]—was matched by a distaste for short sermons. The impatient demand for homiletical brevity—often coupled with appeals for incessant visits, religious bustle and social events—paralyses the preacher and represents "one of the most fatal influences at work to destroy preaching in the true sense of the word. How can a man preach if he feel throughout that the people set a watch upon his lips? Brevity may be the soul of wit, but the preacher is not a wit. And those who say they want little sermon because they are there to worship God and not hear man, have not grasped the rudiments of the first idea of Christian worship."[159] What such seek, Forsyth decried, is "no more than a warm bath or a sacred concert."[160] In an address delivered on the occasion of his public recognition as Minister at Cheetham Hill, Forsyth lamented:

---

156. Forsyth, *Positive Preaching and the Modern Mind*, 112–13.
157. Forsyth, "A Few Hints about Reading the Bible," 531.
158. Forsyth, *Positive Preaching and the Modern Mind*, 5.
159. Ibid., 75; see also p. 120.
160. Ibid., 100.

I: Preaching Sub Specie Crucis

> Among other regrettable tendencies of the hour is the disposition to depreciate the power of the spoken word. It exists both in the pew and in the pulpit itself. I know preachers who regard their Sunday duty with a contempt (which is evident), compared with the so-called practical work with which they fill five days of the week. And we are constantly pressed with the demand for short sermons. I believe myself that short sermons are mostly themselves too long. The man whose preaching is simply tolerated has no right to preach as long as ten minutes. The man whose preaching is welcomed has no right to be always as short as twenty. We listen gladly to political speeches of an hour, and the reason is that we have an interest, amounting to a passion for the subject. Let us have enough knowledge of the subject of religion as to choose only competent men for ministers, and let it be so real and passionate to us that we can take pleasure in what our prophet or expositor has to say for an hour if he likes. I don't hint that all sermons should be an hour long. But I do think short sermons are killing the pulpit and sending the people to the altar or the platform.[161]

Soon after Forsyth's death, T. Charles Williams recounted: "[Forsyth] spoke with solemn emphasis about the perils of the pulpit. He could see no hope except in the return of strong, expository preaching, with a Gospel 'which had not been discovered but received'. His mind pictured the pulpits occupied with elegant young men 'with the Mansfield manner,' as he slyly put it, indulging in beautiful ritual, genial philanthropy and Italian art, and so denying the faith and Cross of our Redeemer and Lord."[162] And W. Robertson Nicoll, writing during the same week, recalled that Forsyth "grew to be a really eminent preacher. He had always the defect of being lengthy, but he put so much life and fire into his discourses that he carried his hearers with him."[163]

It will be clear by now that what was of primary concern to Forsyth, however, was neither the sermon's length nor the preacher's passion but rather the sermon's content. Again, he was well aware that preaching the Bible or preaching theology is not the same as preaching Christ! "It is a light matter," he wrote elsewhere, "having to cast about for a text to face Sunday compared with having to cast about for a message to face our world." He continued:

> Mere theologians try with all earnestness to do things for the Gospel, or correct opinion about it or bespeak interest in it. And, their result is so lean, so ineffectual, because they do not

---

161. Forsyth, *The Pulpit and the Age*; reprinted in this volume, 131–44.
162. Williams, "A Tribute from Wales," 154.
163. Nicoll, "Principal Forsyth," 146.

I: Preaching Sub Specie Crucis

> appropriate what the Gospel has done for them, and they are not broken to it. Many are touched, fewer are seized, and fewer still are broken. We are much too theological, and we need more religion. We believe in the Gospel as a piece of theology, sometimes stodgy, sometimes thin. It is part of our equipment. But is it not possible to preach ardently about Christianity and be a stranger to grace, to hold a brief for Christ ably, eloquently, and even feelingly, and not preach Christ?[164]

We noted earlier Forsyth's lament of those fellow ministers who, while they may have been engaged in some valuable ministry, preach *about* God and *about* Christ rather than actually preach *Christ*. Such, Forsyth insisted, "are only messengers, not Sacraments,"[165] and preachers are called to be the latter. In his series of essays published as "The Preaching of Jesus and the Gospel of Christ," Forsyth powerfully trumpeted that to preach Christ is neither to carry a word *about* Christ, nor to preach the same message that Jesus preached: "His preaching days were to His consummate work of the Cross what the Baptist was to Himself—forerunners."[166] The Church, as the fruit of that consummate work, does not simply restate the message of the Sermon on the Mount, for example, but must proclaim the message of the Sermon in the fuller light of the redeeming work of God's cross and God's Easter. There is wide disparity, too, between preaching *about* the forgiveness of sins and actually preaching the forgiveness of sins. To do the former is to merely make public some information which may or may not be true, to reflect aloud on what may or may not be a possibility, to speak about what is presumably interesting but which may safely be kept at arm's length, so to speak; to do the latter is, in Luther's words, to be one who "calls the thing what it actually is."[167] This is what it means to be a theologian of the cross—a "sacrament" and not a mere reporter, one who preaches him "in whom we have redemption, the forgiveness of sins" (Col 1:14).

To preach the *totus christus* of the Bible means, for Forsyth, to announce the apostolic *kerygma* of the cross. This does not mean that every sermon ought be explicitly concerned with the atonement so much as that the crucified and risen Lord is the content of all Christian preaching:

> To preach Christ is indeed fundamentally to preach His atonement; but it is not incessantly to preach about it. We must always

---

164. Forsyth, "The Ideal Ministry of the Church," 22.
165. Forsyth, "Ordination Address," np. Republished in this volume, 352–55.
166. Forsyth, *The Preaching of Jesus and the Gospel of Christ*, 10.
167. Luther, "Heidelberg Disputation," 40. See also Forde, *On Being a Theologian of the Cross*.

> preach it, but we need not always preach about it. Only it must not be denied or denounced, never ignored or levelled down to the category of man's efforts to atone his own sins. It is true there are historic stages and junctures when to preach Christ in the more theological form is the only preaching relevant to the mental and moral situation. It was so at the Reformation. But today it may be more needful in certain positions to preach the Christ of the cross than the cross of Christ. There is a strategy in the holy war. It is the last crisis that calls the reserves to the front. But whether we preach the Christ who atoned or the atonement of Christ it is still an atoning Christ and an atoning cross we preach. To preach only the atonement, the death apart from the life, or only the person of Christ, the life apart from the death, or only the teaching of Christ, His words apart from His life, may be all equally one-sided, and extreme to falsity . . . Preach the total Christ therefore in the perspective of evangelical faith, but with immediate stress on that aspect most required by the conscience of the hour.[168]

Forsyth's challenge to preachers to "preach the total Christ . . . in the perspective of evangelical faith" recalls his frequent echo that above all else the Bible is "a preaching book," a sacrament which directs us away from itself to Christ. Hence "faith is not faith in the Bible, but in Christ through the Bible; yet there are many preachers who preach the Bible more than Christ."[169] The Bible, in other words, exists to bear witness to the gospel—Jesus Christ himself—and not to provide mere lessons or precepts. It exists to create faith and not to merely instruct. Consequently, Forsyth held that the gospel for whose sake alone the Bible exists has "no meaning whatever apart from dogmatic truth."[170]

Forsyth may not write as a biblical theologian "in the strict sense of the term,"[171] and one might well wish that Forsyth had shared more with us not only of the finished fruit of his Bible reading but also of the processes of his mind given to disciplined and attentive exegesis of Holy Scripture, but at least one New Testament professor observed that Forsyth "bottoms all his theological thinking" upon scripture and that his biblical scholarship was "twenty or thirty years ahead" of most of the exegetes of his day.[172] Forsyth

---

168. Forsyth, *The Cruciality of the Cross*, 81–82, 83.

169. Forsyth, "The Efficiency and Sufficiency of the Bible," 16.

170. Forsyth, "Church, State, Dogma and Education," 830. See also Forsyth, *Missions in State and Church*, 304–6; Forsyth, *The Work of Christ* 38, 55.

171. Jones, "The Christological Thought of Peter Taylor Forsyth and Emil Brunner," 61.

172. Hunter, *P. T. Forsyth: Per Crucem ad Lucem*, 31. See also Jackson, "The Biblical

I: Preaching Sub Specie Crucis

never wrote a commentary, but this expositor—a third of whose library was in German, who read numerous biblical studies journals every week, and who championed the value of biblical criticism to a British audience still hard of hearing—was clearly on top of his game. He was no hypocrite when he wrote, "No man should ask for a public hearing on a theological question unless he has mastered his New Testament at first hand."[173] Certainly Forsyth's sermons betray evidence of a Bible well-worn, affectionately and prayerfully studied, and trusted to interpret the shifting sands of great movements and ideas with which the Church must wrestle and interpret in light of the divine economy.

This was particularly evident, perhaps, when Forsyth turned to Scripture rather than to the creeds of the Church or to the Fathers to construct his christology, and when he defended the notion that it is the *kerygma* itself which is the unifying reality of the Bible, and especially of the New Testament. Richard Lischer put the latter point well, if not in somewhat hyperbolic form, when he wrote of Forsyth:

> His "positive" theology resisted orthodox biblicism and opposed the shallow liberalism of culture-Christianity decades before Barth and the later crises-theology (a term coined by Forsyth). He focused on the kerygma as the principle of unity in the New Testament long before Dodd brought such thinking into vogue. Before Dibelius and Bultmann introduced the academy to Gospel criticism, the evangelical Forsyth made this startling observation: "The New Testament (the Gospels even) is a direct transcript, not of Christ, but of the preaching of Christ." No one since Luther had so firm as grasp on the kerygmatic nature of the New Testament, and no one in the twentieth century translated that insight into homiletical theology with greater passion than P. T. Forsyth.[174]

Forsyth believed not only that the gospel must save the Church and its beliefs, even save the Church from itself—certainly the Church is in no position to save the gospel!—but also that the Church does not require the "permission of the critics" in order to hear the good news. While grateful for sound biblical criticism, "faith," he wrote, "does not wait upon criticism, but it is an essential condition of it." And because of the nature of the subject matter, the fullest critics are believers and not mere inquirers. He continued: "The passion of an apostolic missionary faith is an essential condition to a sound criticism and a safe; and by 'sound' I don't merely mean sound to the

---

Basis of the Theology of P. T. Forsyth"; Jackson, "P. T. Forsyth's Use of the Bible," 323–37.

173. Forsyth, *Positive Preaching and the Modern Mind*, 70.

174. Lischer, *The Company of Preachers*, 98.

I: Preaching Sub Specie Crucis

Confessions, I mean sound to the mind; and by 'safe' I do not merely mean safe for the Church, but safe for the soul. I mean that faith in the Gospel, evangelical faith, is essential for that full, complete view of the case upon which sound results are based; it is essential in order to be fair to all the facts."[175]

Forsyth was no bibliolatrist. An infallible book implies that our primary need is intellectual rather than moral. To be sure, he believed that it should be difficult for us not to believe in verbal inspiration, but the locus of belief is not the Bible *per se* but that word of grace which both creates the Bible and to which the Bible bears faithful witness. The text itself, he insisted, is of secondary value to the holy intent of its inspiration. It is the communication of the gospel itself which elevates the Bible "above a mere chronicle of events to be dissected and discussed by scholarly pedants"[176] and sets it free to be a "sacrament"[177] and "sermon"[178] of the good news. Indeed, Forsyth considered Holy Scripture to be not only a "sacrament" of the gospel, but also Christ's "holy sepulchre"[179] wherein we realise the living Christ who, as we "pore and wait" for him to address us in Scripture, surprises us from behind by announcing his living presence with us. This is evident in his poem, "A Hymn to Christ":

> O sword that finds, O word that binds
> The weakness of the soul!
> O piercing Word! O healing sword!
> Our terror, and our goal.
> . . .
> O light of God! O fire of God!
> And Truth that maketh true!
> Pierce, search us, burn us, bring to dust,
> But, O, create us new.[180]

Evident here is Forsyth's belief in the dynamic action of the divine Word as he who not merely impresses but who "makes and unmakes," who creates and not simply elicits "the power to answer and understand"

---

175. Forsyth, "An Allegory of the Resurrection," 314.

176. Sykes, "Theology Through History," 232.

177. See Forsyth, *The Principle of Authority*, 134–35, 372–74; Forsyth, "Churches, Sects, and Wars," 620; Forsyth, *The Church and the Sacraments*, 132; Forsyth, *The Church, the Gospel, and Society*, 68–69, 125–27; Forsyth, "A Few Hints about Reading the Bible," 530, 542–43; Forsyth, "The Efficiency and Sufficiency of the Bible," 28–29.

178. Forsyth, *The Church, the Gospel, and Society*, 68–69, 80; Forsyth, *Positive Preaching and the Modern Mind*, 7.

179. Forsyth, *God the Holy Father*, 88.

180. Forsyth, "A Hymn to Christ," 133.

I: Preaching Sub Specie Crucis

himself.[181] The poem also betrays something of Forsyth's conviction that the preacher is to function as "the exegete of the eternal," as one who leads "out of the Bible fold on fold of all that is in it," and who expounds the Bible "in its freshest light . . . drawing forth into the interest of our own day the faiths and truths that were already old in God when they first flashed upon the writers of the Book."[182] And like the Apostle Paul, in order to express a reality as incogitable as the revelation of God in the cross, Forsyth too strained language and tortured ideas which he enlisted from any quarter available to him in an effort to communicate the cruciform shape of grace-filled actuality. But Scripture was not the only chalice from which Forsyth drank. Those themes characteristic of his theology also betray a debt to Anselm, Luther, Kant, Carlyle, Ritschl, Troeltsch, Dorner, Kähler, Schlatter,[183] Turner, Dale, Goethe, Law, Harnack, Arnold, Eliot, Kierkegaard (that "modern 'Pascal of the North'"[184]), Maurice, Fairbairn, Denney, Newman, Schleiermacher, Butler, Nietzsche, Milton, Greenwell, Hardy, Zahn, Seeberg, Schopenhauer, Ibsen,[185] Lessing, Ihmels, Loofs, Bunsen, Schelling, Ruskin (who had made Italy voguish for English Protestants), Browning (London Congregationalism's own poet), and many others. Hegel's ghost too, for example, so prevalent in Forsyth's lectures published as *Religion in Recent Art* and *Christ on Parnassus*, also haunts the sermons in this volume, some (like "Egypt," "Music and Worship" and "An Allegory of the Resurrection") more than others, and his presence recalls Forsyth's wide and deep reading habits, and a mind engaged with those ideas and movements that move not only individuals but centuries and nations too. Just as Forsyth described Ezekiel's preaching, so too it might be said of the Aberdonian himself that "the words that he overheard took wings in his genius."[186] So, while his daring mind remained hospitable to innovative ideas, Forsyth did not take ideas over from others directly. Instead, he ingested their insights, he breathed deeply of their vapor; but these were transformed in his lungs so that what was expired was no longer pure Kant or Kierkegaard, but was now Forsyth.

Forsyth, emboldened by his conviction that the preacher's task is to listen for the echoes of Christ's voice and seek traces of Christ's footsteps in the culture and to bring every thought captive to Christ, read broadly; so,

---

181. Forsyth, *The Preaching of Jesus and the Gospel of Christ*, 80.

182. Forsyth, "Things New and Old," 275; reprinted in this volume, 259–69.

183. On the deep influence that Schlatter had on Forsyth's thought, see Goroncy, *Hallowed Be Thy Name*, 90–93.

184. Forsyth, *The Principle of Authority*, 71.

185. On Forsyth's indebtedness to Ibsen, see Goroncy, "Bitter Tonic for our Time," 105–18; Goroncy, "Fighting Troll-Demons in Vaults of the Mind and Heart," 61–85.

186. Forsyth, "An Allegory of the Resurrection," 312.

I: Preaching Sub Specie Crucis

while the Bible remained his principal text, and while he could celebrate the energetic turn in his day towards expository preaching, he was equally free in the gospel to employ other texts, what he called "new texts." In a fine essay on preaching and poetry, for example, he argued that "nothing is far foreign to the Gospel which helps us to acquire our own souls, or elucidate our true spiritual quality. Indeed, it is the divorce of culture with its spaciousness from the power of the cross that has done so much to make culture pagan, and the Gospel either strident or dull." And he proceeded to ask whether modern literature (and we might here add other arts, too) does not offer us "a much neglected opportunity of expounding the old Gospel from new texts."[187] And again:

> May the expository style not be occasionally applied in the interests of Christian truth to the forms of delight with which our modern literature clothes spiritual truth as it follows into the detail of the modern soul the broad principles of Christ? We mean no jugglery with the word Inspiration. We intend no crude identification, in current literary fashion, of the inspiration of today with the Inspiration which breathes uniquely for all time through the first literature of a unique Redemption. But it is one Spirit, even if His ancient movement is "once for all." We gladly accept, and deeply need, the aid of those thinkers who pursue into the complexity of the modern conscience the large and eternal ethics of Christ. Might we not make more use of those men of genius who in the subtle and beautiful forms of literary art enshrine the pearls of the Christian soul. Literary feeling is not religion, and literary religion is not Christian piety. But are we overdone with teachers who can make the spiritual principles of the Christian soul come home to the contemporary imagination, who speak especially to the best of the young, and who would deliver us, if we would let them, from the sentimental fancies which make so much religion nauseous to the robuster mind. A sermon of quotations is usually bad, both as art and as Gospel. Might not the pulpit go a long way beyond mere quotation in occasionally interpreting these great poetic interpreters, who, if not inspired as text, are at least inspired as commentary, and who illuminate from the broad margin of modern time the mysteries of the small immortal page?[188]

---

187. Forsyth, "Preaching and Poetry," 269; reprinted in this volume, 157–63. See also Goroncy, *To Mend the World*.

188. Forsyth, "Preaching and Poetry," 269.

I: Preaching Sub Specie Crucis

Evident here is not only Forsyth's commodious reading habits and firm grasp on matters philosophical but also his Dostoevskian insight into human nature and into the limberness of the Christian message to address every location on the map of human experience. Certainly, Forsyth entertained no illusions about the real challenges and complexities that attend preaching from a "new text"—that it "calls for skill, taste, and tact," that it "requires that the passage be thoroughly mastered, and the preacher saturated with its turns and shades as well as with its ideal unity," and that it was not to everyone's taste—but, he insisted, it is possible to do it "without either wresting the text or forcing the gospel," and it represents a challenge incumbent upon preachers to expound the "spiritual movement" of the culture as represented in its artistry "from the standpoint of the gospel of Christ."[189] Some of his own attempts to so do are evident in this volume, and those interested in meandering further with Forsyth along this path might also be helped by reading his piece "The Pessimism of Mr Thomas Hardy," or his early reflections on Robert Burns.[190]

We have seen that Forsyth considered preaching to be the word of God—God's speech to God's people. He considered it also to be, however, the action of "the Church confessing its faith." "It is less organized," Forsyth said, "but no less collective than the great creeds. And in the Churches where there are no formal creeds it takes their place. The place of the sermon in the more democratic and non-Catholic Churches is due, in part, to the absence in their ritual of a recited creed. It is all that some of them, like the Congregationalists, have for a creed."[191] And insofar as preaching is the word of God, preaching, Forsyth insisted, is also a "sacrament." Indeed, the Sacrament of the Word, he wrote, is "the distinctively Protestant Sacrament" which "invests the pulpit with the dignity, if not the solemnity which elsewhere is bestowed on the altar." Consequently, "the preacher of the Word must regard its distribution as a Sacrament. He breaks to the people the living bread and inspires them with the wine of God."[192]

When it came to the matter of worship, and especially to the sacraments, Forsyth was a high churchman: "Sacraments, and not socialities, make the centre of our Church life and social unity—Sacraments, and not even social beneficence. Make much of them."[193] That said, Forsyth held that there is really only one primary sacrament—the good news of God's grace in

---

189. Ibid., 271. See Goroncy, "Bitter Tonic for our Time," 105–18; Goroncy, "Fighting Troll-Demons in Vaults of the Mind and Heart," 61–85.

190. See Forsyth, "The Pessimism of Mr Thomas Hardy," 193–219; Forsyth, "Robert Burns 1878," 4; Forsyth, "Robert Burns 1879," 4.

191. Forsyth, *Positive Preaching and the Modern Mind*, 68.

192. Forsyth, *The Pulpit and the Age*; reprinted in this volume, 131–44.

193. Forsyth, *The Church and the Sacraments*, 244.

I: Preaching Sub Specie Crucis

Jesus Christ. According to Forsyth—and here he is in harmony with his own Reformed tradition—the locus of the true sacrament is the single event of the incarnate presence of God. Those derivative events, or what the Church commonly calls "the sacraments"—namely, Baptism and the Lord's Supper, and, we might add with Forsyth, the preaching of the Word and the Bible itself—are aspects of the one event. They are, if one prefers, the secondary proclamation activities that bear witness to, are bound to, and are correlated expressions of, the one primary and objective "sacrament" or mystery of God made known in the unique event called Jesus Christ. In these proclamation activities, the original presentation of God to human persons and of human persons to God—the two-fold event or movement that takes place in the hypostatic union[194]—is re-presented in the sacramental life of the Church; that is, the gospel is proclaimed, God makes himself available to us.[195] With characteristically rhetorical power, Forsyth put it thus: "The Word and the Sacraments are the two great expressions of the Gospel in worship. The Sacraments are the acted Word—variants of the preached Word. They are signs, but they are more than signs. They are the Word, the Gospel itself, visible, as in preaching the Word is audible. But in either case it is an act. It is Christ in a real presence giving us anew His Redemption."[196] Or, as he had articulated it in an earlier lecture:

> The great sacrament of Christianity is the sacrament of the living and preached Word of Reconciliation, whether by speech, rite, or work. The elements may be anything; the Word is everything, the active Word of God's Act, Christ's personal Act met by His Church's. That sacrament of the Word is what gives value to all other sacraments. They are not ends, they are but means to that grace. They are but visible, tangible modes of conveying the same gospel which is audible in the Word. In the sacrament of the Word the ministers are themselves the living elements in Christ's hands-broken and poured out in soul, even unto death; so that they may not only witness Christ, or symbolise Him, but by the sacrament of personality actually convey Him crucified and risen. This cannot be done officially. It cannot be done without travail.[197]

I indicated earlier Forsyth's conviction that the pulpit belongs to the Church in a way that the platform never can. Perhaps it is clearer now why

---

194. See Goroncy, "'Tha mi a' toirt fainear dur gearan,'" 253–86.
195. See Goroncy, "John Calvin."
196. Forsyth, *The Church and the Sacraments*, 176.
197. Ibid., 141.

I: Preaching Sub Specie Crucis

Forsyth recognized this to be the case. The great and fundamental sacrament of the Word is "an act and a power":

> It is God's act of redemption before it is man's message of it. It is an eternal, perennial act of God in Christ, repeating itself within each declaration of it. Only as a Gospel done by God is it a Gospel spoken by man. It is a revelation only because it was first of all a reconciliation. It was a work that redeemed us into the power of understanding its own word. It is an objective power, a historic act and perennial energy of the holy love of God in Christ; decisive for humanity in time and eternity; and altering for ever the whole relation of the soul to God, as it may be rejected or believed . . . And it is this act that is prolonged in the word of the preacher, and not merely proclaimed.[198]

And again:

> To be effective our preaching must be sacramental. It must be an act prolonging the Great Act, mediating it, and conveying it. Its energy and authority is that of the Great Act. The Gospel spoken by man is the energizing of the Gospel achieved by God. Its authority is not that of the preacher's personality, nor even of his faith, nay, not even of his message alone, but that of the divine action behind him, whereof he himself is but as it were the sacramental element, and not the sacramental Grace. If our preaching is not more sacramental than the Catholic altar—I do not say more eloquent or more able, but more sacramental—then it is the altar that must prevail over all our No-Popery. For religion *is* sacramental. Where it is not it becomes bald. And the only question is, where the sacrament lies. We place it in the Word of Gospel. *Accedit verbum et fit sacramentum.* Nothing but the Word made Sacrament can make a Sacrament out of elements, and keep it in its proper place. But what a task for our preachers to fulfil![199]

Evident here again is Forsyth's unyielding conviction that preaching is not lecturing, and that the preacher is not at hand to entertain. The preacher's principal work is apostolic, priestly, prophetic and sacramental.[200] First and foremost, the minister exists to serve the gospel and *only insofar as this is the case* does the minister serve the Church. And so the minister takes their

198. Forsyth, *Positive Preaching and the Modern Mind*, 3.

199. Ibid., 57.

200. See Forsyth, *The Church and the Sacraments*, 133, 142–46, 184–85; Forsyth, *The Church, the Gospel, and Society*, 33; Forsyth, *Congregationalism and Reunion*, 37, 57, 74–78; Forsyth, *Revelation Old and New*, 97–99; 112–13; 121; Forsyth, *The Soul of Prayer*, 72–73.

I: Preaching Sub Specie Crucis

job description not from congregational expectations, and still less from the management theories which abound, but from the gospel itself, proclaimed from font, pulpit and table. So Forsyth:

> An ideal ministry is one which is ideal to the Gospel not to humanity. That is, the ideal minister is not the minister of the human ideal, but of the Gospel ideal in the New Testament. The ideal Minister is first the servant of the word, then of man. It is the Gospel revelation that sets up the ideal; it is not the needs, aspirations, or possibilities of human nature. The ideal ministry is not even to be measured by the demands, dreams, or expectations of the churches. The ideal of the church is apt to be a ministry that fills and manages large and busy buildings, undertakes much, and is kind, even to softness; whereas the dominant note of the New Testament, and especially of Christ's teaching, is love's severity. In His lifetime at least, Christ alienated far more than He drew, and made trouble for almost everybody who touched Him. The early Protestants described themselves not as servants even of the Church, but as *V. D. M., Verbi divini ministri.* They served the Gospel rather than the Church, and the Church for the Gospel's sake. A man is an ideal minister not by his success with the public but by his stewardship of the word, by his adequacy and fidelity to Him that called him.[201]

And again, this time in what was possibly his first address to the Cheetham Hill congregation, from "The Pulpit and the Age":

> You have called and I have answered gladly. But it is not your call that has made me a minister. I was a minister before any congregation called me. My election is of God. Paul speaks of 'a faithful minister of the new covenant' . . . The minister of this covenant, therefore, the minister of Christ, has his call, first, in the nature of God and God's Truth; second, in the nature of man and man's need. We have on one side the divine Gospel; we have on the other the cry of the human. His call is constituted both by the divine election and the requirements of human nature. Would that some who are sure of their election by God, were as sure of their election by man, and their fitness to adapt God's truth to human nature. It is not therefore the invitation of any particular congregation that makes a man a minister. It is a call which on the human side proceeds from the needs rather than from the wishes of mankind, from the constitution of human nature as set forth in Christ, rather than from the appointment

---

201. Forsyth, "The Ideal Ministry of the Church," 22.

> by any section or group of men. I am here, not to meet all your requisitions, but to serve all your needs in Jesus Christ. You have not conferred on me my office, and I am Christ's servant more than yours, and yours for His sake. The minister is not the servant of the Church in the sense of any special community or organization. The old Latin theologians used to subscribe themselves V. D. M., Minister of the Word of God,—Minister not of the Church, but of that Christian human nature which our particular views and demands so often belie. A minister may, on occasion, never be so much of a minister as when he resists his congregation and differs from it.[202]

"Only an age engrossed with impressions and careless about realities"[203] could regard the minister's principal work otherwise, or could embrace that monster of *reductio ad absurdums* of treating the sermon as if it were a mere public address, or some assignment whose goal involves anything less than the death of the congregation, and of the preacher! With wobbly eyes and stammering lips, the preacher carries the very word which carries him or her, a word which is an effective deed of God, and which is "charged with blessing or judgment. We eat and drink judgment to ourselves as we hear. It is not an utterance, and not a feat, and not a treat. It is a sacramental act, done together with the community in the name and power of Christ's redeeming act and our common faith."[204]

"I have no hesitation in speaking strongly," Forsyth announced in his first published sermon, "The Turkish Atrocities." "I am not a statesman who has to weigh every word and consult a thousand interests. I have no responsibility upon me but that of uttering the truth."[205] And although this sermon demonstrates that the newly ordained Forsyth was far less concerned with biblical exposition than was the more mature expositor he would become, even here he is as clear as he was in the winter years of his ministry when he addressed, in May 1918, the Assembly Meetings of the Congregational Union of England and Wales, and reminded them—and no doubt himself too—"I am handling powers and not themes. I am not lecturing; and I am not playing with touching things. I am preaching."[206]

Forsyth championed that the Church must recover the dogmatic positivity of evangelical faith. Where the exigency of the Word has been

---

202. Reprinted in this volume, 131–44.
203. Forsyth, *Positive Preaching and the Modern Mind*, 54.
204. Ibid., 56.
205. Forsyth, "The Turkish Atrocities," 4; reprinted in this volume, 69–74.
206. Forsyth, *Congregationalism and Reunion*, 70.

I: Preaching Sub Specie Crucis

abandoned, there seems to be little or no reason for a congregation to assemble each Sunday, no matter how stimulating a particular preacher's personal views might be, or how talented its musicians. Without Christ proclaimed from pulpit, font and table, the Church quickly becomes a harbinger of mediocrity, quackery, and "the gossipy side of life" which is "associated with the small and negligible side of the soul."[207] It is the real presence of Christ crucified, and not great oratory, that makes preaching. And it is the real presence of Christ crucified that transfigures a mere sermon into the good news and self-announcement of God. To cite Forsyth, again at length:

> Preaching . . . is the most distinctive institution in Christianity. It is quite different from oratory. The pulpit is another place, and another kind of place, from the platform. Many succeed in the one, and yet are failures on the other. The Christian preacher is not the successor of the Greek orator, but of the Hebrew prophet. The orator comes with but an inspiration, the prophet comes with a revelation. In so far as the preacher and prophet had an analogue in Greece it was the dramatist, with his urgent sense of life's guilty tragedy, its inevitable ethic, its unseen moral powers, and their atoning purifying note. Moreover, where you have the passion for oratory you are not unlikely to have an impaired style and standard of preaching. Where your object is to secure your audience, rather than your Gospel, preaching is sure to suffer. I will not speak of the oratory which is but rhetoric, tickling the audience. I will take both at their best. It is one thing to have to rouse or persuade people to do something, to put themselves into something; it is another to have to induce them to trust somebody and renounce themselves for him. The one is the political region of work, the other is the religious region of faith. And wherever a people is swallowed up in politics, the preacher is apt to be neglected; unless he imperil his preaching by adjusting himself to political or social methods of address. The orator, speaking generally, has for his business to make real and urgent the present world and its crises, the preacher a world unseen, and the whole crisis of the two worlds. The present world of the orator may be the world of action, or of art. He may speak of affairs, of nature, or of imagination. In the pulpit he may be what is called a practical preacher, or a poet-preacher. But the only business of the apostolic preacher is to make men practically realize a world unseen and spiritual; he has to rouse them not against a common enemy but against their common selves; not against natural obstacles but against spiritual foes; and he has to

---

207. Forsyth, *Positive Preaching and the Modern Mind*, 116.

call out not natural resources but supernatural aids. Indeed, he has to tell men that their natural resources are so inadequate for the last purposes of life and its worst foes that they need from the supernatural much more than aid. They need deliverance, not a helper merely but a Saviour. The note of the preacher is the Gospel of a Saviour. The orator stirs men to rally, the preacher invites them to be redeemed. Demosthenes fires his audience to attack Philip straightway; Paul stirs them to die and rise with Christ. The orator, at most, may urge men to love their brother, the preacher beseeches them first to be reconciled to their Father. With preaching Christianity stands or falls because it is the declaration of a Gospel. Nay more—far more—it is the Gospel prolonging and declaring itself.[208]

More specifically, it is Jesus Christ—who *is* the gospel—preaching *himself* as the eternal Son who reveals the Father, the holiness of the Father's inexhaustible and enduring love, and "the Father's passion to redeem,"[209] a passion flaunted in the costliness of the cross where holiness comes home "bringing His sheaves with Him,"[210] and where God "found Himself."[211]

As Forsyth said of Christ's preaching, so the same might be said of his own:

> His speech was not clear-cut and unambiguous. He set more store by an eloquent flexibility, a suggestiveness in language than by stiff accuracy. He cared more for the pliancy of forms than their correctness. It was more to Him that they should mean greatly than that they should speak exactly and lucidly. He was more ready to keep old formularies, and interpret them, than to found a sect on their rejection for bald new summaries. He was a great Nonconformist, but He was not a separatist, not a sectary. He was always craving to be understood as He Himself understood the past.[212]

This brings us to the matter of Forsyth's writing style, a subject requiring some ink particularly for those readers unfamiliar with Forsyth's penmanship for it might appropriately be said of Forsyth that *Le style c'est l'homme même* ("The style is the man himself").

"The prophet is human, yet he employs notes one octave too high for our ears. He experiences moments that defy our understanding. He is

---

208. Ibid., 1–3.
209. Forsyth, *The Holy Father and the Living Christ*, 86.
210. Forsyth, *The Work of Christ*, 192.
211. Ibid., 224.
212. Forsyth, "Things New and Old," 274.

neither a 'singing saint' nor a 'moralizing poet', but an assaulter of the mind. Often his words begin to burn where conscience ends."[213] So wrote the great Jewish theologian Abraham Joshua Heschel about the Hebrew prophets. Not a few would say that these words might also be appropriately conferred upon Forsyth. Indeed, scattered even among the obituaries that appeared in *The British Weekly* during the week after Forsyth's passing are references to "a tendency to grandiloquence,"[214] and to "a style unusually complex, which did not grow simpler with years."[215] That most prolific of British journalists, W. Robertson Nicoll, who was much loved by nonconformist readers and of whom it was said he had "the keenest nose for a book that will sell of any man in the book business,"[216] observed in Forsyth a style which was both "deliberately adopted" and which "suited him." Still, Nicoll would pronounce of Forsyth: "I have never known a great theological writer who proceeded so much by the way of iteration."[217] Many of Forsyth's students (among whom he "spent himself without stint"[218]) were surprised to hear that others regarded their teacher's books difficult when they themselves "found his familiar lectures not only clear to follow, but a theological education to digest."[219] One of Forsyth's former students, possibly named Elliot, wrote of him: "About his books, I question whether those who knew him only through his books could ever really know him. It was [a] surprise to me when I first discovered that many people regarded his books as difficult. To me they have always been the most readable of theological books. The explanation doubtless is that I had learned, a little at least, to know the man. He took pains to make his thought plain to us students. Though probably our understanding may often have been misunderstanding!"[220]

The reality, however, is that most reviewers comment unenthusiastically on his writing style. One fellow minister famously referred to Forsyth's writing as "fireworks in the fog."[221] And even Forsyth's close friend James Denney confessed to finding Forsyth's book of sermons published under the title *Missions in State and Church* "very difficult to read," and wrote that

213. Heschel, *The Prophets*, 10.
214. Nicoll, "Principal Forsyth," 145.
215. Darlow, "Tributes to the Late Rev. Principal Forsyth," 146.
216. Clement Shorter, as cited in Price, "W. Robertson Nicoll and the Genesis of the Kailyard School," 73.
217. Nicoll, "Principal Forsyth," 146.
218. Darlow, "Tributes to the Late Rev. Principal Forsyth," 146.
219. Ibid.
220. From an anonymous, undated and unpublished letter headed "Dr. Forsyth," in Dr Williams's Library, London.
221. Stephenson, "Letter," 22.

I: Preaching Sub Specie Crucis

"If this is how one feels who is heartily at one with the writer, how must it strike an unsympathetic reader?"[222] Moreover, regarding *Positive Preaching and the Modern Mind*, Denney wrote, "The peculiarity of [Forsyth's] style is such that only people who agree with him strongly are likely to read him through."[223] Certainly few could disagree with the assessment that "the Forsythian style is rugged and some of his paragraphs are enormous. Often he gives the impression in print of a turgid, swift-flowing river, hurrying to hurl itself over some lofty precipice, midst showers of spume."[224] Most criticisms, however, betray a failure to account for the occasional and preached-genre of most of Forsyth's work, prepared in the midst of busy college life and denominational responsibilities, and of the impossible task of speaking and writing about the cross unparadoxically. Moreover, they betray a disregard for Forsyth's theological methodology which nourishes the imagination with displays of breathtaking freedom. To be sure, Forsyth's published work—though evidencing a profound and rigorous mind full of "the stimulus of the spoken word, [and] nuanced by paradox and artful ambiguity," and which "convey the lecture room's privileged immediacy"[225]—remains as curiously undisciplined as it is almost entirely free of the modern concern with footnotes and customary referencing. Even Forsyth's most systematic work, *The Person and Place of Jesus Christ*, was not, Forsyth recalled, "meant for scholars, but largely for ministers of the Word which it seeks in its own way to serve." His stated aim was to "be as popular as the subject and its depth allowed," and he confessed that the lack of bibliographical apparatus is not only unnecessary for lectures, but would give the book "an aspect of erudition which its author does not possess."[226]

But the failure to understand this "patently original thinker"[227] is, I suggest, due more to the taxing nature of his gospel, and to a decline in affinity with the evangelical experience out of which he wrote, than to his writing *per se*. "The merchantmen of these goodly pearls must be seekers;

---

222. Denney, *Letters of Principal James Denney to W. Robertson Nicoll*, 118–19.

223. Ibid., 97. For Denney's fuller review of Forsyth's *Positive Preaching and the Modern Mind*, see Denney, "Principal Forsyth on Preaching," 57.

224. Jones, *The Royalty of the Pulpit*, 131.

225. Binfield, "The Significance of Baby Babble," 1.

226. Forsyth, *The Person and Place of Jesus Christ*, vi. Camfield suggests that there were practical, rather than theological or philosophical reasons for why Forsyth never embarked on a systematic theology: "The truth is that the thought of Forsyth required that 'treatise' which he never gave. Partly, one suspects, from chronic ill-health, and partly, through a disinclination to, and perhaps incapacity for, the work of research." Camfield, "Forsyth," 9.

227. Bebbington, *Evangelicalism in Modern Britain*, 141.

I: Preaching Sub Specie Crucis

and without even divers they cannot be had."²²⁸ Just as T. F. Torrance would later confess that "the difficulty of my style is sometimes due to the difficulty of the subject-matter!,"²²⁹ so too with Forsyth's idiosyncratic writing. One commentator on Forsyth has helpfully drawn attention to an affinity with Gerald Manley Hopkins, noting: "[The] variation in response (to Hopkins' style) is not primarily a matter of *literary* judgement, though it may rationalize itself as such. It depends upon the degree to which the reader is ready to respond to the exceptional and in some ways over-taut intensity of Hopkins' *experience*. Those who have complained that he strove against the genius of the English language have really been complaining that he strained unwarrantably against the measure of human experience which they wish to accept."²³⁰ And Colin Gunton suggested that Forsyth had about him "something of the capacity of Kierkegaard to utter the kind of lapidary judgement that both breaks through cliché and comes, upon reflection, to appear to be undeniably true."²³¹ Certainly at no point does Forsyth suggest that the preacher's task is to promote obscurity. Still, of the accessibility or otherwise of his language Forsyth was well aware: "I own I tax you, and I am sorry, but it has taxed me more."²³² Eugene Peterson was right to describe Forsyth as "a no-nonsense theologian who goes for the jugular."²³³ Forsyth's daughter remembers that although her father could certainly write simply (never simplistically), when writing for trained theological minds he "demands everything we have of mental and spiritual grasp." When writing, this master of English prose was wrestling—like Jacob at Peniel—with thoughts mysterious, unconquerable and beyond human mastery. He also wrote with "a physical and nervous intensity which shook the desk, and which after an hour or two left him utterly spent, stretched out white and still upon his study couch, until the Spirit drove him back to pen and paper."²³⁴ Such intensity was the germane product of the subject itself; "the Browning of theology"²³⁵ entertained no illusions that the truth of the gospel might be lubricated for easier swallowing: "It is not the simple things which make

---

228. Forsyth, *The Person and Place of Jesus Christ*, vii.
229. Torrance, *The Christian Doctrine of God*, xi.
230. Escott, *P. T. Forsyth and the Cure of Souls*, 20–21.
231. Gunton, "Real as the Redemptive," 37.
232. Forsyth, *The Cruciality of the Cross*, 171–72.
233. Peterson, "Foreword," 5.
234. Andrews, "Memoir," xxvi. Another has noted: "[Forsyth] did not usually sit at a table when he wrote, but had a small square board on his knee. He used specially ruled paper, with the lines very far apart." Williams, "A Tribute from Wales," 154.
235. Bishop, Review of *Positive Preaching and the Modern Mind*, 305.

I: Preaching Sub Specie Crucis

the soul," he said. Rather, "the greatest powers are those that break through language and escape."[236]

Writing on the centenary of Forsyth's birth, Gwilym Griffith noted:

> Forsyth did not rank with Spurgeon and Parker, Maclaren and Dale, among the great preachers of his age, nor had he the platform gifts of Hugh Price Hughes, John Clifford and Silvester Horne, though on occasion he could, and did, move great assemblies. Nor, again, was he an engaging 'sun-beshone' personality that makes disciples and devotees through the magnetism of personal contacts. He gained his great, enduring and still-growing influence through his books, which were pre-eminently books of witness. He 'wrote for God and for souls,' and under the stress of inner constraint. He commanded (though this has been denied) an opulent and fluent style, but he sacrifices it when sluggard readers complained of 'obscurity.' He could not 'open his dark sayings,' like the Psalmist, 'upon an harp,' but to meet the infirmity of his critics he sometimes cut up his sentences into short and stertorous predictions—only to be told that he was too epigrammatic, antithetical or paradoxical. But he wrote as a confessor, not as a literary scribe, and his books made their own way . . . One has the feeling that every word he wrote had first been passed through the fire.[237]

Just a few days after Forsyth's death, W. B. Selbie, who succeeded Forsyth at Cambridge but whose acquaintance with Forsyth and his preaching went back to days at Cheetham Hill, remembered the "real power" of Forsyth's ministry. He spoke not only of being "attracted, as many other younger men were, by the note of originality and reality that marked [Forsyth's] preaching," but also of the fact that Forsyth "left a mark [at Cambridge] that will not be easily effaced. Men and women of all kinds found help and comfort in his teaching. His caustic and epigrammatic style appealed to the more intellectual, but he had also a spiritual depth and insight which waked a response in some of the humblest of his hearers, and I have heard these speak of him in terms which any minister might envy."[238] And during the centenary of Forsyth's birth, Hugh Stafford, a retired Quaker schoolmaster from Hitchin, wrote of Forsyth:

> He was my minister for nine years, six while I was a schoolboy in Leicester, and three at Cambridge. Later I often stayed at

236. Forsyth, "The Way of Life," 86.
237. Griffith, "Peter Taylor Forsyth," 1.
238. Selbie, "Tributes to the Late Rev. Principal Forsyth," 153.

Hackney College where he was Principal. I do not suppose that in those early years I ever fully understood his sermons. It was no easy discipline to listen. He seldom preached for less than 40 minutes, and one's mind was kept at full strength all the time. Nevertheless it was profoundly impressive. Every sentence, one felt, came white-hot from the furnace of his spirit . . . One emerged, rather battered perhaps, but humbled, strengthened, and above all filled with the sense of the tremendous import of religion . . . That sense has never left me since.[239]

And, reflecting on a photograph of Forsyth, the President of the Literary and Philosophical Society further fills in the picture in an article published in *The Wyvern*:

Ministers achieve success in their labours by the soundness of the doctrine they set forth, by their energy and earnestness, and by the attractiveness of their manner and style. And any one of these is often sufficient to make a popular teacher of religion: the pastor of the Clarendon Park Church has them all. He is very broad in his beliefs, but he never gets away from the foundation facts of religion . . . Of Mr. Forsyth's energy and enthusiasm in the good cause there can be no doubt. It is impossible to listen to him without catching the seriousness of his themes, and realising that the preacher is pouring out his inmost feelings. Then again, the rev. gentleman has a most happy style. His sermons are not only literary, but even poetical. He is apt indeed in his phrases, and uses exceedingly forceful and elegant English.[240]

Forsyth, of course, would have been horrified at any suggestion that his "elegant English"—forged as it was amidst the "grey skies, great silences, and stubborn glebes"[241] of the Aberdonian soil of his parents—might have placed some obstacle to his hearers hearing the Word of God. As we have already noted, those privileged to hear Forsyth preach on a regular basis, and who wrote about such, testified not only of their awareness of being in the presence of a great personality but, and more importantly, of being in the presence of a personality that had been taken captive by the very reality of which St Paul said that he was not ashamed; namely, Jesus Christ and him crucified.

239. Stafford, "Letter," 8. This letter was Stafford's response to an article on Forsyth by R. L. Child, "P T Forsyth: Some Aspects of his Thoughts," 9. Child's piece was the first in a series of three articles on Forsyth published in the *Baptist Times* in 1948—on May 27 (p. 7) and June 3 (p. 9).

240. Anonymous, "Our Photograph," 67. *The Wyvern* was a Leicester-based "topical, critical, and humorous journal" which ran from 1891 to 1899.

241. Escott, *Director of Souls*, 6

I: Preaching Sub Specie Crucis

Regardless of the text or topic at hand, it was near impossible not to know what drove and overcame this prophet of the cross and what reality he sought to bear witness to, above all else. Furthermore, not only was his assault on the mind concerned to underscore the moral gravity of the human situation *coram deo*, but he also ministered out of that Reformed conviction that it is not only minds or ears that are the barrier to hearing the good news, but wills—"the very centre of our life"[242]—wills, not of a merely battered and bruised human spirit but those of a Lancelot race, a race with weapons in its hands and ever ready to strike against any who would challenge their thrones. It is the recalcitrant human will—"our dearest life, the thing we cling to most and give up last . . . our ownest own"[243]—which is the target of Forsyth's preaching, precisely because it is the target of the God who would be Lord. Forsyth would certainly have agreed with Helmut Thielicke's judgment on preaching: "The aim of the sermon, after all, is to *create* something living and set it in motion. Consequently, it should be directed not only at the intellect, but must at the same time also be aimed at the conscience, will, and imagination. It is addressed to the *whole* person!"[244] So understood, it is little wonder then that every time Forsyth stood up to preach he felt that he was "fighting for the very life of the Faith,"[245] and that consequently no blow could be too hard.

We have seen already that Forsyth never constrained himself to only reading, learning and engaging with "theologians," and that no arena of human activity was off limits. He made every thought an agent of a redeemed personality bearing faithful witness to a waxing world reconquested for God. And it is clear that Forsyth knew that such witness is ultimately beyond human speech (*ineffabili quodam modo*),[246] and ought to be felt more than analysed (as with Kierkegaard), even as the outworking of the atonement itself calls for language. Thus Forsyth strained and tortured language itself, utilizing every human discipline available to him in order to shed light—or rather expunge the light that is there—on one or other facet, vista and panorama of the cross. Forsyth wrote fugue-like, developing endless variations on the one great theme of exhaustless grace. Certainly, as Alan Sell notes, "a reader would have to work very hard to exit from a Forsyth text in absolute ignorance of the author's intention."[247]

---

242. Forsyth, *The Cruciality of the Cross*, 194.
243. Ibid., 192.
244. Thielicke, *Notes from a Wayfarer*, 291–92.
245. Andrews, "Memoir," xxviii.
246. See Calvin, *Inst.*, 2.17.2.
247. Sell, "P T Forsyth: Theologian for a New Millennium?," 238.

I: Preaching Sub Specie Crucis

In the tradition of Bernard, Dante, Donne, Herbert, Milton, Eliot, Auden and R. S. Thomas, Forsyth was a poet's theologian: he believed that theologians, like "first rate poets, must deal with human life. They may not deal with bloodless abstractions or scientific systems whether of anthropology, cosmology, or theology; they must deal with life."[248] This also meant that he continually employed the grammar of "gospel," "religion," "moral," "revelation," "cross" and "redemption," for example, to encompass a broad possibility of meanings. This does make reading Forsyth unnecessarily onerous at times, but it is also part of the joy. It seems that he was not destined to simply repeat the conclusions reached in the past, or the language so employed to do so, even while he greatly appreciated the efforts of his forebears. Donald MacKinnon was fully aware of such when he wrote: "Forsyth explicitly preferred a theology that could flirt with the mythological in its insistence on the primacy of narrative, to one tainted by what he called 'Chalcedonianism,' which seemed to subordinate the concrete reality of Christ's agony in Gethsemane and Calvary to a 'bloodless ballet of impalpable categories.'"[249]

To be sure, this way of doing theology infuriates some, and Forsyth might have done well to concede some ground to his otherwise-sympathetic critics at this point. But the charge that such a style represents some kind of fear of closure or even dogmatic fluffiness around first-order questions simply will not stick. Moreover, it is entirely proper that Forsyth resisted those kinds of analysis all too common in academic attempts to, in Dietrich Ritschl's words, "make God the prisoner of our thoughts or theologies," seeking a "Word with which we could operate, a Word we could 'use', a Word we could judge."[250] The upshot of such an approach is that the real questions posed by the Word of God remain live ones, each time new, which resist, even as they invite, our attempts to forge responses by way of "objective" principles and statements, and which ever and at every moment call for our faithful response. Yes, "the Church sees through a glass darkly; but it sees none the less,"[251] and so it is incumbent upon her to declare what she has seen and heard (1 John 1:1–3), and to embrace a faithful silence about that of which she is ignorant.

---

248. Forsyth, "The Argument for Immortality Drawn from the Nature of Love," 360; reprinted in this volume, 119–30.

249. MacKinnon, "Aspects of Kant's Influence on British Theology," 356.

250. Ritschl, *A Theology of Proclamation*, 68.

251. Shortt, *Rowan Williams*, 5: "The Church sees through a glass darkly; but it sees none the less. These are the two components that Catholic Christianity seeks to hold in tension. Say too little, and you may betray the costly demands of the gospel. Say too much, and you risk sounding fanciful or authoritarian."

I: Preaching Sub Specie Crucis

To this end, Forsyth continues to be a preacher's theologian—a fertile and faithful mentor to those called to kerygmatic ministry. At a time when belief that God's audacious and reconciling speech still arrives though "the foolishness of our proclamation" (1 Cor 1:21) is running thin, Forsyth reminds us that ecclesial pursuits that do not correspond to the Church's cruciform foundation are a vanity, that the task laid upon the preacher is to help the people of God recognize the voice of the Lord—this means, among other things, resisting the temptation to speak for God, recognizing that every sermon tells an unfinished story and is offered in the hope that God has so much more to tell us, and so engaging in a mode of speech that leaves space for the One who alone can finally speak for himself—and that regardless of what others may propose, in the divine freedom and wisdom, preaching is a first-order and not a second-order activity for the Church. It may well be that Forsyth was right after all when he boldly intoned that it is with its preaching that Christianity stands or falls.

II

Published Sermons

1

THE TURKISH ATROCITIES, 1876[1]

ON SUNDAY EVENING LAST, the Rev. P. T. Forsyth, M.A., pastor of the Shipley Congregational Church, preached a sermon having special reference to the barbarities committed by the Turkish troops upon the Christians in the East, the situation in that part of the world, and the duty of England in that matter. There was a good congregation.

Mr. FORSYTH chose as his motto a portion of the seventeenth verse of the second chapter of the First Epistle of Peter—"Love the brotherhood." After a suitable introduction, in which Mr. Disraeli's words, "Our duty at this critical moment is to maintain the Empire of England,"[2] were quoted, and reference made to the selfish policy pursued by successive Governments for many years, the rev. gentleman said: We begin, as a nation, to feel that if our policy is selfishness, we have no more claim to the leading place in a world's affairs than a selfish man or woman has to the homage of our hearts. If our sole object in our foreign policy is one of greed, men of Christian temper feel that we have little standing-ground in international affairs. We have no business to offer to the world, which is panting and struggling for freedom, a gospel whose first provision she makes to be "save thyself." If our duty at this critical moment is to maintain the Empire of England, let us never more talk about England's motto being, "God defend the right." Above all, let us never more claim to be the first Christian country in the world. We may say, "Lord, Lord," from every cathedral and chapel in the land, but so

---

1. The context for this sermon was the 1876 declaration of war on Turkey by both Serbia and Montenegro. The Montenegrin–Ottoman War ended when the Turks (of whom 17,000 had died) signed a truce with the Montenegrins (whose death toll numbered 700) at Edirne on 13 January 1878.
2. From a speech by Benjamin Disraeli given on 11 August 1876.

far as our national religion is expressed in our action, we have no right whatever to the name of Christian. I say this in perfect earnestness, and in full view of what it means. The first and fundamental feature of Christianity is to surrender self—to put it not first, but second. Christians may succeed very imperfectly in realising that, but nobody has a right to Christ's name whose creed does not admit it. Our own views, interest, prestige, even feelings, all in the second place; something else in the first. What would you think of a bishop, a minister, who said boldly in some crisis, "My sole duty at this moment is to secure the supremacy of *my* church, *my* sect, at any price; every other issue is for the moment thrown into the background"? Why, cool politicians would say, "the man is a bigot;" and cynical ones, with a taste for epigram, would say it were well for that church or sect to terminate, terminate its connexion with its leader in the most expeditious manner possible. And yet when that bigotry becomes political—when it is Lord Beaconsfield and not the Bishop of Lincoln who speaks—when, in the throes of oppressed nations for liberty, he says they shall not have a grain more of it than is consistent with the swollen surprise and prestige of England, it is accepted as a principle lying at the basis of our policy, and swallowed by the nation as profound till they are horrified to find they have been fed on human agony and human flesh. I have no hesitation in speaking strongly. I am not a statesman who has to weigh every word and consult a thousand interests. I have no responsibility upon me but that of uttering the truth—I have no object but to contribute, as every man may, to the formation of righteous opinion and the propagation of the Christian enthusiasm of humanity. And I say boldly, the man who can stand up before a people in a crisis like this and declare that our one duty is to seek self and to maintain empire, is a tempter and demoraliser—one of the hundred heads of the hydra of Antichrist. O Milton! O Cromwell! It will indeed be well for your heavenly rest, if it be true that no ripple of this our disgrace reach you when you stand at the foot of the eternal great white throne! I appeal to you, tonight, on behalf of those miserable nationalities with whose sufferings you are, or ought to be, familiar. You have all, I hope, read at least so much of the details furnished by the *Daily News*. I shall not wonder if you found it impossible to read more than the first of the letters. I myself have forced my way through them all. I have done so with pity, with anger, with tears, and, more than once, with suppressed maledictions. This crisis is not without its use—no crisis is purely evil. It has thrown light on one thing to me—it has made me understand as I never did before the vindictive Psalms. It has enabled me to use them. It has supplied the atmosphere of emotion in which their words float and become real. There are junctures when a moment's pity is a momentary sympathy with the crime—when the invocation of a curse

1: The Turkish Atrocities, 1876

is only a handing over to God of miscreants whose atrocities are beyond human power to punish without descending to their own level. But if your reading of these details has affected you as it has me, it will have done something more than filled your eyes and stirred your horror—it will have roused that most terrible of questions, "Is there a God who doeth right upon earth, or are we the sport of callous forces and straws upon the passionate tornado of a blind and passionate force?" It will have sent you in helpless prayer, in stumbling, groping faith, to the lowest steps of the cloud-wrapt great white throne. I can only say Christ saw more than even this, and yet he believed, yet he was patient; he never sought to take the world's reigns out of the hand of God, or to drive himself the chariot of the progressing suns. I ask your help for those people on the ground of these feelings. Your humanity has been killed out of you and lost in the sand of the world. Your own wives, daughters, children, will reproach you with selfishness every time you dwell lovingly on their faces, if you shut your heart and withdraw your hand. I say you are no man if the impulse to do something do not persecute you, as you think of what has been done. I can understand a man feeling as vividly as most of England feels at this moment, and then examining his emotion, to see if it is not misleading him. I can understand a man reflecting in self-control whether the vehemence of his indignation is not likely to destroy the practical and lasting effect which such anger and pity is meant to wage us to. I can understand a man deliberately withholding practical help till the moment he is sure it will be a blessing and not a curse to the miserable. But I cannot understand, I find it impossible to feel anything but contempt for men who give no evidence of any indignation, who treat the whole thing as an affair of diplomacy, who only regard the atrocities as an additional difficulty in a hard problem, and the display of national feeling in the matter an element more hampering and more irrational still. As men and women whose lives are dearer to each other than to themselves, who love each other so well because they love honour in man or woman more, who retain the pure and simple human feelings unsoured by over-refinement and unweakened by criticism, who feel that life would be worthless but for the inviolate sanctities of human affection and the freedom of a free nation and a trustful home, I ask you to help, at present with your money, those who, for the sake of the love, and home, and freedom you always enjoy, have suffered pain and shame such as never have and never will come to you. But you are Englishmen, you say, and you are Christians, and refuse to be guided by sentimental or emotional considerations merely. If you will only swear yourself one of the nation that loved and obeyed Cromwell, that reveres Milton's spirit, that raised Wilberforce and abolished slavery, that spends yearly money, men, and energy in keeping slavery down, that is proud of being called, amid

II: Published Sermons

many faults, the home of freedom; if you will only be true to these traditions, that will do. At the very first blush of it, you must be the friends of the nascent nations that are trying to heave the stones from the tombs where they have been buried by horrible despotism; you must be the deadly foes of a nation that carries on the slave traffic in a more abominable form than negro slavery—the traffic in helpless and unwilling women; you must be on the side of those who are striving to realise in the East the freedom and Christian civilisation of the West; you must be with all your might opposed to a race that has not stirred a step in that direction for 400 years, but has stopped at no cruelty to prevent any such progress, wherever it had the power. How can you, as Englishmen, look without fear—put it on the lowest ground—without selfish fear, on the existence among European nations of brute force which has ceased to be amenable to anything in the shape of a thought, an aspiration, an idea, a sympathy. Apart from the feelings stirred by the horrors of the last months, and standing on the merits of the case between the combatants, can you as Englishmen hesitate on which side to throw your sympathy? Express it, then, and it will carry courage and impulse to the brace endeavours of that miserable nation. It is standing in silent resistance, but turning unspeakably piteous eyes on the horizon of Europe to ask if there be none that will help and none that will deliver. O England, must this little aspirant for its divine right of freedom look to your colossal liberty as a drowning wretch looks up the smooth side of a war-ship at a worser wretch who sees him drown? If it must, thy great freedom has become to thee only a larger and more refined selfishness, and thou art that worst and most pitiful of slaves, who lives and jangles his chains in the mad hallucination that he is free—thou art not the slave of the Turk, thou art his fellow, thou art the slave of the Turk's master, thou art the slave of self and knowest it not.

—The rev. gentleman then referred more particularly to the political aspect of the question. He said that proper vigilance on the part of our diplomatic corps and sympathy more human than Turkish would have prevented these horrors—that, next to the Turks, we bear the responsibility of what has happened. He did not level any charges at the Government. For years this country had pursued a mainly selfish policy in regard to Turkey. Probably our weakest ambassador was at the very point where the strongest was required. Mr. Forsyth then proceeded to substantiate what he had advanced, and went on to say: We are here met in a higher name than that of family, and wider than that of nation. We meet here as part of the widest of all unities—a part of Christ's Church. We are here in the largest, most universal faction we can occupy. We are neither individuals only, nor Englishmen only; we are Christians, we are members of a redeemed humanity. We are parts of a race which,

1: The Turkish Atrocities, 1876

under the influence of the spirit of the risen Christ, is going on to realise perfection and unity in some far-distant future of brotherhood. Towards that, the realisation of national life is but a step: there is a higher unity than the nation, there is the race; and there are higher duties than patriotism. In front of the patriot comes the Redeemer. The Saviour of society is more than the deliverer of a people, and the plain interests of a nation must sometimes yield to the claims of the race at large. That I take to be the chief message of Christianity to the nations of the world today. Christianity shook the European nations into life in the middle ages. It must keep now before the eyes of the nations a higher life—the life of federalised nations, the life of collective humanity, of universal brotherhood. There are countless signs that things are setting in this direction. The best spirits of each nation are striving after this higher unity, and as I pointed out before, we, as a nation, begin to be ashamed of such declarations as that our one object in a great crisis is to save ourselves. This Eastern Question will have been a blessed discipline for us, and the shame and agony of those who have suffered will not have been lost, if it only bring us to our senses and open our eyes to the true nature of the policy we have been pursuing. They will have been sacrificed not for their own country only, but for us. They will have bought liberty of government for their nation, and they will have bought for us the emancipation from not only an obsolete policy, but from an immoral, unchristian, selfish idea.

—After further dwelling on this part of the subject, the rev. gentleman concluded as follows: We must show ourselves in earnest both to the Government, to the Turks, and to the Turkish Christians. They will forgive the past, if the present spirit of the English nation is expressed in its action in the future. But the first step lies with us, not with the Government. We must help those houseless, friendless people who have lost cattle, capital, machinery, stock-in-trade, to say nothing of shelter and food. We must help them to pass the winter. Don't say we should force the Turks to do that. We will force what we want out of them in good time; but diplomacy is untrustworthy and slow, and the winter is coming quick and sure. Contribute of your money. That will be a strong proof that you are in earnest; it will give the poor huddling people hope, and we are saved by hope. They are strong, even now. They gather in despair round Englishmen, who are obliged to leave them without doing anything but reporting to us here, and they cry in fifties, "We are starving, we are starving." If you were in their midst, you would empty your pockets to them, your purse would not be large enough for your heart. Well, put yourself among them in thought and sympathy. See the men fighting, suffering, as only a people choosing between death and freedom can. See the women crying for food for themselves and children, or with that silence of life more pathetic than death bearing about a speechless shame which is no shame but sacrifice, or recurring, with shuddering and pallor, to the memory of their impaled children, and their headless brothers, fathers, and sons. Try to realise these things, and even if you have to go without something you have set your heart on, will you not do it joyfully, and reap from the sacrifice a moral blessing and elevation which no coveted possession can give? You will rise by the amount of such sacrifice so much nearer Christ. You have vowed and sworn to place your sympathies where He puts His. You leave all other sympathy when it clashes with His pity and His cause. If He wept over Jerusalem, how do you think He feels over Bulgaria? And if His spirit brought to birth the nations of modern Europe, is not every struggling nation an embodiment of His cause? Is He indifferent to the issue of this crisis? On which side is He? Can you doubt? Pour your energy this night into His channel; do it at some cost, and you shall not lose your reward.

A collection in [*sic*] behalf of the Servians was then made, £25 10s. 3d. being realised.

2

Mercy the True and Only Justice, 1877

A Sermon Preached in Shipley Congregational Church, on the Missionary Sunday, September 30, 1877.

Preface

It is high time that we should have, on behalf of the young and less thoughtful, more plain-speaking on subjects which the wiser heads agree at least to leave open questions, and which the party of thought in religion as well as in science are tearing open in spite of us. I believe a main obstacle to this with our Congregational system lies in the temper of the laity and the inertia of majorities. Majorities, whatever effect they may give to those practical ends of organisation which are the secondary ends of the Church, are the natural enemies of fresh truth. So that the very machinery of our ecclesiastical freedom tends to become a dead weight on that intellectual, theological, and ultimately spiritual freedom, without which ecclesiastical liberty is licence, having neither source of control, nor indeed cause to be. The freedom that spread the early Church, by leaving huge regions undefined which the later Church has, for its own purposes, closed, is regarded by many of our congregations as their worst foe. We are timid about error because we have a latent and fundamental distrust of truth—a distrust unknown to the Church's warm and growing age.

Blessed with a congregation among whom to be utterly true could never mean to be even faintly a martyr, whose eager sympathy might itself be a keen inspiration to a fruitful soul, and whose Christian temper binds these days of larger light with the days when the members of Christ loved one another, I venture, from time to time, to commend to them from the pulpit such suggestions as these, which now, at their own request, I consign to them in more permanent shape.

Sermon

"Unto Thee, O Lord, belongeth mercy, for Thou renderest to every man according to his work."—Ps. lxii.12.

I wish to speak this morning on a matter which lies at the foundation of popular and indeed all religion. I mean the relation between justice and mercy, and I wish to confine myself to their relation in the eternal divine nature. I shall take another occasion to speak on the mode of their revelation through the incarnation of Jesus Christ.

I assume first of all that we have the means of knowing what God's nature is. Not that we can fathom it; not that we can make out a scientific representation of it. Many theologians have justly incurred the charge of irreverence and intrusiveness from the certainty which they professed to have on the more intricate lines of divine action and shades of divine intention. But if Christianity has any distinctive meaning at all, it is that we can affirm or deny certain things about God, that we are not in a state of utter ignorance about His heart and nature, that we find in the character and work of Jesus Christ a reflection of the character and work and large purpose of God. We get at the fundamental qualities of His moral nature. We get no satisfaction about the metaphysics of the divine, but we do get satisfaction about the morality, the character, of the divine.

Let me premise also that when we speak about God's fundamental qualities we must be careful. All the qualities that go to make up His nature are, in a sense, fundamental qualities. They are all necessary. They are not there in such a way that they might as easily, or as well, be anywhere else. He does not live and move under our intellectual limitations. He is the foundation of all things, and His every aspect is an essential part of Him. There is in Him nothing transitory, careless, ornamental merely. "He is all centre, and no circumference."[1] Wherever He is, and He is everywhere, He is essential; nor can you say of Him that this quality or that is more of His essence than another. You cannot say His strength is a more fundamental quality of Him

---

1. Probably a reference to James Martineau's description of the universe in his *Endeavours after the Christian Life*. Forsyth ranked Martineau, along with Maurice and Newman, as one of the great theologians of the nineteenth century. See Forsyth, "Dr. Martineau," 217.

2: Mercy the true and only Justice, 1877

than His wisdom. His strength *is* wisdom. His wisdom is strength, both to Him and to us. Whatever He is, is eternal—is fundamental.

But our faculties are poor. We must use human language. We cannot conceive the eternal. The moment we give it conceivable shape we strip it of some of its infinity—its eternity. Still, we must think somehow of this great presence realisable behind all our thinking. We must convey and share our thoughts. All we have to do is to remember that these thoughts about God are very faint realisations of Him—significant, but not adequate—progressing towards adequacy—developing, like their physical basis, to higher power in a slow historic scale—always outstripped by the fulness of reality, and therefore always hopeful in the endeavour to compass it—still not adequate. It is not by our modes of thought, or our fashions of speech, that we best realise the divine. We get nearer His reality with our unthinking hearts than with our heartless thoughts. And when we use intellectual formulæ about God, we shall be safe if we remember that a literal interpretation of them makes them false. They are but attempts to realise what is far beyond them. They are "thrown out," as Matthew Arnold well says,[2] at an inconceivable reality which is felt but not grasped—loved but not seen. They are like the scaffolding on which an artist stands to paint divine frescoes on the ceiling of life.

So now, though we can hardly with fundamental accuracy speak of one quality in God being more essential than another, seeing all are equally bound up in His being, yet we may use such language of Him with a real meaning, if we use it with care. If we don't attempt to be very literal, and to define what won't be defined, we may put the question with real meaning to ourselves: Which quality is the more fundamental in God, justice or mercy?

If you examine the other religions which share with Christianity the worship of men, you will find the great religions are those which take their stand upon the mercy of God. I have often pointed out to you the fundamental mercifulness of Judaism; how, though hardened and distorted by priest and scribe, it yet existed mainly for the well-being of the people who obeyed it. You will find this faith in the divine mercy running through the best parts of the Koran, its earlier parts, and you will find it influencing the purest, freshest epoch of Mahomet's life. You will find that, in idea at least, Mahommedanism is a merciful faith. So with Buddhism. Buddha himself was a perfect Hindoo [*sic*] Christ. Nothing was below his pity. It was the sorrow of the world that was his inspiration. That turned him from a prince

---

2. Arnold, *Literature and Dogma*: "The word 'God' is used in most cases as by no means a term of science or exact knowledge, but a term of poetry and eloquence, a term *thrown out*, so to speak, as a not fully grasped object of the speaker's consciousness—a *literary* term, in short; and mankind mean different things by it as their consciousness differs."

to a humble and heavenly-minded and devoted man, ruling a realm his princedom never measured by a humanity stripped of every adventitious aid. These are specimens. A minuter examination will bear out what I say, and Christianity will assure you of it, that the greatest religions of the world are those that take their stand on the mercy of God, and the very greatest makes His mercy paramount.

There is no doubt this is the essence of Christianity. God is Love. Christianity does not spend time debating the fundamental qualities of God. It admits but one quality, which is not quality, but essence—God is Love. All His qualities are but aspects of that. God is endless, universal, unweariable, awful Love. Every other predicate is a quality only, a side of Him. This is His being, His energy, His purpose, His result—Love. But what is the popular conception? It is that God is, above all things and primarily, just. It cannot find any place in the Bible to say God is Justice, but it acts as if it did, and it reads John's text, not God is Love, but God is loving. God it makes to be loving justice, instead of just love, a mild magistrate, instead of a severe father. Mercy had a hard fight of it to get the upper hand, and only succeeded after justice had been appeased by an awful victim, on whom it spent its fires. Justice is held to be the fundamental divine characteristic, tempered by bursts of love or surrounded by a sweet halo of it. It is the idea of business life applied by a successful people to express God's relation with the world. It is the half-truth "Be just before you are generous"[3] expanded into a whole theology. Love is but the flower hung upon the pillar of justice, hard and cold as stone. First justice, then mercy to assuage the justice somewhat. Love is the palliative instead of the principle. And, as a natural consequence of such an inversion, the idea of justice itself becomes corrupt, becomes nothing higher than vengeance. So that the supreme assertion of God's justice in Christ becomes represented as the spending of God's vengeance on Christ, and we have the whole immoral theory of substitution springing out of this original falsity in the conception of God's character which places justice at its basis and love as a flower on the top. God is Love is the faith of Christianity. It is doubtful how far it is its creed.

You know that profound and beautiful collect beginning, "O God, whose nature and property is ever to have mercy and forgive." Turn that up in the Prayer Book some spare hour and ponder it. It is God's *nature* to forgive. Forgiveness is His property, just as it is the property of water to slake your thirst. If it lost that property it would not be water. If God lost the instinct of forgiveness He would cease to be God. He might be as impartial in meting out reward and punishment as a Lord Chief Justice, but He would

---

3. Possibly a reference to a tract that appeared in the popular and multi-volumed *Chambers's Miscellany of Instructive and Entertaining Tracts*, published in Edinburgh from 1847.

not be God. If you will think yourself down to the bottom of that collect, or as far as you can go, you will get clear of all theories of substitution, or such ideas as that Christ took God's wrath and bore our punishment instead of us. It is God's nature and essence and distinctive property to forgive just as it is the nature and fine distinction of some blessed souls among ourselves. You must all surely know somebody who in this respect reflects the divine image, whose impulse is not to resent injury but to cover it over, forget it, and love the offender as before. You parents must all feel that if your child has done wrong it would be easy for you to forgive, and that it is very hard to give even proper punishment. But we are very imperfect and unbalanced. The very tendency to forgive is often a source of weakness to us. Forgiveness degenerates into good nature, carelessness of evil, short-sightedness as to the best good of those we love. Suppose all this weakness done away with. Realise the existence in God of a keen sense and antagonism to evil, such as no man could feel; remember the extent of his vision, both before and after, how He sees all the man has been, all he will be; reflect on the existence in God of a perfect hatred of evil, and a perfect sense of justice, what is due to himself, what is due from man to man, and from himself to man; and then remember that all this does not for one moment interfere with the pure flow of forgiveness, or destroy for an instant the loving harmony of His nature. The forgiveness is as free as that of the most loving and dear of women, while the justice is as strict and stern as that of the truest judge.

But even a conception like that does not fully realise the state of the case. We have only found that God's justice does not stop or poison the stream of His love and forgiveness. We have regarded the two as co-existing in harmony only. That is not enough. We cannot have two centres in God; two circles revolving outside each other, and just clearing each other. God not only is one but is the ultimate unity, and that would make Him at least two. We must find the one to flow from the other in the way of organic connexion. Either justice is at the bottom, and love to a few grows out of it, as so many believe, or love to all is at the bottom, and justice grows out of it, is its fruit, its servant and tool. And that is as John believed, and Paul, and all who have best understood the revelation and work of Jesus Christ.

Justice is but a form and application of love. It is love in action; it is love when it is true and unselfish, purified of passion, seeking not to please itself, but seeking with keen and unflinching eye another's good. Justice is love producing goodness, by mild means or by severe. When a man goes wrong human justice is satisfied with punishing him; divine justice does not want to punish him, except as a means of setting him right. Divine justice aims at making the man who is wrong right, not at punishing him. But it won't hesitate at any punishment needful to make him right. And why? Because divine justice is simply love taking shape, and MERCY IS THE TRUEST, THE ULTIMATE JUSTICE, *"Unto Thee, O Lord, belongeth mercy, for Thou renderest to every man according to his work."*

People tell you that if you committed a single sin you would deserve an infinite punishment for it, because, though finite yourself, you sin against an infinite Being. This infinite punishment would be the just thing, only mercy steps in and reduces the punishment by a certain operation to finite dimensions, or according to some, perhaps most people, relieves you of the punishment altogether, in consideration of its having been taken by another. Now a statement like that contains about as many fallacies as clauses. If it was once just that you should for a single sin bear infinite suffering it must be always just (unless God can change fundamentally), and nothing else could be just. And if mercy procured anything else mercy would be procuring injustice. And again, if it was once just that *you* should for a single sin bear infinite suffering it must always be just, and nothing else could be just. And it would be injustice for anybody else to step in to relieve you of your just punishment, and take on himself a punishment he never deserved. The path of popular theology is strewn with fallacies and moral pitfalls, and perhaps the fundamental fallacy of it all is this, that the sin of a finite being should deserve infinite punishment. That cannot be just. Consider all the weakness and ignorance of men and for which men have not themselves to blame, the weakness of our human condition, of the family, the genus man, of human nature, even where innocent. Consider the sins of circumstance, constitution, or even those which spring from short-sighted love. Can it be just that God should bring beings into the world unprotected by an infinite armour of foresight against the infinite chances and temptations to wrong, and yet hold them liable to infinite punishment when they had gone wrong? Could he have sent the first man here with faculties limited, and experience nothing, and then fix eternal torment as the penalty of his slightest sin? Could that be just? No. But people tell you nothing else would be just, that God could not show mercy till a way was opened out of the dilemma for Him by the death of Christ. Now, that has opened the way for us. It did not open the way for Him. I say mercy to a poor finite creature like man when he had sin was and is the truest and only justice. Punish a man for his sin, that is just; punish him for ages (if in that other world you can reckon time), that may be just; but make no end of punishing him for that sin, reduce him from a man to a devil and keep him there, let him become for ever vile, mainly because he was ignorant to start with, that is not just. The only justice to a sinner in a case like our human one is mercy, is to make his punishment finite, according to his works and proportioned to his offence,

2: Mercy the true and only Justice, 1877

and to make it of such a nature as not simply to torment the man, but to drive him back to the way of good. Mercy, I say then, is the only true justice. Justice is but the severe form of mercy.

Pity must be the first feeling of an infinite towards a finite being. If you had power like God's one of your first emotions would be sorrow for those poor weaklings who were without your strength.

> 'Twas but in giving that thou could'st atone
> For too much wealth amid their poverty.[4]

And as the man of wealth with even a human heart cannot rest content till he has put some or all of his wealth at the service of the ignorant and poor; as the man of knowledge finds not even the joy of acquiring it greater than the joy of bestowing it; as the soul that has found a rest for life has no rest till it can share its discovery with other souls, so He, whose are all the treasures of knowledge, wisdom, and love, who has at His command the resources of infinity, must have an infinite pity for the weak and the bad. The weaker, the more insignificant, the soul—the more room does it leave in the universe, so to speak, for the play round it of that infinite pity which saves. To be small is not to be disregarded by the pity that is infinite. Often we ourselves can more easily pity a little thing than a great. The pity we spend on it is more dewy, tender, and rich. There is something in the greatness of a disaster that brings other feelings into play, and pity is crossed by indignation with some one's carelessness or malice, or it is lost in a feeling that all our pity is inadequate to measure or to help a calamity so great. I say there is something in weakness or smallness which tends to bring pure pity out. It is a sort of compensatory faculty attached to weakness that it has the power to elicit pity in proportion to its weakness, and if we ourselves can pity with such copious compassion a homeless cat, an aged horse, or a noble but hapless dog, what must be spent upon them and the whole brotherhood of misfortune by the pity that is infinite, and grows only more pitiful as it grows more vast.

"Ah, but you say, pity for the weak is one thing, pity for the bad is another thing. Were we only weak we should not so readily mistrust that infinite pity. But it is another thing when we speak of pity for the bad, for that which distrusts it and abuses it. What if the infinitely pitiful is also the infinitely pure? Is the pity for an over-driven horse not crossed by a hot indignation at him who overdrives it? Is God's pity of our weakness not mixed with the deep anger at our sin of the perfectly pure? Grant to Him an infinite pity for our weakness, must that not be crossed and restrained by an infinite indignation with our sin?" In reply I say,

---

4. From George Eliot's poem, "The Legend of Jubal" (1869).

II: Published Sermons

1st: That our mere weakness might be met by something short of an infinite pity, so the infinity of the pity must be reserved for the sin. It is only in the face of sin that pity takes a truly moral quality, and becomes in the highest sense great, infinite. Mere weakness we ourselves can pity with our finite resources of compassion, and pity in an effective and soothing way. So that men and women who are merely weak without being troubled in conscience can find enough solace and strength in leaning on the strong pity of some fellow soul. But when the conscience is roused and the sense of God means the sense of sin, no human pity is enough to rest on, and we must appeal to a superhuman pity, which is infinitely pitiful, because infinitely pure.

For, 2nd: Purity when it becomes infinite becomes redemptive. Finite purity often means fastidiousness and separation. Purity that is reached amid favouring social conditions, by reliance on one's own power of resisting temptation, by trust, that is, in the finite creature, such purity is apt to be mere purism, sometimes little more than prudery. Purism is purity which is fastidious, self-regarding, and sought by finite resources. But the purity that is allied to the infinite, that is secured less by an effort of direct resistance than by an effort, in the other direction, of sublime trust and self-despair, that purity is not isolated, because it does not fear to be contaminated. The purity which is infinite is that which has no fear for itself, that contracts no defilement from the touch of pitch, and that overflows into purification. Purity which is finite is contented only to be pure. Purity which is infinite is purifying also, and is not content till it has subdued all things to itself, and given of its fulness to all who are morally poor. The purity which holds of the infinite is a passionate purity. It longs and yearns; it waits, it prays, it strives; it soothes, and when need is, it burns; it has colour, and soul, and life. The purity which is less than infinite, or which feeds itself only from finite and stoical sources, is like the snow-capped Alp, which powerfully but palely reflects the chillness of the midnight stars. The purity which is infinite, or akin to the infinite, is that same snowy Alp when touched into exquisite colour by the rosy light of the rising sun. Men wait for its lovely appealing; their souls take the warm hue of its rich and solemn face; and they discover in it the true type of the infinite tenderness, which is more of heaven than of earth, and of the purity that because divine is "human to the red-ripe of the heart."[5] I say the infinite purity is redemptive: it draws us into sympathy with it, and where it cannot draw us it will change its face, and drive us. "For a small moment have I forsaken thee, but with great mercies will I gather thee. In a little wrath I hid my face from

---

5. From Robert Browning's poem, "The Ring and the Book" (1868/69).

thee for a moment, but with everlasting kindness will I have mercy upon thee, saith the Lord, thy Redeemer."[6]

3rd: "Everlasting kindness," "A little wrath." That brings me to the third thing I have to say in reply to those who set over against God's infinite pity His infinite indignation, springing from His infinite purity. I have already said infinite purity is not the source of infinite indignation, but of infinite, insatiable redemption. I now say that, though you may speak of God's pity or purity as infinite, you cannot speak of His wrath or indignation as infinite. A little wrath in order to burn in the everlasting kindness; severe justice at those times when it is the only true form of mercy. The wrath of God is the wrath of the Lamb; terrible, but, in the light of eternity, swift and passing; burning up the growth of the soil, but clearing it and enriching it for a sweeter and greener blade. The storm of indignation is the flash of the infinite pity.

Think what you do when you speak of the infinite wrath of God, when you say that to some His anger burns for ever and ever. You make God a devil (I am measuring my words), an implacable spirit whose precedent and example may be quoted by every man who declares that he will not, cannot, forgive his worst foe. Say that the divine anger is an eternal anger, and you credit God with an unappeasable resentment against all who die with their sins on their heads. The moment they cross the frontier of life, and enter on death, that moment God becomes their deadly, everlasting foe. You may say, perhaps, He simply leaves them to themselves—is careless. If that were possible it would be as bad or worse. But it is not possible. The Omnipotent cannot be neutral, and neutrality cannot exist where there is no third party. Between the creature soul and the Creator it cannot be. If He do not save them He is their relentless foe.

Do you reflect, moreover, if you make God's wrath co-eternal with His pity, what disunion you sow in the divine nature. You set up two currents both infinite, both eternal, in awful and eternal collision. Where is then the peace of God which passeth knowledge? Where is the calm of eternity? Torn by gigantic impulses, hurried by titanic storms, which shake an area that could put the sun with its mere fire jets of 70,000 miles in a corner, racked by eternal passions in eternal pain, seeking infinite rest and finding none, eternity, heaving and trembling with the conflict and agony of its eternally divided and warring halves, would then be but the procession of an appalling tragedy, and God—why,

> dragons of the prime
> That tare each other in their slime

---

6. Isa 54:7–8.

II: Published Sermons

Were mellow music matched with Him.[7]

Were the universe but the scene of a rent nature like that, and were God but the name for the supreme discord and agony of spiritual war, well might He come down in a moment of truce, and seek for His rest in the nest of a bird, or the fox's hole; for there would not be one of His creatures but would be happier and more blessed than He, and it would be a grateful ease to Him to feel for an hour only the agony of Judas's soul. A Nero in his remorse would be a resting place for the torn nature of an infinite but self-discordant God. He would deserve neither our hatred nor our contempt, only our pity, and He would stir in us a pity so deep and divine, that we should become Gods [sic] by our infinite sorrow for his infinite pain.

When beliefs like those I resist are preached and held as Christian, can you wonder that the Church often seems a manufactory of sceptics? Can you doubt that there may be ages and churches whose sceptics are but the extreme left of the apostolate? Can you think that human nature does not re-echo its divine origin in protesting? Can you marvel that its representatives in great-souled poets and thinkers with a moral fire, should fiercely revolt and passionately deny? Can you wonder that they should despise and blaspheme so ungodly a God? Through an Æschylus with his Prometheus, or a Shelley, or a Byron, can you wonder that defiance and mockery should be poured on so undivine a king, and He is bidden torture and hate His equals, not His poor finite creatures whom He robbed—because He never gave them—of the infinite power that goes far to keep Him safe? Preach the eternal, unappeasable wrath of God upon lost souls and you offer men a devil to worship. It was from a theological devil that men like Byron and Shelley revolted; it was not from the God Christ worshipped and revealed, for at that time he was hardly preached.

No, no. God's wrath will last while sin lasts, but its purpose in lasting is not to perpetuate the sin, but to destroy it. It will pass away when it has done its purifying work. The wrath of God is not infinite and eternal in any sense such as His pity, His mercy, His love is. It is but a passing phase of these which are His eternal essence.

One practical word. If justice springs from love and is not its foe but its weapon, then to be just men and women you must be loving men and women. Justice is a function of the heart. The true impartiality springs from wise love. Its type is the mother and her family. The foundation of an orderly life and home is love, and the world will never be made the abode of justice till men recognise it as the abode of love, not of an unknown power but of

---

7. From Alfred Tennyson's poem, "In Memoriam A. H. H." (1849).

2: Mercy the true and only Justice, 1877

a love whose gleams or whose possibilities are to be caught even in heathen eyes and savage breasts.

> Father of all—we urge as our strong plea—
> Thou lovest all; thy erring child may be
> Lost to himself, but never lost to Thee.
>
> All souls are thine; the wings of morning bear
> None from that presence which is everywhere,
> Nor hell itself can hide, for thou art there.
>
> Through sins of sense, perversities of will,
> Through doubt and pain, through guilt and shame, and ill,
> Thy pitying eye is on thy creature still.
>
> Wilt thou not make, Eternal Source and Goal
> In Thy long years, life's broken circle whole,
> And change to praise the cry of a lost soul.[8]

---

8. A slight modification of John Greenleaf Whittier's poem, "The Cry of a Lost Soul" (1862).

3

THE STRENGTH OF WEAKNESS, 1878

"When I am weak then I am strong."
—2 CORINTHIANS 12:10

THE MOST PROFOUND UTTERANCES of the spirit sometimes betake themselves to paradox, as if the soul spurned and mocked the world in the act of using its speech. The spirit, in an intoxication of heavenly power, seems to glory in the powerlessness of the spoken word to pinion its wings. When faith is weak it is the slave of the things that daily seem. The laws of the understanding, the weight of investigation, the frosty rigidity of science, and the ordinary formularies of life lie upon it as if they would crush it. But when faith is strong it takes its revenge. Language then is not only inadequate—it is sublimely inadequate. The soul laughs at it and plays with it. In a fit of generosity it condescends to use it. In an immediate fit of irony it flies away, and mockingly bids speech follow if it can. Then it flies down in pity, and again speaks with human tongue. In another moment it has vanished into paradise—it has forgotten the existence of its lame ally—it is hearing things which is not lawful for a man to utter. There is an old fable that Vulcan, the artisan, the blacksmith god, displeased Jupiter, the king of heaven, who caught him and flung him in a rage sheer over the crystal battlements of heaven. Nine days he fell, and when he lighted on the earth he met with a fracture that left him a limping god the rest of his immortal days. As Jupiter to Vulcan, so is soul to speech. Language is a marvellous structure, a divine workmanship. But it limps as it goes. It is for ever nine days fall from the heaven that is the home of the soul. A paradox is the fall of Vulcan at the hands of Jupiter. It is the hour of the soul's triumph over the forms of the human heart.

3: The Strength of Weakness, 1878

It is not only complex minds that have to betake themselves to paradox to utter their spiritual experience. The simplest soul that intensely lives the highest life wants sometimes to utter things that defy its power of utterance, and its earthly state is in such miserable contrast with its heavenly visions that it can only express the relation by what seems a mockery. I die, but yet I live. I live, yet not I, but Christ in me. I glory in persecution. I am cast down, yet not forsaken. I have nothing, yet I possess all things. I am poor, yet I make many rich. I am blind, but yet I see. My case is hopeless, yet I am saved by hope. I am lame, but from time to time I go to the beautiful gates of a distant heaven. I lie at rich men's doors, but I nestle in Abraham's bosom. I have a hard fight only to live, yet I am kept fighting by a life that never leaves me. I am sadly alone, yet I am not alone, I am a foolish child, yet I am wise unto salvation. The weak things of the world I see bringing down the things that are mighty. Babes and sucklings utter perfect praise. A man that hath no music in his soul, yet is adding daily to the music of the world. Some that have little sense of beauty are leading the most beautiful lives. And some who seem to themselves to have a thorn in the flesh, marring half their usefulness and depressing their whole lives, yet become the source of an almost infinite spiritual power. Such was Paul. "When I am weak, then am I strong."

There may be a faith in you for which you can give no reason but the noble life it sustains. There is a divine foolishness which upsets at once the laws of a systematic reckoning and glories in the strength with which it feels itself weak. There is a secret assurance of inexhaustible power which can afford to set forth its infirmities in the world's very face, which makes a man feel most victorious when he is confuted by all the tests of world or Church. There is a glory which so excelleth that all a man's weaknesses are positive gain if they do but make room for this supreme glory to enter in. There is a kind of strength which does not appear till every other power has gone in. When all the common stars have gone down, the sun of this strength arises with healing in his wings.

This is a spiritual strength, and it shows itself only in spiritual results. There are people whose self-confidence will carry them unabashed through every exposure of their incapacity. There are men who think themselves better qualified to settle the knotty points of an intellectual war by their innocence of all real acquaintance with the subject. They seem to feel, as has been said, that to know the subject would prejudice their minds. The very absence of grammar becomes a presumption of power in theology, and favour with God is in inverse ratio to favour with men. There is an echo of truth in these absurdities. Carry the matter into the purely spiritual realm, and it is true that a peasant *may* know the mind of God better than a pedant. The absence of grammar need be no hindrance to a Christlike humility of soul, and a despised beggar may *feel* God as a whole university cannot. But never think to rely on a paradox in a region where speech and logic can easily cover the problems. Don't think you are better qualified to decide on the fourth gospel because you are untainted with either Greek or philosophy, and let alone the metaphysics of God if you haven't done something with Plato or Kant. But when you are in a world where the Father meets and converses with His child's soul, when you are laid on a sick bed where you see visions and dream dreams of Him, when you are ruined in business so that you are built up in fortitude, love, and grace, when all your mental powers, through some continuous fleshly thorn, fail you till you are humbled to receive a God you cannot acquire, then glory in your weakness, sport with speech, rejoice in tribulation, be strong in the very fact that you are weak, and feel in great humility that you have in you more of the world's chief power than in the time of health, wealth, and unbroken ease. The *spiritual* is the home of paradox. There alone a man may be strong in proportion as he is weak.

Do you see that man who moves about among his neighbours as if he were enveloped in a felt but unseen cloud of sanctity? He breathes an air which is above controversy, and yet he has no Pharasaic feeling that controversy is below him. He is swift to hear, but slow to speak. When human sin and wrong call for a condemnation, he condemns firmly, with an unspoken reserve of mercy for the sinning soul. When human weakness meets with the penalty of weakness, he has a tear in his eye for the weak one, while he says the judgment is just. He is painfully fair to all sides, and almost weakly distrustful of his own verdict or powers. Yet his opinion is weighty, his presence carries every matter into a higher plane.

> His converse drew us with delight;
> The men of rathe and riper years,
> The feeble soul, a haunt of fears,
> Forgot its weakness in his sight.
>
> On him the loyal-hearted hung,
> The proud was half disarmed of pride
> Nor cared the serpent at his side
> To flicker with its double tongue.
>
> The stern were mild when he was by
> The flippant put himself to school
> And heard him, and the brazen fool
> Was softened, and he knew not why.[1]

---

1. From Alfred Tennyson's poem, "In Memoriam A. H. H." (1849).

3: The Strength of Weakness, 1878

He is above sects, above parties. He has power like a great mountain to banish thoughts of littleness; and his is a witchery like that of the soft blue sky, to draw forth the cramped energies of a distrustful soul. The breath of envy that blows upon most cannot wither him. He is heaping up an influence he never seeks, and by the simple elevation of his life, he is drawing all men round him. Few men are weaker, he would tell you. You can see that not one in a thousand has his power. What is the secret of this contradiction? It is only the paradox of the earthly and the heavenly. By himself it is true, as he says, few men are weaker. Joined with that power to which he has given possession of his life, he is a very tower of strength. Years ago there was an experience which shook to its roots his self-trust, and cut the ground clean away from beneath his self-will. The world may have forgotten it, or may never have known it. Those who remember have long forgiven it. He has done neither—neither forgotten nor forgiven it. It is not present with him to torment him, but it is present to control him. It plunged him into hell, and then gradually, by the grace of God, carried him up into heaven. His own will was irremediably shaken, but it gave place to the will of God, and henceforth all life took a changed aspect. It was to be conquered less by effort than by submission. Any strength of his was to come henceforth by the power and the persistency with which he knew himself weak. If he ever thinks of this late won and unsought power of his among men, he can only say "When I am weak then am I strong." He does not say the weakness is the cause of the strength. Paul does not say so. Strength must come out of the strong. He only, like Paul, puts the two together. They exist together. The one is but the occasion of the other, not its cause. When I had lost myself, I found myself. But I found not myself in my lost self. I found a new true self in Christ, in God. My weakness opened a door for the influx of divine power. My fall gave God the opportunity to lift me up. I fell from my pedestal. God set on it a new man.

You must have marked or felt the sanctifying influence of perpetual pain. Have you never known a case where the thorn in the flesh was a ceaseless hindrance to almost every plan, and yet a constant impulse to sweet patience. You must have known of men or women who had, under pressure of bodily weakness, to give up every suggestion of natural ambition, and retiring, inch by inch, to accept a life other than the life they had framed. Have you never heard of cases where powers that would bless a nation almost were made useless for that end, and had by daily struggle to be bent to feed a prolonged patience, and build up a single beautifully-resigned life with the force that might have forged a name. Where did these powers go? To waste? What became of the old ambitions? Did they die? No, they took other form. If they died, they died to live transfigured. There is a dignity that doth hedge a king. The play of great power invests a man with worshipfulness, and we greet with profound admiration the statesman who, with unique insight, steers a nation to glory by the path of truth and right. But what is the dignity of the heroic king compared with the sanctity of the suffering king? The king uncrowned has a kind of power which the king crowned could never wield. The queen who goes to a revolutionary prison between wild guards, bareheaded, unjewelled, with an open-breasted gown, lays a spell upon human hearts which a whole coronation service cannot raise. And there is round the silent sick-bed of a paralysed genius who embraces, after a dreadful struggle, his new doom cheerfully, silently, with smiles as deep as those that cover the sunlit sea—there is round his head a halo which shines only on sorrow's kings, and his is a nobility that none can touch but God's princes of the blood. Princes of the blood! All heaven's princes are princes of the blood, and the King of Saints is the King of Sorrow.

Go to Rome and they will show you the wood of the true cross. Go to Jerusalem and you may see it again. Visit Florence and they will show you another piece. Try Naples and you will find a bit there. You laugh at the relic-mongers. Why I can show you fragments of the true cross without your going so far from home. I can take you where a life-long pain is developing a perfectly gentle intelligence and an utterly sweet will. I can walk you further, and show you where domestic torment is being bravely born, and the crucified ones, though they fall sometimes beneath their load, rise again and go on, hopeless, but for the hope that daily looks in on them in the smile of Christ. I could take you where women, out of sheer pity, take upon themselves gratuitous trouble with children who are neither kith nor kin, and with invalids in whom they have neither part nor lot except in the bond of Christ. I could show you, if I go far enough, quiet women growing pinched in face and grey in hair, yet bearing up, and hoping against hope, with devils of husbands, who are irritable when sober and malicious when drunk. I could show you husbands paying fine after fine for wives that have grown fiends, in the hope that some time, some time the weight of patience would prove too much for the strength of sin. I could show you women slaving for invalid husbands, and racking inventive brains to support their children. I could tell you of husbands nursing with infallible cheerfulness invalid wives, and widowers trying with rough and untaught hands to wash, dress, and feed an orphan of two. I could find for you sister and brother bearing up together, each leaning on the other under disaster, poverty, wrong; and the woman developing out of her sex's weakness an astonishing strength when the man fell down in her slender arms. You need not go very far to find noble souls wearing the mask of a smile upon a heart that is without hope, till the very muscles of their face are sore with the effort, which is one of will alone. The dead smile more calmly, but not so sweetly as these. They would be happier if they could but look more miserable. But a look of misery from them means a pang of misery to some they love; and they go about wearing on their face a gracious lie, because a dear life may be kept in if hope can be kept up.

Ay, the true cross has left plenty of relics behind it. It grows the faster as it is cut and carried away. It will strike from a slip. Bury your fragment and it will live. Wear it in the silence of your heart, in the depth of your renouncing will, and it will multiply itself till your silence and what seems your weakness become a broad green tree for the weary birds of the air to shelter in. Strength is not measured by your power to do only, but just as often by your power to endure. And, whether in doing or enduring, strength is always to be measured by your power to believe. The strength of a life is in proportion neither to intelligence, nor passion, nor will, but to faith. It is the eye that sees when all other eyes fail that we look to for help. And it might conceivably be that in some great crisis of the world, when all trust in large intellects or powerful wills had broken down, that men's faith should be kept alive by none of these, but by the persistent and unshakable belief of some suffering soul, powerful only to suffer, and yet to believe; lying, perhaps, on a bed of pain, but yet with clear, calm soul, calling out to the world in suspense, "Still I see, still I see. God holds the world still, and is guiding it to the perfect end." I say such a crisis is a conceivable thing, though it would mean a second Incarnation of the Son of God. It is the very essence of the first. And as that is eternal, we need no second. Christ saved the world by His eternal, indestructible faith. In total physical prostration, in the abeyance of every high faculty which men most praise, deserted by His dearest, with the hateful or the indifferent for His nearest, He yet, by the simple power of faith, by His belief both in God and man, has made that weak hour to be the source and centre of the only world-wide moral power. From Christ's cross streams the impulse of the strong and the comfort of the weak.

> Is it not strange the darkest hour
> That ever dawned on sinful earth,
> Should touch the heart with softer power
> For comfort than an angel's mirth?[2]

The world in its common hours asks for joy. It praises and feasts the man or woman who can bring it only joy. The buoyant spirits, the bounding health, the indiscriminate mirth, or even the gaiety of old pagan life, the men who bring those to us we crown with garlands, and we set at the chief seats in our feasts. Alas! the day has gone by when joy was the world's highest aim, and simple gladness the pervading thought. The gay old pagan life

2. From John Keble's poem, "Good Friday" (1827).

vanished when the spectacle of Christ's awful purity appalled the world with the terror of a new and higher ideal. "If that is what we ought to be, is there much cause for joy in the thought of what we have been?" So joy ceased to be the world's highest aim. Sorrow filled men's hearts, and the idea of joy gave place to the idea of peace. Never more shall joy, delight simply, be the ideal of this world. That dark, strong hour, that sad sweet life, that mystery of sorrow and strength, that Titanic power of conquered pain, that Divine undying faith, that unquenchable and deserted love, those thirty little years of infinite greatness, that strength for all time weighed down with the weakness of the hour, that life in death, have changed all that. The victory of weakness has swallowed joy up in comfort, and the impulse to life is now forgiveness, not delight.

"The gods were feasting," says a modern poet, "the old gods were feasting. The nectar went round, the laughter was full and free. Apollo unsealed his lyre, and the muses fell in with their gracious and stately tones. When suddenly there came slowly panting in a pale and blood-stained Jew. On His head was a crown of thorns, on His shoulder He bore a great wooden cross. And He threw down the cross on the lofty table of the gods till the golden goblets rang, and the gods turned dumb and pale. And paler they grew and paler, they whitened and whitened away, till at last they melted entirely into mist. The world grew grey and dark. The happy gods were no more. Joy had gone, but comfort came. He can bear his sorrow easily who sees his God sorrow with him. These merry gods of old who felt no pain, knew nothing of how it goes with poor tormented men, and a poor distracted man in his trouble could find they had no heart for him. They were holiday gods these. Men danced round them and only gave them thanks. They were never beloved from the heart of hearts. To be loved like that one must see sorrow and know pain. Sympathy is the last consecration of love. It is love itself, perhaps. Of all the gods who have ever loved, Christ, therefore, is the most beloved. And the weakest—the women—they love Him the most."[3]

To have written these words one might be glad to have lived and sorrowed much. They contain the secret of Christianity. Strength perfect in weakness. Love made certain by death. Sympathy made exquisite by sorrow.

A suffering God. You touch the two infinites there. The infinite of glory and the infinite of pain. They met in Christ. Whoever will take up the fellowship of His cross conquers in His strength. Sorrow like His makes us strong, for it binds us in unity with God in His divinest hour, and unity there is strength indeed. Sorrow gives us a rare advantage for understanding

3. This appears to be Forsyth's own translation and paraphrase of words from Heinrich Heine's *Reisebilder* (English translation, *Pictures of Travel*).

Christ, and whoever understands Him is strong, if he be as weak as a straw. The will that can truly resign and receive, that is the perfect will, not the will which can dare, do, and defy. "My will at all costs"—that is to be weak. "Thy will, not mine"—that is to be strong. Christ's is the final religion. For Divine love can do nothing more when it has resigned all. Christ's is the universal religion, for all men can surrender if all men cannot achieve. It is not always possible for us to live. It is always possible divinely to die. And a divine death means a divine resurrection. The cross involved the empty tomb, and the empty tomb means the fulness of a new and living world.

4

THE BIBLE DOCTRINE OF HELL AND THE UNSEEN, 1879

Sermon by the Rev. P. T. Forsyth,
Preached in the Bradford Road Congregational Church,
Shipley, November 23, 1879.

At the outset, the rev. gentleman said that in the study of this question we are to be guided by Bible principles rather than by Bible texts or the opinions held by its different writers in different ages.

The Bible does not supply any dogmatic utterance on this point. It gives principles which enable us to form our opinions. We may find—and shall—that the express utterances of the Bible on this point are either conflicting or indefinite; that the Old Testament, for example, contradicts the New Testament in some important particulars, that both are indefinite and not final, and that we have to deal with a developing idea and not a dogma at all. The life after death may be treated in several ways—(1) We may ask, is there such a thing?—The fact. (2) How does it exist?—The mode. (3) How long does it exist?—Duration.

(1) Does it exist? Does the Bible say that it exists? This is partly a question of immortality, but not quite. The Jews believed in a life after death before they believed in immortality. Their views took three stages. (*a*) In the earliest age, this life was all. There was hardly any thought of the future life. Justice was done in this world. God in this world filled men's thoughts. The reward of keeping the commandments was longevity of the individual or of the nation. The patriarchs were so full of the sense of God that they did not trouble much about their own future. So on the subject of an existence beyond death, this part of Jewish testimony is very silent. Expressions in the narrators betray the

4: The Bible Doctrine of Hell and the Unseen, 1879

position of their later age on the subject, but there is little or nothing in the proceedings or words of the great figures to indicate that they had the idea. (*b*) In the next period there is the belief in the continued existence of the dead elsewhere in a dreary lifeless fashion, which I will describe presently. (*c*) In the last period there was a more vivid belief in immortality—not mere existence of a dreamy and shadowy sort, but continued life and fulness of it—an intensification of all the interests and passions of this world, instead of a diminution of them. The belief in immortality does not appear till very late in Jewish history. The belief in some sort of feeble continuation of existence appears much earlier. There is no certainty of immortality in the Old Testament.

(2) Now as to this second stage of thought. When the belief gained ground that men did not cease to exist when they died, what was the mode of that existence? How were they conceived to exist, and where? As this is a form of belief which covered the whole time when the Old Testament was written, we may ask as our answer to this question, "What is the Old Testament view of the state after death?" Well, it was very like the conception of the Greeks and Romans. Their Hades corresponds to the Hebrew Sheol. Hades was a dreary and vast palace or realm of Pluto in the heart of the earth, where departed souls entered never to return, but to lead henceforth a joyous, passionless existence, and continue a sort of subdued vitality. The Hebrew Sheol is so similar that they had probably a kindred origin. The word signifies a gulf or abyss. It was understood to be a vast cavity in the heart of the earth, where the dead passed when the breath left the body. It opened once to swallow Korah, Dathan and Abiram. The expression "He was gathered to his fathers" refers to this and not to burial, for both are mentioned together, as in Gen. 25, 8 and 9 verse, "Abraham . . . was gathered to his people. And his sons buried him in the cave of Machpelah." The conception was rude at first, but gradually grew more terrible as the clinging to life grew and the horror of leaving it. All passed there with very few exceptions such as Enoch and Elijah, who went at once to the presence of God. Abraham and the fathers were all there. This exemption grew to be the hope of many a pious Jew. Ps. 73, 24. There were two currents of Jewish thought. To see God is to die, and to see God is to live. It is chiefly in the poetic and prophetic books that the hopeless horror of Sheol is developed. The existence there was lifeless and spiritless (for the life had been in the blood), and shadowy. Communion with God was broken off—the supreme energies of worship were possible no more. See Ps. 6, 5. "For in death there is no remembrance of thee; in the grave who shall give thee thanks." Ps. 30, 9. "What profit is there in my blood when I go down to the pit? Shall the dust praise thee? Shall it declare thy truth?" Eccl. 9, 10. "For there is no work, no device, nor knowledge in the grave whither thou goest." Sheol is a place of silence,

darkness, and forgetfulness. It is described in Job as a "land of darkness and the shadow of death, without any order, and where the light is as darkness."[1] All glory is over there, pain too, and trouble cease. Absolute equality exists, for "there the prisoners rest together; they hear not the voice of the oppressor. The small and great are there; and the servant is free from his master."[2] It is represented as a prison with gates, bolts, and bars (Job 17, 6), open only to the eye of God (26, 6). It is a final state; there is no evasion, escape, or return. Job 30, 24. "Howbeit he will not stretch out his hand to the grave, though they cry in his destruction." Job 7, 10. "He shall return no more to his house, neither shall his place know him any more." Ps. 49, 8. "Too costly is the redemption of their soul, and it must be given up for ever," (the grim irony of which is lost in our version). God's presence is there, but not his activity. Yet certain excitements are represented as possible in this dreary state. The highest passions are impossible. Any knowledge or sympathy with this life is impossible. Yet, such is not always the representation. "Hell from beneath is moved for thee—to meet thee at thy coming. It stirreth up the dead for thee."[3] We are told in Isaiah of the excitement caused by the entrance to Sheol of the Chaldean King. There are indications, too, that certain sections of the people believed in a possible communication between this world and that. The belief in necromancy, so strongly discouraged in the Old Testament (Witch of Endor) shows that. And just as the belief in a continual existence, however dreary, gave a basis for the doctrine of immortality, so this belief in the possible recall of the dead gave a basis and soil for the belief in the resurrection at a later date. This, then, is the testimony of the Old Testament. The sight of God was a splendid hope of awful boldness. What a bold verse that was in its time (Ps. 73, 24). "Thou shalt guide me by thy counsel, and afterward receive me to glory." It was the intuitional germ of what has since grown from a splendid guess to a splendid faith. In the New Testament the popular idea is vastly changed and contrasted. The Apocrypha supplies the missing link of development where in our Bibles a great gap occurs. After the exile the Jews were scattered—some in Palestine, some in Alexandria. The Apocrypha contains Palestinian books and Alexandrian books. The Alexandrian books are influenced by Greek philosophy. There are two ideas of death in the Old Testament; one that it was a curse, and in the nature of things should not be; the other that it was the ordained and natural end and consequence of life. The Alexandrians adopted the former belief. Death should not be; in the case of the just it is not; they do not

1. Job 10:22.
2. Job 3:18–19.
3. Isa 14:9.

die; it only seems so to fools. Wisdom 3, 2. There is not a promiscuous Sheol to which all go, good and bad. Sheol is only for the bad. The state in the next life is conditioned by character in this; the good, after some purification, go to God, in Heaven. Instead of a very few like Enoch going to God, all the good go, and eternal destiny is fixed at death. When the appointed time comes, there comes judgment, and those in Sheol stay there; those in heaven stay there, after assisting in the judgment. This idea of the judgment is a new idea, an importation. The Palestinian books differed in their conceptions. They too had the new idea of judgment, Sheol was the intermediate state into which all souls, good and bad, went to wait. At the judgment the good received resurrection to Heaven, the bad remained in Sheol. In Sheol, therefore, there were two divisions, one for the good, one for the bad. That for the bad was the valley of fire called, after the valley of Purification near Jerusalem, Gehenna. A great gulf was fixed between the two, but communication was possible. There was no passing, however. The spirits in prison to whom it is said Christ preached were the pre-Christian saints waiting in Sheol. The good part of Sheol was called "Abraham's bosom," for Abraham was there, "Paradise," "Eden," etc. When Christ came, this last was the popular idea, represented by the Pharisees. It contradicted the Old Testament in not making Sheol final, only part of it, Gehenna. It varied from the Alexandrian and philosophical idea in putting the finality at judgment rather than at death. At any rate it did not allow the good, as the Alexandrian did, to pass to glory at once, but made them sojourn in Sheol. The grand addition to the old idea in the Apocrypha is the idea of judgment in another life. The prophets had insisted only on the judgment in this life, either on the individual or the nation. This of course gave Sheol a more vital connection with the world, and added intensity and significance to the life there. It is hardly now a dreamy life, but on one hand the expectation of resurrection, and on the other the deeper agony of the bad in the new region of Gehenna. The idea of immortality—continued life, not mere existence—had by this time gained ground, coming partly from Greece, partly from the East, and the thought of a future life was becoming a powerful one among thinking men as well as in the popular view. The mere *existence* of Sheol develops into the *life* of immortality. Immortality was coming to light, emerging from Hades, from Sheol. The gospel was at hand. It is a good description of the change from Sheol to immortality to say that Christ brought life and immortality to the light. He intensified and certified the faith in immortality—the fact of a continued life under moral conditions, and bound up with a judgment. But did he throw any new light on the aspect of the matter we are considering—on the mode of existence beyond death? Except that the conditions were moral and spiritual, did he reveal any further conditions or circumstances of that life? Did he tell us anything about how the judgment would happen, and in what definite way the departed spirits lived? You say yes, there is the parable about Dives and Lazarus; there is the outer darkness; there is the worm and the fire, undying and unquenched. There is the passage about the Son of Man coming in glory with all his holy angels. Well, I reply that all these representations are not quite harmonious. Taken altogether they do not make a consistent picture. And for that, as well as for other reasons, it is more probable that Christ, in the pursuit of his great, moral and spiritual end, took the imagery, which he found ready to hand in the popular belief. He used those popular and material representations as a vehicle for inner truth. He used them, but did not stamp them. We are not committed to them as having Christ's authority as descriptions of the mode of life in the unseen. Immortality, judgment, retribution, justice, love, *God*, these were the realities he directly conveyed. These were the words he would print on the soul. The imagery was but the moveable types which he used for the purpose. The representations were but symbols, not realities in themselves. Before leaving this question of the modes of existence in the unseen, I will dispose of the other New Testament representations. Paul is indefinite. He says nothing directly on the point. Some of his passages point to the state immediately after death as a brief sleep till Christ return. Others of them, written in other moments, point to it as an immediate union with Christ in Heaven. He oscillates between the two views in the Apocrypha, he probably could not make up his mind, and never made great exertions to do so. Such questions for him were overshadowed by vaster and more infinite bearings of the spiritual world. The Apocalypse goes into much detail—too much, but it is not to gratify curiosity. It is to magnify the victory of Christ. Here too we have the Jewish popular conception employed in a poetic way, and probably in a symbolic way.

(3) How long does the state after death exist? We pass from its mode or shape or conditions to its duration. This is the great question today. And it will be settled one way if we use Bible texts; another, if we use Bible principles and ideas. (*a*) In the Old Testament we saw that from Sheol there was no escape or return. If the people of those days thought of eternity at all—which is doubtful—then Sheol was everlasting. (*b*) The same applies to those who at the judgment were left in the Sheol or Hades of the Apocrypha. There is no indication of any provision for their release. If the question rises it is repressed as fruitless, for want of data. (*c*) The teaching of Christ gives but slender foothold to the idea of restoration. I mean the direct and express teaching. The question was never then put point blank. It is not an enquiry of that age but of this. Its earnestness is a fruit of the Christian spirit after all these centuries of growth. But neither can it be said that Christ has pronounced definitely for the endless

4: The Bible Doctrine of Hell and the Unseen, 1879

duration of torment. In this respect also he used the language and symbols of his time. He did not come to set men's minds at rest on the question of the duration of punishment. He came to reveal God's judgment in the soul, moral not temporal realities. When he speaks of everlasting punishment, his words are not to be pressed as if he was replying to the express question which so many are asking today. The great gulf was not between Heaven and Hell, but down the middle of Sheol. Paul never faces the question of the duration of punishment. It was not presented to him, and his mind did not willingly raise it or dwell upon it. He delights in the idea of being for ever with the Lord. It seems to expel the other idea. There is but a single reference in his writings to the idea of the underworld, and that is rather in quoting other people's words—Romans x, i. It is a most striking fact that Christ has far more to say about Hell than his greatest apostle. Just as the thoughts and presence of God left no room in the earliest Jews for the desire or hope of immortality, so the thought and presence of Christ left in Paul no room for the idea of Hell. Even John, the Apostle of Love as he is called, is more prolific of references to Hell and future punishment than Paul, especially if John wrote the Apocalypse. There the lake of fire means an eternal doom. There is no Restoration. All we can suppose the writer to have in view at best was the annihilation of the wicked in it. It is all the stranger in Paul if you remember this was the same injurious persecutor who, breathing out threats and slaughter, haled men and women forth to torture and death for the name of Jesus. What a shock of change had passed over him. How was this stern man softened, and the harsh made mild in the discipline of those years after his conversion of which history is silent. In what conflict of the spirit and inward fighting had he learned the secret of Jesus and tempered his passionate propagandism to the tender and loving reasonableness of the Cross. The fact is that Paul has so little to say about Hell, and Christ so comparatively little, for this reason, that both were full of the destruction of Death and Hell. Instead of teaching what the underworld was, it was Paul's business and inspiration to declare that by Christ Death and Hell should be no more. Christ had abolished both, taken away the sting from Death, and robbed Hell of power and victory. His kingdom had overthrown the kingdom of darkness. He had the keys of Hell and Death. He was the deliverer therefrom and their destroyer. The preacher then went on to state that this was one of the points on which that which Jesus was and did is perhaps of more importance than what he said. It is by the spirit of Jesus' life and revelation that we must be guided in this matter. If the presence of Christ and God in Paul banished Hell from his consciousness, so the presence and operation of God in existence will banish Hell from that. Endless Hell is not reconcileable with the character of God as revealed by Christ, both in his person and work. If God and his Love is to be all in all, then no place is left for

II: Published Sermons

Hell in the end. It may be answered that the existence of evil is not reconcileable with God's character; the reply to which is that it is more so than the permanence of evil. If evil is to be permanent in any part of the universe, then God is there foiled and the Cross of Christ of none effect. After stating that God's gift to the world is life, overflowing, infinite life, Mr. Forsyth said: It is life we want, and the eternal life is goodness—being like Christ. That goodness is consummated in Heaven, we say. There is fulness of life. But there there is no pain. Where life is full there is no pain, *i.e.*, where goodness is full and free, there is no pain. Pain then if not caused is occasioned by evil. So long as evil lasts there will be Hell. If evil should cease, Hell would be burned out. Now if Christ's cross means anything, it means the destruction of evil everywhere and for ever. The work of the cross is not done while there is a single soul unwon to the mastery of Christ and uninfected by his spirit. The destruction of evil means the redemption of evil souls. Evil simply means evil souls. If we believe in the cross then we believe there will come a time when evil shall everywhere cease and sin no longer be. And remember that there is but one way of destroying evil. It is by making souls good. It is a moral and spiritual state to be met by the contrary moral and spiritual state. The cessation of evil means that spirits cease to do evil and learn to do well. I insist on this in order to repudiate the "miserable doctrine of annihilation,"[4] as it has been called. Some have been shocked out of the falsehood of an endless Hell without being shocked into the opposite idea of universal salvation. They stop half-way across the street and run for refuge to one of those little islands in the middle crowned by a feeble gaslamp where nobody can stay but for a time. They escape by supposing that the finally impenitent are annihilated, or, to put it at its best, that they go out, expire, and cease to be for want of the immortal sustenance given by union with Christ. I do not think that from the point of view of the divine character it matters much whether you say they are annihilated or simply go out. If they are annihilated it is by God's act. If they go out it is also God's act who made them so that they should at a certain time go out, and withheld the endowment of infinite vitality. If a man make a machine it is much the same for his reputation for wisdom whether he crush it because it won't work, or whether he made it so weakly that it broke down and collapsed after working a certain time. Well, these people say—Yes, evil will be abolished, but by the destruction of the soul which does the evil. It is the stamping out process. It is not curing but killing. It is to say in effect there is a way of getting rid of sin other than by conversion. It is to say, we have got no good out of these people, we will stop their chance of more evil, or good either. It is to confess that a section of the human race has been successful in withstanding

---

4. A reference to Brown, *The Doctrine of Annihilation*, vi.

4: The Bible Doctrine of Hell and the Unseen, 1879

the power of the cross of Christ and must be exterminated in order that the cross may have imperial and universal sway. That may be *imperium et libertas*,[5] but it is neither the empire nor the liberty of the cross as it appeared to Paul. Such an exit from the difficulty is about as damaging to the character of God as the old one from which it professes to escape. It is one of the timid half-measures which aggravate the evil. The true wisdom is to be bold; the true safety is to be daring. Such was the wisdom of Paul. We must fearlessly grapple with the arch-fear, and to destroy this last of foes tax the vastest energies and potentialities of the cross. Neither divine justice nor human freedom can suffer in the process. The Cross is their reconciliation. And I say, according to my reading of the Bible, the Cross and an endless Hell are incompatible. Not that the Cross and Hell are incompatible. It is just as far wrong to say there is no Hell as to say it will last for ever. The reality of Hell is and will be far more terrible than your horriblest dreams of its endlessness have been able to make it. But it is not material fire and it is not for ever. It is a spiritual condition. And if it give you relief to think, Oh! it is only spiritual, that only means that there is a new order of agony in store for you, that you have never known the meaning of the word spiritual, that your being for all you may have suffered has never been searched as it can be searched and sounded by a spiritual woe. It is because Hell is not endless that your agony will be so deep. If it were endless you could take some refuge in a just challenge of the infinite cruelty that made it so. And in your agony you would be in some sort heroic. You would be a kind of martyr to infinite power. You would have the partial sympathy of all the most just natures, and the pity of all the most loving hearts. But you will be robbed of that refuge. You will not be able to call the conscience or the pity of the world to your relief. You will not have the ghost of a pretext for heroism of any kind. For the God who has made Hell has made it in a love which it will be seen by all to be utterly ignoble to resist and defy, and not heroic at all. It is the consciousness that you have sinned against a God of such love that he must terminate and destroy even Hell, it is that knowledge that will fill the cup of your remorse and embitter the sting which wakes you up to repentance and true life. You will then know that the pains of love are more awful than the stings of force and hate, and the chastisement of the Lord more dreadful than any torments of Satan could be.

---

5. Empire and liberty.

5

Egypt: A Sermon for Young Men, 1882

Preached at St. Thomas's Square, Hackney,
Sunday, September 17, 1882.

My sermon this evening is to young men, and the subject I have chosen is Egypt. It is easy to see how I came to choose such a subject. If young men nowadays read nothing else, they read the papers. Their morning portion is the *Telegraph*, and their evening portion is the *Echo*. The *Daily News* is like the early, and the *Globe* is unto them like the latter rain. And the papers, of course, are full of what has been filling the minds of all of us. Egypt has been, for the last few weeks, and this week especially, a land of Goshen for the newspapers, and the war has come down like the fertile fulness of the Nile upon the empty and thirsty public mind.

Apart from this it might seem somewhat paradoxical to select such a subject as a text for young men. It is a case of extremes meeting. When Tennyson speaks about Chaucer he says he comes "the youngest to the oldest singer that England bore." So when we join Egypt and youth, we bring the oldest to the youngest civilisation that the world has born. The Sphinx wears a shade of still more mysterious and sublime contempt on her placid yet passionless face when she sees at her venerable feet the anxious merchant and the journalistic scribe, and overhears the youth of the period betting on the prospects of Arabi's success.

And yet, surely, there is something that might for a moment solemnise even the Stock Exchange in the shadow of that hoary and mystic land. It is a strange destiny which forces us English so often to invade the grey silence of a burned-out past, and play our engines of war upon the embers of extinct civilisations. It is not our lot to measure weapons with European nations

5: Egypt: A Sermon for Young Men, 1882

of a culture coeval and equal with our own. Our soldiers and our sailors are sent to slay the slain, in a sense, and their expeditions carry them to gaze upon the wrinkled age of Chinese conservatism, the gigantic temples, idolatries, and castes of Hindoo [sic] antiquity, or the monuments of a civilisation which might be the grandfather of either—the Egyptian has. Mexico alone I suppose among the dead majesties of extra-European civilisation has never been troubled in her eternal sleep by the din of our camps and the roar of our fleet. The mushroom antiquity of Greece or Rome is too modern for the antiquarian taste of our military enterprise. We prefer to fight under the shadows of nations that Greece and Rome deemed ancient, and we have once again roused the sleeping millenniums of the pyramids. Their millenniums; centuries are nowhere when we speak of this cradle of government, science, and art. I turn up a small reference Bible, and I find at the top of the marginal column, beside the first chapter of Genesis, the date 4004 BC. The suggestion is that the world and man were created in some week during that year. Why, that is very nearly the date of the first historical dynasty of Egypt. The flood, I find, dated in this bold Bible at 3317. Why, by that time the pyramids had been long built. And, if you will reflect on the centuries it must have taken to develop the arts of government, of writing, of building, and of burying which we find in such perfection there, you will feel that even in the fourth millennium BC Egyptian society must have reckoned itself old, and the first historical dynasty must have been preceded by several Governments, of which we find but an inferential trace. Now, just think of all it takes to make up a great and enlightened civilisation. Think of the congeries of cultured religion, science, industry, the awful aggregate of passion, thought, hope, fear, love, plots, crimes, enterprises, tragedies, and victories of all sorts. Reflect that that Egyptian people were no dullards, but joined much of the Greek intellect with no little of the Hebrew seriousness. They were more deeply religious than the Greeks, and more nimbly intellectual than the Jews. The ready fertility of their Nile-watered soil did not furnish an excuse for that indolence of mind and body which is the curse of tropically fertile lands. It rather gave them a material basis from which they could work, unhampered with the coarser cares of life, towards the higher regions of knowledge and faith. They taught the Greeks mathematics. They might have taught the Jews immortality. The temper of the people was cheery and light. Don't suppose "that because we know them chiefly from their graves and temples, they had no other interests than temples and graves." Their monuments bear trace of their love for dance and song, comedy, caricature, and even the grotesque. And yet their seriousness was such that they thought the Greek light and childish. The thought of the infinite future lay upon them as it did not upon the Greek, and it sobered and cheered them at once. It is their faith in the future life, and their consequent care of their dead that have chiefly made them known to us. They have become immortal, because they believed in immortality.

We look with some respect on an aged yew. We are touched with the antiquity of an ancient castle, or abbey, or town. We lay bare with eager, careful, and pious hand the vestiges of ancient Rome and the relics of ancient Sparta, Troy, and Jerusalem. Their very dust is dear to us. We finger their stones with reverence; we gather up their fragments, that nothing may be lost. But what are stones, utensils, weapons, buildings or even books and statues compared with a whole civilisation; and what is their antiquity compared with a culture 6,000 years of age. One lesson for us from our contact with a land like Egypt is the lesson of reverence. No spot utters such a rebuke as Egypt does to the picnic view of history; the spirit, born in teeming centres of materialistic and squalid civilisation, which regards the relics and monuments of the past as proper places for excursions, dances, and shows, to be strewn with a litter of unclean papers, or carved over with a vulgar record of vulgar names. If antiquity can ever be venerable, it is in Egypt. These monuments, whether from their age or their size, warn off the thoughtless touch. They symbolise a culture that may well make us modest, with all our nineteenth century achievement. The past is not the region of fogeyism that the common mind loves to believe. There is no surer sign of a true and sympathetic culture than a high sense of what the past has done and what we owe to it. It is not the tendency of the public mind, especially in the business world, to be overburdened with reverence for anything, the past included. And there is a school of youths which regards any tenderness for the great objects of human reverence as an unmanly weakness. My brethren, refuse to go after this conceited insensibility. Refuse to think that little children and winsome girls are the only fit objects of gentle and tender feeling. It is comparatively easy for one who is not entirely a brute to be tender to that whose sweet weakness appeals to him. That is common manhood. But it is uncommon and noble manhood to dare to feel tenderly towards something that stands over you, that awes you, that is not weak and appealing, but majestic, and that calls forth a tenderness not playful, but deep and almost solemn. Most people, as I say, who have any heart left can be playfully tender. Few people—but those of the highest and finest sort—care to cherish a solemn tenderness. And yet this is the feeling that a great and most venerable but extinct past should rouse. And if it be an education for us to become only acquainted with such a past to study its ways and realise its mere age; if that bring us face to face with a great presence, with whose relics we can converse and feel ourselves great, how much greater must we feel when we are drawn so close to that solemn greatness as to love and cherish it and feel that we are warmed and fed, and not repelled. There is

5: Egypt: A Sermon for Young Men, 1882

no lesson harder for the youth of an inquiring age to learn than that of true reverence, and there is none so indispensable for the safety of his progress. It is another form of the one great need, the need of a true religion, the need of an *Eternal* God. If a tender reverence becomes and adorns us in the presence of anything so solemn as the memory of a mighty civilisation and the organised relics of old human hearts what must we not feel when we realise about us and within us a living presence, which was before time began to be, and who walked in their midst. It may be doubted, in view of the constant flux of physical life, and the change of material particles, if the sun and moon we see be the same that gave shape to the Egyptian worship, and imperturbably watched the dynasties rise and set. It is certain that we do not look on the same Nile, the same water, or the same sand and slime upon its shore. But we do stand under the eye and breath of the same venerable and eternal God as watched and inspired the civilisations of old. When the thought first flashed through the mind of Cheops that he would build for himself and his line an immortal tomb, that thought was known to Him who stands among us at this hour, and is searching the ambitions of your heart and mine. How strange, how dreadful is this place. For here is a living Being by our very side who stood by when the pyramids were raised, when Egypt was the foremost of teeming empires, and who has by heart the whole weird story of that mysterious land. If it dignify us to feel tenderly to so ancient a past, if such a past truly realised extort from us an awe which is not wholly fear, how it must exalt us to have tender contact with Him who was by when the world was framed, and who built His own pyramids in the everlasting hills. That, indeed, is the source of all true dignity in human life, to touch the Eternal, to have fellowship with the Father, and stand upon the rock of ages. To know Him is glory, honour, and immortality, and he that doeth His will shall abide for ever.

The Sphinx is well accepted as the symbol of that hoary civilisation of old Egypt. Now what is the Sphinx? It is a figure with a human head and the body of a beast, a human face upon the figure of a brute. Now what does that symbolise in the light of spiritual development? It symbolises a stage at which the human spirit or intelligence has just emerged and got its head clear of the lowest and animal nature. The civilisation of ancient Egypt was a stage further on than the civilisations of the remoter East, where the worship of nature lay like a crushing and unbreathing load upon the nobler spirit of man, "Westward the tide of empire sets its wave."[1] It is in the West that man has realised the freedom of his spirit and the compass of his intelligence, and it has taken place in these later and Christian centuries chiefly.

---

1. This appears to be a play on Bishop George Berkeley's famous words, "Westward the tide of empire holds its way."

II: Published Sermons

Now, Egypt occupies a middle place in this development. It is the transition point from East to West. It is not so strange, therefore, that it should now threaten to be the battlefield of the two. The civilizing forces of the West roll back to pay to the East, in spite of herself, the debt of obligation so long due. The East resists, and naturally resists, such missionaries as we mostly send, and declines to answer a summons by tuck of drum. It is in Egypt, it seems, that two forces must meet. Egypt has now become what the Judea of the prophets used to be. Little Judea was the earthen pipkin between the two iron pots when the huge empires of Assyria and Egypt came into collision for the mastery of the Eastern world. (Isa. xix. 24.) And between the two, Judea was, after much diplomacy and some heroism, crushed. And all the tragedy and pathos of her expiring life are uttered for ever in the writings of the prophets. But the conflict has changed, and with it the battlefield. The mastery now sought is not that of the Eastern World, but that of the Old World altogether. The combatants are not two empires, but two civilisations, two continents, two religions. And the battlefield is little Egypt, little among the nations, but endowed with a strange position between them, a strange destiny, and strange memories. Shall Egypt be extinguished between the two forces as Judea was of old? That probably depends on Egypt herself, if she still retains the spirit of a people and the germs of nationality. The civilisation of the West has learned one lesson unknown to the empires of the old East. It has felt the nobility of helping the weak and setting upon their feet a feeble folk that has still the spark and promise of life. The situation of Egypt, at the meeting-point of those continents, will always make it an important commercial centre. The days are by when it was a great centre of culture and the focus of light. What Alexandria was for early Christianity it will never be again. It was the headquarters, then, of all the most cosmopolitan influence and fine Catholic culture of the day. The schools of Alexandria were the headquarters of a wide paganism and a liberal Christianity. True to her geographical place and function, Egypt was the intellectual meeting-point of East and West, the seat of the greatest effort ever made till our own day to harmonise Hebraism and Hellenism in man's higher thought. That I suppose Egypt will never be again; but it will be due to the Egyptians alone if their country, with so commanding a situation, ever become the mere dependency of a foreign and aggrandising power.

Egypt, then, never was an originating power among the nations so much as a harmonising and connecting power. Its spiritual as well as its geographical position was central rather than original. It was from the beginning half-savage, half-civilised. It was grossly sensual, but it was something more and better. It was intellectual with an upward look even at the spiritual. It is well typified by the sphinx. And when we remember that look

5: Egypt: A Sermon for Young Men, 1882

of inscrutable mystery, and aged hereditary secrecy on the fresh face of the sphinx, we feel still more how truly this precious monument incarnates the people that set it there.

It has been said that Egypt, in this sphinx-like transition from the animalism of the East to the spiritual intelligence of the West, represents the boyhood of the human spirit just passing into youth. It is true, at any rate, that the sphinx is a striking symbol of that perilous stage. It is in early youth that man has the first sharp sense of his double nature. It is in early youth that he begins to feel that he is half-animal, half-soul. The boy is hardly troubled with that conflict. When you begin to realise it, you begin to be men. You are passing into a nobler region. You are inheriting sublime possibilities. You are at the transition point between mere nature and intelligent controlling will. You are getting your head, the spiritual part of you, clear of the body, the mere animal part of you. It is a momentous and a dubious time. The face you raise out of mere boyish naturalism is like the face of the sphinx—in this, too, that it is full of mystery. Nobody can read it, nobody can foretel your future or decipher your secrets. You cannot yourself. Egypt was not only the land of dawning science and rising mind, it was the land of mystery. It was the home of the occult. Its culture was like its river, whose source and secret springs men for ever sought and never found. So you find youth is for you the land of Egypt. Your mind is dawning, your meaning is mysterious, your will is maturing, your future is vague. Sense and soul are beginning their war. What will the issue be? That is wrapped in more than Egyptian darkness. Shall this undiscovered country, this land of mystery before you, become to you the house of bondage? Your youth lies all before you with the promise of rich life, much pleasure, freedom, ease, success. As the famished Hebrews of old went down to the rich plenty of that Egyptian land of Goshen, so your young, eager, and hungry spirits march into this luxuriant and prosperous tract of youth. The Hebrews became slaves in their Goshen. Will you in yours? Having got your head clear of the mere animalism of eating and thoughtless boyhood, shall it sink again in shame and be re-absorbed in the sensuous nature from which it rose? Having once felt aspiration, and longed to be brave, high, and beneficent, shall you wander at ease among these flowery pastures all day till you are overtaken by the night, in which no man can work? The Jews came out of their Egyptian slavery. They came out by faith in God. They were led forth by the intervention of God; but the Egyptians themselves fell into a slavery from which they never escaped. Sense in them was coupled with intellect—yes, even with religion, but not with powerful faith and living piety. And so sense got the upper hand. The great old civilisation faded. The intellect died away. The Egyptians had besides the sphinx other representations of the double form. They had figures in which the head was the head of a brute, and the body the body of a man. They had their belief in immortality and resurrection, true; but they also had their worship of animals: bulls, cats, crocodiles, beetles. The sphinx represents the dawning, aspiring aspect of the Egyptian spirit—the power of the soul, the faith of immortality. The image of Anubis, with its dog's head, represents the decline and fall of the Egyptian spirit, the power of sense, the relapse into animalism, the worship of the brute. It was Anubis, and not the Sphinx, that became the type of Egypt. While Hebraism bred Jesus, Egypt produced Cleopatra. The heart sank again into the brute, the face lost its soul, and sense ruled all. Egypt became a land of lotos-eaters [sic]. How do you know that it will not be thus with you? Your aspiration, now pure and high, may sink into a sensualism far worse and deadlier than mere boyish and thoughtless naturalism. No intellect will save you from this lapse, or deliver your whole body from the bondage of the brute into the perfect beauty of the balanced man. Love and faith—pure love and high faith, the faith, fear, and love of God—will do this. They will bring you through Egypt refreshed and fed by the plenty of Goshen, but not enslaved by its luxury, or made faint with its lotos-flowers [sic]. These alone will send you on to share in the well-knit growth of strong manhood, as Egypt, had she had them, might have lived on into the forward march of the growing West, whereas now it is her old slaves, the Jews, that have most moulded the West, and she is its slave, its victim, and its drudge. The revengers of Time are strange. The Egyptian bondsmen of old are the great and crushing Egyptian bondholders today. Young men, is it to be the bondage of Egypt, or the freedom of God? The narrow world, or the broad liberty of the Cross? Is it to be Cleopatra, or Christ?

6

Pessimism, 1884

Preached at St. Thomas's Square, Hackney.

"And God saw everything that he had made, and, behold, it was very good."

—GENESIS 1:31

"I have seen all the work that is done under the sun and behold, all is vanity and vexation of the spirit."

—ECCLESIASTES 1:14

WHAT COULD BE MORE different than the tempers of mind which uttered sayings like these? What could be more extraordinary than the contention that both utter the message of the same spirit and contribute to the same consistent and infallible book?

Creation and life very good. Creation and life, vanity, delusion, hollowness, and vexation of spirit. Both cannot be right. They cannot be reconciled except by a forced and elaborate process, which might be used to reconcile anything with everything.

But statements so diverse are easily enough explained if we remember that in the Bible we are dealing, not with a book, but with a library; not with a literary work, but with a nation's literature. It is not a pure revelation we have, but the strange eventful history of one. We may expect, therefore, to find in it great variety, and almost hopeless difference of view. Were it not so, it would be an impoverished literature, the product of a meagre and slothful national mind. We must expect to find in the literature of a gifted people extreme variety, even among the products of the same age and stage of civilization. But the variety will be greater still if what we have is the fruit, not of one age, but of many developing centuries. In this very matter of optimism and pessimism, your own correspondence at twenty would probably betray a more ardent hopefulness and joy than the letters you write to your familiars at fifty. And so the Book of Genesis, or this part of it, will wear a very different hue from the Book of Ecclesiastes. At least 500 years of stormy and changeful national life lie between them. Totally new experiences and new forces had in that time been infused into Hebrew civilisation. The first vigorous poetic and believing age had given way to an age crushed by the extremities of national disaster, and sicklied with the pale hue of foreign thought. The present *form* of that chapter of Genesis may be regarded roughly as bearing the impress of the eighth or ninth century BC, the sanguine stamp of a great prophetic time. The Book of Ecclesiastes, on the other hand, is not earlier than the third century, when the disruption of the two kingdoms, the insecurity of an absolute and semipagan monarchy, the captivity of the nation, the setting up of the hierarchy, and the conquest by both Greek thought and Greek arms had deeply changed and saddened the spirit of Hebrew dream. The problems of society had become more intricate, more pressing; more poignant. On a certain section of it there was settling down a melancholy, which was not the fantastic and beautiful melancholy of youth, but the cynical and *blasé* melancholy of wasted and cumbered age.

Our own generation finds a special attraction in this Book of Ecclesiastes. We too have fallen on an age when the first free fearless vigour of our Elizabethan time has gone by, when even the John Bull view of England is collapsing, when the condition and prospects of our crowded society are raising questions which only the stupid can face with a light heart, or treat with the old answers. The old pharmacopeia of politics has no medicine for the new disease. And in this respect England is not alone. Here too, she maintains the European concert. She is in this matter a limb of the great body of the civilised West. The continent is even in some respects worse off than we; the disease exists in a form more acute, and it has gone deeper into the system. We in England doubt and fear. Abroad they deny and destroy. We think we have fallen on a bad time. They think they have been cast into the worst of possible worlds. Our scepticism is practical, constructive, and hopeful on the whole. Theirs is theoretical, destructive, and desperate. We have a measure of social ease and prosperity, arising partly from our enormous wealth, which is denied to the impoverished malcontents of foreign countries. Our centuries of broadening freedom have taken the most fatal sting out of political rancour. But abroad the discontent is exasperated by a more eager poverty, maddened by repression, and embittered by an inflexible despotism. We English in the mass have patience, and we have not "lucidity." We do not think out problems to their logical conclusion. We have

6: Pessimism, 1884

not time to do so. We have a knack of suddenly changing the whole problem by concessions yielded just at the hour prescribed by a kind of instinctive and hereditary wisdom. Our problem is by our practical tact constantly changing. Abroad, however, where government is so much less flexible, and relief so much more slow, time is given for the full working out of the situation in thought. The thinkers abroad face the same social problem so long, that they have time to elaborate in connection with it theories and systems, which then become their principles of action. Our happy position relieves us of the necessity of maintaining that standing army which is ruining every State on the continent. The incubus has pressed so long there, and the misery flowing from it has become so chronic in the lower levels of the political mass, that society seems to them simply to repeat in an aggravated form all the cruelty and inhospitality of Nature instead of fortifying men against them. The long and constant presence of such an evil then, I say, gives time for the philosophers to reason and that rebellious despair which is the habitual tone of the masses for whom they feel. Popular pessimism is shaped into reasoned pessimism. The religion of irreligion receives from the philosophers a theology of atheology. And the moral side of the same greedless creed is Nihilism, under its various names and nationalities. Pessimism and Nihilism are connected as faith and works, principle and practice. If life is as bad as it can be, there might be some hope in reducing everything to anarchy and chaos, because out of that might possibly come a slightly better or less bad order of things, and in any case death in the attempt leaves one no worse than before. So thorough-going pessimism is practically translated into reckless Nihilism. Though I ought to say, I think, there is a nobler side to many of the Nihilists, and they are impelled by a true principle of sacrifice which needs only to be guided by a truer principle of wisdom and faith. There is enormous moral power lying germinal in Russia alone, waiting the fulness of the time when, under the guidance of a better creed, it shall bless and exalt Europe.

In this country we are not as yet seriously troubled with the more thorough-going forms of pessimism; but I do not think we have escaped it, for the reason that we have not yet come to it. We are as yet only in the Agnostic stage, but we are fairly well through that, and are beginning to get dissatisfied with it. From that stage we must go either up or down. We may go up. A truer philosophy (not even now without a witness) may restore the vigour of a nobler faith. Or we may go down. We may descend to the next level of unbelief, to the lower cycle in the mind's inferno. That next level is pessimism. I feel sure that the pessimistic wave will engulf many more in the course of the next few years than have succumbed as yet. I should think so if for no other reason than because the chief work of the representative German pessimist is about to be issued in an English translation, and because he is the writer of a style as lucid as Mr. Spencer, and far more full of insight and fascination. The number of people who can read, and who care to read such works, has very greatly increased. And there has increased at the same time the number of people whose enervated frames and their overdriven and high-strung lives predispose them to a view of life which cannot be said to be hopeful or even cheerful. These two factors, our increased education and our increased pressure on the means of livelihood, combine to make a soil for the teachings of a pessimism which is the grave of all life worth living, whether social or individual. Things seem worse because there are more of us, and our ideal is higher.

An evening paper pointed out last week that though "in increased consumption of the chief commodities, in better education, in greater freedom from crime and pauperism, and in increased savings, the masses of the people are immensely better than they were fifty years ago,"[1] yet there is not more, but less contentment, and revolutionary schemes are more rife than ever. What is the reason? Is it due to the inherent wickedness and folly of the mass of the people? Is it the love of sin and enthusiasm for theft that is at the bottom of the new land schemes? That is the old woman's explanation. It is like the view of our grandmother Church, who finds in atheism the sole explanation of the Liberation Society. The true explanation is that while all this material progress has been made, another kind of progress has also been going on at a rapid rate. I mean ideal progress, progress in people's ideas of what life ought to be and by proper exertion and opportunity can be. There is a sense in which things are worse at the present day than they were half a century ago. The distance between the ideal of life entertained by most people and their actual life is greater than it was. The standard of comfort has risen with greater rapidity than the means of comfort. Hence the discontent which prevails, the restlessness, the indications and preludes of social change. Were there no scope for the new activity set on by the new needs the discontent would develop or degenerate into a settled, gloomy, and subversive pessimism; were we governed by a military caste which, with the sharpest of arguments, forbade full ventilation of the subject, repressed action, and precluded the possibility of a new adjustment, all the horrors of Nihilistic pessimism would be in store for us; and we might have our foremost literary man of next generation preaching suicide, and retaining his own existence, only that he might persuade other people into the blessing of parting with theirs.

1. These words, slightly modified, come from Robert Giffen's 1883 inaugural address as President of the Statistical Society, "The Progress of the Working-Classes in the Last Half-Century."

6: Pessimism, 1884

Pessimism, then, is the bottomless, godless abyss that lies between the ideal and the actual. It is applied Atheism. It is in one respect a result of over-education. Its home is in over-educated Germany, where intellectual has inordinately outrun practical activity, and local thought has left local self-government, i.e., self-help, far behind. And that is the danger of a certain class of ideals. They don't carry their own coal on board. They are not able to provide the motor power by which they are to be realised. Culture may easily plunge men into an abyss of despair and bitterness if it only shows them ideals which their actual position must continue to mock and deny.

To deal with pessimism and to prevent pessimism we must have an ideal which is something more than an idea of ours, something more than an ambition of ours. We must have an ideal which is the fountain head of our ideas and ambitions, one which is working incessantly to bring us to its own image; one in whose presence we feel inspiration and attainment at last and surely blended; one that is gradually filling up the abyss of pessimism by drawing together its edges and reconciling what we are with what we long to be. We must have a God, in brief, who is at once our Mighty One and our Redeemer. The morality of pessimism is based upon pity. Whatever the noble pessimist does is to be done out of compassion for those who are fellow victims with himself of the same gigantic mistake that stumbled on such a world. But pessimism has no piteous God. I do not read that the foremost pessimists credit with this beautiful emotion and moral inspiration of pity the huge Will over all that blundered into us, and might best pity and compensate the creatures of its own error. Let us be provided with a Deity not only wiser, but of more tender mercy than this, who by no mistake or blind passion of His own, but in His deliberate will begat us; who long before the pessimist arose with his compassion, saw no eye to pity and no arm to save, so in His love and in His pity He redeemed us, and bare us and carried us all the days of old. There is, in the pessimist's pity, no mean degree of bitterness, and no great trace of the sweet peace which sent forth and clothed the pity of God in Christ. Ah, it is no small thing to have known the evil of the world as its Redeemer knew it, and yet to have poured on it a pity which was all peace within, unsoured, not acrid, but deep fixed in an eternal seat of love.

And the Saviour knew the evil that is in the world as even Schopenhauer did not. I do not find much in that strange passionate, and loveless character to impress me with a sense of moral dignity, to say nothing of moral exaltation or insight. Like his creed he was more sensible of the pains of the world than of the sins of it. Pessimism, indeed, is the vengeance of God on an age that is prone to do right more for the pleasure than for the goodness of it. The creed has nobler sides, I know, but it is in no small measure now what it was in the Book of Ecclesiastes, the drivelling of an emasculated spirit, *blasé* and exhausted by the enjoyments of life. It is not the gross pleasures only that produce that condition of soul, but even the more refined when pursued as pleasures merely. Pessimism is not only the fruit of an overdriven age, but of an age that idolises mere culture, and picks daintily amongst all the resources of taste, till it come to patronise a religion whose Deity is the pink of all exquisiteness in shade, movement, and thrill. Pessimism is the Nemesis of a society whose grand and fundamental distinction is not right and wrong, false and true, but simply pleasure and pain. It is a sybarite religion, and a finicking philosophy, with a blunder for its first principle and annihilation for its forlorn hope. The chant of its worship is, "Thou art our King, O Death; to thee we groan."[2] And it has no noble ethical feature which does not find a more solid ground, and an equally good expression within the limits of Christianity truly judged. As, indeed, Schopenhauer once admitted. He said the nature of his ethics was identical with the ethics of Christianity, though Christian ethics had a different terminology, owing partly to what he called the "Jewish dogma" underlying them. And is not any philosophy reduced to an absurdity along with the comfort-worship it represents when the inevitable inference from it is that all the kindness and love you can bestow on a friend is the worst possible service to him because it helps to attach him to a life which is the worst of ills?

The solution of life is not to be found in grappling with pain, but in the conflict with sin. The strongest soul that ever lived was crushed by sins rather than pains, by sins not His own, not by the pains which were. Here lies the centre and secret of Christianity, not in the miracles of healing, but in the miracles of forgiveness, and in the cross, the greatest of them all. And here lies the key and reason why Christianity, with all its melancholy, with all its Divine sadness, can never be pessimist. It is not simply and generally that, being a religion of faith and hope, it cannot give way to despair. But it is here, in this principle, viz., that in Christianity we never become aware of the worst till we are in possession of the best. Pessimism is the form assumed by the scepticism of an age unprecedentedly sensitive to pain. It is a revolt more from pain than from evil. If it engaged the larger foe, it might find a strength it did not expect to be with it in the night. It is in the moral world we read the secrets which make all the mysteries of life tolerable and even just. It is there, in conflict with good and evil, that we find the means of dealing with pleasure and pain. And in the Christian moral world, what most beneficent principle do we find? A scheme of compensation, a sliding and self-adjusting scale far

---

2. From William Wordsworth's sonnet, "Methought I Saw the Footsteps of a Throne" (1806/07).

more indicative of a God than all the theology of design. For we find this principle, that the sense of evil is deepest only in those who have laid hold of God and final good—i.e., in those who have realised the evil by first grasping the cure of evil. Who ever realised sin and its awful meaning like the pure and holy Jesus? Who are so full of self-accusation and self-condemnation as the great apostles and saints among His followers? Who are they that have the most tenacious memories? Why, the lovers of Divine loveliness and the good who never forgive themselves their own sin. Memories of pleasure fade and memories of pain. Our first affections die, and our once bright and young ideas that stung us into intellectual life these tarnish and lose their charm and their power. But two things stay with us and deepen as we age, if we grow in grace and good—our one deep love and our one great sin. They who are most with us in our latest hours are those whom we most loved, and those whom we most injured. And blessed are they who are forgiven much for that they love much, who have injured most where they love most, whose sin and whose love are toward God.

The deepest sense of evil is possible only to a believer in redemption—not a redemption that shall be one day, but that is now going on. How could we bear to see the worst and utmost evil and sorrow, but for the sense and certainly that it has in it the sentence of its own death. How could we, as a race, face death successfully—death, that great ravager of love—except in the loving faith that death itself is wounded unto death. The deepest sense of evil, therefore, in Christianity can never lead to despair, to bitterness, to destructiveness of soul. The faith that most feels the ravages in life is the faith which sets us by the Maker and builder of life. Faith is moral courage, and it is moral courage we need to face life with. Good nerves may serve this man or that, but what mankind needs, what the soul needs that does not rest in stupidity or ignorance, is the bravery of faith. And to this courage there is no pessimism. Gethsemane, indeed, it may enter, and the cup may be bitter, but the lips that drink it are sweet. The soul is sweet on which the bitter sorrow falls. The suicide of hopeless pessimism is as far from it as the selfishness of mere breezy optimism, or the smugness of small content, or the morbid robustness of physical verve. The best, in revealing to us the worst, abolishes it, and the light of God, which maketh all things manifest, brings sin out only that it may die in the great and terrible daylight of the Lord.

> For sudden the worst turns the best to the brave,
> The black minute's at end,
> And the elements' rage, the fiend voices that rave,
> Shall dwindle, shall blend,
> Shall change, shall become first a peace out of pain;

II: Published Sermons

> Then a light, then thy breast,
> O thou soul of my soul! I shall clasp thee again,
> And with God be the rest.³

But to end on another note, Pessimism is not a pure curse. There are many people, and Christian people too, who are not pessimist enough. They go to war "with a light heart." They are sanguine because they are ignorant. Perhaps the sanity of popular Christianity is due more to its ignorance than to its faith. Perhaps the bulk of people are secure in virtue rather of what they do not know, than in virtue of what they do believe. One of the most pessimistic features of the age is the way some people manage to escape pessimism. For there is no more hopeless sign of a doomed age than the prevalence of cheery prophets, who neither see nor foresee, who heal the wound of their people slightly, and who say "Peace, peace," where there is no peace, but smouldering war. But I must say the pooh-pooh school of Christians seems to be losing strength, and they abound only in the less intelligent denominations. We are being forced into anxiety, not by abstract sin but by concrete sins, individual and especially social, here and now. We are being forced out of our ignorant optimism by the spread of social information, and by a truer idea of the real dangers science brings to soul. Our faith is becoming less a cherub's creed, and more a warrior's breath, less a thing of seraphic strain, and more a thing of battle and scars. The glory of life is becoming less the smile of the angel, and more and more the glory of the crucified. We understand better, because we feel more, the considerations and the sorrows which make men pessimists. We sup more full of horrors than our forefathers did with their weekly paper, and their precise creeds. The new music of the world, like the "music of the future,"⁴ takes great part of its power from its new ear for minors, and its masterly use of discord. New action is shaped by the aching sense of new needs. New victories presuppose new pains, new enemies. We are able more clearly to say, "Well, seeing what the pessimists see, I should be a pessimist too, were it not for seeing something the pessimists miss."

While the catalogue of our horrible civilisation is being read out to us, and the dark side of our progress thrust on our dismayed attention I must remind you of this. I must remind you that on the great mass of people who can take no direct part in reducing these horrors, the effect of reading about them may be a mischievous one. It seems to me it must be mischievous if it simply lie in the memory and be turned to no moral account It will turn *itself* to pessimistic account, and, while soiling our minds, will also

---

3. From Robert Browning's poem, "Prospice" (1864).

4. A reference to Richard Wagner's essay, "Zukunftsmusik," published first in French in 1860 and in the original German the following year.

6: Pessimism, 1884

demoralise them, by filling us with a sense of our impotence in the kingdom of God. We shall gain the truly pessimistic feeling that these evils are an essential and inevitable factor in the aggregate of society, which is thus absurdly shown to be possible only by what it exists to fight against. To believe that is demoralising to mind and morals. But how to avoid believing it? How to turn the dreadful knowledge to real account? Few of us can act directly; but if we simply let the information soak into our minds and settle there, we are not better, but worse; and society is not mended; and so there is a clear net loss. I venture to say that these facts will not in one case out of ten be turned to real and good account. And it will be because they are not turned to purely religious account. They are too awful to be treated as a mere extension of our knowledge. But, in the absence of direct practical action, what remains? Why, the religious use of the facts. What use did Christ make of such knowledge? He did not erect on it new social schemes' He did no employ it as matter for sermons or ground for collections. No, it was, by prayer and thought, turned to account for His own supreme task—that is, for the soul and salvation of the world. It evoked in Him spiritual antagonism of the silent and omnipotent sort. Gethsemane and those nightly hilltops, with their awful vigils, were witnesses of the way such things were dealt with by one who applied the radical remedy to the evil in the world. He met it in the power of an endless life, in the silent clash of the soul's Armageddon. I am a little afraid of the excitement going on about our East-end horrors, especially in our churches. They can at present do little or nothing of what has immediately to be done; but I am afraid that when they have been agitated into demanding that something shall be done, they may not always be urged and instructed how to deal with these terrors in the purely religious way, in the way of edification—i.e., in the way of drawing from them, by prayer and lonely thought before God, that new solemnity of earnest spirit which the world's sin and sorrow bred in the soul of Christ. The immediate remedy will oust what should be a deepened sense of the eternal problem and the eternal cure. And we may feed our philanthropy (or amuse it) at the expense of what most truly constitutes our soul.

And one of the most pessimistic features of the time is the possibility that, even among the religious, a reference to prayer and thought as the supremely efficient treatment of such matters may be met with the infatuated sneer of an over-practical and Protestant race, who call Jesus "Lord" and yet hold that His grand method is one rather to be admired than reproduced. It is spiritual evil that is at the root's root of these things. And it is evil which is far from wholly theirs, whom in their slums we shudderingly pity and evangelise. It is evil in which we by our prosperity share. And yet he would by most be reckoned an amiable dreamer and a Romanistic pietist, who should retire

II: Published Sermons

from the active world in the faith that he was, by a lifetime of intercession and thought, engaging our social foe at his citadel, and dying with Christ upon the Spirit's cross for the redemption of society. But these ills are not a local eruption, but a social disease; and the only final cure is one which will regenerate our social soul, and possibly revolutionise our social body.

All knowledge has its responsibilities, and, depend on it, knowledge like this will not leave us as it found us; and the question for us is, How shall it leave us—with the good fruit, of pessimism, or with the bad; with a new solemnity in our sympathy with the sin-bearer, or with a new cynicism born of the better sense of impotence against the world?

7

THE ARGUMENT FOR IMMORTALITY DRAWN FROM THE NATURE OF LOVE: A LECTURE ON LORD TENNYSON'S "VASTNESS," 1885[1]

THE POETS OF THE first rank may be divided into two great classes, marked by a difference which is not quite welcome to the criticism of the day. That criticism, with all its exquisite taste, just severity, and ideal sympathy, belongs mainly to the Humanist School, and its analysis is guided by a philosophy which has no room within its borders for anything that breathes of theology. But the distinction which I now allude to between two classes of poets, both in the first rank, is just the distinction between theological and non-theological. You have on one side names like Homer, Æschylus, the Old Testament prophets, the Indian and Scandinavian Epicists, Dante, Milton, and Browning. On the other side you have Euripides, Shakespeare, Goethe, and what I may term the whole Pagan School, without using the term Pagan in any opprobrious sense. I mean by it the Naturalist, Humanist side of the poetic succession as distinct from the Supernaturalist or distinctively Christian side. And the distinction corresponds so far with the old division into the Classicist and Romanticist Schools. Poets, to be first rate poets, must deal with human life. They may not deal with bloodless abstractions or scientific systems whether of anthropology, cosmology, or theology; they must deal with life. But the distinction between the two classes is this, that while the Humanist, or Naturalist, or Pagan, or Classical poets treat life in relation to this world, the Theological, Supernatural, Christian, or Romantic poets' view is always, expressly or implicitly, in relation to a world beyond. The one class view life in its finite aspects; the other in its infinite. The one

---

1. Alfred Tennyson's "Vastness" was first published in 1885.

II: Published Sermons

regard it in its attitude to Nature; the other in its attitude to God. The one hears life bearing lovely witness of itself, of humanity alone; the other hears in its testimony the solemn chime of God and immortality. To the one class, our little life is rounded with a sleep, and they treat the life beyond with the deep silence of the daily Press; to the other, life is not rounded at all, but full of all chaos and angularity, till it is bathed, filled, and opened in the atmosphere of a life to come. "On the earth the broken arc, in the heaven the perfect round."[2]

Now, I will not so far anticipate a verdict which, perhaps, is possible only to posterity, as to say that Tennyson belongs to the first ranks of poets. It may be enough for the moment to admit how very high in the poetic hierarchy he stands. And I may go on to say, what is more to my present purpose, that of the two poetic lines he belongs to the theological side. It is a very remarkable feature of our non-theological age that its two very greatest poets are not only theological in their spirit, but almost aggressively so. Theology, driven from life and science, has taken refuge with poetry. Browning and Tennyson are not simply religious, they are men of a range of intellect which makes religion alone insufficient. Moreover, they are the denizens of a scientific age. Their religion is, therefore, much more than emotional; so much more as to be almost systematic. And while the religion of that side of the Church which professes to draw nearest to the science of the day threatens to thaw into intuitional sentiment, the religion of our contemporary poetry is lifted from the miry clay of emotion, and set upon the rock of knowledge and truth. It has often been said that the teachers of the age's religion are to be sought rather among its poets than its preachers. But it seems as if we must look for our noblest theology also to our poets, rather than to our clerical schools. I could justify the apparent paradox best by some exposition of Mr. Browning's poetry; but the case of Tennyson is sufficiently in point.

The age which exalts these two poets calls itself an untheological age. Even preachers set upon popularity disclaim the suspicion of being theologians, and their congregations welcome the abdication—with the same good sense as would mark a like reception of some brazen politician's declaration that politics should not be hampered by any acquaintance with economic science. The age is deeply theological, and does not know it. It is like the man who was amazed to find that all his life he had been talking prose without being aware of it. We are theological, and don't know it. Hence part

---

2. From Robert Browning's poem, "Sordello" (1840): "On the earth the broken arcs; in the heaven, a perfect round."

7: The Argument for Immortality Drawn from the Nature of Love

of our unhappiness. It is like the sorrow of some young Werther[3] who bears in his bosom the ferment of a genius not yet apprehended, and the germ of a revolution not yet realised. Our atheology belies our true deep selves, and our great poets are in this but prophets. They steal upon our less aggressive hours, and reveal our soul and future to ourselves. They foreshadow our destiny, and they tell us that, in spite of all the *savants* say about the impossibility of a theology, it is the passion for a theology which is at the root of our mind's unrest, and the possession of a theology which alone can lay our mind's anarchy. In this respect, as in others, Tennyson is both the index and the mirror of his time. He expresses its soul for other ages, but he also reflects and explains it to itself. No poet has given finer voice to the age's doubt; but his voice is still finer as he sings to the age a congenial faith, and forces it to feel that below the surface of its articulate denials are the living roots of a latent and irresistible belief. He is preacher as well as poet. We give him a position which to his genius we cannot withhold. He gives us a message which to his conscience he cannot suppress. Many poets have only a vocation. This is one that has a gospel.

And something is to be said as to the quality of his theology. His genius is of full and opulent nature. It breathes the air of English midlands, cathedral closes, and all abodes of ancient calm. But its wealth is even richer and ampler than that. There is something Oriental about it, a hint of the lotus, and a taste of all the poppied syrups of the world. His poetry might be described in many of its features as "lines to an Indian air."[4] And there is one feature of the Indian mind which is strikingly reflected in his genius. It is the imaginative sense of mere vastness. India, with its enormous levels, its colossal Himalayas, and its teeming population, and its historic waves of levelling conquest, is the land of vastness. Its systems of thought and religion are vastness distilled in imagination—inorganic vastness reflected in a merely cumulative, and not shaping, spirit of imagination. Its Pantheism has been called the Pantheism of passive imagination as distinct from the Western Pantheism, of creative thought. It piles infinite upon infinite without fusing them into any supreme infinite which would give them all an organic unity and life. It is the imaginative vastness of comparative chaos, and the dim welter of pessimistic world on world. Now, Tennyson has many Pantheistic sympathies and tendencies; but it is Pantheism of the imaginative rather than the philosophic sort. He has a sufficient acquaintance with the enormous scientific results of the day; but they appeal to him not so much on the

---

3. A reference to Johann Wolfgang von Goethe's *Die Leiden des jungen Werthers* (trans. *The Sorrows of Young Werther*), first published in 1774.

4. A reference to Percy Bysshe Shelley's poem so named, although first published in 1822 as "Song written for an Indian Air."

II: Published Sermons

philosophical as on the imaginative side—perhaps, one might even say, not so much on the healthy as on the morbid side. For there is a morbid thread in his genius which, in one sense, makes it all the truer as an expression and reflection of a more or less morbid world. He is here in vivid contrast with Browning, whose vast knowledge is held with much more achromatic clearness, healthy vigour, and ruling power. The one is Oriental and pessimist; the other is Western and optimist. And so, when Tennyson looks out upon the world of knowledge, and round him on the world of experience, what he feels, first and most deeply, is its enormous range and compass, its pure immensity, the bewilderment of its infinitude. It was easy to dogmatise even a hundred years ago. But now—

> Knowledge every way
> Is infinite, and who can say?[5]

The field under our vision is so huge that, if the knowledge which saves is to be got at only by induction, it would seem as if its possibility must move off with every expansion of our science. And so soul is at war with mind. The wider our grasp of variety the poorer our knowledge of unity. The faculties are opening year by year, but opening only to expose a wider surface of starving soul. I say, if we are dependent only upon induction from particulars for the greatest laws of life, then we can never begin our induction really, can never begin the ultimate induction, because, at the present rapid rate and infinite range of possible knowledge, we can never feel that we have the bulk of the instructions for our brief. We never can feel, facing our infinity of knowledge, that we have got that majority of particulars which would supply ground for a safe generalisation. Meanwhile, the soul is starving while the food is growing. Our infinite heart is dying for a knowledge which the mind says must be infinitely waited for. And we are offered, accordingly, by the inductive philosophers, a religion of Agnosticism, of ignorance, the worship of a pure mystery. This is a tragic state of things, and it is a tragedy which it is the spiritual poet's function to feel. The poet is the man of love, and he is not satisfied to look forth upon the world and see only a fragment of law. To the poet, no less than to the sage, confronting the world, the question of questions is that which Tennyson puts in this poem: "What is it all? What does it mean? What is the law of all laws—is it love or is it not?" From the confusion and contrariety of things the Evolutionist escapes upon the wings of natural law, and development explains all—all that he sees. For he does not see all. The philosopher escapes from the mystery upon the back

---

5. A play on words from Robert Browning's poem, "Christmas-Eve and Easter-Day" (1850): "Mercy every way is infinite—and who can say?"

7: The Argument for Immortality Drawn from the Nature of Love

of all-pervading thought. The Stoic takes refuge in defiant, invincible, and righteous will. The poet says: "Love is enough." While the Christian flees also to love, but it is the love of God.

Well, Tennyson as a poet, and a spiritual poet, looks forth upon the enormous range of the known and knowable world, and he certainly does not see it with the complacent eyes of the Evolutionary fatalist. He is not entranced with the splendour of sweep and range in the known. It *is* the known that moves him. It is knowledge, not ignorance, that is the spirit of the time, and it is to what we know, not to our ignorance, that the poet responds. He does respond to it; he is impressed. But what sort of a response and impression is it? I say he is not entranced. It is not the panting exultation of the explorer who has emerged through a continent upon the sea—the infinite sea. It is not the silent ecstasy of awe which the conqueror of a new world feels, as he looks on some Grand Pacific of Science, he

> With all his men,
> Silent upon a peak in Darien.[6]

It is not the youthful ardour of "Locksley Hall"[7] over the fairy tales of science and the federation of the world. It is the strain of an older man, and an older, complexer world. The heats of young enthusiasm are cooled, the hardy, ruddy faith of dawning powers has abated. The natural man and his noble enthusiasms have run their course. And in his closing years the poet is forced back on some ground of ardour and faith, higher and deeper than the high spirits of manhood and youth. For his response now to the world of knowledge and experience is dismal and tragic in the extreme. Instead of the equable reign of uniform law, and the complete symmetry of Evolutionary process, what he rather sees is a world out of joint, teeming not only with incongruities, but with calamities, and not with calamities merely, but with wrongs, not only with wrongs, but with wrongs enthroned and even consecrated. He looks into the world not with an intellect alone, but with a heart, a conscience, a sense of fitness and measure, a thirst for moral order and spiritual rule. With such eyes he looks abroad upon the world of Nature and the natural man. And the inevitable experience in such cases is also his. Naturalism slips into pessimism. Development, without spiritual source, principle, or goal, becomes simply an extended degeneration. It is not the vastness, only, that appals his imagination and crushes his soul. The title of the poem is not quite happy. The enormous scale of the world and human affairs stuns him, not because it is so vast, for that might stir the sense of the sublime; but it is the emptiness

---

6. From John Keats' sonnet, "On First Looking into Chapman's Homer" (1816).
7. A poem written by Alfred Tennyson in 1835.

of the vastness that terrifies him. It has no revelation of God, only an echo of his magnified self. The echo of his own soul returns upon him, as a child's cry might reverberate in a ruin where he had strayed alone, only to terrify him by the gaping horror of the dim, distorted, and elaborate aisles. It is the sense of an empty infinitude, in which the grotesques on the capitals become hideous, and the shadows in the corners the shadows of death. But an empty infinitude is no infinitude. It is a limited, not an infinite, thing; for infinitude is fulness, and it is really not the vastness of the world and of life that is at the source of his misery, but the pettiness, the sense of limitation arising from the sense of mortality. The imaginative horror may arise from the loneliness and dreary vastness; but the moral horror rises from the pettiness of life, both in its interests and its range. It would be more true to say that it is the complexity of experience that appals him; and, still more than its complexity, its disorder of complexity—its confusion—and, perhaps, most of all, its futility.

"What *is* it all?" is the question in Stanza XIV, on which the whole poem turns. And what is meant by "it" is explained in the thirteen stanzas which precede it. It is the whole range of experience open to the highly cultivated mind, which looks out on the world without the one spiritual centre and clue. There seems one end to the righteous and the wicked. Men are as the fishes of the sea that have no ruler over them. Everything speaks of the vastness of force and the insignificance of the soul. The very destiny of a nation, or a race, or a planet is taken up by this giant force as a very little thing, and swallowed by this brute vastness as a drop in the bucket. It is as careless of a bereaved hearth as of an extinct planet, peopled once. The causes which shake peoples and shape politics are no more than the flutter of an ant-hill amid the infinities of the astronomical heaven. Amid the lies and brutalities of Democracy, coming in like a flood, the voice of the wise is unheard. Men are dying for wrong causes as well as for right. Mothers, on the one side, are selling away innocence; charity, on the other, is buying up the time in works of salvation. Quackeries of religion and of society flourish, while the purest faith shines in a fog of gloomy doubt. Pleasure is passing through lust into pain. Lascivious wealth and flattering courtiers, grasping greed, and honest poverty, hates of nation, hates of neighbours, vows firm unto death and vows that go like flax in fire, men dying in vice and men nailing their flesh to the cross, all the changes of the fashions, the seasons, the empires; all the medley of science, art, and religion; of philosophy, poetry, prayer; of noble and base, of foul and fair—what is it all worth, what does it all mean? What is all to one who looks on it with no background of eternity, either to the picture or to his soul? What is it all, if each man dies like a dog; if we only become, at last, "corpse-coffins," our own souls' sepulchres; if the body festering there have more life creeping in it than there is now in the soul which it once encased? What is all if we

7: The Argument for Immortality Drawn from the Nature of Love

have simply gone out like a spark, lost irrevocably in a vastness which can spare millions of such atoms and never miss them? What means all the welter and chaos of life, all effort for one cause rather than another, all preference of good to evil and fair to false, if the end is a level desert of infinity, varied only by the extinct volcanoes of passion for right or wrong? If the soul be a thing of such utter, such ineffable insignificance, that it has no greatness of its own to oppose to that mere expanse of vastness, flat, insensate, and all-erasing, what is the meaning of all that heart-agony and soul-conflict which here we see? Is there no response beyond the world to all this striving, crying, and tears within it? Is there no voice from without, no revelation, no light—all the outer darkness and utter silence? Is the past voiceless, meaningless? Is its face just stolid, no eye in it, no expression, no warmth, no interest even, no life? Meaningless, indeed, the past would be even if it were in the most perfect order of unbroken law, but no more. To have order is not to have meaning, any more than to make a solitude is to bring peace. Order without revelation is death, a lifeless eternity of frost and iron. Order which is utterly silent is vastness without meaning, mechanism without significance, and movement without life. Is this our end, to be

> Swallowed in vastness, lost in silence, drowned in the deeps of a meaningless past?

Is our infinite something which crushes us and our effort? Has it no speech nor language? Has it no revelation, no expression of soul in its face, but only a fixed, glazed, and meaningless stare upon the turmoil of a few ill-tempered gnats or bees?

These are the reflections of the natural man raised to the pitch of genius after a survey of life secluded from the influences of the supernatural. And the end of these things is death. The whole world is gained, but the soul is lost. Experience is multiplied and enriched till the soul sinks under it. The meat has grown more than the body, the raiment than the life. And Naturalism, after going up in a train of genius like a chariot of fire, has gone out like a rocket in the darkness of pessimism. The glory of Nature, cut off from the supernatural glory which excelleth, carries about in it its own death sentence, and fosters, by its very nutrition, the germ of its own dissolution. Like an eagle, transfixed with a feathered shaft,

> 'tis doomed to feel
> It nursed the pinion which impelled the steel.[8]

---

8. From Byron's poem, "English Bards and Scotch Reviewers" (1809): "Keen were his pangs, but keener far to feel/He nursed the pinion which impelled the steel."

II: Published Sermons

Am I wrong? Am I using pulpit exaggeration and religious one-sidedness? Am I back at the old Christian trick of villifying Nature for the sake of the glory of God, and cursing the beauty of the earth to enhance and splendours of the sky? Well, you shall listen to one of the apostles of Naturalism, one of the foremost of them, armed with all the best culture of the school, but who is, above all things, a man of dignity, candour, and truth. Professor Seeley, in "Natural Religion," after clearing the supernatural off the board in the sense of discarding a personal God or Immortality, uses language which is the very echo of mine, but which, if I used it, might be put down to Christian superstition and the Christian love of insulting Nature. Here are his words, words of candid misgiving, almost of fear, at the close of his book. After admitting that the supernatural may be necessary after all, as a supplement to "Naturalism," he says: "No sooner do we try to think that the known and the natural can suffice for human life than pessimism raises its head ... The more our thoughts widen and deepen, as the universe grows upon us, and we become accustomed to boundless space and time, the more petrifying is the contrast of our own insignificance ... A moral paralysis creeps upon us. For awhile we comfort ourselves with the notion of self-sacrifice; we say: 'What matter if I pass. Let me think of others.' But the *others* now become contemptible to us less than self; all human griefs alike seem little worth assuaginy, human happiness too paltry, at the best, to be worth increasing. The whole moral world is reduced to a point: the spiritual city, the 'soul of all the saints,' dwindles to 'the least of little stars.' Good and evil, right and wrong, become infinitesimal, ephemeral matters, whilst Eternity and Infinity remain attributes of that only which is outside mortality. The affections die away in a world where everything good and enduring is cold; they die of their own conscious feebleness and bootlessness. Supernatural religion met this want by connecting love and righteousness with Eternity. And if that is shaken, what would Natural Religion avail then?"[9] I think that is a wonderful commentary on this poem.

To the poet's dilemma, the philosopher has the answer of Pascal. "If the universe rolled over me and crushed me," said Pascal, "I should be greater than the universe, because I should *know* what was being done."[10] And that is, in substance, the only answer to be given. The merest conscious speck has a greatness and a mystery greater than all the vastness of time, space, or force. The great and standing miracle is here in me, that I at one and the same moment am and know myself to be. Here, at least, in this direction,

---

9. Seeley, *Natural Religion*, 261–62.

10. Pascal, *Pensées*, 97: "But, if the universe were to crush him, man would still be more noble than that which killed him, because he knows that he dies and the advantage which the universe has over him; the universe knows nothing of this" (#347).

7: The Argument for Immortality Drawn from the Nature of Love

lies the true nature of infinity, the true sphere of greatness, the true note of superiority. The unconscious cannot crush the conscious, for the reason that it cannot produce the conscious. To get at the true greatness and escape from mere brute greatness we must pass from quantity to quality, and be prepared to find things transpiring on minute spots of space or time which are of far more real consequence than the extinction of a whole burnt-out planet, tenanted by no conscious life. Tragedies take place, and victories are achieved at single points of time, which are of more eternal moment than all the course of years. And there may reside upon a point of space a spirit of more infinite value than all the infinites together which radiate from that point without end. The gravest, most eternal truths are not those which are drawn from careful induction, for we have already seen that we should then have to wait to Eternity to eternal truth. But they arise from the nature of human being and human thought, from that high miracle of our conscious selves, in which we are at once ourselves and not ourselves, and we live yet not we, but God liveth in us. The miracle of revelation is, at bottom, no other than the miracle of personality.

But though the poet takes this line, he puts it in other and more popular form. He declares, too, the infinite value and greatness of the soul, the living individual, in the face of mere outward vastness. But he does it not in the name of the consciousness which knows, but in that of the soul which loves. The true infinite is the infinite of Love. God is not the immensities, any or all of them, but God is Love. When infinity meets infinity, it is the loveless infinity that must go under, not the loving one. Love is more eternal than either space, or time, or force; and, indeed, gives them any eternity they have. They are the shadows of which the substance is love. The philosopher says: "There must be some thinking Being outside man, for human thought insists on a cognate objective to complete its own subjective reality." But the poet says in more intelligible speech: "Love is impossible without two souls, as impossible as a stick without two ends, or a magnet without two poles." A solitary being could never feel love. There must be two. And when one of them is removed it is only that he is put out of sight. The very fact that I go on loving implies, of necessity, that he goes on living, just as surely as the one pole of the active magnet implies the other. Love is indestructible. "Its holy flame for ever burneth."[11] This or that passion or affection of love may fade. But love is imperishable; and so long as men go on to love what has passed into the unseen, so long is it certain that in the unseen there is answering life. It is the existence of that life in the unseen which is, unknown to us, the condition making it possible for our love to continue. If our beloved were

---

11. From Robert Southey's poem, "The Curse of Kehama" (1810).

II: Published Sermons

extinguished in death, the fact would be signalled from the unseen by the expiring of our love in the seen.

In one of Shakespeare's lyrics, of obscure, mystic, and somewhat affected style, there is the suggestion of a like course of thought as to the nature of love:—

> So they loved, as love in twain
> Had the essence but in one;
> Two distincts, division none;
> Number three in love was slain.
>
> Hearts remote, yet not asunder;
> Distance and no space was seen.
>
> . . .
>
> Reason, in itself confounded,
> Saw division grow together,
> To themselves yet either neither;
> Simple were so well compounded.
>
> That it cried: "How true a twain
> Seemeth this concordant one;
> Love hath reason, Reason none,
> If what parts can so remain."[12]

The whole reply of Tennyson's poem is in its closing line, and it is in the vein I have indicated:—

> Peace, let it be! for I loved him, and love him for ever: the dead
> are not dead, but alive.
> In just the same strain he says, in "In Memoriam":—
> If e'er, when Faith had fallen asleep,
> I heard a voice: "Believe no more,"
> And heard an ever-breaking shore,
> That tumbled in the godless deep,
>
> A warmth within the breast would melt
> The freezing reason's colder part,
> And, like a man in wrath, the heart
> Stood up and answered: "I have felt!"[13]

And in similar reply to the suggestion of human insignificance, when confronted with the vastness of the universe, Mr. Browning says:—

> For a loving worm within its clod

---

12. From William Shakespeare's poem, "The Phoenix and the Turtle" (1601).
13. From Alfred Tennyson's poem, "In Memoriam A. H. H." (1849).

7: The Argument for Immortality Drawn from the Nature of Love

>   Is diviner than a loveless god
>   Amid his worlds.[14]

Of course, it is not meant that a thing is true because you deeply feel it to be true. That is a criticism, I admit, to which the isolated verses I have just quoted from "In Memoriam" are open, though the whole poem is not, nor does it lie against this poem. But the reasoning is not from your feeling of love, but from the existence and nature of love. And such is its nature, whether men feel it feebly or strongly, that it not only redeems from insignificance the heart capable of it, but it casts into real insignificance, by comparison, whatever is incapable of it, though it be the whole universe. Love is in its nature eternal. Its double nature is our true eternity. And nothing else is eternal except as some factor or necessity of love. Our idea of eternity is not endlessness, but the idea which is in love. And that which is loveless can never destroy love, any more than the unconscious can destroy the conscious. It is our eternal life to live in love, to be its factors, its members, its organs. We are immortal, not so much because we love, as because love loves through us. For God is love, and our life is in God and in His working within us. And our true infinite is not one which rolls over us and crushes, but one which pours itself into us, and quickens us and gives us his own power of an endless life. After all, it is not on our own love we must build. That is but a stepping stone. Other foundation can no man lay than that is laid, which is the love of God in Christ Jesus our Lord. If the nature of love is Divine, the essence of love is God. And for our own immortality the best warrant is not so much our own affections as the love towards us of God. We only love because He first loved us. And when we say that Christ brought life and immortality to light, we say it because in Him we realise the eternal love of God, and we say love like that could not be holden of death or overcome by it. If that could eternally die, nothing else could for a moment live.

There is nothing in the argument of this poem that is very new to anybody who has made a study of "In Memoriam." Even in that great poem it is at bottom the old argument for another life drawn from the absurdities to which we are otherwise reduced by the incompleteness, the incongruities, and the inequalities of this. But if it be the old theme, it is the old theme enriched by its passage through a true poet's soul. For the justice which of old demanded another life is substituted the demands of love—not of lovers, mark you, but of love. The contention is that love if it is not immortal, must perish, even as mortal. The moment it feels its own mortality it is smitten with blight. It becomes, as "In Memoriam" well puts it, "half dead to know that it must die." If, however, love goes on loving, the lovers must go on

14. From Robert Browning's poem, "Christmas-Eve and Easter-Day" (1850).

living. And the argument, plainly put, is thus: The nature and idea of love is such that its continuance as a reality here, when one factor has passed into the unseen, involves the continued existence of that factor in equal reality there. The old argument is in this poem uttered with new passion, but not in a new aspect. It is an argument so deep and true that for a vital mind it is always new. It rests on the foundations of the heart. What life is can only be answered, explained, fulfilled, by including what it shall be. And what it shall be is a question that can be answered only by appeal to the power that has it in hand. If that power be love, we are immortal; for love hath need of the poorest of us to complete and share his fulness of being. But if that power be not love, if force has in it no revelation of a greater than itself, of moral nature and spiritual quality, then we are not immortal, and we are, of all creatures, most miserable; because, being the most insignificant of all, we were tortured with dreams of an infinite wrath which made us battle for the true and the just, only in the end to be sealed within the iron hills or blown about with the dust of the desert.

From which dream we are delivered in the revelation and cross of Jesus Christ our Lord—the ever-present revelation which breaks the silence of the past and gives expression and meaning to the Eternal Universe. Because He lives we shall also live. The principle of His immortality is the principle of ours. So come out of your doubt, gloom, or despair.

> Peace, let it be! for we loved Him, and love Him for ever: the dead is not dead but alive.

8

THE PULPIT AND THE AGE, 1885

PAUL WRITING TO THE Galatians takes his stand upon two points: First, his own personal position in relation to the Gospel; Second, the intrinsic nature of that Gospel in relation to the larger needs of the age. Something like this I will also venture to do.

You have called and I have answered gladly. But it is not your call that has made me a minister. I was a minister before any congregation called me. My election is of God. Paul speaks of "a faithful minister of the new covenant." Now, to a covenant there are two parties. In this covenant they are God and man. God's fulness meets man's need. The divine nature meets human nature, and the union is a wedlock, first made in heaven. It is visibly set forth in Christ. The minister of this covenant, therefore, the minister of Christ, has his call, first, in the nature of God and God's Truth; second, in the nature of man and man's need. We have on one side the divine Gospel; we have on the other the cry of the human. His call is constituted both by the divine election and the requirements of human nature. Would that some who are sure of their election by God, were as sure of their election by man, and their fitness to adapt God's truth to human nature. It is not therefore the invitation of any particular congregation that makes a man a minister. It is a call which on the human side proceeds from the needs rather than from the wishes of mankind, from the constitution of human nature as set forth in Christ, rather than from the appointment by any section or group of men. I am here, not to meet all your requisitions, but to serve all your needs in Jesus Christ. You have not conferred on me my office, and I am Christ's servant more than yours, and yours for His sake. The minister is not the servant of the Church in the sense of any special community or organization. The old Latin theologians used to subscribe themselves V. D. M., Minister of the

II: Published Sermons

Word of God,—Minister not of the Church, but of that Christian human nature which our particular views and demands so often belie. A minister may, on occasion, never be so much of a minister as when he resists his congregation and differs from it. But neither is he any true minister if he differs from his congregation in a way to forfeit their affection and respect. I will not undertake always to agree with you, but I will undertake to extort your respect, to pursue your co-operation, and wistfully to strive after your affection. The man who is always in opposition is either an inspired prophet like Jeremiah or Carlyle, or an impracticable fool.

As the Minister is the servant of the Church in the sense I have explained, so the Church is the servant of the Kingdom of God. It is one of the best signs of the Church today that it is more ready than ever before to recognise the Christianity outside the Church, and to admit that God has a controversy not covered by ecclesiastical discussions. That Church is the best Church which is most free to serve the needs of mankind and the kingdom of heaven. The Church, no more than the Minister, exists to meet men's expectations. St. Paul speaks (if we have the courage rightly to translate him) of the God of the period, the fashionable God. It was a deity in the most vivid contrast with the Hebrew God—the Eternal. Well, every period does not insist on stereotyping its own religious fashion. The enormous freedom entrusted by God to His Church is there because of the enormous wealth and variety in the Kingdom of God. So rich and diversified is the Kingdom of God that His Church, which is to serve and hasten it, must be extremely flexible and free; it must resist, at least it must be free to resist upon occasion, the public outcry for this or that special mode of action as sole or supreme. To take one example: Mr. Arnold and a large portion of the public hold that the Church is a society for the promotion of goodness, or the production of right conduct. But the Church says, "No, the Kingdom of God is not primarily behaviour, but a right spirit, a new heart, a regenerate man, not simply and altered demeanour." And so the Church says, "Our object is not to produce this or that course of conduct, but to produce men and women, and not men and women of a type either, but souls representing all the various wealth of individuality in Christ." Again, no one mode of action will give scope to all the energies of the Christian sphere. A very large section of the Christian public makes an imperious demand that the Christian Church shall devote itself to philanthropy. Well, no Christian Church is true to its Master if it do not stimulate men to philanthropy, especially amid the misery of an age like this. But Christianity is something more than philanthropy after all, and the Christian has other virtues than benevolence, imperative as that is. And it must be open to any section of the Church, without prejudice, to devote itself to the cultivation of any branch of the kingdom's energies which seems to lie nearest to its hand and resource. It must be open to any Church to say, if it so deem, that it is a question for discussion how far even philanthropy is not a function rather of society in general than of specific religious communities. It is dangerous for a minister to also be an almoner, and it may not always [be] safe for a congregation.

And generally, it may be said that a Church is in itself an organic living body and therefore, as such, beautiful and valuable for its own sake, like a human being or a human family, apart from such purposes of outward utility as it may be calculated to serve. Those who urge the aggressiveness of a Church do well. A Church should be aggressive, and if it is vital will be. But the case is sometimes overstated in the interests of what is conventionally called Christian work. As there are some sects who believe they alone preach the Gospel, so some admirably laborious Christians speak as if their form of work were the only kind of Christian activity deserving the name. To depreciate a Church which is not organised to the very utmost for this kind of thing, is like denying a family its right to exist because it fills no public office, or makes no direct contribution of labour to the community. A Church is like a family. It is a social unity in itself. It is the tenement of an unspeakably precious life, and its contribution may freely be more to the quality than to the area of Christ's kingdom, without being for that reason less acceptable to Him.

But there is a perversion of the social idea of the Church which needs to be deprecated on the other hand. It is the case in America, and it is to a somewhat grave extent the case here, that the chief expression given to the social idea of the Church is in the way of mere sociability. The true idea of Christian fraternity degenerates into the mere notion of religious sociability. Now, Jesus Christ did not come into the world to foster sociability. The best culture of the Christian life requires much more seclusion and reserve than it mostly receives. It was human brotherhood that Christ came to set up. We are more intimately bound in the truth of Christ to some whom we have never seen at all than to some whom we meet every week. The grand expression and distinctive act of the Church fraternity is in the Sacraments—in the tender dedication and reception of the young soul in Baptism, the solemn sense of the unearthly brotherhood in Communion and the less awful and more frequent association of ourselves for the sacrament of the Word in worship and preaching. I regret the tendency to make little of the Sacramental side of our common religious life. It is our neglect of the Sacraments, our abandonment of their culture to the priestly party, that makes the strength of sacerdotalism. The more we dignify the Sacraments and assert our part in them, the more we weaken the power of the priest and destroy his exclusive place. We are prone to make too little of the Sacramental side of our Christian life and too much of the I, in the way, for example, of tea parties, entertainments, recreations. I should be sorry to see these things banished, but let them go if they are impoverishing the life which finds at the table of the Lord its chief refreshment and its chief fraternal bond. The Church, which for the sake of social intercourse, or even benevolent work, neglects its proper, special, quieter and more solemn Sacramental functions, is killing its Christian life in the eye. Its worship is not healthy, nor is its work. It is sacrificing the Sacraments, the sanctities, and will go on to sacrifice (like the Salvation Army) even the decencies of Christ to an order of activity which is in its nature lower, more external, and sure itself in the end to deteriorate for want of the inward food.

I have spoken of a third Sacrament, the Sacrament of the Word. It is the distinctively Protestant Sacrament, and it invests the pulpit with the dignity, if not the solemnity which elsewhere is bestowed on the altar. Among other regrettable tendencies of the hour is the disposition to depreciate the power of the spoken word. It exists both in the pew and in the pulpit itself. I know preachers who regard their Sunday duty with a contempt (which is evident), compared with the so-called practical work with which they fill five days of the week. And we are constantly pressed with the demand for short sermons. I believe myself that short sermons are mostly themselves too long. The man whose preaching is simply tolerated has no right to preach as long as ten minutes. The man whose preaching is welcomed has no right to be always as short as twenty. We listen gladly to political speeches of an hour, and the reason is that we have an interest, amounting to a passion for the subject. Let us have enough knowledge of the subject of religion as to choose only competent men for ministers, and let it be so real and passionate to us that we can take pleasure in what our prophet or expositor has to say for an hour if he likes. I don't hint that all sermons should be an hour long. But I do think short sermons are killing the pulpit and sending the people to the altar or the platform.

The preacher of the Word must regard its distribution as a Sacrament. He breaks to the people the living bread and inspires them with the wine of God. His speech is an act and generates acts. And the preaching of the Word in this high ideal of it is based upon two beliefs.

1. On the belief in a Revelation.
2. On the belief in the persuasibility of men.

1. The preacher must believe that God has revealed Himself and that that fact alone makes religion possible. Religion is not mere longing, nor

8: The Pulpit and the Age, 1885

is it the worship of our own ideas. It is a response to God's revelation of Himself. Without revelation religion is not possible. The preacher must have something to preach, a message from God. He does not imagine his Gospel; it comes to him. But this means nothing else than that God has first spoken. The first preacher of God was God Himself. He is not a lonely God, nor a silent. He never was nor can be such. It is His eternal nature and function to reveal Himself: to impart Himself. His going forth is from everlasting. Christianity starts from the eternal necessity and reality of revelation; or in other words, Christianity stands upon the Incarnation, which is the principle and summary of all Revelation, and a fact, not historic only, but historic because spiritual and eternal.

But is this by any denied? Yes, it is a truth which is thrown into the sharpest outline and definition by its denial on the part of those philosophers who are known as Agnostics. The plain Saxon of their position is that God has never spoken; that the power, whose product they confess we are, flung us sullenly forth without a word which we have any ears to hear. If He gave the word, and refused us an organ to lay hold of it, it is all the same as if He gave no word. If the power that produced us denied us ears, that means that He had either no desire or no power to be heard by us. No human soul has ever had a message from God, they say, and no human faculty is capable of receiving such message. The power that produces us was unable to maintain His communications with us, and must sit at the centre, like the polar ice from which the icebergs float clean away to melt and vanish in the infinite azure of the seas where the ice cannot live. God, they tell us, is not only relatively a mystery, but the absolute mystery, of whom nothing whatever can certainly be said. And Christ, when he called Him Father, was under a rash delusion that anything about the divine nature could be known. Many Christians, while they deny that Reason is the criterion of Revelation, yet vigorously assert that it is its organ. But the Agnostics deny human faculty of Reason to be even the organ of Revelation. And yet they try to save Religion as a vague sense of mystery and an awed consciousness of power that besets us before and behind. But Religion is not possible without the Revelation which they deny, and which is the preacher's charter and ground to be.

One the other hand, I cannot utterly refuse to regard these Agnostics as teachers sent from God. They have been in great measure called into existence by exaggerated and immodest statements made by some of the believers in God as to the extent of their knowledge of the divine nature. That nature has by some systematisers been so surveyed and mapped, its currents, processes, and transaction have been so fathomed and charted, with such minutes of details and such pretence of special information, that the natural modesty of the human soul has revolted and as usual the revolt has gone to the other extreme. We do not know everything about God, nor half as much as some believe they do. And it is well we should be brought to our sober senses on such a matter. But it is just as untrue to say we know and can know nothing about God. It is not Atheism it is true, but it is something which in the long and practical result will not be very far removed from it.

The statement of Christian doctrine has always been more or less determined by the dominant philosophic creed of the age. The Christian creeds grew out of conflict with the heresies, and were shaped in view of them. And the modern heresy of Agnosticism determines for us the most urgent, timely, and relevant significance of the Incarnation. It is in its shape as opposed to Agnosticism that it is the Gospel of the Age. The Incarnation is to be asserted as the principle of Revelation essential to Deity, in contrast with the principle of no Revelation or Agnosticism. All Christian philosophers must start from the principle of Revelation. Mysterious as God is, He is no absolute mystery. No religious philosophy is possible with a dumb God or deaf men. And Religion which has no philosophy has no solid ground.

But the preacher, who is also a Christian apostle, must preach more than the mere illumination under the head of Revelation. The Christian thought of the Incarnation has two factors—Manifestation and Redemption. There is John's favourite idea of the Word, and Paul's of the Cross. There is revelation by light—the light which lighteth every man—and there is revelation by darkness; revelation on the one hand by Life, on the other by Death, of Him who is Lord both of Death and Life. The message of God is no mere statement made by God, but a person and an act embodying His own Self and Nature. It is God Himself that speaks. "Only God can represent God." We preach *Christ crucified*—a person in an act. It is not Revelation in the mere sense in which a Greek philosopher would have conceived it—as a flash of discovery—but Revelation by Death. It is a religion not of cheery radiance only, but of sombre glory, stifled splendour, luminous gloom, and tragic might. The character of Christ is inseparable from the work of Christ, the image of the Father from the world of the Father. The character needed the cross. God could not only live but die. The living God is the dying God. The Sun of the divine righteousness could not only shine, but set and shine the more. The cross is imbedded in the very principle of Revelation. It is for the putting away of sin, but not for that alone. It is also for the illumination of the pure. The cross was in God before sin was in man, and it will be our central and vital principle still when sin has been clean destroyed. It is not an expedient or a medicine only. It is the Eternal principle of Eternal Life, which is always and only possible even to God by an Eternal Death.

8: The Pulpit and the Age, 1885

This, then, is the first belief of the preacher or apostle—that God has spoken, that He is ever speaking in such overwhelming fashion as to us seems silence, that the whole nature lives, moves, and has its being in the Supernatural and the whole of human life issues upwards in a Supernatural Christ.

2. His second belief is in the persuasibility of men. The grandest grandeur of God comes softliest home to man.[1] The divine Word or Reason is the utterance of God's intelligence to the intelligence (not merely the intellect) of men. The preaching of the Word is something more high and wondrous than the declaration of truth merely ancient, traditional, and authoritative. Declamatory and denunciatory preaching is the cheapest of all and the feeblest. It is your Forcible-feebles who do so much to bring the *Word* of the Gospel into public neglect and good-humoured contempt. But the preaching of the Word is the declaration of the *whole* counsel of God,—the whole reason, thought, and will of God. And by *whole* is meant in its proportions not in its extent. The whole of God was involved in our Creation and Redemption. It is a Gospel, therefore, which appeals to man in his completeness,—to man not as an emotional, or as an intellectual, or as a sinful vessel, but as a man, one and indivisible as God Himself is. It is the utterance of the Love of Him who *is* Love. It is the expression of Love in its most sweeping and masculine as well as its most tender and feminine sense. "Amor est virilis," says the sweet author of the *Imitation*.[2] Preaching tends to become too feminine, and many favourite preachers differ from the great preachers of earlier times, in that their beauty of sentiment is not infused and braced with the like vigour and sinew of understanding. Robert Hall was almost the last of that order. The preaching of the Word is the exposition of the Word of God with a passion and grasp something like adequate to its intrinsic dimension of Truth. Preaching should be like what God is—impassioned thought. But it is thought rather in its depth than in its range, and it is the passion whose whisper is often more piercing than its shout. It is more effective by quietude than by magnificence, and becoming incarnate in much humiliation it impresses rather by its victorious calm than by its militant force. The quiet preacher, if he have mind enough to get to reality, and enough morals to ring true, is among the mightiest pulpit powers. His reality preaches for him in much plainness of speech. The passion and tragedy which thought sees in life may beat in the simplest phrase. The sweetest and most potent words in human

---

1. "Knowing the terror of the Lord, we *persuade* men." [This footnote appears in the original text.]

2. "Love is manly," from Thomas à Kempis' *De Imitatione Christi* (c. 1418–1427).

language are neither gilt with the charm of sentiment nor ranged in the pomp of a period. Yet they cover the Eternal passion and conquer the Eternal sin. They stand not in "an endless peace without passion, but in an endless passion without dispeace," and they are perhaps these, "Come unto me all ye that labour and are heavy laden, and I will give you rest. Take my yoke upon you and learn of me, for I am meek and lowly of heart, and ye shall find rest unto your souls."[3] And the exposition of the Word is more than the exposition of Scripture. It is the exposition of the Bible within the Bible. It is the exposition of a Word that shall endure when all the Bibles of the world are burned up. The identification of the Bible with the Word of God has much hampered preaching, which is the exposition of Christ. Yet I, for my part, mean to do more than I have ever done in the expounding of Scripture. The Bible in our age has been almost rediscovered. It has undergone what classical literature underwent at the Renaissance. It is glowing and bursting with new and rich life, thought, and emotion. The Bible was never so rich as the abused critics have made it; and depend upon it the Bible cannot take its true and supreme place without Christ taking a truer and supremer place than before. Christ has in some quarters suffered from a wrong kind of respect for the Bible. Claims have been made for the Bible which many people, who are not yet sons of perdition, have resented. But such people are open and longing for the light of the Word, Christ, who is the power and the wisdom of God. No religious need of this age is deeper than the need for the Revelation of God to its mind and thought. If the *mind* of this century were Christian with all its enthusiasms of humanity, what a volume of faith and power would be brought to deal with the age's sins, and misery. But the Christian instincts of the soul are chilled and bewildered by the gulf between its religion and its thought, and the general air is too cold and incredulous for the best blossoms of Christian achievement.

Yet the mind and spirit of the universe is Christian. God is Christian. The soul of things is Christian. The conquest of human thought by Christ can be but a matter of time and freedom. Give us room and light and air. Christ is the truth men's mind were made for. Let us preach Christ. Let us take courage. Let us only believe in our Christian selves. If only we had a little more courage, a little more magnanimity in our religion, a little more faith in our own Gospel, a little more trust in what our creed can do for us, rather than we have for our creed! We want outspoken men,—men not afraid of strong things, and men with enough knowledge for ballast; and we want them both to preach and to act. The strongest things ever said in

---

3. Matt 11:28–29.

8: The Pulpit and the Age, 1885

the world were said by Christ and by Paul, and the most reckless things, if they were not true. So let us ask if statements are substantially mightily true, rather than if they are measured. The measure we want is the measure of the fulness of Christ. But what we must have—the Christ, I mean, as well as the fulness. We want men, it is true, and fearless men,—men able on occasion to withstand their very brethren to the face. But above all, we must have men who are able and obliged to do this for a particular reason and in a particular strength. We want men who are men because of Christ,—men whom Christ has made men, and who feel they owe their manhood to Him It is not a pagan but a Christian manhood we want in our pulpits and elsewhere. It is a manhood that is debtor to Jesus Christ for its own self and is never weary of constantly and variously, directly and indirectly, consciously and unconsciously, acknowledging the obligation.

The ministry cannot go on as a mere tolerated survival from an outgrown age and a creed out-worn. Your minister cannot with self-respect hold his place as a mere social or religious propriety. He is beneath himself if he be there as a mere utility-man or religious hack. He is in the idea of him your blessing and your pride. Do you believe the minister of Christ has a *real* place in modern society? Does he satisfy a real need or a fictitious one? Is he deeply indispensable or sadly inevitable? Is he a real producer, factor, contributor in the body politic? I could lay my hands on a small book on political economy where he is reckoned with as a non-producer. It all depends on the quality of his Gospel. Has he anything with which to meet, and not only to meet but to kindle and satisfy the peculiar aspirations of the age? Can he still help God to make men? If he can, then no producer is so indispensable as he.

The minister of a Christian Gospel is deeply required by the spirit of a time which is so Christian in many of its best and most characteristic instincts. He has much to teach and much to learn. Let him gladly do both. I welcome the spirit of the age. I do fear the spirit of the world. Nothing is for Christianity so formidable, so hard to eradicate as that. But the spirit of the age I do not fear. The Father worketh hitherto, and we work. The results which please Him best in His world may not always be those which His believers directly see and consciously produce. There is such a thing as the Spirit of God over and above the Church of God, and purposes of His are ripening in the growth of human faculty, which He may see cause to prize more than some very eager efforts of ours. God is leading the world where we have no hold of and He may be trusted not to lead it backwards. The Christianity required today must be at least four things.

1. It must be real and positive. It must have the air of reality which the best public of the day demands in the treatment of great affairs. More

and more, religion must part, and the pulpit must part, with its unrealities, its *finesse,* its men-of-straw issues, and its slaughter of the slain. More and more, religion must come to correspond with the absolute nature of God and the absolute needs of man. Its work must be like every other kind of honest work,—the real fulfilment of real and not fictitious needs. Such work is well described in the Epistle to Titus, iii. 14. "Let our people learn to profess honest occupations for necessary wants that they be not unfruitful." [R.V. margin.] A real religion, a religion which has the air of realism and not of mere strategy, or mere sentiment, or mere orthodoxy about it, is one that is not accommodated to any figments or legal fictions imported into the processes of the divine nature. Nor must it, on the other hand, deal with the merely superficial, artificial, and accidental demands of men, but with the essential requirements of human nature. We must labour to meet real difficulties in a real, *bona fide,* and sympathetic way. We must learn to treat critics as friends, and make our enemies our helpers. They see what we don't if we see what they don't. We must court knowledge of the worst that can be said against us. We must not live in the fools' paradise of those who hold all criticism of our creed to be carping, malevolent, and gratuitous. We must learn to dread a security which rests more upon ignorance than open-eyed faith. These objections against us mean something. What do they mean? We, who profess to have the key to life and the clue to truth, are bound to show that, and from our unique position, not simply refute scepticism, but interpret the sceptics to themselves. That is a process we can never go through without priceless gain on our part. No heretic or sceptic was ever yet sympathetically and rationally dealt with without a clear gain to our own position, the removal of parasitic growths or the dispersion of haze and mist. Nothing brings religion into more discredit than the air of unreality it acquires by secluding itself: in a spurious and valetudinarian sanctity, from vigorous direct and wholesome contact with the most real and vital problems and interest of contemporary life. This is a too prevalent blight upon the plants of God's planting. It is the phylloxera of the true Vine.

The second feature of a timely and needed Christianity is that it shall be—

2. Rational. I do not mean of course Rationalist. Rationalism is an outgrown phase of thought which is only not out-grown in England, because England is so far behind in everything pertaining to religious thought. The Reason of Man is the total and aggregate power of his spirit. It is the complete unity and faculty of all that constitutes him man. Faith is one of its prime functions and Love its joy and crown. To this, above all things, Christianity above all religions appeals. Its appeal is not to the logical faculty

8: The Pulpit and the Age, 1885

alone; nor to the emotional, but to the combined unity of heart, thought, will, and social nature. Nothing is so permanent, nothing so universal, as what is reasonable. A universal and eternal religion must be rational. To be vigorous and fertile, it must be rational. Sweet reasonableness is not a flabby things. If it ever seems weak it is one of the weak things of the world that confound the dogmatist and the bully at last. It is the dogmatisms of vigour and rigour that are not permanent. It has often been said that it is the ultra Conservatives who are the true revolutionaries. It is these rigid dogmatisms that are the least permanent, because they are most left behind. We shun the man of dogmatic unreason in private life, and the world resents and deserts his counterpart in a church or an age. Men are very persuasible, very teachable, to rational methods. For man is after all the reflected mind of God, and it was no Gospel of Unreason that the Son of God came forth to preach.

But in the third place, the Christianity which is to be timely must also be—

3. Liberal. The Spirit of God is a most subtle and persuasive Spirit, and His commandment is exceeding broad. The Spirit of Christ is the Spirit of the created world. As the world and the soul grow, there grows also the Spirit of Christ. If it be God's Eternal Nature ever to reveal Himself, then the religion which answers to such Revelation must be progressive. Only if God ceased revealing Himself would it be possible to make any stage of revelation final. The Bible is not a *terminus ad quem*,[4] it is a *terminus a quo*.[5] It is not a sea, it is a source, perennial indeed, but final, no. It is a great injustice to any past to invest it with that absolute despotism which history makes it its business to undo. It is a libel too upon the processes and purposes of God, and it is no less unjust to present and future. The half has not yet been told, and modern art, science, and politics contain a revelation of God no less real than any uttered by holy men of old. Not less real, I say. I do not say exactly the same. I do not say superior. I only say no less real. The Revelation of God in man is at least *as real* in the history of man at large as in the forecast of man in Christ Jesus. Nature and history reveal God as truly though not as profoundly as Prophet and Christ. The principle, the criterion, and what scholars call the Norm of revelation is given once for all in New Testament, with its Christian idea, consciousness and personality. But its horizon is infinite and its fertility unbounded. And it is a principle which commits us to the widest sympathies, the keenest receptiveness, much docility of demeanour, and a respectful recognition of the Christianity outside the Church. And it is not because we are not sure that we are so ready to learn.

4. A finishing point.
5. A starting point.

II: Published Sermons

It is not the mere seeker after Truth, but the man who has found Truth, that is most able and eager to deal with new Truth. It is not the inquirer that is modest—he is often pert—but the finder; and the modesty of science is due not to its ignorance and its quest, but to the great confidence and reserved strength which it has in the possession at last of the true scientific method. And such is the confidence of faith which we have in Christ. We have found the method of Humanity.

A liberal Christianity being a rational Christianity, is opposed to a Christianity merely authoritative, traditional, and crystallized. No age of the Church, from Christ's small company downwards, has enjoyed total immunity from error. No age, therefore, or its products, is beyond criticism, or beyond development. Nay, the test of a great past age is just its capacity for being left behind, its faculty of outgrowing itself: its wealth of germinal power to become superior to itself and pass into something which includes itself. Dead small ages will not develop, and cannot be outgrown; they can but be swept away, like the sterile civilizations of Mexico or Cambodia.

Christianity, at least in Protestantism, is a perpetual self-regenerating power. As the Christian man must examine himself, outgrow, correct, and readjust himself to his infinite standard, so with the Christian community, and the Christian creed. Protestantism is Christianity in its aspect of self-regeneration. It represents that property of ever-living spirit, that instinct of self-preservation on the part of Christianity, by which it varies to meet new condition, and so escapes from death by the fixities and falsities of history. Onward, onward, ever, but in Christ Jesus. It will be time for us to stop and return when we have left Him far behind.

4. The religion required by the needs of the hour must be, fourthly, a social religion. This does not mean, as already said, a Christianity given up to many meetings and much recreation, but a Christianity which has the secret of the social idea, and so is capable by its very nature of organising and dominating human society. If man be the product of the Love and Reason of God, then the Love of the Living God must be the influence which co-ordinates all his parts, and the music to which his members fall into beautiful place. The great test for Christianity in the future is the social test. It is competent to carry out the re-organization of society on a basis of reasonable love? Has it power to meet the aspirations, heal the wounds, and reform the abuses of society? Can it readjust the social machine, and give us all the blessings and none of the dangers of Socialism? Can it give us, without Revolution, "Liberty, Equality, and Fraternity,"[6] and raise these to godly significance? Can it provide

---

6. The motto—*Liberté, égalité, fraternité*—originated during the period of the French Revolution and was formally accepted as France's national motto during France's Third Republic in the late nineteenth century.

8: The Pulpit and the Age, 1885

a career to talent, room to labour, security to enjoy the fruits of labour? Can it assure every man of a future, and so expand for every man his present? Can it lift the load of hopelessness which weighs down whole classes, and makes thrift and prudence either futile or impossible? Can it do such things as these, and set current society on the basis of a social idea which is eternal, and a Social Being who is God? If not, let it make room for one that can.

A social religion is one opposed (1) to the spirit of caste, privilege, and monopoly, especially in respect of religious conviction or of pecuniary position. It aims at stripping the social idea of its worldliness, and making an unworldly earth wherein dwelleth righteousness. Its aristocracy is a spiritual aristocracy, its warfare knows nothing of militarism, its priesthood is royal of soul, its peerage is the roll of excellence and the record of goodness, its politics is the pure application of our principle, and its commerce is the glad satisfying of the brotherhood's need. A social religion is opposed, first to the spirit of caste and the mere clash of interests. But it is (2) to a Christianity merely popular, numerical, and common-place. Christianity is just as little to be sacrificed to the poor as to the rich. To make it serve either end of the social scale exclusively is to limit and weaken it. The Pharisee, with his popular religion, was no nearer Christ than the refined, superior, and exclusive Sadducee. Indeed, it was the popular religionists of the day that slew Christ. The Church and the Church idea is the meeting point of the whole community. It is a spirit, power, and presence which, like God in the Universe, places, holds, binds, and balances all. No man or class has more right to the love of God than another. Why should the rich be robbed of the Christianity can give them to endure their wealth any more than the poor of its help to abide their poverty?

These things and many more are not only demanded by the age from our religion, but demanded by our religion from us. Our concessions must not be compelled but inspired. We do not serve a Christ who comes laggardly forth at the repeated call of an alien time. But the Christ we serve is the power who inspires the time's great needs and prescribes its high demands. To keep us of the Church meek, our Lord's voice comes to us often by the mouth of the world; but woe be to us if we know not His call in whatever guise. The spirit will then have departed from us, as from some of us it has all but gone, and we shall be left to wither and die while from the very stones God raises up children to Abraham.

Let us, my dear friends, rise to the height and breadth of our high vocation. Let us court the things that are of noblest seeming and of godliest report. Let us repudiate the pride which sometimes goes with our Faith, the prejudice which is apt to go with Love. Let us eschew the banalities of belief, and the trivialities of doubt. Let us rise to the measure of our Christ and live on the

II: Published Sermons

wealth of His most excellent glory. Let Him refashion life for us and renovate duty. Let us be rigid first with ourselves. Let us pass into His Life by His Death. Let us widen all our views by letting Him widen our heart and increase our Life. Let us labour in the presence of an Infinite destiny, and grow in the bosom of the Illimitable God.

9

Sunday-Schools and Modern Theology, 1887

OPINION ON SUCH MATTERS has now gone so far that reasonable objection can no longer be taken to the claim of a recognised and honourable position for the new views alongside of the old. The religious temper of the time sets in favour, not of exclusion, monopoly, and persecution, but of inclusion, comprehension, and mutual interpretation. I suppose we are quite done with the days when anything that challenged or unsettled the old forms of theology was regarded as an emanation of the evil one, or an exhibition of original sin. Theology is the queen of the sciences, and must exhibit, in royal measure, the vital feature of a science; which is to change, progress, grow full and rich, and escape from the inevitable limitations and mistakes of the past. My only quarrel is with the blind conservatives who would let nothing go, and the wild revolutionaries who would hold nothing fast; for these two are one flesh.

It is not difficult to see which aspect of religious truth is likely to attract the young mind in these days of ours. And, therefore, I venture to say: Be sympathetic to the spirit of theological change and progress, even if you cannot see your way to adopt this or that change in particular. The conservative who is friendly and interested towards liberal tendencies is the only conservative who can render real service to his party, or obtain for it the sound influence which conservatism should always have. No teacher is likely to do much, either for his creed or his pupils, who sets only a denunciatory face to the newer tendencies of religious thought.

It is possible, of course, to say that theology and its movements have very little to do with Sunday-school work. And this, I regret to think, is a sentiment held by several who, so far as their own creed goes, are orthodox. But they have been infected by the spirit of the age towards theology, to an extent which leads them to consider that it has but little place in connection with the education of the young. Their idea is that the chance afforded the Sunday-school teacher should be used for impressing the young, whatever becomes of instructing them. Now, we may go so far as this: we may say that a theology like that of the Shorter Catechism is not in place in the Sunday-school. But, unfortunately, the rejection of systematic and metaphysical theology has meant the rejection of systematic and methodical instruction, which is a very great loss. It is not easy to say how far conversion should be the direct aim in a Sunday-school, but I am sure it should not be the sole aim. And the Sunday-school will not perform its full function till a great deal more is done than now in the way of Christian instruction. I hold that the greatest interior danger to Christianity in England is the most miserable condition of the religious intelligence in all classes. We are not an instructed people, and our creed is the consecration of our pet ignorance. Much of this is due to the popular disrepute into which theology has fallen—a discredit which is one of the modern influences in religion not entirely wholesome. Religious feeling is divorced from religious intelligence; we are pious agnostics, and in a school for the *teaching* of religion that is a great misfortune. I do not find that the same thing is the case abroad. It is one of the base distinctions of the English mind. Even the most advanced sections of the Church in Germany and Switzerland have innumerable manuals and guides for religious instruction, which are admirable in their scope and idea. They are not metaphysical, but they have a system and order in the exposition of the main principles of Christian doctrine and Christian ethics. They supply the skeleton which the teacher must make it his business to clothe with warm life and sound piety. Dr. Abbott's "Bible Lessons"[1] is the only thing in English worth naming in this connection. It is most admirable, but too expensive, and perhaps not sufficiently elementary.

My complaint is that so much of our inculcated piety is flabby, and the simplicity of Christ becomes pietistic wish-wash. And I think the sentimental and untheological nature of some of the new tendencies in religion has much to do with this defect. We abuse the proverb that the heart makes the theologian. But to be untheological is to be irrational. Theology is a science, and the teaching of a rudimentary theology ought to form part of our elementary science teaching. It will be long probably before the British Association have a department of theology, and as long before the theological chaos of the public mind permit of any scientific instruction in religious truth in our Board-schools. Meantime, it is the opportunity of the Sunday-school, and much would be gained if it were possible for the Union to construct a manual

---

1. The Rev. Edwin Abbott Abbott served as headmaster of the City of London School and penned, from the late 1860s onward, a number of volumes of "Bible Lessons" in the form of dialogues between a teacher and a pupil.

9: Sunday-Schools and Modern Theology, 1887

which each teacher could amplify at his discretion. Even those teachers of religion who ought not to teach theology will teach their religion a great deal better, and will teach a better and manlier religion, if they have some theological order in their own mind. Probably most of us would rather hear Professor Huxley on birds than a pigeon fancier. If you look at ulterior results a full heart alone is a poor substitute for an ordered mind.

Our forefathers, who really read theology, and thought theology, and discussed theology at the fireside, were better equipped than we are in this respect. Their answers to questions might not always satisfy our contemporaries, but they had a grasp of their own side of the subject which lent vast force to the weight of their character. They had rational convictions. But we, nowadays, too often try to rear character without conviction, without knowledge, and by means of religious impressions or moral sympathies only. The result is not as satisfactory, in some respects, as the old way. We follow the age and rely on a religion of love—but love which is, in most cases, more amiable, perhaps, than effective. We make love a sentiment rather than a principle, and we work by emotion to the neglect of character. We become afraid to do or say anything the children will not like, lest we lose influence over them, or drive them to some other more indulgent school. We pamper, and coax, and bribe them, till it is the settled belief of many of them that they do us a great favour by attendance. And with cruel tenderness we relax discipline sometimes till the tone of the school is so flabby that it lowers the moral system of the scholars beyond the power of any class teaching to brace it. Or, the class teaching itself potters anxiously about the children's souls, encourages an unnatural self-scrutiny, keeps pulling up the roots to see how the plant is growing. The teachers want to save the children, and to do it at once, instead of trusting their salvation to the truth and word of God, expounded, pressed, and moulded into the realism of life. Anyhow, we lose the enormous leverage upon character supplied by clear conviction, firm belief, and sound objective knowledge of truth. And if that be absent no mere culture of the affections or sympathies can do its work.

I am afraid it is a great but indubitable misfortune that we do not get for teachers the cream of our adolescent intelligence. Our regret for this fact can hardly be too deep. There is nothing that needs mending so much in connection with our Sunday-schools as the quality of the teaching. I do not say the teachers, observe (for in the matter of their character and devotion I have nothing to say), but the *teaching*. And I am bound to say that there are few who feel this so much as many of the best teachers themselves; and they evince it in their eagerness to profit by such classes or manuals as are likely to prepare them better for their work. Our Sunday-schools, being educational institutions, are forward to feel the unhappy divorce between popular religion and intelligence; and we need, for the moment (far more than enthusiasm and devotion, which abound) that admixture of brains which is so necessary for continued success in any great enterprise. No great enterprise can flourish upon little minds, be the devotion what it may. And the same curse which is beginning to handicap England in the markets of the world is robbing her grand Sunday-school idea and organisation of half its influence. I mean under-education, and, what is worse, a distrust and contempt of education. The education of all our religious teachers has fallen far behind the general pace of the world's intelligence, and our Sunday-school staff shares the misfortune. I am apt to think that our schools would gain vastly from any system which, like evening classes between the ages of fourteen and eighteen, would carry on education just when it begins to be education, and becomes something more than mere instruction. The more you look the more you find how we suffer from lack of mental freshness and power of accommodation to new circumstances. Of course, my remarks apply more to the senior classes than to the junior; but it should be remembered that it is the senior classes that give the school its tone. With this qualification, however, I say that for a Sunday-school teacher the appropriate knowledge is just as necessary as piety and zeal. He ought to have an adequate knowledge of the subject he is going to work in. And my regret is, therefore, deep at the abstention from Sunday-school work of the more cultivated intelligence of many of our churches.

It is a fact whose explanation is complicated. First, there is no doubt that the liberal views in religion, which come with quickening intelligence, have, with many, a tendency to breed, not exactly religious indifference, but evangelical indifference. I do not say religious indifference, for the consuming interest to such minds remains religious. But it is evangelical indifference, for the old faith no longer overflows into the operation of saving love, and its lines are too blurred to afford the practical stimulus flowing from definite conviction on the deepest things.

A very general spirit of doubt and question is current, as we all know, in respect of points once deemed fixed. Now, I do not call doubt a disease; but I do call it something like a searching East wind. It is wholesome, but it needs a healthy constitution to profit by it. The questions are often such as need far more mental vigour and equipment to settle them than to raise them. Amateur thinking is, therefore, at a great disadvantage. But young men, even if very intelligent, cannot be expected to be successful business men and expert theologians too. Hence their minds remain often and long in a state of dilettante uncertainty about matters very important to a religious teacher, with the result that as teachers such people are not available. Take the question of miracles. There is just enough doubt about them floating in the air to infect a good many minds who are interested in the

9: Sunday-Schools and Modern Theology, 1887

question without being competent to settle it, or, at least, to settle it soon. I have several times asked persons of intelligence to take a class, and have got the answer that they did not know what to say when the critical mind of boys put point-blank the question—which probably was first heard at home—"But did this really happen?" A preacher might simply not select such a subject, or might treat it as a parable; but a teacher has it very pointedly forced on him.

And in like manner we have young men in our classes who have heard current secularist talk, and who easily think superficial difficulties fatal to profound belief—we have them asking, *e.g.*, how Jesus could die if He was Immortal God? What is a teacher to say? Is there any educative value in simply dogmatising and reiterating that, nevertheless, He was God and did die? Rather than do that, many refuse to become teachers altogether, and so not only rob us of what help they could give, but lose that chance of enlarging their own minds which teaching always brings.

I am not blaming young men of intelligence who may grow hazy about their creed. For in an age like the present such a period of transition, with its lowered vitality can by some minds only be avoided by intellectual death. And it is even a worse death to profess a definiteness of conviction which is not really possessed. I would only blame where this condition of mental fluidity is accepted and acquiesced in, where the mind settles down into unsettlement, where instability acquires fixity of tenure, and where the vigorous intelligence does not rebel against such a vagrant despotism as intolerable. And I mention the thing here to illustrate the way in which one of the tendencies of the modern religious mind affects the Sunday-school, by withdrawing a considerable number of people from teaching who would otherwise bring to the work the intelligence whose absence is deplored. I feel sure more use could be made of the Sunday-school in dealing with the intellectual difficulties of the day. They have far more influence than the secluded pietists recognise. Here is an experienced evangelist like Rev. W. H. M. Hay Aitken [*sic*],[2] at the Church Congress, bespeaking sympathy for the vast number of cases where there is "the desire to believe without the intellectual capacity to do so." What is the Sunday-school doing as an institution to give this sympathy any practical form?

But is there not a second cause for these abstentions which is blameworthy? I allude now to the attitude not unfrequently assumed towards such minds by those robust and inelastic believers who are so invaluable in Sunday school as in other good work. I may be wrong; but I regard the

---

2. Canon William Hay Macdowall Hunter Aitken (1841–1927) was an Anglican evangelist who spoke at a number of Keswick Conventions.

inhospitable attitude of the missionary societies (and especially of their rich lay supporters) towards modern views as one of the great causes of the startling decay in the missionary sympathies of the public. And the same thing holds good, to an extent which I will not venture to define in connection with the great mission effort of the Sunday-school. There is a general feeling abroad, especially among young men, that the *personnel* of the ordinary Sunday-school is the preserve of a somewhat severe orthodoxy, and that those who sympathise with so-called heretical views are unwelcome as co-adjutors, and will be made uncomfortable. I will leave the decision whether the impression is justified; but, for my own part, I have no doubt of its existence. And if it exist, you can well believe that it has a very deterrent influence upon the very minds who, as teachers, might both give and gain most. And it is one of those influences connected with the new theology which cannot at present be said to make for the interests of the Sunday-school.

I mention these things to show that I have no indiscriminate admiration for the modern temper as compared with the old. We are not in every respect better than our fathers. Those who are for going with the times, must not make the mistake of supposing that all that is new is all that is true. Nor must they think that an easy Gospel is any improvement on the noble severity of the old.

But I go on to point out one or two aspects of a better influence exerted on our work by the change in theology.

1. And, first, there is the more rational, humane, and sympathetic spirit in which theological views of every shade are coming to be held. We differ in another temper. And this is a change which cannot fail to have a beneficial influence on the attitude of the young to religion. The arrogant and exclusive dogmatism which is perishing was no good passport to the youthful mind. It created a certain instinct of repulsion, which neutralised much of the good that its element of truth was calculated to do. The spirit of doctrinal rigorism is not the best atmosphere for educational work. For one it rears it dwarfs a hundred.

2. There is another great feature of the newer schools of theology which is of vast influence in favour of Sunday-school work. I allude to the redoubled, and more than redoubled, study, of the first order, recently given to the Bible. Never were those who had to teach from the Bible in such a rich and happy position as they have now been placed in by the labours of the more modern-minded scholars upon Scripture. Many of the revolts against the old theology have been forced on men by the truer study of the Bible. It has been studied in a truly scholarly and scientific way, by men unfettered by dogmatic prepossessions, and anxious only to know what in His Word God the Lord does say. The Bible has been restored to history and to humanity. It has ceased to be

9: Sunday-Schools and Modern Theology, 1887

the theologian's monopoly; and it is a vast gain for teaching purposes that it should have had breathed into it a new historic colour and life. In some senses the Bible has been rediscovered during this century, and its events and characters reclothed in a garb which comes very close to our modern situations and sympathies. There are now few manuals of the higher politics equal to the prophets, if we will study them for principles instead of predictions. The Bible has been made a more human book, but only ignorance can conclude that it therefore loses in divinity. It has certainly been made a book far more interesting to youth. Its literary side has received huge attention and exposition. Its charm has been raised, and its power is so much the higher, finer, more penetrating, and more commanding. It has been charged afresh with the most perennial and enkindling ideas, and brought into sympathy with the human heart and imagination. How terribly and fatally religion has been divorced from the popular imagination! What a lay figure Christ has been made in some Christian quarters!—how official His function!—how unreal His work! But the whole effort of recent study of the Gospels has been to reanimate their great figure, to reconstruct the lost mind of Christ, to trace the movements of His living soul, and to find in His character the key to His saving work. We are coming to see that the question of all questions is one as to the consciousness of Christ—its nature, its contents, and its implications. The object of all Biblical criticism is to distil this true word of God out of Scripture, and it is to facilitate this that the best claims for critical freedom are made. Christ is being raised from the dead, in a figure, to the amazement and disquiet, it may be admitted, of many faithful guardians of His tomb. But what results may we not hope for upon the young when teachers come to be infected with such ideas and aims, when they are able to offer to the children the Man Christ Jesus, as one whose true Deity vitalises and transfigures His human life and thought, instead of being merely tacked on to it? Much is doing among teachers in this way; more will be done as they find, and cannot help finding, that this method gives them a power over the sympathies of their pupils afforded by nothing else. But they must not omit fearlessly to use the best means of Scriptural interpretation which the popularisation of the best scholarship puts into their hands. A teacher who can reanimate the Gospel narrative of Jesus need never fall back on the indolent and miserable expedient of angling for the imaginative interest of the children by reading for a lesson slip-slop tales.

    3. The modification of the old doctrines of total depravity and eternal torment have given a new worth to human life, even in its germ; drawn more loving care to the study of it, disposed us to lead it rather than drive it, and given a great stimulus to the study of child-nature. We are led to reverence the human nature of the child more, and to adopt more carefully our methods to its laws, as being the laws of God. The vast

and thoughtful interest now devoted to children is a true result of our humaner thoughts about God and His purpose with man. It would be strange if we realised the universal and indestructible Fatherhood of God, and yet were unaffected in our own spirit of fatherhood, and unchanged in our treatment of the child. It is impossible to treat children when they are believed to be children of God in the same way as when they are held to be children of the devil. We have had a fair trial of the latter system of culture, and a sad crop of crabbed and stunted men and women we have raised in many quarters by our repressionary methods. To masses we have made God unlovely in His love. We have pollarded too many of our young willows by the water courses, we have kept down the level of the Christian stature, and gnarled the Christian mind into grotesque travesties of the tree of life. But we have also lived to see a better day. The softening, not to say vanishing, of the more gloomy views of God, man, and the future must be the removal of a great obstacle in getting at the generous sympathies of the young. It is true there is a greater tax made on the teacher. He has not only to teach, he has to reveal God. And he has to reveal Him, as the great Revelation did, through a life, a heart, a behaviour. It is far more easy to teach a system than to reveal the Father by living the Son. But while the former may make religious pedants, it is the latter alone that can turn the children of men to the children of God. I say we have gained more for educational purposes by an increased grasp of the Divine Fatherhood and the humanity of the Eternal Son than we have lost by all the doubt and question raised round other points. Whatever doctrine has suffered, time will show that the great doctrine of the Incarnation has gained infinitely in its practical, educating, redeeming power. And, in illustration of that, you have only to remember how near Christ is brought to the successive stages of our tried human life by the increased stress laid, in these latter days, upon His true development and genuine temptation. The ecclesiastical Christ may suffer, but the truly Scriptural cannot.

4. There is one feature of the present day which seems to me, on the whole, more beneficial than mischievous in its bearing on the religious treatment of children. You will, I fear, not all agree with me when I say it is the temporary decay of the sense of sin. The gain is not unmixed—far from it. To illustrate from another sphere, I certainly think the decay or modification of old notions about the fate of the heathen and their share in hell has seriously affected the foreign mission field, and reduced the number of those who rushed in to pluck brands from the burning. And so in our home missions our views are relaxed as to the finality of death for character, and we contemplate at least the possibility of the redemptive function of hell. Well, so far as that goes we have relaxed also one force

9: Sunday-Schools and Modern Theology, 1887

which led to an almost passionate concern for the unconverted souls of the young. We have lost a certain stimulus to a certain aspect of Sunday-school work—a stimulus without which it is doubtful if the Sunday-school would ever have risen to what it is. But we have now, as always, the motive of salvation from sin. That was the substance of the old enthusiasm, however perishable its form. But we have also different notions about dealing with sin in the young—healthier notions, I venture to think, and notions less apt to do violence to the culture of the Christian character. I can only be brief; but you will probably admit that it is easily possible to do great mischief to the young conscience by unwise efforts to force on it a premature and unnatural sense of sin. We may regret the present deadness of the public mind to moral guilt, but I am inclined to think it has had one good effect, in discouraging some of the efforts unhappily made to impress children with a deep contrition. I need not point out how easy it is thus to make young Pharisees, who begin a career of imposition on others by first imposing on themselves. And this leads me to indicate another and kindred feature of the time which predisposes the public sympathies to Sunday-school work.

5. A certain amount is lost of the reliance that used to be placed on conversion. It is not denied, but it is much more cautiously treated than it used to be. We have more faith than we used to have in education. The natural man may be Christianised by a conversion of some violence; but the natural child, if you would only begin in time, and respect its naturalness, is Christianised by education. "Except ye are converted, and become as little children."[3] The man is converted to the child, but the child is educated to the man in Christ Jesus. The increase of public confidence in the methods of education may, indeed, be regarded as a factor of the vaster faith in Evolution which has taken such possession of the age, and made it at once patient in its intolerance of evil, and hopeful and judicious in its treatment. Evolution has done more for the world than convulsion. Convulsions, indeed, are themselves only unusual links in the evolutionary chain. So the larger idea to which conversion is tributary is the idea of education. It is part of the evolutionary sympathies of the time that we are more anxious than we were to encourage agencies like the Sunday-school, which place the young in the religious environment of a Christian society, mould them by the gentle action of Christian character, and feed them with the nurture of Christian principle and truth. After all, what does a Christian education mean but that we spread the conversion over a longer period. It is really only the sudden and violent conversion of the

---

3. Matt 18:3.

adult that is more suspected than before. It is not the need or the reality of conversion from self as a centre to God. That must always be expected, whether swift or slow. The school is one of God's slow agencies. We try to make the school do for children what a truly Christian home would do if they had it—make sudden conversion unnecessary by a preventing grace, by an insensible conversion, by the slow, ingraining influence of Christian knowledge, Christian care, and Christian life. The comparative discredit into which sudden conversion has fallen has not acted injuriously on the Sunday-school and certainly not on the public sense of its value. Nor has the Sunday-school suffered—nor is it likely to suffer—from a prevalence of evolutionary ideas as to the creation of character, and the slow, solid rearing of the Christian mind.

6. This leads us to remark upon the extraordinary stress laid by the newer views on the ethical side of Christianity. The ethical aspect of the Atonement is the side which, under the name of the moral theory, has done so much to modify, if not to expel, the old forensic idea, with its *quid pro quos*[4] and its dubious ethics of substitution. It is a tendency of the day which has drawn forth from the hidden riches of Christ a marvellous new store of moral beauty, humane charm, and social power. It is the ethical rather than the strictly evangelical aspect of Christianity which it has been the function of our day to turn to the light. A time may come, I admit, and may not be distant, when we shall have to do what Paul did. It was chiefly in his conflict with Judaism that he pressed the expiatory aspect of the work of Christ. It formed the substance of His protest as it formed the essence of Luther's. And a protest may be forced on us which will cause us to renew our emphasis on some theory of Atonement for the sake of a true view of Incarnation. We may have to go back on the more strictly evangelical aspect of Christ's work to save us from one sided morality, from a despotism of propriety, a deification of "conduct," and an ethical pharisaism which is all law and no Gospel, all practical, with no food or kindling for the living spirit at all. But I doubt if the Sunday-school has, on the whole, reached this point, or adequately risen to its opportunity in expounding ethical Christianity, or inculcating the elements of a distinctively Christian morality. If a teacher wanted to do this he would find great difficulty in getting any help. I do not think any Sunday-school union has published an approach to a manual on this subject. And yet how necessary, how imperative such teaching is! The fact is, our children grow up without any instruction worth the name in the duties and relations which for a social being are the most important of all. They have no schooling in the Christian laws of right conduct. I am not saying

---

4. One thing in return for another.

9: Sunday-Schools and Modern Theology, 1887

that increased attention has not been given to the moral beauty of Christ's life, or that there is any failure in the inculcation of moral precepts; but what is desiderated is not moral *precepts*, but some elementary acquaintance with the *laws* of our moral relations in Christian Society as distinct from a society merely natural and pagan. Our preachers and pastors even are turned out to guide and inform the public conscience without any serious instruction in Christian Ethics. They get some theology and a degree in science, but of the system of Christian Society, or the casuistry of Christian relations they are taught nothing in an effective way. They are unequipped for the great and indispensable task of moralising English freedom and converting it to the Christian thing of the same name. There is an agreement upon the Christian morality among those who differ on every other point. Why is more not made of it? Why should not a teacher be in a position to give at least one Sunday a month to a lesson on Christian morality, if he were provided with such help as he might find (for lack of a better), in Mrs. Bray's "Elements of Morality."[5] Granted that the book is dry and imperfect, that is just what a teacher who can teach needs. He can vitalise it, and follow it out, if he will take the pains to master it, and to watch life for instances and illustrations. The notes of the most interesting and moving sermon would be very dry reading. There is no practical faculty which gets so little education as the sense of duty. We have no technical schools for the art of life. And for all that people prate about their conscience, there is nothing rarer than a *trained* conscience. Even among Christians what passes for conscience is little more in most cases that social heredity, moral tradition, rule of thumb, or light of Nature, baptised with a Christian name. It is not a faculty educated to independent vitality in the moral principles of Christ.

If Christianity is to guide more than ever our social life, it must provide some better education than it is doing for the conscience of the young public, and for their idea of the contrast between society as Christian and as pagan. Where, but to our Sunday-school, can we look, at present, for any instruction in the elements of social morality. There is but little chance of such a thing in the Board-schools. All that they can turn out is a set of clever young individualists, to whom religion, when it comes, is apt to mean no more than the saving of their own souls. In how many Board-schools, I wonder, or even Sunday-schools, are children ever taught anything of the sanctity of public property in connection, *e.g.*, with school furniture? I deeply wish the powerful Sunday-school Unions would pay some very competent person to write a shilling manual of Christian morality, explaining and illustrating, in a suitably elementary fashion, the duties of Christians

---

5. Bray, *Elements of Morality in Easy lessons, For Home and School Teaching.*

not only to God but to themselves and to the social bodies of which they must form a part. We want something more thorough-going, more systematic, more piquant, more in touch with modern conditions than the trite lessons which are incidentally drawn from the passage of Scripture for the day. It would be the teacher's care to hide the system of such a book, to cover it well with the flesh of actual life, to illustrate it by concrete instances drawn from literature (including good novels) or experience, and make it, instead of a fetter, a frame for his living work.

In conclusion, I offer a word conversely on the influence of Sunday-school teaching upon theology. It is very great. It has been said that the test of a theology lies in its capacity of being prayed. Another lies in its capacity of being adapted to the young. It is really the same test. We all pray as children, and the theology of childship is the theology for childhood. Many parents have had their first real difficulties about the views they were reared in suggested by the attempt to teach them to their own children. The like has happened with venerable professors from their contact with young students. And so with Sunday-school teachers. As usual when we begin to teach the children, the wand of the Divine irony waves, and, lo! they are teaching us. There have been doctrines which no parent could teach his children in a feeling way without violence done to the human nature of both, and the effort has led at last to their abandonment. Magistrates may believe in Total Depravity, fathers really don't; and they will not go on trying to think they ought, in the light of their children's eyes. It is hard for many a man who wishes to be orthodox but has daughters like goodly pearls to believe even in Universal Depravity. No mother who realises what it means can ever believe in Eternal Torment, even if she refuses to dogmatise about Universal Redemption. And if the question be of vicarious *punishment*, no man of Christian feeling can look on a sick child without piteously asking, "These sheep, what have they done?" The more we try to teach our religion to the young the more we shall be led to purify its theology. We shall not only have our attention directed with some force to the subject, but we may find some reason to doubt whether the best interpreters of the Divine Fatherhood have always been those celibate thinkers who framed, with such acumen, the creeds of the Church in the creed-making age; and we may find that these are due more to the expositors of Scripture than to its Inspirer. The care of children has always brought people close to religion; it may not impossibly have a considerable effect on our theology, and there, too, as beneath the Star of Bethlehem, "a little child shall lead them"[6]—even the wisest of them.

6. Isa 11:6.

10

Preaching and Poetry, 1890

Much is said for the moment on the duties of the Church in connection with the recreation of the people, and the question is, doubtless, important, whether it lies within the Church's sphere or not. There is some room for doubt if the popularity so won may not be too brief, costly, and sterile for spiritual use. But there is a cognate region where the Church might, perhaps, with profit do more than is mostly tried. To purvey for the masses pleasure which, though harmless, has no teaching, and though elevating, has no inspiration in it, may before long be recognised to be one of the duties of the municipality rather than of the Church. But there is a pleasure which has teaching and kindling in it, a delight which does not just leave us in spirit where it found us, which is more than recreative, and which does not so much relax as brace us; or if it do not brace, yet at least, enriches us, and enhances us to ourselves. With pleasure of this kind, surely the Church has something to do. Nothing is far foreign to the Gospel which helps us to acquire our own souls, or elucidate our true spiritual quality. Indeed, it is the divorce of culture with its spaciousness from the power of the cross that has done so much to make culture pagan, and the Gospel either strident or dull. Is there any real reason why the Church, the pulpit, should not do more than heretofore for the pleasure of the soul and the delight that goes with ideas? Is there not some good reason why we should be slow to fritter our Christian energies on the pleasure which stirs no noble memories or hopes, but only strives to make the jaded man forget both tomorrow and today? Has the Protestant Church not gone a very long way in the wake of the Roman, in accommodating its methods to men's weakness instead of making demands on the strength which it professes to supply? And what earnest man but knows how deep is George Meredith's truth: "The reason why so many people fall away from God, is because they cling to Him with their weakness rather than with their strength."[1] In a word, does our modern literature not offer us a much neglected opportunity of expounding the old Gospel from new texts?

We are returning with amazing energy to the expository style of preaching. As the Reformation goes on to its completion, it carries us both backward and forward to the rehabilitation of Scripture. The true reform of the Church can only proceed from within. And a reform the Church from within means a repristination of the charter on which the Church rests. The Church, reviving in power, in taste, in learning, and in social ideas, rediscovers the Bible. Literary science and Christian feeling combine, at a little cost to some traditional views, to make Scripture richer than ever. A growing Christ entails a glowing word. God draws nearer, and the bush flames anew.

If we must be ultimately bound to the Bible, must we be slavishly bound? If our Gospel must rest for its final authority on the principle of Scripture, must every discourse keep the form of starting from a Scriptural text?

May the expository style not be occasionally applied in the interests of Christian truth to the forms of delight with which our modern literature clothes spiritual truth as it follows into the detail of the modern soul the broad principles of Christ? We mean no jugglery with the word Inspiration. We intend no crude identification, in current literary fashion, of the inspiration of today with the Inspiration which breathes uniquely for all time through the first literature of a unique Redemption. But it is one Spirit, even if His ancient movement is "once for all."[2] We gladly accept, and deeply need, the aid of those thinkers who pursue into the complexity of the modern conscience the large and eternal ethics of Christ. Might we not make more use of those men of genius who in the subtle and beautiful forms of literary art enshrine the pearls of the Christian soul. Literary feeling is not religion, and literary religion is not Christian piety. But are we overdone with teachers who can make the spiritual principles of the Christian soul come home to the contemporary imagination, who speak especially to the best of the young, and who would deliver us, if we would let them, from the sentimental fancies which make so much religion nauseous to the robuster mind. A sermon of quotations is usually bad, both as art and as Gospel. Might not the pulpit go a long way beyond mere quotation in occasionally interpreting these great poetic interpreters, who, if not inspired as text, are

---

1. George Meredith, *The Ordeal of Richard Feverel*, 2:117: "For this reason so many fall from God, who have attained to him; that they cling to him with their Weakness, not with their Strength."

2. Heb 10:10.

10: Preaching and Poetry, 1890

at least inspired as commentary, and who illuminate from the broad margin of modern time the mysteries of the small immortal page?

We have the old Gospel in new lights, the old flame in new lamps. The greater poetry of the day is Christian poetry. Wordsworth, Tennyson, and the Brownings are not only religious and Christian, but theological. Matthew Arnold, as a poet, is almost persuaded. And the death of Browning made even Swinburne a preacher of immortality. Men like these have depths of rich, moral wisdom, of which our popular teaching stands much in need; and they may have spiritual vision of true Christian sort, which God has put at our disposal to supplement the dull sense, which is all that many believers attain to, of their Lord. The commentary which brings Christ nearest is, doubtless, our own incommunicable Christian experience. But what we gain in nearness we are apt to lose in size and scope, in depth and grasp. In such regard the poets with whom God has blessed our outward, material, and luxurious age are among the finest of all commentators on Scripture. They might be made the most influential of all teachers (especially for the young) in the contemporary, but yet spiritual aspects of that Christian truth whose wellhead is in Scripture itself. The spirit of Christ is the testimony of poetry as well as of prophecy. Our great poets have in them "something of prophetic strain"[3]—in the higher sense of the word prophetic, which implies looking into the things of Christ no less than speaking them out. Much use might be made of the poets to convert to Christian instruction the current craving for delight; and especially might this be useful to those whose poetic years and tastes are not yet over, but whose interest it is most difficult to bespeak for religious teaching. That teaching is either conventional, and does not attract them, or it is fully adequate, and so beyond them. They have passed from boyhood and girlhood. They begin to feel the suggestions of dawning mind and manhood. They turn, well disposed, to the things that are pure, lovely, and of good report. But the sources of Christian religion do not become really interesting to them. Scripture speaks after all with an archaic accent. A veil is on its face. Christ seems so ancient, so distant, so irrelevant, and the objections to Christ so near, so modern, so intelligible, so plausible. He appears a Christ of yesterday. It is the anti-Christ that is of today. And they know not what is forever. They grow indifferent for want of some living mediating spirit between the Christ of the story and the Christ of the age. Mr. Stopford Brooke's admirable *Christ in Modern Life*[4] is an in-

---

3. From John Milton's "Il Penseroso" (1631–1632?): "Till old experiences do attain/ To something of prophetic strain."

4. Brooke, *Christ in Modern Life: Sermons Preached in St. James's Chapel, York Street, St. James's Square, London* (1872).

adequate book, but its many editions prove how real is the need it meets. Why cannot a more evangelical belief do something to meet that need? The class alluded to is often shy of sermons and their makers. And even if they are not very learned they turn away from feeble homilies with a garnish of music, and the general aspect (as a witty bishop puts it) of "a text floating alone in a quantity of soup." They might be saved for religion if they were saved from the impression that it is so very irrelevant. At their age, perhaps, they cannot be expected to have a mature sense of its actuality in personal experience, even if Christians round them made their religion more actual in practice than they do. The young seek a Christ for the age as well as a Christ for the vicissitudes of the individual soul. There may be a precocity, not to say sometimes a conceit, in the demand, but in intelligent quarters it is there. Who would prefer it away? And they would at least be more prejudiced in favour of Christ if He were made to speak to them oftener, as men of piercing genius can make Him speak, in the large language of the age's heart, not in the quaint piety of the past, or its stately inflexible forms. We cannot put a genius in every pulpit, but we might let genius speak through them all the same.

With what is only pretty or sentimental in poetry, the pulpit has not much to do. And yet by using poetry chiefly as illustrative quotation the pulpit too often inflicts on poetry this stigma. It perpetuates the public delusion that poetry and sentiment, poetry and fancy, are the same thing. People learn to think that a poem is a triumph of language, or of imagery, with a thought let in here and there which it is useful to remember and not amiss to quote. But of the large movement of organic thought pervading even a small poem of the true sort, like Wordsworth's "Ode to Duty," they have no idea. They have dissociated poetry as completely from the deep and real issues of life in some quarters, as religion has been dissociated from them in others. So that while we have one party asserting in the name of religion that poetry has little to do with the saving of the soul, we have literary people like Matthew Arnold in an extreme reaction, waiting for the coming age when poetry shall be the great guide and sweetener of the soul, and treating the Bible as little more than literature contributory to that end.

Religion is not sentiment; neither is poetry. Nor is religion poetry; nor poetry, religion. Such talk is not surprising in a half-educated age like our own, especially among the "young lions" of art, literature, and rambling religion. But religion and poetry have much in common. They deal seriously and largely with life as a unity—with the soul itself and not with its sides and occupations. They are practical and creative. A poet is a "maker," and religion is the great maker of men. Like poetry it is a spiritual maker, a maker of large minds, and of hearts uplift by sacred sorrows, infinite thoughts, and

10: Preaching and Poetry, 1890

endless hopes. Such was the heart of Christ—our Man of men. For years He lived upon the literature of His nation as His spiritual food. Can it be quite His will that we should neglect the literature of *our* nation—especially those parts of it that are most redolent of Himself and of a like seriousness in aim? May we not, ought we not, in the name and interests both of our Christianity and our youth, to try to do a little more in the way of correcting by the weight and grandeur of poetic thought the tendency of religion to pretty sentiment, and of making our faith not only a creed or a precept but a real discipline to the moral imagination and the truly public mind?

These words may not improbably be read by people of both views on the question of religion and the nation, of Church and State. But it may be presumed that they only differ as to the best mode in which religion may be made the ruling factor in national affairs, and, at the same time, saved by interests of national dimensions from the close piety of conventicle or sect. Religion needs to be made national no less than the nation needs to be made religious. It is not theology that has made the sects mischievous so much as the severance of faith from the unity and volume of the national soul. Indeed, we should be much depressed if we had not in the progress of theology our chief hope for the erasure of the sects. But it must be a theology which is not unprepared to place itself in tune with the unity of the nation's soul as uttered in its great literature, and especially its great poetry. As religious teachers of every communion, we have a function to the nation as well as to the Church. And we have a unique position and advantage as mediators of both, as interpreters to the people both of their present soul and of their destiny *sub specie eternitatis*.[5] Again we repeat that the literary man is not the priest, that poetry is not the guide of life. But these extreme positions would never have been assumed if the Church had not provoked them by a corresponding extravagance and one-sidedness. The public soul in some of its finest utterances tends away from Christ, chiefly because Christ has been secluded from the public soul. It is in its literature and chiefly in its poetry that the nation's soul finds vent, and unity, and distinctive expression. In its poetry a people is more truly itself than anywhere else, except in its religion. The severance of the popular religion from the national poetry is such a divorce of the nation from its faith as must be fatal if it cannot be healed. The true nationalizing of our religion cannot be effected without a good understanding set up between our literary and our Christian soul, between our spiritual unity as a people in our poetry and our spiritual unity as mankind in Christ. It is a huge blessing that our great poetry is so Christian. It would be a vaster blessing still if we better understood how Christian it is. It would

---

5. Under the aspect of eternity.

II: Published Sermons

help to prevent us from seeking the nationalizing of religion in false and less spiritual forms.

There is another point. Though our first-rate literature is Christian, and probably never was so distinctively Christian, it is otherwise with our second and third rate literature. That is either conventional or agnostic in its creed. It is not always aggressively agnostic. It does not always preach Spencer or Strauss, and probably does not care for them. But its task and temper is agnostic. It is humanist at best. It is pagan when it is worse. And at its worst it is pagan, pious, and fashionable, all at once, and goes to church with Becky Sharp[6] in her last saintly years. We do not deny that our current literature is healthy in the main. All we say is, that viewed in its spirit, and from a point distinctively Christian, its drift and temper are agnostic. Its religion, where it is not traditional and clerical, is but humane and philanthropic. It is one of the elegancies of life. We do not even venture to complain that this is so. Perhaps it is well that the depths and realities of religion should be kept out of any but first-class literature. And it may be that the religious novel, like the religious press, is, on the whole, a less healthy thing than the sweet and natural products of pure humanism. Give us Dickens and Besant before either Mrs. Ward or Miss Schreiner still. All we urge is this, that it is a misfortune if the mass of those who, for lack of imaginative power or intellectual vigour, do not read first-class literature are left with the delusion that the attitude of literature to faith is only what their acquaintance with literature would imply, and that all the passion is on the humanist side of life. And this is an error which something might be done to remedy (especially on behalf of the growing class of educated women) if the pulpit would from time to time boldly take an English poem for a text, and expound its spiritual movement from the firm standpoint of the gospel of Christ. We believe it is possible to do this without either wresting the text or forcing the gospel. Of course it calls for skill, and taste, and tact. It requires that the passage be thoroughly mastered, and the preacher saturated with its turns and shades as well as with its ideal unity. It is a task in which some will succeed better than others, just as there are some who excel in the expository treatment of Scripture, while others are at home only in the topical style. We are not alone in this suggestion. One well-known preacher has taken up Dante in this way. Several (though not from the pulpit) have gone through "In Memoriam." Browning has been turned to account. What could be less foreign to the pulpit than the *Letter of Karshish*, for instance, with its realism, its unearthliness, its spell of Christ, and the searching passion of its solemn close. There is much that is serviceable in Wordsworth. Milton waits to be relieved from the underserved neglect into which his obsolete theology

---

6. A character in William Makepeace Thackeray's *Vanity Fair* (1847–1848).

has cast his spiritual splendour and moral depth. It is a style of preaching which ought to be congenial in Scotland, at least, with its power and taste for sustained attention and serious treatment in pulpit themes. Probably enough the chief suspicions and objections may come not from the pulpit, but from the pew, which, if its beliefs ever are of iron, is in its methods as the northern iron and the steel. But what is suggested here might do something to prepare the way for the time when, as in Dante's or in Milton's day, the literature of passion and the literature of faith shall be either one or at one; when we shall no longer hear complaint, with old Isaac Watts,

> O why is piety so weak
> And yet the muse so strong;[7]

when faith shall get wings and imagination a conscience; when piety, as in Israel, shall be grand and yet sincere, and poetry in Christ be true to the fact and inspiration of man's central soul.

---

7. From Isaac Watts' "Two Happy Rivals, Devotion and the Muse" (1706?).

11

Mystics and Saints, 1894

THE PRESENT WRITER PUBLISHED last year, in a book called *Faith and Criticism*,[1] an essay in which he laid some stress on the harm done by mysticism, with its exit in metaphysics, to the true idea of revelation. To his great surprise he has occasionally heard that essay described and distrusted as mystical. And the reason seems to be that it insisted on personal intercourse with the personal, historic, and living Saviour as an indispensable condition of any revelation, in the true and religious sense of the word, namely, as bearing less on God's nature than on His will and work for mankind. If that be mysticism, of course faith is essentially mystic, and so is the revelation it answers. But that is not mysticism in the word's convenient and distinctive use. As a tendency in human thought, mysticism is, first, the reduction of religion to knowledge, to insight, to a γνῶσις [gnōsis], or to a philosophy, which makes contemplation or intuition the goal and essence of the perfect life. And, in the second place, it is the rejection of all mediation as a permanent element in this contemplation, and the insistence on direct contact between God and the soul in the region of ideas. It is the tendency in religion which is impatient of what is positive and historic. It promises a presence of God which is at once more real and rational than history affords. The God who directly touches a living soul can so easily be made to appear a real presence in comparison with the God who acts by a historic figure. And the God who is an object of knowledge or reason taxes the natural man less than the God who is an object of moral experience in such a reconciliation

---

1. Bennet, ed., *Faith and Criticism*. Forsyth's contribution to the volume was his essay "Revelation and the Person of Christ." Other contributors included W. H. Bennett, W. F. Adeney, Eric A. Lawrence, R. F. Horton, H. Arnold Thomas, F. Herbert Stead, E. Armitage, and Thomas Raleigh.

11: Mystics and Saints, 1894

as Christ's. Hence mysticism is a favourite resort of those who resent the authority of any tradition, as well as of those whose reason is more active than soul or conscience in their religious habit. Mysticism is mostly rational in the affinities of its theology. Indeed, its religion is at bottom simply a variety of the rational process. Its true antithesis is not rationalism, but history. It is a mistake to say, as some do, that "the mystic is one who at any point in the quest for truth or God deserts his reason for a higher, or seemingly higher, guide." Mysticism is essentially rational, and tends to be rationalistic. What Hegel plants at the foundation of certainty, and calls "the intuition of thought," is the root of mysticism. The vastest speculative systems are in essence mystic. They view religion in the form of knowledge, and they tend to make light of history and of volition and mediation as essential to religion. Mysticism is not a "denial of the sufficiency of reason," even of transcendent reason. It is still the action of reason in so far as it reduces faith to some form of philosophy, subjects it to some form of science, keeps it noetic in quality, and closes it in beatific *vision*. It transplants religion from the will to the intelligence, and makes belief a matter of evidence or rational sight rather than of faith, of personal influence and self-committal. It does not matter whether we take the more systematic mystics or the more vague and emotional. At the heart of all, mysticism is this union of two intelligences rather than two wills: and it may degenerate even into the union of two substances disguised with the name of spirits. It regards religion as fundamentally metaphysical, as a form of the knowledge of ultimate being, a phase of natural knowledge spiritualised. This is something different from the act of faith, which is moral, not an act of knowing, not a process of the natural intelligence spiritualised, but the one true supernatural act, the one true organ of the supernatural, finding its object in no mere object of noetic perception, however present, but in a historic person equally present. His union with us is not the mystic interfusion of two substances, however rarefied and dubbed spiritual; but it is real personal intercourse, and the ground of that certainty which is the deepest of all—the certainty which rests on a moral being like our central selves. Opposed to all mysticism is the faith (but not the uncritical faith) in a historic personal Saviour, intercourse with whom is the standing condition for ever and ever of all that is properly to be called religion. The judges of Christian truth are not, in the first place, reasonable men, but redeemed men. If our Protestantism mean anything distinctive it means that. And if it be weak for the hour, it is because the habit of the hour is to accept Christ, not as the Creator of a new creature, but in so far as He can be shown to commend Himself to lovers of truth, human instincts, social ideals, or æsthetic taste. We judge and elect our Judge. The mystic, be he visionary or rationalist, measures Christ by His precious but passing utility for effecting the union of the soul with God. The Christian finds that union only and ever in Christ, the historic and exalted Christ. This difference may seem either trivial or oversubtle. We believe it is just as trivial as the displaced molecule in the brain, or the little misbehaviour of a heart-valve. And it is just as subtle as the intangible gas which in time extinguishes life.

It will further illustrate my meaning if I take up another point. It is sometimes asked how, if we insist on the reality of direct contact with the living personality of Christ, we can deal with a Romanist who declares that he has the same evidence as ourselves, in personal experience, of communion with the Virgin Mary or any of the saints.

To which I should reply thus:—

1. The final certainty by which we test all, is a moral certainty. It is a matter of conscience. Conscience is the authority for truth no less than action. This is a world where truth exists ultimately for the sake of action, and we cannot therefore have two standards. This ethical standard is the distinctly Christian, and is in flat antithesis to the pagan nature worship which speaks in this wise: "If the miracle of the soul and the world does not touch men, if through its veil they do not see the face of God, neither will they believe though one rose from the dead." Thousands of Christian believers who had seen no God in the soul disprove that.

2. But we do not go far in a serious way into moral certainties till we discover the sense and certainty of guilt. Kant will soon take us there; however many Kantians may refuse to follow, who have more sympathy with his intellectual agnosticism than with his moral sense.

3. But if we are not to be left there, we must pass in our moral experience to the deeper and still more earnest sense of forgiveness, of reconciliation, of a world reconciled, a redemption, and atonement.

4. And there lies the world's last ethical certainty, the basis of all ethic which is at once humane and imperative—in a religious experience, the experience of guilt abolished by holy love. It is not the moral philosopher, nor the poetic Stoic, like Emerson, with his lucid but limited moral insight; it is not the man of mere insight or genius at all, however fine or holy, who is in possession of the fundamental moral experience, and the ultimate certainty of the soul. It is the man who really experiences the redemption of his conscience from guilt. The true foundation of modern ethics, and especially of the ethics of the future, was laid in the restoration of evangelical Christianity at the Reformation, and then faith became a new power and fashion of life, and the grace-renewed will displaced the illuminated mind as the highest thing in man.

11: Mystics and Saints, 1894

5. But to take the next step, this experience, in the great volume of competent testimony, is inseparable from the experience of the living presence and action of the historic Jesus as the Redeemer. Wherever that has been denied, the habit of thinking or speaking of guilt or deliverance from it has decayed, and religion is founded upon philosophic axioms and various intuitions, instead of moral experience of the most serious, profound, and passionate sort. The experience of redemption, and of Christ as the living Redeemer, are one and the same experience, one and the same act. We know our guilt and our pardon in the act of faith by which we realise the nature and presence of the Redeemer. He is identical with our very ultimate conscience and our final moral certainty.

6. He becomes, therefore, for us the test of all else. He is, in this capacity, the evangelical seat of authority. The seat of authority for the whole human conscience, and therefore the whole of human history, especially in the future, is the Redeemer. The ideal has often as much power to mock as to allure. The moral imperative may damn as many as it inspires. Neither ideal nor imperative can save—not even Christ as the ideal. Authority invests a dying king. Our Lord is our Redeemer. Conscience itself is but an occasional voice from this everlasting throne of the cross.

Of no saint or virgin, even in Catholic experience of their presence, has this been said. Nor could it be said without stepping, in the very statement, outside the Christian pale. The saints that are invoked are not prayed to in the sense in which the Saviour is. They may be auxiliaries in certain crises, but they are not the redeemers of the soul in its grand crisis, either individually or historically. The statements made about the presence and visitation of the saints must be brought to the test of our certainty in Christ. And if denied, they must be denied on the ground of that certainty and its implications.

7. The question under notice takes account of nothing beyond the mere subjective intensity or vividness of an experience. That goes for little in reality; though in an age when mere impression is prized, as it is today, it goes for far too much. It is not a question of subjective vehemence in the experience. It may be conceded that the experience of the visitation of saints felt by some Catholics has been much more intense than the experience which far better people in Protestantism have had of the Saviour. And, indeed, this communion of saints has in these Catholics themselves been more vividly felt than they ever realised the Saviour's nearness; and yet the reality of the Saviour's action has not been thought by that Church to be for that reason less than the action of saints. It is not a question of the vividness of the experience, but of the nature of it; and especially its ethical quality, its historic origin, and its effect on the conscience in connexion with guilt. And when that is realised, when we turn from the amount of an impression

or the vividness of an experience to its moral nature and result (as Protestants should who have not unlearned the soul of their own faith), then the question which seemed intellectually so plausible will display its religious inexperience. In a word, the criterion is not subjective, mystical, individual, and intense but objective, historic, positive, universal, and morally imperative where the deep decisions lie in a soul that is thorough with itself.

8. It is really a question which turns chiefly on the difference in kind in the objects of the experience. The most entrancing sense of the Virgin's glory is, after all, an æsthetic impression. It is not ethical in the sense in which the Redeemer's presence is. It is the impression of a vaguely glorious, spiritual presence; it is not the response to a Saviour's power. It is a state of the religious imagination rather than of the conscience. It is something the soul possesses, not something which possesses the soul. It tends to ecstasy rather than to assurance, to delight and comfort us rather than to remake and control us. It does not place us in the grasp of a mighty personality who has the right to our whole life, yea, to the conscience by which we stand against all the world. How can it? We know less than we crave to know about the historic personality of Jesus, but we know vastly less about the personality of His mother. We can establish mystic relations with her enlarged and glorified image, but we have nothing like the character, and especially the death, of Christ, which seizes us in a moral grasp and opens a heaven for the conscience more than for the imagination and the heart. This mystic devotion is not surprising in an age when women are asserting and securing a position they have never had before both in life, faith, and unfaith. But for their own sakes it must be corrected from sources more ethical and historic. It is not in Catholic lands, the lands of the religious imagination, that their new career has become possible. Woman worship means woman slavery. They have won what they have in lands where the Christian faith was more Protestant and moral, less of the imagination and more of the conscience, less mystic and more ethical, less inspired by the beatific vision and the sweetness of charity, and more controlled by the love of truth, the righteousness of faith, and the cleansing of the conscience, by the certainty of forgiveness in Christ alone.

12

THE WAY OF LIFE, 1897

A Sermon Preached Especially to Students, and More Particularly to the Freshmen (and Women), at Emmanuel Congregational Church, Cambridge, on October 18, 1896.

"The wicked have waited for me to destroy me: but I will consider Thy testimonies. I have seen an end of all perfection: but Thy commandment is exceeding broad."

—PSALM 119:95, 96

WHAT THE PSALMIST MEANS is this: all earthly perfection is limited; but God's law is limitless. It is set in the heavens. It is rooted in the earth. It is higher than the sphere of the sky; beyond the solid dome of the firmament. It is deeper than the depths of earth; none can dig through and pass beyond it. It is deeper even than Sheol which is under the earth—"If I make my bed in hell, Thou art there."[1] It is broader than the sea; beyond the horizon the reign of this law goes.

The whole passage is like a piece from a modern scientific poem, glorifying the universality of law, or the majesty of cosmic order and stability. Beyond all the forms of power that we see there is a world of power unseen, inexhaustible—a realm of law complete and infinite, embracing all the finite and partial laws which seem to us to clash and break. No sooner does a thing come to perfection than it begins to succumb to decay and death. No

---

1. Ps 139:8.

sooner do we reach one goal than another range rises on our sight. But there is a perfection that does not wither, and a law that succumbs to no other law. It is the perfection of the Eternal, who is above all change and embraces it. It is the law of the Almighty, which limits all law and itself is limited by none and cut short by none.

That is a great inspiration of the psalmist. What is the inference he draws from it?

That which lay in his heart next to the law of God was Israel. He writes anxiously, though inspiredly, faithfully. Israel was in peril. "I am Thine, save me."[2] "The wicked have waited for me to destroy me." That was Israel speaking in him. He was speaking for Israel. He was thinking, hoping for Israel! And the inference he drew from his inspiration was this: Would the law, the order of God, be so infinitely perfect if He allowed Israel to be destroyed, the Israel who honoured and prized that law in their worship and in all their national hopes and dreams?

Well, we have the history behind us and clear, which for the psalmist was still future and dark. We read centuries of national doom, and centuries of scientific progress. We know from the science and thought that the law and order of God are vaster than the psalmist dreamed, more stable and more broad. And we also know that Israel fell, and fell by its very worship of that law which the psalmist trusted for its endless security. He thought it linked Israel with all the stabilities of nature, conscience, and soul.

I. Inspiration and Inference

I beg you to notice, then, as the first suggestion from the text, the difference there may be in the Bible itself between *inspiration* and *inference*. It is an important thing when we come to interpret the Bible. The psalmist's inspiration was right. The law, order, plan, and purpose of God is infinitely broad. And because infinitely broad it is eternally stable. Being so broad, it includes under its control every power which could possibly rise up against it. And being master of every hostile power, of course it is eternally stable and sure. It was the spirit and law of God that taught the psalmist this certainty about itself. The inspiration of the Almighty gave him understanding.

But when it came to inference he was on different ground. His inference was that Israel's law and Israel's constitution were for ever indispensable to the vast designs and infinite purposes of God. He thought, like any Anglican or Roman Judaist, that his Church, his ritual, his priesthood was for ever bound up with the well-being and continuance of the world, material

2. Ps 119:94.

and spiritual. That is an inference which history has upset. Not only does the world get on very well without Judaism, but Judaism has to be destroyed that the world may get on, that the law of God may be made truly spiritual and infinite, and the soul redeemed to feel its greatness and its eternity.

Do not forget that in the Bible we have a mixture of inspiration and inference. And it is the great task laid on us in its study today to distinguish and separate these two. The great contribution which God has demanded from our age to the Bible is that we save its inspiration from its inferences. And the great contribution which He is making to our age by the Bible is to save us from its inferences by its inspiration. For instance, the writers of the Bible believed that God made the world in six days. It was inspiration to believe with their power and glory that God made the world. It was inference (poetic inference if you like) to believe that the world was made in six days without any evolution at all. We have learned on the strength of the inspiration to discard the inference. God has taught us in redeeming the world that He made it. He has taught us that He is Creator by the New Testament in a way that Genesis could not. But He has also taught us by a newer testament still how exceeding broad His making of the world was. It was a limited idea of perfection that supposed it to be done by six successive sweeps of creative power in as many successive days. God's way with the world was larger. His commanding word was broader. His time and patience with the world were longer. His method was deeper. But His power was no less. There was profound inspiration in the great vision of these six creative words. The idea of a vast creative *word* is grander than the idea of a great *wave* of creative power. For a word is the act of a will, and a wave may be but the movement of a force. So the *inspiration* of Genesis is right. And we hold to it. And it saves us from being much troubled when the *inference* of Genesis is upset, and evolving ages of creative will take the place of six sudden steps crowded into a week.

So in other parts of the Bible. Remember always the difference between passing inference and permanent inspiration, between the spirit of the age and the Spirit of Christ, between local and temporary belief and eternal, ageless faith.

II. The Inadequacy of Perfection

There is another point I ask you to notice, coming now to the ninety-sixth verse alone. It is an experimental verse. It expresses something the man had found out for himself—*the inadequacy of perfection*. He had *observed*, and *experienced*. He had *observed* in the course of his life that all visible perfection came to an end, that it was outgrown and left behind, that prosperity had its meridian and then its decline, that there was in all visible perfection some law which was its death sentence. But he had *experienced* the reality of a law which was final, perfect in itself, not to be outgrown, a complete, eternal, changeless whole, embracing all change, and inspiring all change. It was a law so perfect, that it could not be expressed in any earthly form or any human life. The forms of beauty burst or withered. The loveliest lives were checkered or brief. The finest health was not adequate to the whole power and destiny of the soul within. But the law of God was both perfect and eternal, broad beyond all the finished products of time, stable beyond all the chances of life, adequate to itself always. The loveliest, most perfect flower, statue, woman, or man was at the mercy of a brute with a hammer. But there was a perfection which could make that brute an angel and more. Earth's perfection first blossoms, then dies. God's perfection first dies, then blossoms and saves. The psalmist did not see the cross, but the cross was in what the psalmist saw.

That was his experience. Now the same result has been borne home to the great human experience in history. There is a kind of perfection that soon perishes, and there is a kind so vast that it hardly seems perfection; but it saves from perishing for ever. There is the perfection of *form*, which soon reaches its limits and becomes inadequate. And there is the perfection of *soul*, which every form breaks down more or less in the effort to express. And I say we have this written large in the long experience called history. As soon as the real power and infinitude of God's Spirit entered history in Jesus Christ all the existing ideals and forms of perfection became inadequate and imperfect. The soul broke through all possible forms of earthly expression, and triumphed in their very wreck, as it had always done in their perfection. If ever you think scholars are wrecking the Bible, recall this Christian relation of body and soul.

And for illustration take two things. Take a Greek statue and a Christian picture. Take the Apollo Belvidere or the Venus of Milo. You have nothing in the world more perfect in form. They express the height of earthly perfection. Art in that way could no farther go. The spirit of Greece uttered itself perfectly in such finished things. Place either of them by the side of one of the great Italian pictures—a Christ, a crucifixion, a saint, a resurrection, a paradise—by one of the great religious masters. You have in the picture a volume of meaning and power which makes the correcter statue seem even poor. You have a wealth of spirit and suggestion which makes the expression on the face of the statue insipid. Perfect as the form of Greece was, it became imperfect when you reached the face. There is no expression there. Greece had no soul, no heart, to express. In the light of the broad new perfection of God's Spirit the exquisiteness of human perfection soon came to an end. And the statue was too poverty stricken, with all its perfectness, too icily

12: The Way of Life, 1897

regular, too splendidly null, to express the vast spiritual wealth and infinite value of the human soul enriched with immortality by the Redeemer.

These statues and philosophies, so finished, so imperishable!

> Growth came when, looking our last on them all,
> We turned our eyes inwardly one fine day
> And cried with a start—What if we so small
> Be greater and grander the while than they?
> Are they perfect of lineament, perfect of stature?
> In both, of such lower types are we
> Precisely because of our wider nature;
> For time, theirs—ours, for eternity.
>
> To-day's brief passion limits their range;
> It seethes with the morrow for us and more.
> They are perfect—how else? they shall never change:
> We are faulty—why not? we have time in store.
> The Artificer's hand is not arrested
> With us; we are rough-hewn, nowise polished:
> They stand for our copy, and, once invested
> With all they can teach, we shall see them abolished.

And these Christian painters, even when they painted broken saints with faulty drawing,

> Made new hopes shine through the flesh they fray,
> New fears aggrandise the rags and tatters:
> To bring the invisible full into play!
> Let the visible go to the dogs—what matters?[3]

These words are from a poem of Browning's, "Old Pictures in Florence." Take it down and try to make something of it. It is not simple. But it is not the simple things that make the soul. The greatest powers are those that break through language and escape. I cannot put into a sermon all I want to say on this text. But Browning has it. His reach mostly exceeds his grasp. And that is why he was so sure of heaven.

Only think of the lordly Plato and the Lord-led Paul—the leisurely Plato and the passionate Paul—the splendid poet-thinker and the broken, tender, persecuted, mighty apostle. Which of them represents the true perfection of God, the final, real, universal perfection of the soul, the perfect action of the spirit in history? The perfection of Greece broke down. It broke from within. It was broken from without. So did the perfection of Judæa. The elaboration of law killed the soul. But the new law of faith and love triumphed. The infinite

---

3. From Robert Browning's poem, "Old Pictures in Florence" (1855).

perfection, the unutterable love, of the miserable cross was the only thing capable of saving man and setting him on a new and nobler career. Modern history stands on the broad, deep law of Christ. "I understand more than the ancients, because I keep Thy precepts."

You are in this university, many of you, to learn the best pagan idea of perfection. You ought to know it and often pursue it. But you are here, in this and every church, to learn how limited, how worldly it is, how inadequate to the real greatness of the soul, how imperfect before the perfectness of Christ. You must learn how much more perfect is good heart than good form, and how much broader is the glory of the crucified Christ than the gleam of the radiant Apollo. Our perfection is not our inward harmony, our personal harmony; it is not in the exquisite relation of our parts to each other as in a statue. It is not a character in perfect taste. It is not a balanced nature; it is not self-contained. *Art,* even ethical art, is not perfection. Nor is it our social harmony. It is not in our kindly relations to each other; it is not in readjustment of conditions; it is not brotherly love and social peace. *Socialism* is not perfection. But our perfection is in our relation, our attitude to the Father. It is the harmony of reconciliation in Jesus Christ. It is *faith*. The man of faith with many faults and some shames is more perfect than the flawless man, the perfect gentleman, who has no relations with the unseen, no dealings with its God, no trust in its love, no sense of the unspeakableness of heavenly things by earth's finest forms, chords, colours, or tongues.

III. The Broad and the Narrow

Lastly, I would speak of the final clause in the passage, "Thy commandment is exceeding broad." And first as to the word "broad," and next as to the word "commandment."

1. The present time is one to which the word "broad," appeals. Many people are escaping from narrow and rigid laws of religious truth. God is leading them out of Egypt. A new study of the Bible has made us feel in what a large, free world its writers moved. It is a world of imagination, of soul, of infinite spiritual range and power. Then science has opened to us world on world of the vast and the small. The universe has become an infinite thing. Politics have taken the note of freedom and enlargement in all parties. Society is undergoing a new emancipation. Two great hosts—women and workmen—have become conscious of new possibilities, a new career. The awakening of these two sections alone has made a vast change and will make a greater still. Even the young are infected with the like spirit. They are interested in many things they did not care for before. They form societies to discuss them. They are

12: The Way of Life, 1897

not content to take the traditional lines. They have their intelligence roused. They begin to feel that they were meant for better things than athletics and singsongs. They dimly perceive a new, great world breaking into view around them. They have more access than ever before to the world of knowledge and action. They are full of confidence, which it is easy to snub, but better to guide. It chiefly needs to be tempered by a deeper acquaintance with their world and with themselves. They are full of sympathy for things broad, free, genial. You come up here some of you, men and women of you, and you pass into a new world which is larger than you have yet known. You have lived at home, perhaps, up to now. It has been a dear world, but a smaller than you enter here. Perhaps it has even been a world of narrow interests, parochial interests, and you come into one of the great intellectual centres of the world. The religion in which you have been reared, though very genuine and very deep, has perhaps been of a narrow and timid kind. You have had no real preparation for the stir of new, vivid, and wide ideas which may meet you here. You cannot learn to fly in a hencoop. For you soon, if not already, the word "broad" will have a fascination. You will meet people, and make friends of people, perhaps, who may tempt you to despise and revolt from the circle of things and thoughts you have grown up in. The old creeds may seem antiquated in the light of new science. The old faith may seem perhaps good enough for those you leave behind, but not for you. The Bible of the apostles and prophets will suffer by comparison with the broad new science, and the broad new literature, and the broad new thoughts of the age. The society of your native place may seem a poor, narrow clique compared with the freedom offered by the advanced society of the modern woman and the modern man. The Church you were reared in, converted in perhaps, may come to seem to you a little sect which you want to leave behind when you hear from your new companions of their no Church, or their old Church, their high Church, their broad Church. You may be invited to consider your Nonconformity a narrow affair compared with the imposing constitution and ritual of the Church most influential here and elsewhere. You may even be led to think (for there is no limit to their audacity) that there is more devotion in the services of the Established Church than in the worship of your own. You will forget that that rests with you. And, unlike many a simple great one gone, you will not "abide among your own people."

I sympathise with you greatly. I know the spell of things broad, great, boundless, free. It is a spell you ought to feel. Your education here will not do what it should for you if you do not feel that. Religion has suffered unspeakably from narrow notions and infinitely from narrow hearts. But it suffers so much because it is in its nature free. It is the eagle that suffers from captivity, and the lark; it is not the mole. In faith's name let us be broad. It is God's commandment.

But remember this. Do not mistake breadth of view for breadth of soul. Faith is not a thing of views nor a thing of feelings. It is a thing of soul. It is greatness of soul that is the glorious liberty of the sons of God. There is a breadth which is very shallow. I have found it very common among people who were always talking of breadth of view. God is exceeding broad. The soul of Christ is broader than all the world and the great souls in it. But remember the breadth of God is *deep* and *high*. The ideal city was foursquare every way, equal in height, breadth, and depth. You gain little if you gain in breadth only to lose in depth, if you are broad and low, if you grow just as shallow as you grow wide. There is a breadth which is mere indifference. And a man may have very wide and free notions about life because he has no real notion of God or his soul at all. The breadth of God is deep, and it is intense. There is no religious narrowness more narrow than the breadth which outgrows all depth, intensity, reality of faith, all trust of the heart, all positive belief about things unseen or a world to come. To *see* broad is not to *be* broad. And the real broadening forces are not those that extend our vision, but those that enlarge ourselves, our souls, our manhood, womanhood, our faith. There is a saving narrowness. All the breadth of the world present and to come entered by a narrow way. It is narrowed down to Christ; narrowed down, down to the cross of Christ, to the soul, greatness and glory there. And if ever you grow cold to that, if ever you lose the sense of infinite greatness in that brief life and obscure death, you are growing into the narrowest narrowness of all—the smallness of the thin, shallow person whose ambition and whose speech aim at being thought broad, liberal, emancipated, advanced, rational before anything else.

2. So I come to the word "commandment." The breadth of God is in His commandment. It is a focused breadth. It is moored, concentrated, a breadth gathered in intense centres and positive lines. It follows the lines of positive truth and positive law. It is a matter, first of all, of conscience and heart. It is not the vague freedom of the winds, but the rooted and grounded freedom of an established soul. Yes, that is what we want—not an established Church, but an established soul; not free thought at first, but a free soul. And a free soul is a good soul, a redeemed soul, vowed to the moral law of God, acquainted with repentance, full of faith, given up to the law of love in Jesus Christ. Let no broad notions lead you to think that you can trifle with God's law in your conscience, or ignore His wide love concentrated for the world in the cross of Jesus Christ. The cross is a mere speck in the tract of time, but it is the living centre of broad and full eternity. The depth, intensity, height, and breadth of all spiritual being is there. The whole freedom of the soul is there. The largeness and hope of all the future are there. The obligation of the cross is the first commandment

and the last. This is the one broad commandment, that we believe in Christ, live in Christ. This is the real condition of moral freedom, of soul freedom, of heart release and largeness, of human greatness and spiritual range. This plants us in infinity, breaks the one narrowing power of sin, brings life and immortality to light, unites us, redeemed, with God, who is the eternal amplitude of all we can be or know. You find all great things, broad, free, kindling things, thus. Christ is the Lord of them all and the Giver of them all. "For I am persuaded, that neither death, nor life, nor height, nor depth, nor length, nor breadth, shall be able to separate us from the love of God, which is in Christ Jesus our Lord."[4]

---

4. Rom 8:38–39.

13

THE EMPIRE FOR CHRIST, 1900

Preached in the City Temple on Tuesday Afternoon, May 8, being the Annual Sermon on behalf of the Colonial Missionary Society.

> *"The little one shall become a thousand, and a small one a strong nation: I the Lord will hasten it in its time."*
>
> —ISAIAH 60:22

WE BEGIN WITH A creative point, and we end with a collective world; we begin as mere tribesmen, and we end with a mighty nation. We begin as single souls, and we end and rest in the collective Personality of God. We begin with a forsaken cross, and we end with the glorious heavenly Church that filleth earth and heaven. That is God's way with His work. It is the way of growth, of progress, of evolution, and all by way of humiliation. It is not a ready-made creation that we see around us; a creation that God had done with would be a creation dead. God is always creating. He is Creator in His nature; wherever He is and works there is creation. Providence is itself creation. Creation and increase have the same root; they have the same root as words, and they have the same root as realities. The little one becomes a thousand. It is not that nothing becomes a thousand, nor is it that the little one is a thousand in the twinkling of an eye. There is a growth, a becoming, a path, a process, between the one and the many. Along that path the Creator goes as creator. The creative presence and principle rules every point of the evolutionary process. It is only the hand that made you that makes you grow. There is an old saying that the perseverance of the saints is made up of ever new beginnings. The cross which justifies is the perpetual source of the Spirit that sanctifies. And the same is true in its measure of the evolution of things. The Creator is a faithful creator, who, having created His own world, creates it unto the end. The race which began in love is continued by love. We are often told that creation is creation by evolution, but we must also remember that evolution is evolution by creation. The action of God is not separable from the presence of God. The Creator is not only in His own creation, but in His creative growth. He not only sustains, He unfolds. He not only upholds what is permanent, He adds what is new at every point. Or is there at every point something new? That is the real problem of evolution in a word. In the process of change we have not just something else, another of the same, but we have something more and something better.

And what is the explanation of God in the little one, the presence of God in the atom, it may be? The physical explanation is the thing which fascinates us for the hour, but that is still a riddle. The real explanation does not lie in that direction; the real explanation is a moral one. God's indwelling in the little one is an act of humiliation. The secret of the new-born Christ is the miracle of the primal germ. The second creation explains the first. In Christ and in Him as crucified the world was created no less than redeemed, and developed no less than created. It was God's self-humiliation which redeemed the world that also created it, whether it be the world of the thousand or the world of the little one, whether the universe or the atom or the babe. It was the same act of self-humiliation which made Godhead to be born as a little child and to appear as the first speck of life or the lone atom of matter. The height of omnipotence was the power to humble Himself, to empty Himself, to go out of Himself and His own bliss. He leaves His native and eternal blessedness and settles in a foreign world. The eternal Father expatriates Himself, and in His Son becomes a Pilgrim Father to found a new world. Some speak of the world as due to emanations of the Divine, I would speak rather, if I reverently might, of the emigration of the Divine, of His going forth in His person, and not of His sending forth His waves. Might I venture on the expression that it was by a Divine emigration and settlement in Christ and His Spirit that earth became a colony of Him and the Church a mission colony upon the face of the earth? The real idea in the heart of creation was not by almighty magic to make something out of nothing, but it was by moral miracle to make Himself of no account, to become a child and an alien on the earth, to suffer and to die. The thousand, the million, the Infinite, becomes a little one; and that is the only way in which the little one ever becomes a thousand.

I have spoken generally; may I speak in more detail? This way of growth is God's patient way of creating and completing the world. First,

II: Published Sermons

God is in the world as force or vitality. The course of our physical world, since it arose out of the fiery nebula in ages incalculably remote, has been the action and the reality of the forces of God, but about that I will not speak further upon an occasion like this. I will go on to say that the presence of God the infinite in the little one means the presence of God the most pitiful, and on that may I dwell for a little.

The Pity of God

The ruling passion of the infinite God towards the little one surely must be pity. You have that patient process illustrated in the growth of man from the infant. All the most excellent faculty of the greatest man was once in the puling fashion of a helpless child. To his mother he was not great at all, but only dear. The mightiest monarch or genius or saint could once do no more for himself than the beggar's baby, and when they were stripped and washed you could not tell the one from the other.

Naked we every one came into the world—naked of all those distinctions which grow upon life, and turn its first simplicity into so complex a thing. Naked, helpless, pitiable, the baby man appears, needing all manner of care, more care than the young of any other creature, and for a longer time. He appeals to pity and affection, and without them he must die. He moves the pity and love of women, and his true guardian angel is his mother. And if it be a long time since any of us said "mother," in heaven our angel doth always behold the face of our Father in heaven.

But the poor little one moves more than a mother's pity when it is plunged so utterly helpless into such an old and clever world, he has the pity of God. Like a father the Lord pitieth these feeble things, bewildered and stunned at their entry on such a cunning world as this. May we not let fancy go? May we not figure the helplessness and speechlessness of the babe as due to its utter bewilderment with the shock of emerging, naked and alone, upon such an awful stage, and a house so full and fine?

But there falls upon the child, like a sheltering cloud, the pity of God. That is also unspeakable, like the amazement in its own wild, unspeculative eyes. And so these two look at each other and say nothing. The pity of the Lord shelters the child in a cloud of ignorance, and that pity is the first and closest swaddling clothes the infant wears. And it is the pity of the Lord that rears it by all the sweet nursing mothers and all the strong nursing fathers, and all the stern and helpful shocks of life; it is still the pity of the Lord that makes a world for the soul to unfold in, and it is the faithful merciful Creator who adds the cubits to its stature and the faculty to its will. By the Lord's pity and grace the little one becomes a thousand, and the poor thing a great hero, and the manger-born a mighty saviour. May I not go further, may I not whisper this? At last all the kingly faculty of man falls upon its second childhood; here-enters the manger in the shape of a coffin. He has to accept the humiliation and the new birth of death; he has again to enter a vast strange world. Do you not think, when he emerges into that unseen world, and into the awful wonder, wisdom, and glory there, he will feel alone, bewildered, and stunned again as when he was born here? The old man is but an infant of days as he enters that world in which this world is but as a womb. And can you not believe that there God, the faithful Creator, awaits him, the measureless infinite pity of the Lord will be beforehand with the poor soul, and will prepare a place and take him up in His arms and call a nurse who (like Moses's) may be his mother, or his Beatrice, like Dante's, and slowly that Grace will open his second life to the Love that moves the sun and all the stars. And our immortality, like our mortality, will thus begin in the same Lord's merciful care which has borne us and carried us all the days of old.

God As Thought

God is in His growing world as thought. I would illustrate the same principle from the history of the human race and its civilisation. What a creative miracle! What a world out of nothing! What have we today, and what had we at the outset of it all? What we have today is unspeakable. Who can take stock of the whole store of human achievement? What adequate encyclopædia could be issued by our times? What account could there be of the amazing wealth which the human spirit has acquired in its career to this day? What report could do justice to our inheritance from the past, our faculty in the present, our resource and promise for the future? Where could it be registered and appreciated in its totality? Nowhere except in the sympathy of the soul-searching God, whose own inspiration has given us this understanding. And who but God Himself can assess the vast and various wealth of the human heart and soul and will at this late day—the silent quality of our conquest over nature, over the slothful self, and over the problems of the world? Pass outside England and its splendid isolation. Enlarge your sense of splendour by placing your own land in its proper place as a member only of the European system. Make an effort, and realise something of foreign achievement and pre-eminence. Do but think of the art, the science, the enterprise, the thought, the passion, the hope, the faith, the social victories, the material triumphs, the fabrics, the constitutions, the spiritual ideals and the spiritual conquests, aspirations, tragedies, heroisms of our time. Think of it all and multiply it all, and then ask yourself what it all sprang from. From a first simple pair in a garden you may say, with your fathers. Or from a few pairs you may say with newer science; or, at least from a crude and primitive stage, whether the first human pairs were few or many. But, in any case, does it not all stand upon the five simple senses of some very simple people? Faith itself comes by hearing. The solemn increase has grown out of five barley loaves and a few small fishes. Of course there is the soul, the reason within: but its writing is invisible till it feel the fire of experience; its speech is unheard till it find a sounding-board in the sensible world. The reason is not the product of the senses, but it does not get to work till sense presses the button and releases the power. "The reason of a man within him," as one beautifully says, "is like the blind old Theban prophet to whom his daughter described the flight of the birds; he prophesied upon the report."[1] The thousand thousand glories of man's greatness today are the constant creation of an ever-present God residing in soul as soul resides in sense, interpreting soul as soul interprets sense. They are His creation from beginnings mean and small, and the splendours of man's heaven are but a galaxy of God-glorified dusts. It is because God divides Himself without end that we multiply and increase, and it is because He never loses Himself, however far out of Himself He goes, but He forever finds Himself in our increase, that it is growth and greatness at all. The majesty of human progress is the humiliated God finding Himself in man and rising again in Christ Jesus to be in a Church what He has always been in the Eternal Spirit. If the little one ever become a thousand it is because the Infinite became a little one.

The Choice of Destiny

I should like now to ask your attention to this. I should like to point out by way of illustrating the subject more practically, how our immortal destiny turns on a choice of the will which is brief to our experience but final in its effect, empirically brief but of eternal moment. "Choose well, your choice is brief but yet endless."[2] When we enter the moral world we are in a world where we do not follow simply the pressure of a mighty force behind but we are ourselves called upon to become the greatest of contributory forces, and to make revolutions in ourselves and the world which are more than all the evolutions that went before. But I cannot dwell upon that. I want to pass, if you please, to the latter portion of the verse, "The small one a strong nation." That social growth

---

1. This appears to be Forsyth's own translation of words from Johann Georg Hamann's early London writings (published in Volume One of Frederick Roth's eight-volume edition of *Hamann's Schriften*).

2. These words of Goethe's were widely quoted during the nineteenth century.

13: The Empire for Christ, 1900

also must carry God as truly as the cosmic growth does, and the same God who works by humiliation always. His public relations are as real and constant as His cosmic relations. Social development is only safe and permanent if God, who made the worlds in Christ, go with every step and guide every great step in the extension of states, no less than in the spread of the Church. State and Church do not show forth the cross in the same way; but can there be any sound principle for the evolution of the State which is not the principle of the evolution of the human soul? And can there be a real evolution of the soul except by the principle of redemption which makes the Church? If the cross guided the cosmic process, the cross also rules the social march and leads the generations on. The methods are different, but the principle of society, the principle of the Church are the same. I say you certainly have this principle of Divine evolution in the growth and spread of the Church towards the Kingdom of God. The little one becomes a thousand, and even a mighty nation. First, to begin with the Lord Himself, you have the feeble little Jesus; then the obscure saint; then the neglected prophet; then the unregarded Saviour, the crucified Son of God; then the invisible King of Glory. First you have only the Saviour's own faith in Himself and His Father: yea, you have that faith reduced on the cross to a spark in the night, but a spark which was really the sun for our system. First, I say, you have Christ's own faith, then you have a disciple or two blundering along to light, then a band of apostles easily excited and easily rebuffed, stunned and dubious in the great crisis; then 120 waiting in an upper room, then the establishment and endowment of the Church with power from on high by the Holy Ghost. Then there were added to them about 3,000 souls; then you have the real primate of the apostles in the person of the great colonial missionary. I mean St. Paul. You have St. Paul, the great emigrant, nay nomad, of the faith, with his itinerancy among the Jewish colonies, and his founding of churches by their means. Like the other apostles, Paul was a missionary who acted through the colonies of his race; and he mastered their dream of Jewish imperialism with the subtler saving imperialism of the cross of Christ. He always made for the Jewish colonies and their synagogues first. He made the colonies advance agents of the Church.

I should like to invite special attention to the part played by three ideas in the evolution of Christianity and its conquest of the world. These are: first, the imperial idea; second, the colonial idea, the idea of national expansion, peaceful and free; and third, the idea of the cross upon this public scale, the idea of sacrifice, service, and reconciliation in their large and political sense.

II: Published Sermons

The Imperial Idea

As to the first, I shall only remind you of the universal, permanent, and commanding quality of the Gospel idea both in Christ's own mind and especially in the imagination of Paul. It aimed at nothing less than the world, nothing lower than the mastery of the world, nothing short of its perpetual mastery by a simple, absolute Head. The imperial institutions of the times were not without a great effect upon the ideals and the language of the first Christianity—only not upon its methods. For instance, there is growing evidence from Roman inscriptions that show that the striking phrases and notions of the Imperial Government were quickly caught up and fitted on by the early Christian faith, especially in the East. The deity of the Emperor offered at least a terminology for the deity of Christ. If an emperor was "Lord" in the public edicts, the Saviour was still more so in the Christian faith. If the title was carved on the monuments which Christians daily saw, it was the more readily engraved upon the Christian imagination of faith. To call Christ "Lord" had a very definite meaning for an Asiatic Christian, and a very dangerous one, one very likely to provoke State persecution. It was setting up not only another king but another Emperor, one Jesus. The Greek adjective which describes the Supper as the Lord's Supper in 1 Cor. xi. 20 (and which later came to describe as the Lord's the first day) had been nowhere else found, and was supposed to be an invention of Paul's—till now we read it in the Government inscriptions of Asia which Paul and many of his readers saw and heard daily. It means there Imperial, pertaining to the Emperor. For Paul the Roman Empire was but a sketch, a first draft and framework of the universal Church, and the *locum tenens*[3] of a Christianity also imperial. And the imperial language was none too large for his dream either of Christ or His kingdom. By its very nature Christianity was imperial. It was universal, imposing, insatiable, aggressive, even overturning, but always conquering. It was commanding, exclusive, nay absolute in its claim; it was stable, nay eternal; it aimed at a wide franchise and a world-wide peace. It was not military in its methods, nor commercial, but it was imperial in its range, its style, and its devotion to one crowned Head, whose spirit was its genius and whose will was its law.

The Colonial Idea

But I wish to say more about the other two ideas—the colony and the cross. However imperial, Christianity was the product not of an empire but of a

---

3. A place-holder.

13: The Empire for Christ, 1900

nation. It was a national extension, the spiritual extension of a certain nation within the empire, that really paved the way for the extension of the Church. The Church arose in a nation with a tendency to disperse and colonise. And it was a nation whose every effort at military extension was foiled, a nation whose cosmopolitanism was on quite different lines from the great empire it outlived, a nation whose extension (as became the mother of Christianity) was not the organised extension of conquest, but the free, pacific, and informal extension of colonisation; a nation, too, not beloved by the military nations around, and making no effort to be beloved till its spirit was changed by the Gospel and a new landless Israel rose from the ruins of the old. Universal Christianity was planted by the Christianity of an insulated yet a colonising race, whose doings were not State expeditions, but casual emigrations; they were free, therefore, to become the organs and agents of a faith still more free than their patriotism, for the use of a spiritual and supernatural God. Such seems the method of the outgoing God, the self-exiling God, from the days of emigrant Abraham to those of Christ and His outcast cross.

The spread of the Kingdom of God owes most, perhaps, to the great colonising races—to the Jews, the Germans, the Anglo-Saxons. To the mere conquering races, like Spain or France, it owes little but misfortune. The upbuilding of the kingdom has been brought about not by centralisation, but by a dispersion; not by a vast organisation, but by a mighty principle; not by the French and Roman policy, but by the Teutonic. Emigration became missionary. The first missions from England went to follow up her colonies. They went to the recent American plantations, and they were the work of that wonderful commonwealth and its protector's teeming genius. Little England has gone on since then to dot the world with the English genius and faith. Little Nazareth mastered Israel, but before that little Israel had spread itself on the Roman world, and its creed laid a spell on the better Pagan mind. The Jewish colonies and their synagogues were stars on the Pagan night, and some of them, kindled by Christ, grew suns. The dispersed of Israel were the points of origin for the kingdom of Christ. And the dispersed of England have in her colonies carried the principles of that kingdom over more of the world than it ever covered before. And now, if a missionary movement were to sweep over our principal colonies like that which swept over the motherland when the colonies themselves were rising a century ago, what might the effect not be for the world! Think of what the seizure of one of our American colonies by the missionary spirit has already done for the heathen world. I mean America. America is an English colony which began as the whole teeming creation did, in an emigrant pilgrim fatherhood, a humiliation, an exile, a self-expatriation of the divine. But I am thinking most of the mission which a colony is, and not of the missionaries it may send out. Trade, I am aware, has a mission which few of the traders know, and single evangelists certainly have theirs. Missionary societies have repeated in the last century the conquests of the Church's first age. But political societies, like the colonies with their free institutions, have a part to play which is all their own in the saving of the world. The great missionary on earth is the Church, and the mission of the Church exhibits the great principle that only a society can save society—under Christ.

Now these colonies are free societies, like the Church. I mean they are not like the old classical and mechanical colonies of Greece, deliberate and organised expeditions of the State. They have grown up spontaneously, they were not manufactured. They are political bodies of a natural and not a fabricated kind, which have grown with an amazing speed and power. And for the purposes of the free kingdom of God such political societies have a great part to play if they will; and so has the old mother State through them. A colony is a settled missionary. The very existence of colonies from a Christian race opens a kind of missionary action which is denied to individuals or boards. A prolific race with the adventurous temper and the governing faculty may be, by its colonies, the vastest influence for covering the world with Christian society and institutions. If the little primitive Church has in these last days grown upon the earth to thousands and millions, why is it? Is it not chiefly because of the colonising, the self-multiplying, the self-settling power of the races who believe most in a self-respecting God—an out-going, home-bring, all-subduing God? God took up our own isles as a very little thing, but now they sit upon the circle of the earth in which their inhabitants are as grasshoppers. Britain covers the globe with little Britains, which not only make up the greater Britain, but do something to make and extend the Kingdom of God. The expansion of England has, on the whole, meant the extension of the Kingdom of God. There are many shameful deductions to be made, but on the large whole is not that so? Boasting is excluded when we know the facts, and know ourselves. But is it not true what John Stuart Mill said, with his severe ethics and his calm judgment: "We are the power which of all the world best understands liberty; and whatever may have been our cross in the past, we have attained to more of conscience and moral principle in our dealings with foreigners than any other nation seems either to conceive as possible or recognise as desirable."[4] Our colonists have taken their religion with them, and in

---

4. A slight misquotation of words from Mill's *Considerations on Representative Government* (1861): "[Great Britain] at least keeps the markets of the different countries open to one another, and prevents that mutual exclusion by hostile tariffs, which none of the great communities of mankind, except England, have yet completely outgrown. And in the case of the British possessions it has the advantage, especially valuable at the present time, of adding to the moral influence, and weight in the councils of the world,

13: The Empire for Christ, 1900

many cases their living faith. The action of God has thrilled along our far-flung line. And the colonies have developed forms of Church life freer and more spontaneous than the Motherland. They have shown that Christianity not only can flourish without a State Church, but better without it. That a fee people, left to itself, requires that its Church be free, as an establishment can never be. The Imperial idea is the centralised sense—in the military Roman or Napoleonic sense—is hateful and fatal. But it is another thing in the sense of free racial federation. That federation is a Free Church idea. The Free Churches represent the unity of a principle in the face of an organisation, and it is made possible by the existence of our colonies. They set forth the difference between a military empire of the Latin type, with a dominating centre, and a constitutional empire of the Teutonic type, whose parts cohere in honourable freedom about a centre of affection, and whose ports are open to the traffic of the world. The little one has not grown to a huge one, but to a thousandfold. Yet! Yet! What if the thousand should mistake the moral conditions of their freedom? What if the thousand in their recoil upon the motherland should smother the little one in an unspiritual embrace? What if a young, lusty, and prosperous race should scout the vigilance of the old liberty, the source of the old freedom, the obedience of the old faith, and the moral conditions of the old power? Is it certain that Empire, even in our pacific sense, if left to itself, might not relapse into Empire in the godless and soulless sense? Man in high place is, as it were, in office in the inverse; and the exercise of office increases the love of power. And we English in particular are a governing race, with pride enough, not to say insolence enough; and it might easily enough turn us merely into a domineering race if we do not take the cross with us, if we leave behind us the moral condemnation of the Divine growth. English imperialism has more than any other been accompanied by the moralised and missionary spirit. Like other Empires, it has too often taken the sword; but oftener than other Empires it has taken it by the blade, and repented and made it the cross. There was never such converted and missionary politics seen in the history of the world as our Indian Empire, or even our present Egyptian policy. We have striven to atone by the way we keep for much that needed atoning in the way we won. But I have only said that our Imperialism has been accompanied by the missionary spirit; I have not ventured to say that it is permeated by it, controlled by it. There are many problems far from simple yet to be solved in the importing of Christian ethics into affairs on the political and historic scale. I admit that the mode of applying the Christian principle differs

---

of the Power which, of all in existence, best understands liberty—and whatever may have been its errors in the past, has attained to more of conscience and moral principle in its dealings with foreigners than any other great nation seems either to conceive as possible or recognise as desirable."

in the public from the individual's case. It is less direct, more elastic, more opportunist. It is not so simple and off-hand as ethical enthusiasts think. But is it possible in the long run to separate Empire from ethics? I mean, of course, Christian ethics. There is no other now that we need consider. Is it possible even for our free colonies to grow in Freedom and cohere in a commonwealth without public and private Christian faith to rule their lusty vigours? Can even the British type of Imperialism be saved from sinking into the coarser type apart from a real control by the cross of faith? I do not speak of British hearts. I have little faith in patriotic ardours, historic tradition, or in racial prestige for anything so great and long as the ultimate destiny of an Empire. Races deteriorate; they sink by their own weight, and the national soul becomes debased by its own power, unless progress is sanctified by the Divine and humble action which makes extension real growth. Every step of the evolving world is possible only by the indwelling energy and purpose and principle of God; we have no power even to crucify Him except He gives it us from above. So at every step of the expanding realm we need Christ and His public principle of conscience above convenience. Are you going to shut Him out of all but Church history? Is He to become a mere ecclesiastical Person at home or a President of missions abroad? The greater the society the more it needs a Christian sanction and a Christian cement. "Rule Britannia" will never keep Britain fit to rule even herself, and mere patriotism can never carry the power or peril of a great realm. But there must be living faith, and the public morals that grow from living faith in Christ and His moral redemption. The question is, Shall we gain the Christian conscience fast enough to save us and our own rule? The Church itself is but imperfectly moralised as yet; whole sections of it are but religious, and little more. But the Church has a staying power that the State has not—in her faith. The State has only its righteousness, its morality. Shall the State be moralised in time to save its vast material empire from ethical collapse? What I want chiefly to do is to urge the need of cultivating the Christian bond between ourselves and our colonies, even more than the patriotic. I want to urge that our vast national expansion must carry Christ with it, and the Christian type of public conduct if our prosperity is not to recoil upon us and make us topple over like a broken wave. The Church must save the Empire. We hear speech sometimes of the State protecting the Church. It is absurd. It is to speak of the sinner protecting the Saviour, or philosophy the Gospel. It is the Church in the sense of the Gospel that must protect the State, save the Empire from the risk of its own inflation, and enable it to carry its needful weight of mail. It is the personal vital faith which makes the Church that must be the moral regulation of the growing State. We need the cross for Church and for State, but for State and public purposes our direct need is the cross that moralises more even than the cross that forgives. Our churches are entrusted with the reconciling power of the cross for the peace of the soul, but what directly concerns the State is the moral authority of the cross, its public and social principle, its responsible type of righteousness, and its reconciling imperial action. We have now entered on the epoch of the moralising of the two great public passions, patriotism and religion. They were already gallant and noble, but the note of righteousness, the full power of the cross's edict of sacrifice, has not yet had its true place in them for the general mind. Yet it grows and swells. More and more we ask in all great national movements the question good men ask of their own conduct, "Is it just?" and "Is it generously just?" And what is this but inviting into our growth God who alone gives increase—God who grows by scattering, who finds by loss, and rules by service? The true Imperialism, especially in a people of colonial dispersion, is based on sacrifice. Yes, you admit it cannot be unless each live in a spirit of sacrifice to the whole. But I mean more than that, I mean the sacrifice of the whole to God. And I could not mean that in a vague way. I mean the avowed subordination of national conduct to the public moral principle into which God Himself condensed His whole action upon the world on the cross. I mean sacrifice whose nature and object is not simply to consolidate, but to rescue and to reconcile. I mean the idea of reconciliation as a public principle, at the cost of the pagan idea of retribution.

State and Church

I have spoken of what the Kingdom of God owes to the colonising principle. That is historically so. But it is so in a deeper sense. The Kingdom of God rests not only on the outgoing of certain races, but still more on the outgoing of God Himself. The salvation of the world is due to the settlement of God on it in His Son, His Spirit, His Church. Earth becomes a colony of heaven because of the migration here of God and His organising of a free community in this outlying part of His universe. You will tell me this is a fanciful idea; will you pardon me? It is the cross of Christ which is the historical focus, the actual and the moral lever of the world. There is the ancestral fire where all our fresh altars are kindled, and our fresh enterprises hallowed; there our fresh ideas are guided and sobered. They are sacred if they carry with them not the mere banner of the cross, but the control of the cross. Empire means for any people of the cross not self-assertion, not aggression, not capture, but responsibility for the world, sacrifice for it, the purpose of the passion to reconcile it either in evangelical or political form. That is the real national establishment of the church. If our ideas are large let them not be loose. Let our piety not be vague. Let us force our dreams into moral definition. We are not literary men, but prophets of the pressing conscience. Let us be perfectly explicit with ourselves and the public. Self-sacrifice does not mean self-immolation or self-extinction. To lose the existence of self is to lose the power of sacrificing self. A nation with no self has nothing to serve the world with. Let us avoid vague altruisms on the one hand and vague patriotisms on the other—vague patriotisms varnished but not hallowed by vague pieties. Large empire and vague piety go ill together. Large missionaries ardours do not go well together with raw tribal moralities of the natural man. No zeal for missions can make national raids honest. Let us carry with us wherever we go the sense of justice and the love of conscience before convenience. But again let us not be vague; let us be sure that by justice, by conscience, we mean more than mere fair play, mere reward, or mere retribution. Let it be Christian justice, Christian justice is very much more than that. The justice of the cross means work. The justice demanded of us by the cross is the justice which was met by the cross. Let the stroke of justice fall, the severe stroke of punishment if you will. But when the stroke fell at our moral centre it meant something very different from vengeance, something much more than equity. It was justice, it was condemnation, it was punishment, but it was a world more. It was all these with a higher intention. It was more even than justice mitigated by mercy. It was not a mollified justice persuaded to take less and go. It was not curbed or thwarted justice. It was justice free and full and magnified, justice taught by pity its place, justice active not subdued, justice healing, saving, sacrificing, reconciling. Our religion should not simply sit by our moral action to temper it. It gives it its inspiration, and principle, and type. It is no use sending our Church to mitigate the severities of our politics. Our Church is there to permeate our politics with its principle, and to make them politics of sacrifice, politics of reconcilement. What shall it profit a people if it gain the whole world and lose its own soul? And it might lose it by the feebleness or the falsity of the church to which it gave its soul to keep. War may be inevitable. It may be the Divine word of condemnation, the stroke of punishment. But the thing is there, can it be conquered, converted, made to serve the kingdom of God at all? Only if it can be made a means of recovery and reconcilement. The blood of brave men flows mingled with the tears of those who love them. Blood and water come from our pierced side. For what does it cry? Vengeance? No. It is not a shriek but a prayer. Let us pour out before the god of the cross the blood of those who go in jeopardy of their lives. It is not a massacre but a sacrifice when they die. Since Christ died the blood of the brave speak to better things than that of Abel. The bravest who bleed would not be satisfied with revenge, but with peace. The bravest brave are content to die if it may be in sacrifice; they are unworthy to be sacrificed

13: The Empire for Christ, 1900

if they do not seek at the long last by their sacrifice to reconcile. Do not say that a nation is something too large for self-sacrifice, that sacrifice is a principle which has its field only in individuals or in small communities, and that it is mere inflation of style and want of judgment to apply it to a people. I might reply that it is the principle of a larger Empire even than the British—I mean the Church. And consider this. If you exclude self sacrifice from the morals of the State you leave an undue influence in the hands of the Church. You give an institution within the State a monopoly of the greatest moral influence on the public. The State ought not to control the Church, but it ought at least to be the critic of the Church. And it cannot be that if it exercise no self-sacrifice on its own part. A man who sacrifices nothing has no right to sit in judgment on a man who has sacrifice for the spirit of his life. To acquire the right to criticise the Church and keep it in its place the State should be the Church's moral peer. And it cannot be that unless it is also a self-sacrificing community in its proper way. I would ask you to note the present decline in the influence of Parliament, and the increase of the influence of the Church. Is it not because there is in Parliament a decay of moral earnestness and a corresponding growth of that in the Church? And the standard of moral earnestness is self-sacrifice, in Christian ethics at least. But, you retort upon me that the very largeness of the Church's empire is due to its neglect of the principle of sacrifice, and its lamentable loyalty to the principle of self-assertion, aggression, monopoly, and dominion. That is greatly true; but I cannot stay to ask if it is the whole truth. I will not ask either whether there be in the Church a spirit of self-rebuke and self-reform, a holy spirit, which is not in the State. It has saved and will save the Church from its own past no less than from a present evil world and a future judgment. But I will go beyond the Church, and ask if the principle be not the very life, power, and permanence of a far greater society than the Church—namely, of Godhead itself, of God Himself in His manifold and social nature as a triune God. I beseech you not to believe that this is mere extravagance of speech. Is there, in the very nature of the Godhead and behind its members, no principle of subordination, of surrender? And does not that principle carry its unity through, even when the conditions cease to be those of bliss, when they become those of sorrow and pain, when the word is not harmony, but reconciliation; Is it not by virtue of His sacrifice that He rules us forever? When His omnipotence has no power over us we are held by His self-humiliation. Where the prestige of His majesty becomes no more than an oppression, are we not moved, and always justly moved, by His loving Will in the cross? Is it not by His meek sacrifice that He goes on to inherit the earth? Or is He the chief instance of the failure of His own promise? and shall He never inherit the earth? Is then a nation greater than its God, or the most imperial of peoples above its Lord? Can it live upon other principles than its God? Is there any prestige of empire or secret of sway so great as that of suffering service and universal responsibility? Is the ruling race today not on the whole the most helping race? Is the white man's burden not inherited from the white man's God? Does He ask any sacrifice from men or nations which He has not made and outdone?

It is the great burden bearers within a people that are its heroes and kings: royalty is by sacrifice, and heroism by renunciation. *Within* a nation's own public life must the rule be different without for the nation's own place in the world? Our great rulers are those that carry the people. Is it not the nations that carry the world that shall rule the world? Meekness, of course, does not take the same form for a nation as for a man. Your Englishman is not meek, but, as policies go, the policy which the Englishman serves is meek in the sense that it is not Napoleonic, it does not crush but uplift, it sets free, it obeys a mission rather than an ambition. In man or nation meekness is the principle of sacrifice and service, it is the opposite of mere self-assertion, aggression, and aggrandisement. In this sense will it not be increasingly true as we grow in moral culture that the meek shall inherit the earth? It is the nation charged with responsibility, help, and emancipation that has the career. Worth by duty, nobility by service, royalty by sacrifice—that is no longer a principle only of private morals and personal character. It is the principle of public worth, national royalty, and venerable state everywhere. It is only the cross that has the true Imperial significance, for the cross is the badge of the King of Kings, and the stability of the great white throne.

Queen, Premier, and Commander

I suppose there are three figures that stand out today beyond all others in the sympathy and affection of our English race, and their cross is their crown, the source of their prestige is their burdens, and the seat of their fame is the load they bear. There is first the queen, aged, widowed, lonely, wise, and brave; burdened like few of her subjects to the very end, and bearing her doom of greatness with a gallant heart and kind; inured to sorrow, private and public, but still more inured to plain duty, vast concern, royal dignity, and human sympathy; at eighty-one devoting her season of rest to the reconciliation of her realm; who is worthy of England, and who has done much to make England and its courts worthy of her—our dear, revered Queen. Who would covet a throne, but for the recompense of vast and passionate love it may win? And how can it win such love but by duty, grief, and care on a royal, an Imperial scale?

13: The Empire for Christ, 1900

There is next her aging Premier—widowed, too, of late—his son shut up in the grim leaguer of Mafeking, weighed down by a war he did not choose, stooping under the load of a realm which is too wide for the peace he loves, and too proud for the allies he needs, charged with our most delicate relations to a Europe that distrusts us, guiding bravely a democracy he distrusts, facing a rent Church and a State that has transient peace at home only because at war abroad. This courage, devotion, and burden of care his political opponents may honour, and they may rest from political antagonism at a moment like this to say so.

And there is last the Commander-in-Chief upon the field, also old, also bereaved, and bereaved by the very war and hour that called him from the rest he had earned well, swift and patient in a breath, able, noble, and humane, not only a master of war, but a redeemer even of war. Each comes out of a venerable retirement that might have been enjoyed without shame, and from griefs that might have justified an abdication of responsibility long ere now; and each comes out to bear the far burden of the realm, and to save it for its place in the saving of the world. This war may be a young man's war in the making of it, but it is the old people's victory, glory, and praise.

The Burden of the Lord

Yet these valours, triumphs, and splendours will pass. New occasions will arise, and new crises will tax us. New heroes, heroines, and heroisms will spring up—the man coming with the hour. What stirs us so deeply today will take its place at a later and perhaps more laden day,

> With old forgotten far-off things
> And battles long ago.[5]

These things, I say, may come to live but in the historian's page, and in the memory of those well-taught. But what shall never die is the divine death triumph and spell. What never shall be forgotten is the burden of the Lord, the load that is borne by the Eternal, the reconciling sacrifice, the outgoing of the ancient of days, of the King of Kings; the reconciling victory of the captain of our salvation. What cannot die is the forthgoing of the Eternal to the recesses and rebellious fastnesses of His kingdom, to war, to suffer, to sympathise, to conquer, and to save. When there is no more saving to be done there will always be the saving God to be glorified, and His saving

---

5. From William Wordsworth's poem, "The Solitary Reaper" (1805): "Will no one tell me what she sings?—/Perhaps the plaintive numbers flow/For old, unhappy, far-off things, And battles long ago."

grace to be praised, and His saving cross to be established in the human and heavenly society which must crown the policies of the earth. The memory of that shall grow into our ruling presence and the spirit of it into our ruling power. No kingdom on earth is too great to own in its conduct the cross which is God's principle for life and leading among the armies of heaven, and the seat of His everlasting empire over the inhabitants of the earth. The God of our personal salvation is the God of the universal future. And the morality of a social Godhead which redeems the soul is the ruling principle of human society redeemed. The only justice that justifies war is the spirit of God's holy war, the justice of reconciliation and reunion.

The Mother and her Colonies

Every part of the Empire must aid every other in this crucial war for the moral dominion of ourselves. The colonies have something to teach us. They have made experiments in advance of us. They have led the way that we must follow in some social directions. They have done so in ecclesiastical and educational policy. But we have also much to teach them and much of the higher help to give. The frontiers of an empire are in peculiar moral peril from their direct contact with inferior races and pioneer conditions. The frontier men are in danger of being mastered by those they master, or of being captured by their very passion of progress and secularised by mere material advance. English men and women often return from India far below the men and women they went. The expansion of England has suffered in quality from contact with the very races she went to bless. But for renewal from the centre there would be decay. And the colonies which have not suffered from this infection have yet felt the secularisation that imperils new countries whose energies are taxed in securing a material base. And they may have suffered by some seclusion from the ethical advance of an old and experienced culture. For the local knowledge of facts is one thing and the moral principle of treating them is another. But the difference between the mother country and the colonies in this respect lessens rapidly. Powerful influences from home are at work. The universities are missionising them, for instance. Their universities and colleges are staffed by men who carry out the ideas and methods of our seats of learning, especially in science. Many of their men and women come to Oxford and Cambridge, and they are among the most interesting and illustrious of our students—some of these from colonial congregations. And the universities yonder are affiliated with ours here. The Press of this country, again, has a great effect on their public. English men and women also in increasing numbers travel in our

13: The Empire for Christ, 1900

colonies; and our colonists come still more freely here, and each party carries forth the ideas and influence of the motherland to ferment in the young receptive soil. Our home literature is as yet a far greater influence upon our cousins abroad than their home-grown genius or their native art. In the æsthetic region in particular we subtly mould their imaginative life. Their very superiority to us in the matter of education and general intelligence enables them to take advantage of all these things in a rapid way. Are we, then, to send them only our civilisation and culture? And are we to do nothing to aid them in Christian faith and truth? In ecclesiastical politics they can set us an example; but in some forms of Christian culture and life it is possible for an old and mature country to offer a help and guidance which I hope the younger lands are not too proud to take. Christianity can go out to affect the vigorous life of our colonies, are we to hang back with aid to that form of Christianity which we believe in most? It has such affinity with colonial democracy, and yet it has a severe conflict with the condition of a new country. The organised churches can take care of themselves, but the Congregationalist churches, which have to pay for their independence here, have to pay for it still more severely yonder. Isolation is bad here, but it is worse yonder. And in these days of Free Church Federation it would be a mistake to leave out of our sympathy the churches and groups which are insulated by thousands of miles from their religious home. The Colonial Missionary Society is not so much a missionary society as a church extension society. It is a Church Aid Society. The colonies are but English counties located abroad. The Cape churches are a remoter Cornwall, and Canada is a more distant Cumberland. The little mother should not disown her thousands nor the small one the great nation she has grown. If Congregationalism be worth preserving for English freedom it must be worth helping for still freer lands. "The spirit of liberty is freer in the British colonies than in any other part of the earth."[6] It is British liberty itself set free and liberalised. Has such a climate no affinity with our principle of faith and our Congregational doctrine and practice? It would befit a speech rather than a sermon if I were to plead the case further on these lines. I will only say a little heart goes as ill with a great nation as a little mind.

We are today in the midst of a great national change. A new public situation has been created, in which precedents guide us little, and principles must come to our aid. Old party lines are being erased, and new issues are arising which deeply involve us with the colonial parts of our race. The old political moralities are being tested, challenged, and revised. The duty imposed on the church as the great moral educator of the people grows more exacting. And

---

6. From Edmund Burke's *Speech on Conciliation with the Colonies* (1775).

II: Published Sermons

I am bound to say a deeper sense of that duty exists in every section of the Church. She has not only a renewed vision of her own central truth, but a new sense of its demand upon the State and conduct of Society at large. As she is disestablished in the political sense she becomes established in the moral sense, and the less she seeks to rule the more she grows in influence upon the public ideal and the public career. She must seek to be thus established in the social constituency. She must go behind measures, and educate that public mind and soul, which the passing years will push to the front of affairs. She must give herself with new earnestness to the moral understanding of her own faith, and the public translation of her own morals. She must escape from the pietisms of the cave, and speak with the large utterance of a public Saviour, and the high demands of a jealous God. She must not fear to plant human society upon her own morality, and her own morality upon the fastnesses of her theological faith. For a great nation is ill fitted with a petty Church. And a great humanity is the native speech and the lordly home of a great, glorious, righteous, and everlasting God, who from the throne of His ageless cross made unto us wisdom, power, holiness, justice, goodness, and truth.

14

THE SLOWNESS OF GOD, 1900

"The barley in the appointed place."
—ISAIAH 28:23–26

Isaiah was first a speaker then a writer. His books were addresses printed. And these addresses were short, "occasional," practical. They were themselves deeds, contributed to the public and social action of his day. Each of these brief and close packed messages to his age was a living act. He was neither a committee-man, an organiser, an agitator, nor a parliamentarian. He had little to show that would have been called work by people who think speech to be waste. He did not preach a gospel of work in the interest of a gospel of silence. Our own prophet of the gospel of work and silence was the most voluble of men, both by tongue and pen. Isaiah's words were themselves deeds, like every word which proceedeth from the mouth of God.

Probably Isaiah prepared his messages. They are too elaborate, concise, and compact with passionate thought to be extempore. Therefore having delivered them he took care of them. Then he published them, first, perhaps, as broadsheets, as ballads used to circulate. Then he collected them, arranged them in some connexion, and made pamphlets of them. Then the pamphlets were collected into those thirty-nine chapters which form the book we now have in our hands. May I take it for granted that you know that the second half of our Isaiah, from chap. 40 onwards, is parted from the first by more than a century! It came from the bosom of the Captivity in Babylon, and from the genius of some inspired servant of God, whose name and personality are quite unknown to us. Whereas the only Isaiah we know lived in the time of Ahaz and Hezekiah.

II: Published Sermons

This twenty-eighth chapter alone is made up of three addresses given to different people at different times. The first part, vv. 1–13, is a vehement denunciation to the sneering drunkards who were ruining Samaria. It was therefore before the destruction of Samaria in 722 BC. The second part, vv. 14–22, is a like denunciation of the rascality of the ruling class in Judea, the ring of Pachas, as we might say, who surrounded the palace at Jerusalem, and who hoped to bribe calamity when it came, and avert by diplomatic chicanery what could be avoided only by righteousness. And the last part, vv. 23–29, is a kind of parable of judgments, couched, like the true parable always, not only in the speech but in the habits of the life that his audience knew best. It is quite a separate address, though it is likely enough that Isaiah himself in publication added it to the other two. In these he had denounced judgment, in this he insists that if judgment is delayed it is never forgotten. The bolt which seems to come so suddenly from heaven comes really from the heart of a storm which gathers long, works round the horizon, draws off and returns, and bursts now here now there with varying force. That, however, is not Isaiah's image. He does not go to the heavens but to the earth. He speaks to the farmer of his ways with the soil. Such, he says, are the ways of God with the people.

It was a quiet time. Hezekiah was on the throne. It might be about 710 BC. There was little stirring in foreign politics. No great enemy was on the horizon. The Assyrian wolf had for the time retired from the fold. He was occupied with some troubles in his own lair. Hezekiah had not yet revolted from Sennacherib as in 705 he did. It was a time of vassalage, and its peace was a vassal peace. It was not a very noble one. The soul of the people was feeble. Its vices grew on it. It had no high ardour, no fiery faith, no spiritual vision. It took things as they came, and forgot them as they went. With this ease and levity of life came scepticism as usual. But it was not of the theological but of the moral sort. It did not turn on science or philosophy, which had little entrance to the Jerusalem of those days. It was the deadlier moral sort, scepticism not of God's existence but of God's righteousness. They would not deny that God was, but they thought He was careless or irrelevant: or He was venal and could be bought over when the crisis came. If God is irrelevant His word is impertinent. It is a frequent enough habit of mind at certain stages of history. It speaks thus to this very day. "We see no trace of Him. He gives no sign. Judgment is an old-fashioned idea. We are out-growing calamity. We are learning to protect ourselves from disaster, and we fail to feel the presence or need of another protector. We prosper. We grow enlightened. Law rules all, and we learn law and control all. Science banishes pestilence. Diplomacy and the growth of humane feelings avert war. Wealth and shipping prevent famine. Free institutions prevent revolution. Calamity, even if it comes,

14: The Slowness of God, 1900

is not to be viewed as judgment. Judgment is an outworn superstition. Let us eat, drink, and be merry—all in measure, all in comfort. Let us fleet the time carelessly, as they did in the golden worlds. Why place the righteousness of God as a spectre at our feast? If He wish to be recognized, why does He not speak infallibly? Why does He not act urgently? Let us see His judgments, and we will believe in them. 'Let Him make speed, let Him hasten His work that we may see it. Let the counsel of the Holy One draw nigh that we may know it.'[1] The oracles are dumb. The miracles are sealed. Apostles are dead; and prophets are vain. 'Where is His promise of His coming? For since the fathers are fallen asleep, all things continue as they were.'[2] And even if they change, we perceive neither the finger nor the scheme of God, neither His presence nor His policy, neither His power nor His justice, neither His help, His judgments, nor His kingdom."

We speak like that in our prosperous today. The men of science, for instance, discard a God who does not speak or act according to the canons and methods they are used to. If He do not behave as they prescribe, He is for them practically not there. If He cannot approve Himself by the established philosophic proofs, He need not be regarded. As if faith were not in default of proofs, and the spirit in man had no power to meet God's Spirit in human affairs, and discern His presence. So we speak today. They spoke like it in the prophet's old yesterday. Samaria had been swept away, indeed, as the prophet saw and said it would. But that was a dozen years ago. "We are as bad as Samaria are we? You lie, prophet. For if we were the judgment would have swept over us too. But we stand. We are at rest. We are more comfortable than when we were zealous for Jehovah. Let Jehovah bring on His judgments that we may believe. Let Him speak as we dictate, if He would have us believe. Meantime we are not sure that He is not held in check by Baal, or has not other things to do than judge us. We will treat Baal with some respect, as we do not know when we may need him for a friend. He serves us fairly for the present. For the rest we have treaties, arrangements with foreign powers. We learn to understand high policy. We keep our eye on foreign affairs, and domestic matters, like righteousness, do not seem alarming." So they said, and so they might have said for another hundred years and more. For it was more than another century before Jerusalem followed Samaria to the dust and her people to Exile.

Isaiah is called on for a theodicy. He has to vindicate the ways of God to men. He has to take up the prophets' and apostles' task in every age, and force home the conviction that the absence of God is not the sleep of God,

---

1. Isa 5:19.
2. 2 Pet 3:4.

nor His hiding of Himself His absence, nor His silence His unrighteousness, nor His slowness His feebleness. The slowness of God is the patience of God. His silence is His omnipotence. His hiding is the subtlety of His omnipresence. His absence is a form of His vigilance. His forbearance is a stage of His judgment and a phase of His wise justice. If the thunder of judgment do not follow fast on the flash of sin, it is not because the Judge is not at the door. At least He is in the town, and is making His way to the inquest in your house. God's procedure is a great procedure. It is perfectly infallible in its working, and sure in its event. But it will not be hurried for outcry or for defiance. He is not a passionate God, like His accusers and sceptics. There is everything to be considered, and everybody, and the righteousness not of the moment but of the long last. With Him a thousand years are as one day, and one day as a thousand years. There is method in His procedure. There is plan, patience, completeness. He stays to gather up everything, to take everything with Him, to bring everything home. The home of everything is its place in the justice of God, its function in His judgment.

This is what Isaiah had to bring home to his public, as we have to ours. We have our resources; he had his. And ours are vaster, more complete, than his, though we do not use them as he did. We have God's own theodicy in Christ, in the justice and judgment of the Cross. But Isaiah had his prophet's vision, his insight into Providence, his sound judgment of God's judgment, his inspiration for judging of the Judge (which is God's Spirit reading Himself aloud). Isaiah had his sense of reality—of the reality of common life, and the reality of the spiritual principles beneath it. He had his gift of speech, of vivid observation, of fiery, fearless passion, of packed phrase. He had the skill of homely, deep parable that settles never to be dislodged, and teems from its place with God's truth pervading men's ways. And Isaiah put his theodicy in the shape of a parable from the commonest pursuits of rural life. It was there that he found the principles to God's dealings, not by excogitation, not innate in the soul, but saturating the healthy occupations of men, and ruling their practical relations with the good brown earth. He did not only illustrate his truth from their familiar toil, but he found *the same principles* in their work and in God's with the world. Just as in our fatherhood we have the rudiments of God's.

Listen, he says, you who think God sleeps because His chastisement is not incessant. Is the ploughman *always* ploughing? Is there no rest for the soil? Is there no sowing after the ploughing? Does he not let the earth alone after the sowing too? Does he fold his hands when he has torn up the ground and levelled its clods? No, he proceeds, only he changes his procedure. He puts in his seed. And he puts in different seeds different ways. He not only goes on; he discriminates as he goes on. He scatters the fitches, and

14: The Slowness of God, 1900

the cummin; the wheat and the barley he sets with more care in rows; and the spelt he puts in for a border to these. How comes he to do this? God hath taught him, says the prophet. We should say now he has learnt by long experience. Both are right. If we do learn from experience, it is God's laws that we learn, and we learn by God's schooling. If the experience of generations has taught us, it is none the less God's teaching. Creation by evolution is as compatible with a Creator as creation by a stroke. God taught him this, says the prophet. And God taught him so, because it is God's own way. God's theodicy is rooted in the very soil. His righteousness springs from the earth. God's way with the earth is His way with its dwellers. It is just so that God tills man and farms history. Providence is the Great Husbandman. We are God's planting and God's estate. As you do not forever plough down the soil and break up the ground, so neither does God. There is in His procedure both method and discrimination. His judgment is not a monotony of chastisement. It is not His way to mow down Samaria and Jerusalem at one sweep. He does not treat the scoundrelism of Judah in just the same way as the drunkenness of Ephraim. Drunkenness does bring a swifter judgment on a people (as on a man) than rascality, though not a surer. But as after the ploughing comes sowing, and after sowing a time of rest ere the sprout appear, so God rests and lets men rest. This is His mercy, His wisdom. He will give the one judgment time to have its effect on men before the next comes. There is method and patience in His ways as in yours which He taught you. There is method, but no monotony. There is discrimination. He is not moved by passion, else he would sweep clean the whole wicked earth. He adjusts judgment to time, place, people, and the great end in view—the great harvest at the close of all. What indeed is judgment but adjustment? God does not move like a man in a hurry, by short cuts. He does not go to His end with blunt directness like your common plain-dealer, who sees but one small near thing to do, and straightway does it and is done. With God each judgment contributes to the next, and the next may be less severe or more, according as the interval is used. The Almighty is the Almighty strategist. He moves in great orbits and roundabout ways. But His forces are always on the spot at the right time. The hour comes and the God. And He sweeps the country clean as He advances. He leaves no foe to harass his rear. His judgments are slow, circuitous, lingering, it may be, but they are patient, merciful, final in their nature. They serve a purpose, they follow a plan, they discriminate, they strike here, they lift there, here they pull men up, there they let them go. Some they only shake, some they tread, some they crush and grind to powder.

That is how the prophet goes on with his parable. He has been speaking of the soil and its treatment. He goes on to draw the like lesson from

II: Published Sermons

the produce of the soil and *its* treatment. Your farmer is as skilful and discriminating with the one as with the other, with the grain as with the soil. That is his art and craft and mystery. Is there no art, craft, and mystery in the great Harvester of the world? Is there no judiciousness in His judgment? Is it but a monotone of vengeance? Your threshing now, says the prophet, is it all done one way? Do you treat all seed alike? You thresh with a stick for a beater, or with a heavy sledge with teeth, or with a heavy wheel behind a horse. The succulent produce like fitches you beat with a rod. It is enough. The heavy implement would make them a pulp. The harder stalks and grains you thresh with the sledge or with the wheel. And even in your threshing of them there is measure and skill in your conduct. You know when to stop before you crush the grain to dust. Bread-corn has to be ground. That is another and a later process. You do not thresh, thresh it till it is as good as ground up in the litter of the barn floor. You will not be for ever threshing it. Your implements are heavy and their work severe, still they are only for separating the grain from the stalk, not for grinding it. There is care, method, judgment in your proceedings. There is a differential treatment, there is a time to stop. Who taught you all this? This also is from the Lord of Hosts, so wonderful in counsel, so excellent in working. It is His own method. What in you is rural skill in Him is historic strategy. What in you is art in Him is providence. But it is the same spirit in both. Your small prudence has the same root as His vast providence. Providence is but a longer prudence. Judgment is sure, however judicious. God gives long rests but never lets go. His lessons are severe but He allows much time to ponder them. He judges one to save another. He speaks to Judah by Ephraim, and gives the lesson time to sink in. So He has spoken to the world by Israel. Beware how you turn His forbearance to your deeper damnation and His goodness into a deeper severity. He does not cease to besiege you though He draws his forces for a time out of sight.

Judah was getting over the fright of twelve years ago in the fall of Samaria. And that is always a dangerous time. People then are angry with themselves for being frightened and with the prophet who scared them. They tend to be defiant, more reckless in sin, more ready for temptation, more sceptical, more contemptuous of the slumbering power. You have seen the growing boldness of a boy in teasing a dog which he has found to be chained, till the animal with a bound tears the chain from the staple and has him in his teeth. You have heard how the glutton and drunkard will presume on a magnificent constitution, and break nature's laws daily, till he snap and collapse with a crash. You have read how a savage race will calculate upon the patience and reluctance of a European power in its raids, insults, and cruelties, till civilization is roused and they are swept from the spot by a stroke. So it was in a way with Judah.

14: The Slowness of God, 1900

The effect of Samaria's doom was wearing off, and the prophet would fain save them from the like. He enters into their frame of mind and reasons with it in this parable. He can remonstrate and plead as well as denounce. And he does it here.

Now, is this passage so hopelessly obscure? Is it not full of profound and luminous truth? Is the Bible not worth studying—and most worth, perhaps, just where it seems most dark? Every tangle means more of the gold thread.

Let us discriminate too. The prophet was dealing with a nation. He was amid public affairs, public sins. *There* there is both more scope and need for the preaching of judgments. With individuals there is another and a mightier word; and we live in another and more gracious time. God is the Judge and King of *nations*—but He is in Christ the Lover of *souls*. We do not do well to appeal to nations chiefly in the name of the love which so stirs and melts the soul. And we do not do well to preach incessant judgment to the souls which are the objects of the love of God. Preach righteousness and judgment to peoples, with love for the soul.

To souls preach love and faith, with righteousness for its public garb and judgment to brace the air. The judgment for sin upon the soul Christ has taken for us, if we will but take Him. The judgment of national sin may reach a point when there is no more repentance but God's unforgiveness and destruction.

Finally, for your private conduct take a suggestion from v. 28. You are not called on to grind the corn that you have to thresh. Beware of incessant judgment! Beware of acquiring the habit of incessant criticism! Beware lest you come to be known as nothing if not critical, like the villain Iago. You must judge, you must condemn at times. It is your duty to express condemnation, censure. Do not let this censorious habit master you. It loses the dignity of judgment and becomes mere grumbling and mere nagging.

And when the censure is over let it rest. Do not cast things up. No generous mind does that. Especially do not do it with children. It exasperates them in one way and crushes them in another. Fathers provoke not your children to anger lest they be discouraged, *i.e.*, dumpish, sullen, resentful, through being always dropped upon. Do not always be plowing, raking up the old soil and the old sores. Let the past be. Let there be some rest for the moral ground. Sow your seed, but let it germinate in peace. Use the past, but do not be always thinking of it. Dwell with hope and faith on the future. Your Judge is your Redeemer. Never judge but in the spirit that redeems.

15

AN ALLEGORY OF THE RESURRECTION, 1902

"Son of man, can these bones live? . . . O Lord God, thou knowest . . . Ye shall know . . . when I have opened your graves."

—EZEKIEL 37:3–13

EZEKIEL DIFFERS FROM THE other prophets in this: that he stands before us as half-prophet and half-priest. He has been described by a great authority as a priest in a prophet's mantle. In him the two streams met and parted; prophetism ended in Ezekiel the prophet, and the hierarchy began in Ezekiel the priest—at least, the hierarchy in its full power. In this passage, however, Ezekiel is no priest, but he is pure prophet, and he is in the great prophetic line. And we are, perhaps, in a position to trace the growth of this famous parable, perhaps to reconstruct the process by which it arose in the prophet's thought. It was built from a hint; he took fire from a spark, and that spark seems to have been a phrase he heard among his fellow-exiles in Babylon, quoted in verse 11, "Our bones are dried up, our hope is lost." The words that he overheard took wings in his genius. They gave him a bone, and he made a bird, like the great naturalist. The metaphor swelled in his imagination to a vision, and it became one of the great dreams of the world, which is so much more than a dream, because its inspiration is the sleepless purpose of God. The prophet stands up amid lassitude and indifference, and he is a prophet because he is a man of hope. In dark days he did not despair of the State; he had hope for the people, and it was because he had faith in its God. "Not for your sakes do I do this, but for my own name's sake, which ye have profaned among the heathen."[1] What we have here, then, is an allegory—an

---

1. Ezek 36:22.

15: An Allegory of the Resurrection, 1902

allegory of the resurrection. But it is not the resurrection of the body, nor perhaps of the dead as individuals, but of the nation; the resurrection of the individual dead was perhaps no part as yet of the Hebrew faith; at any rate, what was promised in the mind of the prophet was the resurrection of the nation. And I may perhaps be allowed to call your attention to the whole allegory under these three points of view—(1) the Scene, (2) the Action, and (3) the Result.

I. The Scene

It was the scene of so many visions—the valley by the river Chebar. Now, however, it was a hideous place. It seemed a valley of desolation, it was a vast charnel-house; a skeleton army, to the prophet's vision, lay there. It was ghastly, not with the fresh horror of festering corruption, but with the gaunt squalor of dry ruin. The plain was white with the chronic leprosy of death; and it was the chill of old death—death grown grey and sere, death itself turned dead—because it was death with its beauty dead, death with its pathos dead, death which was not redolent of a life just gone, but death long hopeless of any life to come. It was death long settled down into dismal possession, death established and privileged, throned and secure. That meant Israel—defeated and wasted and strewn by the heathen. Its old soul was extinct and its old hope gone; its sacred laws were like limbs dismembered and parched. Israel was crumbling into the deadly soil of a paganism which had slain faith. They were left to die a second death, some not hoping, some not wishing, to revive. And the vision would stand for any people whose soul had become extinct, for any class or section of people who were treated as aliens, whether deported or not, if they are cut off from interest in their native soil, if they are oppressed until energy is dead and faith dried up; whose hope no more sings, but has only a hard rattle of coarse mirth, like the bones stirred by the wind, or the British workman's ditties today.

The bones were many, and they were very dry. The multitude of the slain was unable to avert death. No multitude can outlive death; death always has a majority on its side. "And they were very dry."[2] The dryness and the death of a dead community is something more dead than the same number of dead scattered up and down; a community of the dead city is worse than the death of the same number of people scattered abroad about the country. Nests of iniquity are more iniquitous than the scattered crime; therefore pull down the nests and make the rooks flee; scatter the alsatias, erase the slums, spread the hotbeds out on the land, and destroy the ferment

2. Ezek 37:2.

of corruption. The death of a great multitude is very dead, but when it lives the life of a great multitude is very high; it may be an army that no man can number, it may be the very city of God.

II. The Action

I speak, in the second place, about the action. The prophet passed by the bones round about. He did not go through them, he did not tread on them as a lout in a cemetery steps upon the graves. They had been trodden enough. The Spirit of God moved in the prophet; his God had been the God of these bones also, and therefore he is respectful, reverent, to them. The Spirit of God does make us reverent to human wrecks, whether they be black or white. Faith alone, with its power of light, has the true reverence for death. When a woman gathered for burial the mutilated and detested remains of the Emperor Nero, the pagan world, it is said, surmised she must have been a Christian; only a Christian would have been likely to conceive so chivalrous a devotion towards wretchedness. And the preacher of the Lord has no right to treat otherwise than respectfully the dry bones that he confronts in the world around him—faithfully but respectfully. Abuse is not Divine judgment, and who with a right heart would treat otherwise than respectfully the disinherited in any people, the dispossessed and deadened, the serfs of our civilisation, whose hope is worn to the bone, and their life-joy wasted to a skeleton? Whoever does otherwise does it from a low heart. Man fallen and dead is yet an object of some respect to his brother. For what is he to his God? "Can these bones live?" Well, at least, they are relics; they are not merely remnants and mere things, they are things with memories, things with tears in them, things once wedded to life, although now in such tragic divorce; they are things which appeal to loves and memories in the living God Himself, whose love once gave them life and watched over them. They are bones, not stones, a very mummy of a man lying beneath the wrath and curse of God may not yet be the victim of God's neglect. The hardened heart has the distinction still of God's anger, and in so far it has also some of God's promise. His anger is not out of relation to His love, it is not beyond His pity or foreign to His grace. It was those under His wrath that He was moved to redeem. To have the anger of God, I venture to say, is at least some melancholy dignity; it is one that stocks and stones have not, nor the orbits of the heavens, nor the cold infinities of space; nor could they have that anger if aught went wrong with them. If the heathen themselves are under the wrath of God, they have some claim upon our respect from that point of view alone, to say nothing of the transcendent claims upon out pity and our love.

15: An Allegory of the Resurrection, 1902

Faith and Criticism

"Son of man, can these bones live?" This question to the prophet is put anew to his posterity every time he reviews the past. Is there ought in that dead past with life for the present; has the faith of the past moral rescue for the future; has past knowledge and action the power to enlarge and correct itself and to grow; or is the past dumb and done, dead and dry? "Son of man, can these bones live?" It is a question that God is asking by the mouth of historic criticism today. The valley of secular history in the light of today is strewn with unhinged historic facts, and some proved historic errors; and Scripture itself is like the very cockpit of the valley, where the battle has been most fierce, and where to many godly eyes the slaughter has been severest and the desolation most sore. They seem to see but bones left; they are unsure whether the precious past can survive the critics. I would bid them take heart, fear not, only believe. Faith is absolutely essential to sound criticism. We may have been trusting certain conclusions of the Church, at any rate, too much to the corruptible flesh of changing creeds. Let us invoke and stir up the Spirit of God. It was a too-proud flesh, perhaps, that had come in certain quarters to clothe these sacred bones in the Church's course, a flesh to establish, indolent and unspiritual. At the Reformation, for instance, some of the systems that had grown up to cover the historic facts needed the invader with his critic's blade and his destroying skill. The fierce Assyrian and the proud Babylonian, who assailed a too-rank Israel, were still, with the prophets, the servants of the Lord. But the bones are there, the facts are there, and amongst them and over them stands still the prophet of prophets, the soul and spirit of prophecy, the Saviour stands over them and the Spirit of God is there.

We have what the first century had even when it buried Christ, we have One who cannot be holden of death, and we have the Church's faith. God would be able, if we were ever reduced to that—so improbable it is—of these bones to raise up children to Abraham, and from these facts to make believers in Christ. Why, the Gospels which have done so much are comparatively meagre, they are but as bones in a mound, compared with the fulness of the whole historic Christ, but they fix for ever the saving revelation of God as a historic revelation and a revelation in power. The Spirit of God is a spirit of history; the true history of spirit is always the Spirit of God, and history in God's hands goes to cure the wounds that history makes. Let us never give the Gospel's case away, nor even seem to take it for granted that critical methods must only have destructive results. Faith, I venture to repeat, is an essential condition of sound criticism. It was to faith that the first facts came; they came to the Church, not to the world. Is the Church to wait upon the world's permission to believe? History which is at once scientific and spiritual will cure not only the diseases of old history, but the surgical wounds made by critical history today. The history that constructs will take the tool from the hands of history that destroys. Critics' swords will grow to ploughshares, and their spears to pruning hooks. And what threatened the life of the old faith will be found to have prepared for more fruit.

These very bones, if we were reduced to that, I have ventured to say, are more than remnants—they are holy and potent relics. They are not the residuum of criticism, they are relics for our faith. They are clothed not only with memories but with power. There is virtue in them and miracle in them; there is life and healing in the touch of them. Did He not say He came to give His life as a ransom for many? Did He not know what He was about? Did He not say that His was the new covenant blood shed for many for the remission of sin? Did He not invite the whole world to come into His capacious soul, His divine soul, and there promised them rest? Did He not declare that every soul that confessed Him before men would be confessed by Him at the long last when it was judged of all? Did He not declare that no man knew the Father but the Son and those to whom the Son should reveal Him?

"Sound" and "Safe" Criticism

Why need I go on multiplying points like these? If you choose to call these bones relics, from bones and relics like these from His own account of His own cross, could we not if the need arose rebuild our Jerusalem with the aid of the Holy Ghost? It is the Gospel that must save the Church and its beliefs; it is not the Church that can ever save the Gospel. The historic Gospel saved everything at the Reformation; it saved the Church from itself, and it must go on doing so. We must not come to the Gospel with the permission of the critics, we come to criticism in the power of the Gospel. Faith does not wait upon criticism, but it is an essential condition of it. The complete critic is not a mere inquirer, but a believer. It was to believers, not critics, that the things appealed which are criticised most today. Critical energy is only just and true when it is in the hands of a Church whose heart is full of evangelical faith. The passion of an apostolic missionary faith is an essential condition to a sound criticism and a safe; and by "sound" I don't merely mean sound to the Confessions, I mean sound to the mind; and by "safe" I do not merely mean safe for the Church, but safe for the soul. I mean that faith in the Gospel, evangelical faith, is essential for that full, complete view of the case upon which sound results are based; it is essential in order to be fair to all the facts. It must enter in, not to decide whether we shall expect proved results, but to decide the results we are to count as proved. Faith is not only

15: An Allegory of the Resurrection, 1902

an asset which criticism must include in its audit, but it is an organ that criticism must use. The eye cannot say to the ear, "I have no need of thee."[3]

> And God has a few of us whom He whispers in the ear,
> The rest may reason, and welcome, but we musicians know.[4]

It must affect my view of the evidence of the resurrection of Christ if I have been met by Christ, dealt with by Christ, had personal dealings with the Redeemer. There is great truth in those words, "If ye do His will ye shall know of His doctrine."[5] I venture to suggest that there is still deeper truth in these words, "Ye shall know that I am the Lord when I have opened your graves and brought you out of your graves, O my people."[6] The man who was struck down on the way to Damascus had every essential evidence about Him who was raised up at Jerusalem. The faith of Pentecost makes a great difference about the Easter creed. It is by Christ within us that we can take full measure of the Christ without. We cannot judge of our Christ properly until we have been judged by Christ, the judge of all; and His evidence is Himself, and the history of the Risen One in the experience of the Church for these 2,000 years must interpret and must supplement the historic evidence of His resurrection.

Historical Valleys of Dry Bones

Experience verifies the Gospel; my history makes strange things credible in the history of long ago. And the evidence, the leading evidence, is not confined to the first, second, or third centuries, but is vital and mighty in every century, and not the least in the century in which we live. The Spirit that quickens is as essential as the vision that sees; the faith which felt what those bones could be was as real to the case as the eyesight which saw them on the plain. The history of the future, indeed, can have no new revelation. The Christ which is to be is the Christ which has been, is now, and ever shall be, the same yesterday, the same today and for ever. There is nothing conceivable beyond the salvation and the Saviour that we have, but the future may re-reveal the revelation which is fixed in the history of the past. It will elicit its infinite resource. Its history was God's first channel of revelation, then by way

---

3. 1 Cor 12:21.
4. From Robert Browning's poem, "Abt Vogler" (1864): "But God has a few of us whom He whispers in the ear; The rest may reason and welcome: 'tis we musicians know."
5. John 7:17.
6. Ezek 37:13.

of history will come the revelation of the resources of that revelation. The students of history must not work alone, they must work along with the makers of history; not only the study of past history, but the course of future history is the way of God's Spirit in the deep. Personal history and public history—that is the way of God's Spirit. It is the nations that God must win, not the cloisters; and the great revival, which is to move no mere sect or coterie, but which is to change the spirit of our national life, will show its genius, its public and historic genius, in this, namely: it may recast here and there the history of the past, but it will enlarge by new races the Christianity of the future; it may reread the history of the Church, but it will rediscover the Bible's exhaustless power, it will realise afresh in man's affairs the life of Christ Himself. And are we not always realising afresh the Lord's death? For the Lord hath yet more light and truth to break forth from His holy Son. The past is not dead, but speaketh and prophesieth until now. And from age to age God confounds the pessimists, He revives the bones by miracles by historic resurrection.

God takes the man of little faith, takes him like Ezekiel, carries him back in spirit through history to the dark ages of Europe; plants him beside a church with its faith dried and enterprise dulled into mere orthodoxy beneath the Pagan empire. He sets you in the valley of the dark ages, when the Spanish Moors had more light and life than the Christians of Europe. He asks you, "Can these bones live?" You cannot say, but God's answer is the wonderful eleventh, twelfth, and thirteenth centuries. The past was not dead; the Church is never without its recuperative power somewhere. As the body of Christ, it must rise, and cannot be holden of death, howsoever long the torpor may be.

Or again, God takes you onward, and sets you in another dismal valley, the church of the Borgias and Medicis, amongst the parched bones of faith, when the former revival had shrunk to a mere renaissance, when Paganism was not in the Empire but in the Church's own heart and head. He points you to the wicked Church of all the cultures at Rome in the valley of the fifteenth century, when the faithful had all but ceased to be. "Can these bones live?" You see not how. God's answer is Luther, Calvin, and the sixteenth century, the rediscovery of St. Paul, the coronation of faith, the vitalising of Europe, Puritanism, the birth of democracy, the rise of constitutionalism, Free Churchism, and the dawn of modern times. No, the past is not dead.

And once more He plants you by the English Church of last century, with Deism outside, and drought within, but no thirst. Can they live? God's answer is Wesley and the Evangelical revival, Newman and the Oxford revival, and much more that I cannot name because I must single out the feature which has gathered us here—modern missions. I doubt if any such answer has ever been given to the prophet's question as this. We have the

15: An Allegory of the Resurrection, 1902

answer before our eyes. The world has it, and it is often as smoke in its eyes. But the men who first faced the problem, and first moved in these missions had not this answer before their eyes, they had it before their faith alone. They were prophets indeed, in the true inspired line, for they had it in their souls only. They had it surer there in their faith than many of us who have it in our sight. They lived in the valley of the eighteenth century, but their souls stood upon Pisgah; they saw the Promised Land, and all things delivered unto Christ of the Father. They had Imperial minds, but they had also holy methods. They saw the bones stirred and clothed, and men trooping from their living graves at the call of the Spirit alone. They saw races roused, rescued, civilised by the Gospel. Nay, they saw more; they saw the Church itself converted to missions, a bony Church quickened, fleshed, and marshalled anew. They saw that the Church must be reconverted if it was to survive, but they also saw that it would be reconverted, because they had the Spirit that makes the Church, and felt the first flutter of His breast. And the Church did need this reconversion. There was not among the heathen more contemptuous opposition to missions than these men met sometimes in the Church at home. When we speak of the great effect of the Church on the heathen, let us not forget the great blessing of the heathen to the Church. The receiving of them has been to the Church itself life from the dead. The Church has more faith in its own Gospel because of its proved power abroad; it is more sure of its own word, and it feels that it is not only a mighty word, a true word, but a more genial and pitiful word. The old bones live again in a humaner life. Every missionary is preaching to the Church that sent him no less than to the churches he found. When we speak of the action of grace, think also of the reaction of grace, the force of its recoil; deep calleth unto deep. The Gospel's word to the world includes also its echo to the Church. Missions are an integral part of the Church and a source of new life to it, and the missionaries are prophets that call flesh upon our bones. To convert the heathen is to bless and serve the Church. These missionaries are not hobby-riders that the Church patronises; they are organs, agents, and deputies of the Church itself. They do not act alongside of us, but for us; they are the long arms of the Church and the limbs by which it covers the breadth of the world. The man to whom missions are a fanatic fad, and not his own concern, has yet to learn the soul of the Christian Gospel and the secret of the Church's life.

II: Published Sermons

The Universalism of Missions

It is upon the universalism of missions that our Church's own foundation rests. We live upon the Word we give. It is always a tendency and temptation of the Church to conquer a certain region, then settle down, to turn self-contained, to seclude itself from humanity in a side valley, and from other Churches. It becomes a sect, a mere national Church. It forgets that the Church is humanity in the germ, and that its health is in its human range; and then it becomes inhuman, and sceptical about humanity; finally, it becomes sceptical about its own Gospel, and credulous about its own rights. To limit the Gospel is in the end to deny the Gospel, and it is from this that missions save us; they force us to realise that the Gospel is for man and man for the Gospel, that the Church has the world for its parish. Nothing teaches us like missions that English Christianity must have more than an English Gospel. The foundation of our British Church was a mission; it was a Spirit from abroad that stirred our Pagan bones. We are not Jewish converts, we are heathen Christians. I don't mean that we are Christian heathen, but we owe our Christian selves to an ancient mission to the Gentiles. Where should we have been without Paul, Boniface, Augustine, Columba, and a host more? We are Christians because we were caught in the wider sweep of the Kingdom's net; prophets in exile invoked the Spirit upon us. Ages ago, we were made Christians by men of the very stamp and vision of those who a century ago rose amongst ourselves to continue that true apostolic succession. It is down the line of the ministry that the true apostolic succession comes, not down the line of bishops. That continuity is nothing else than the inextinguishable missionary energy of the Gospel. No, the past is not dead while we keep that, nor the present, for, whatever the Churches are that they should not be, and whatever they are not that they should be, at least they are not dead. They are neither corpses nor are they mummies—whatever some of their members are. And some of these are great problems.

Dry Bones in the Heathen World

Some members of the Church—yea, some Churches themselves—make a greater problem than even the world or the heathen does. They make us ask, "Can *these* bones live?" These people who go to church, who uphold their Church, who would fight for their Church, would make civil war for its privileges, who have more fight than faith in them, whose souls are exceedingly filled with contempt, and they have a name to live, but are spiritually dead, who care for their Church chiefly as partisans, or because it is a centre

15: An Allegory of the Resurrection, 1902

of social rank or of juvenile amusements—can they live? What preacher but is cast into occasional despair by that question as he looks upon many spiritual skeletons about him? What preacher has not many a time to answer with Ezekiel that they can only live by some miracle of God; he, poor son of man, has failed, and is hopeless. He is preaching, perhaps, out of duty more than inspiration; he often prophesies in obedience rather than in hope. Well, preach hope till you have hope; then preach it because you have it. "Prophesy over these bones; call out to the Spirit," says the Lord. At the Lord's call, if not at your own impulse, call; call with a faith of life when the sense of life is low; speak the word you are bidden, and wait for the word you feel; and then the matter is the Lord's, and you win a new confidence in the midst of self-despair.

But it is not with bones or mummies that the preacher has chiefly to do. He comes, let us say, and lifts a vital voice. He is a man of parts and force; he collects a following, he is the centre of an interesting congregation. It looks well, comfortable; it is no skeleton crowd, it has flesh and blood. What is lacking? Perhaps the things that are not revealed to flesh and blood, the unearthly lustre in the eye, and movement in the mien, the Spirit of life. It is a congregation possibly, not a church; it is not dry, but it is not inspired; it is cultured possibly, but it is not kindled. The spirit has not come to stay, and there is not amongst them the shout of a king. So far, perhaps, it is only education, culture, that the preacher has supplied; it is mere religion, not regeneration. The bones are clothed, but not quickened; they know about sacred things, but they do not know about the Holy Ghost.

So prophesy once more, Son of man, saith the Lord. Prophesy to the Spirit of life; preach, but, still more, pray; invoke the abiding Spirit to enter these easy forms. They are less dismal than they were, but still too dull. Court for their sake the spirit and cultivate the discernment of the Spirit. Amid the many airs that fan them, amid the crowd of vivacious interests that tickle them as they pass by, make the Spirit of a new life blow on them. Above every other influence woo and wait upon the Spirit. Trace and press the Spirit of God; in every providence seize the Divine grace, subdue the spirit of the age to the Spirit of God; set up among the critics the Judge of all the earth. Preach the Spirit which not only clothes the skeletons decently and comfortably, but set them on their feet in the Kingdom of God. Preach what cast down imaginations and high things to the obedience of Christ; proclaim that Spirit which turns mere vitality into true life, mere comfort into the mighty peace; turn your worldly skeletons, by all means, into living congregations, but, above all, turn your congregation into a living Church.

And how shall you do that if your appeals to men have not been preceded by your cry to the Spirit, if your action on them is not inspired by your wrestling with God? Only then can you turn a crowd into a people, and a people into the Kingdom of God. That is the way to turn your Aceldama into the habitation of a multitude, and your multitude into a spiritual phalanx. Prophesy no more to the bones, preach no more as if it were dead worldlings you had; pray to the Spirit of God and preach to the spirit of man. Preach as to those who have begun to live and seek life. Never mind about current literature, mind the deep things of God. Preach to them great things. Let the trivial rubbish alone that occupies too much of our Church interest. It is possible to lose the soul in the effort to win souls. Dwell less upon the minor truths, dwell more upon the mighty truths which grow mightier by iteration. Take care of the spiritual pounds, and the current pence will look after themselves. Preach character by all means more than has been done, but preach it through a Gospel which takes the making of character out of your hands. Preach the Lord's Supper more often, and the tea-meetings less, as the Church's social centre and family hearth. Do not preach about goodness less, preach about grace more. Do not preach self-denial, preach a cross that compels self-denial. Don't mistake fervour and ardour for the Holy Ghost; do not take the flush for the blood or the blood for the life. Bring to men the Spirit, prophesy to the spirit in them; bring to them great demands—it is the demands of life that make men, is it not? Tax them, ask of them great sacrifices. We grow up as we lay down. Sacrifice before faith? No, first the sacrifice which is faith. There is no such tax on self-will as faith, no such sacrifice of our self-satisfaction as true faith, faith of the right kind, faith which is a cross as well as a trust in a cross and a resurrection, too. Trouble them, trouble them with the stir of a higher life. Living water is always troubled, it is an angel's trace upon the pool. Leave them not at ease; do not stop with putting on the flesh that just saves them from being skeletons. Infuse the flesh with the spirit; propose a great task, a thing incredible, and keep it before them till they rise to it. Does not the spirit make demands on us which no preacher can venture to do? Does not something in our own soul as he prophesies stir us, rebuke us, exact from us more than we dare? All the movements the true prophets stir escape beyond their dreams and demands.

Missionary Passions and Missionary Methods

And on this missionary occasion, I will confess that wonderful as the missionary record is, I should not be able always to retain my own faith in missions if I went merely by the reports and palpable results from the mission-field, unless they prophesy to the spirit in me, unless they appealed

15: An Allegory of the Resurrection, 1902

to faith in the Gospel more than faith in missions or missionaries. This is the real basis of missionary interest and action. It is our own experience of the Gospel, and not our acquaintance with the fields. For missionary methods you must know the field; that is the affair of the missionary statesman. But for missionary passion you must know the Gospel, and know it in the Spirit. And you must prize it so that you must give it away, you must not despise it so much that you keep it to yourself. It is to the Spirit as we have experienced it that missions appeal, it is to this Spirit they prophesy when they really stir us and give us stay. The missionary passion is proportionate to the Evangelical faith, and what it has done for our souls. If we feed our central fires with the oil of grace we can work our machinery at the world's end and keep it going in all weathers, in spite of travellers, traders, newspapers, and politicians. So, then, when the results of missions fail us, we fall back upon our own experience of the Gospel. But if that fail us? When the objective results fall short, can faith live upon a subjective experience which has its seasons, and may flush or pale? Is not the first necessity for faith an adjective? Are there no hours in the experience even of the best and boldest when the vision fades, the fine gold dims, and the glorious hour grows grey?—no times of dereliction, and seasons when the brook runs dry that we drank of by the way and lifted up our heart? Are there no times of lassitude, distraction, and other preoccupations in the Church at large? If results do not come in, and the confidence of hope goes out, what then? Then, then is the greatest hour.

Night it must be, ere Friedland's star shall burn.[7]

It was on an hour of dereliction that the whole world's fate hung and its Saviour won; when feeling ebbs we anchor on fact. Failing the results we see, and the experience we feel, we stand on a faith in which we know. When our experience wanes we turn to the experience of Christ and His apostles. Christ's faith in His own work stands when ours wavers. When it is hard to believe, we believe in His belief; we turn to Christ's sense of His own sure lordship of the world, Christ's faith in His own cross. We hear the command of Him who knew the power and range of His own victory. We discern the missionary necessity in the very nature and grace of the Gospel itself.

And so I draw near to my third head. Christ's redemption was the reversion of the world; it is the pledge of His final lordship of life; it is our impulse and our law, our steam and our compass. It gives the spiritual certainty which masters the world, and it gives the moral principle of its safe mastery; it brings both the spiritual courage and the moral method for

---

7. Thomas Carlyle, cited in *Letters and Memorials of Jane Welsh Carlyle, Prepared for Publication by Thomas Carlyle*, Volume 1 (1883).

handling the world. The power of the new life to come has the promise of the world that now is.

III. The Result

I speak in the third place about the result. "Ye shall know that I am the Lord, know what lordship is, when I have opened your graves, O My people."[8] The true, profound, and spiritual insight into things is by spiritual resurrection. Lordship is by knowledge, and this knowledge is by resurrection. We know what must rule the earth by knowing what has changed us. This is the source for men or nations of true conquest and final dominion of the world; the power and method of the world's final lordship is a power of which we know nothing until we are saved men. We cannot use that power till we share its life and experience its control; the final lordship of the world can only be on the principle of the missionary Gospel. Redemption is the condition of empire; there is but one morality, and its source and principle is the cross. The world is to be ruled at last by those men and by that society that know the laws and powers of the new soul. You cannot know God and God's way with the world unless you give your whole manhood as the pledge; to command the world you must die and you must rise with more command of your soul than when you died. You must come out of the grave of your dead self with the power of God. This is the moral truth of all Divine dominion, personal or collective, private or public. "When ye possess the land, and thy son asketh thee what mean these statutes and judgments, thou shalt say, 'We were bondsmen, and the Lord brought us out of Egypt with a mighty hand.'"[9] The spiritual power makes its own procedure and manages its own machinery. Inspiration is the true principle of organisation; the social fabric must grow out of the spiritual fact, and the social form reflect the social power. The Church is but self-organised inspiration; its form is given by the nature of its truth, and the forms of human society must finally take their shape from the need, the life, and the redeemed destiny of the human soul. I suppose there never was a time in the history of the world when organisation went for so much, for good or ill, as it does today. Societies have been called into existence for all manner of purposes, till they oust the home and threaten to submerge even the Church. Philanthropy is organised as a serious business; the Churches themselves organise and federate in a way unheard of, and some seek to organise themselves that never were organised before; missions are now conducted by societies which are in themselves small states; politics

8. Ezek 37:13.
9. Deut 6:20–21.

15: An Allegory of the Resurrection, 1902

and parties are in the hands of wire-pullers, and death is organised as well as life. Drink is organised into a solid, selfish interest, anti-social, inhuman, and deadly. Armies were never such perfect and costly machines, and wars were never so scientific; the bloodless war of industry is entering on a phase of trusts and syndicates, when vast organisations threaten to extinguish private enterprise altogether. The commercial swallows up the national; it is the newest Catholicism, that of finance. Labour is organised no less than capital in a way that seems sometimes to threaten both the life and the conscience of industry. Civilisation itself becomes organised, by wire and rail and Press, into a concert which is not always in tune, but is still in action. But is there no grave danger in this passionate rush to the mechanical side of existence? As we perfect the form, what is to become of the spirit? Can we organise human nature and land this leviathan with a hook? Can we organise ourselves into eternal life, or contest with Christ the monopoly of souls? Do we not already know more than we have power to manage? Have we not more skill and education than we know what to do with? If we have but organisation to lean on, and but trusts to trust, what is our future to be? How are we to work this load of machinery, and carry this steel nail? How are we to escape a crustacean doom and a tortoise future? Where are we to find the increase of life which is to save our organisation from becoming our grave? How is society to be saved from the growth of its own tissue, the hardening of its own shell? If the new organisation spread without new life, what does that mean but relapse, servitude, and suffocation? We die pot-bound; we may multiply the people, but if we do not increase the vital joy which is to save us from an outbreak of anarchism we shall pull the new fabric about its own ears and perish in the wreck.

The mere national spirit cannot save the nations. Human nature cannot secure its own liberty against a skilful conspiracy of intellect, will and money for its capture. Have we no source of new life, no treasury of moral power, no spring of moral initiative, no surety for our spiritual freedom, no security against the tyrants that bribe us, and find too ready allies in our own greeds and passions? If organisation grow, there must grow also a new volume of life; where is this life to come from? "Ye shall know," saith the Lord, "when I have brought you out of your graves." The efficiency of the world must be carried by a sufficiency of the Spirit, and its machinery worked by new Divine life. Empire must obey inspiration; the worldly spirit cannot hold the world; the increase of sources must be controlled by an increase of faith. Economic adventure must be balanced by spiritual enterprise. Christ must rise in us more than we rise to the hour; the energy of our adventure must be ruled by the power and purpose of His resurrection. What we need is power to manage power; it is moral insight and spiritual courage; it is courage and resource to confront the problems and perils that do not occur to our common thoughts, our common Press, our common Parliament. It is courage to conquer a dread of ourselves that would overwhelm us if we saw and knew ourselves; it is power to confront the inevitable time when our tough self-satisfaction is rent from top to bottom, and we shall have to know ourselves for the common laggards, traitors, or rebels that we are to the Lord of the moral world. The Titan is weary, because he is worldly and defies the holy gods.

Conquerors Because Redeemed

What troubles and threatens us most is not the pathlessness of a dark world, but misgiving about our own self, disenchantment with our schemes, and despair of our own fidelity. What we need is the kind of power that will enable us to go on and still conquer when our robust assurance fails, when we have gone through the disillusionment which comes from exhausting the world we range, from neglecting our conscience or betraying it, and then finding ourselves out. Is there no spirit to find us then, where we have hidden ourselves away among the stuff? If we have no such Discoverer, Redeemer, Quickener, we have no God, no kingdom, no courage, no future. It is in His Redemption that we must find our power to master life, and our ethic to rule the world. It is in His forgiveness that we find the humility that has the promise of freedom and the imperial secret; it is in His cross that we find the ethics that inherit the earth. The future of the world is theirs who have the secret of the moral world. When He has brought us from our graves, then we shall know how heaven's missions are spread, worlds are won, and stable empires made. The secret of Christ is the empire of the world; the missionary Gospel is the only imperial principle. How can we master where we do not know? and we only know life, man, and the moral world in the cross. We only know them when we do much more than know, when we trust and experience their moral salvation. The world was made for the cross. We conquer fate because we are so much more than conquerors; we are redeemed. The hero who remains hero stands upon the saint, and any final heroism of man and beneficent valour of greatness is due to the redeeming holiness of God. It is the breath of a Spirit which quickens and masters, because it is a Holy Spirit, and works in a holy way. Patriotism and devotion are things that worthily lay hold on our imagination; they are fine virtues, but they are not by themselves things whereby a soul lives or a people. The final human weal depends not on magnanimity or devotion, but on righteousness whose source is the principle of the cross. And

15: An Allegory of the Resurrection, 1902

by that I mean much more than a spirit of sacrifice of idealism. It is possible to combine with much toil and large sacrifice a total lack of moral quality or Christian faith; it is possible to combine with a life devoted to vast visions conduct released from moral scruples. Napoleon's order of greatness was as unscrupulous as it was large; it was red with ruin, and it cursed a whole people with visions of glory which quenched the passion of duty and debased the public soul to the Second Empire and its sequels. Our ethics today are suffering from the literary and religious glorification of love for its own sake, and the idea of sacrifice is becoming debased by an æsthetic idolatry of mere sacrifice and mere bravery. Both the love and the sacrifice hear so much about themselves that they grow self-conscious. They "fancy themselves," they dress for the public and count on the Press. How nauseous are the ideals of love and sacrifice that nourish the young Briton of both sexes in the sixpenny magazine! They are not lost in a moral inspiration and a holy end, they are cut off from faith. Before I admire sacrifice or any ardour, I wish to know its object, its inspiration, its methods. What brought a world from its grave was not the ideals [of] Christ, not Messianic visions nor self-sacrifice; for them it was done by refusing some of those grandiose visions for those of secret, severe, and holy obedience to the Holy Law; it was by His hallowing once and always, in the world's most vast public and decisive act, God's Holy but dishallowed Name. It is not ideals that save, nor guesses—not dreams, sacrifices, nor genius—but sanctity.

The Mightiest Personality in History

I do feel—we all feel—the spell of huge personalities, forceful and imaginative; but I feel their limits still more. The man of blood and iron was bewildered and beaten by the spiritual power of Rome; the Armada was broken upon a people it despised. Cromwell himself ran the hilt of his matchless sword into his own mighty and making hand, and he gave his work the sentence of premature collapse. The most colossal personality succumbs to death, but death itself has succumbed to a personality more than colossal in Christ—more than colossal, not because more forceful, but because He was the Holy and the Just. The mightiest personality in history is the Holy One. He is the first, and He will be the last. The greatest power we know is holiness; the holy Christ is the chief of the great powers of Europe today. It is not from Him that holiness has become for the world a negative idea, cloistered and feeble. The first care to Christ was not that He should sacrifice Himself for an ideal, it was that He should glorify the holiness of God. He died to bless man, but still more to glorify God, and upon His people the first charge in Church or State must always be, not the happiness of men, but the holiness of God. The Christian man's chief end is to glorify a holy God in all things, public and private. Our aspirations must follow our prayers, our public dreams must follow our most common prayer, which always begins, "Hallowed be Thy Name, as in heaven's affairs, so in earth's."[10] When the Church can make that note practical in human affairs, then the Church will call the people from their graves; she will set up realms based on something more missionary than the egoisms and rivalries of race.

The Real Key of Empire

It already means much that in the present war so many of our people on both sides have sought justification beyond England's rights in England's duty to the righteous purpose of God for the world. Our very divisions have that new and ennobling feature. I wish to say this lest I might seem guilty of the indecency of passing any political judgment here on current affairs. Generosity and sacrifice can silence many tongues and stir much praise; but are we not all convinced that it is public righteousness that exalteth a nation, and holiness that hallows sacrifice? How can we prosper if we are moving about in a world not realised? and the world is not realised till we stir its moral nerve, and God has exposed and stirred that nerve in Christ's cross. God, His existence and His Kingdom, is for many of the mighty potsherds of earth but an even chance; and their huge schemes for history fail and break their necks because they put their feet into the little molehill of this "perhaps." But knowledge that makes long history and holds the far future, is the knowledge of a kingdom-making, nation-making God, righteous even to holiness, and holy enough to redeem us from our moral graves.

In a word, it is the missionary idea, the missionary faith, and the missionary policy that has the key of empire and the long last reversion of the wide world's future. If the Christian Church go to the heathen with one word, and the Christian State with another, where is hope? There is no sure future to godless dreams, godless commerce, yea, or even godless ardour for the just, the free. It is possible to spread even justice and freedom by ways which civilise but debase, and which exploit the world far faster than they can save it. The missionary spirit is the spirit which brings men and nations out of their graves through a holy resurrection, and a resurrection unto godliness. Do you tell me this is a preacher's extravagance? Nay, it is apostolic penetration and boldness; it is not mine; I do but paraphrase the New Testament. At any rate, it is there, at this faith, that the great audacities

10. Matt 6:9–10//Luke 11:2.

15: An Allegory of the Resurrection, 1902

of the missionary passion are fed; and I confess to you that I see more that is grand, sure, and practical in the visions of an original missionary pioneer than in those of the greatest empire builders. I think more of the dreams of Carey than of Clive; Clive no doubt was a great man, and he attracts the national imagination, but the least in the Kingdom of Heaven was greater than he; the violent may take, but it is the meek that inherit and the just that keep. The spirit which possesses the earth and keeps possession is inspired at the folly of the cross. "The weakness of the cross!" From beyond these walls I can hear the scorner say, "It is the greatest decadence in history, and can become the most nauseous." And this voice of Nietzsche finds an echo in the secret heart and practical conduct of many a spirit less bold. The greatest decadence! It is the sublimest irony of history. So quiet, so awful, so absurd, so irresistible, it mocks the wisdom of the wise and the valour of the brave. The terrible ones are brought to naught; it is as mighty as the heavens, that see all things, and outlive them, and still smile subtly, securely on. "The weakness of the cross" is the greatest pitfall on earth, and it mocks the empire makers as it establishes its power upon their wreck, and thrusts its fine spells through the crevices of their untempered walls. This is all very ridiculous, of course, but they laugh best who laugh last. One sits in heaven and laughs. I think I do measure with some adequacy the power of Paganism at home and abroad, and it does seem very ridiculous to think of the conversion of the races of the East to Christ, or of the peoples of Europe to the principles of the Gospel. It is as ridiculous as Christ before Pilate, as ironical as the Judge of all the earth sentenced by a forgotten Sanhedrin. Oh, I know that ridicule and folly; I know it for the very power and irony of God. If you ask me whether these wrecks and relics of conscience in Europe or elsewhere can live, I must frankly say, "I do not know; I doubt it." I do not wonder that many doubt it, and that the world disbelieves it.

Out of the Prison-Graves

I do not know it from any deduction, but I believe it—I am sure of it. And I do because I know this: First, I know that God has made life out of my shipwreck; that is my experience. He has opened my grave and made me live; He has clothed my bones with flesh, and stirred me with life and hope; and if He has done that for me, then the incredible miracle is in principle done that saves the world. For the second thing, I know is this, that, according to the mind of Christ and the experience of His apostles in every age, I have only been saved by something which in the same act also saved the world. It took a world's salvation to save me, and what I know in this matter for me I foreknow for mankind. My salvation has been the prophetic spirit of a world's redemption. The prophetic spirit is not knowing the future, but knowing Him who does. Missions depend not on a foresight of the Church's triumph, but on an insight into the Gospel's purpose and power; we see not yet all things subdued, but we see Jesus. I am saved by the cross and resurrection of One who was not one, but all mankind's epitome, promise, and surety. This I know—namely, "O Lord, Thou knowest." If I do not know the world's future and its possibilities, God knows. And this God has told and moved me how to act. He has told me to treat every man as saveable; therefore every man is, and He has commanded and inspired His Church to act as if from these wrecks of men He could by His own breath make armies of the Lord. Therefore, by faith I know they can be. He has made man's possibilities the Church's opportunity, and man's needs the Church's way—nay, its safety. If I refuse His Word I derange my own soul; I can only go on to my own salvation if I recognise that God has charged Himself with the salvation of my kind and put some of the responsibility on me. Our missions cast us upon the fundamental right and faith of the Church itself. The charter of both is the same; to lose faith in man under God is, in due time, to lose faith also in a God over man. But it should not be so hard to believe in a missionary future if there were not something wrong with our Christian present, nor to believe for the dark races if we were more sound about the white. We are straitened in ourselves. We are still in our graves buried alive. And when the trouble is lack of power, what is there to do but pray? We are alive enough surely to believe in prayer.

O Lord, bid us come forth, we are in our graves; Lord, raise us up. We are bound in graveclothes, loose us and let us go; we are tied up in our habits, our views, our pursuits, our prejudices, our egotisms, our politics, our interests, our fears, our passions, our fashions, our friends, our sects, our creeds; and our life is stale, our bones are dry, and we are weary; our little souls are easily weary of so great a world; it presses on us like a weight of earth. All we often seem able to do is to turn in our coffin. Lord, Lord, open unto us! Open our graves, clothe our bones with flesh, and inspire our flesh with freedom by Thy Spirit; Thou hast given to us for our deepest passion the passion to be free, because we are made in Thine image and freedom is Thy passion; Thine own deepest passion is the passion to redeem us and set us free. Raise us from the dead, loose us and let us go, set us on our feet, put us back in our own land. This is not our own land; we are exiles, and we are too content. We are secluded, buried in a valley out of the way; bring us forth into the great traffic of Thy kingdom; there is our native land. Lord of life, we can only live in Thee, Thou art our native land. Restore us to Thee. We can but know Thee by sharing Thy life, and win Thy world by sharing Thy victory. Breathe into us

15: An Allegory of the Resurrection, 1902

Thy breath; lift us with Thy Spirit. We faint, we fail, we die, we lie, we parch, we bleach upon the valley of battle where Thy enemies prevail, and the fowls of heaven pick us bare. Clothe our bones, quicken our flesh, kindle our powers, and create us anew, and the valley of death shall be a gate of hope, and because we have fallen, we shall rise to a humbler life and move to a holier land.

O Christ, Redeemer of the world, Thou Open Door, and Thou Living Way, Thou Certainty of Truth and Assurance of Salvation, by the open mystery of Thy Holy Incarnation, by Thy cross and passion, by Thy precious death and burial, and by the coming of Thy kingdom, have mercy on those who are dead and buried here. By Thy glorious resurrection and ascension, and by the coming of the Holy Ghost, good Lord, open our graves, enlarge our hearts, and deliver our souls into their native land. Give us our brethren for a care and the heathen for our desire. Roll away the stone of our self-concern, break the seal of our slumber and the delusion of our dreams. Fulfil with the fulness of the heathen the fulness of our salvation. We are not what we might be to Thee, because they are not what they should be to us. Lord, lay them on our heart. On Thy heart we have all lain, and so Thou wast our Saviour. Bring us into the fulness of knowledge and strength of salvation through the risen might, grace, and glory of Jesus Christ our Lord.

16

DUMB CREATURES AND CHRISTMAS: A LITTLE SERMON TO LITTLE FOLK, 1903

"She laid him in a manger."
—LUKE 2:7

IN THE CHURCH OF England and in the Church of Rome they have what are called saints' days. These are days set apart for the special remembrance of good and holy men and women. It does us good to remember the great and faithful who have passed away. It makes us a little ashamed of ourselves that we are not better. And it makes us remember that we can be better if we like.

But there have been more people holy and good than there are days in the year. So in order that none of these worthies should be left out or forgotten there was one day set apart for a memorial of all of them together. They called it All Saints' Day, and it falls upon November 1.

But that was not enough for the Christian heart. We are taught to think not only of the good but of everybody, not only of the living but of the dead. God sends his rain and his sunshine upon the good and the evil alike. He tells us to pray for the bad as well as to praise for the good. And we are particularly told to consider the poor and insignificant. Accordingly, there was a day set apart for remembering everybody—good and bad, living and dead. That was called All Souls' Day, and it is on November 2—the day after All Saints'.

But there was more than even that. There was a day set apart for remembering all children. Was that not very proper? If we are to remember those who have ended very good, why should we not remember those who are beginning to be very good, and who are good just a little? I mean the

16: Dumb Creatures and Christmas: A Little Sermon to Little Folk, 1903

children; and I say they are just a little good because there is not very much of them to be good; and also because they are just beginning to be good, and have not got so far on the road as they will one day. And, again, if we are to remember everybody, including the dead who have just died, why should we not remember those who are just starting to live and who have all the hard road of life before them? It is very proper that we have a day of all children. But there is no day with that name, if you look down the almanack. No. It goes under another name. Christmas speaks of a little Child who was, as you might say, all little children gathered into one. In this baby the childhood of all children was gathered up and put in a small and precious form. In foreign lands they take roses in millions and they extract the essence out of them; and out of thousands of roses they get only a tiny quantity of this essence. Its scent is very powerful, and they put a small quantity into little phials, and it sells for a great deal of money. Now, in the baby Jesus it was as if the childhood of all rosy children were there in a small and costly form. Thus when we celebrate the day of His birth we celebrate all children, and all that is childlike. And so Christmas Day is really All Children's Day. It comes to cheer us up in the very middle of winter; just as a little grandchild might come to two people who are getting old and have the snow coming down upon them in the shape of grey hairs.

The first Christmas lesson then is that you remember all children, especially all forgotten and neglected children. And I hope you will learn not to sit down to your Christmas dinner in comfort till you have seen that some child has one who, but for you, would have had none.

But I want to go further than all saints, or all souls, or all children. I want to take in all creatures, especially when we are thinking of God.

> For the dear God that loveth us
> He made and loveth all.[1]

Now what day should we have for All Creatures' Day? You will not find that in the almanack either. But what better day could we have than this selfsame Christmas Day? For was Jesus born among other children? Was He born into a nursery? Was there a crowd of other children all eager to see the new baby, and all clapping their hands when they did? Nothing of the kind. You know He was born in a stable, with a horse-trough for a cradle, with straw for a bed, and the cattle for company. There was the ass on which His mother rode, there were the asses of the other travellers who had got rooms in the inn; there were the cows belonging to the farm, and

---

1. From Samuel Taylor Coleridge's poem, "The Rime of the Ancient Mariner" (1798).

II: Published Sermons

the fowls pecking in the straw; and there were the sheep—well, the sheep, of course, were in the fields, where the angels' message came to the men who were taking care of them. The animals were nearer to the infant Jesus than any children were. And how often He spoke of the animals when He grew up; and He never spoke as if he despised them, but always as if He watched and loved them. And how very much the animals owe to Jesus! How much better the religion of Jesus has made people treat animals! The animals owe Jesus a great deal, if they but had a tongue to tell it. Yet they have tongues. I once saw a very old carving of the Nativity over a great church door. Now, I have seen several old pictures of the Nativity with the animals standing by or looking in with great interest at the stable window. But in this case they were still more interested; they were very affectionate to the baby, and their tongues expressed it. For it was two cows, and they had come up to the manger. You may know, perhaps, how curious cows are about clothes. They eat the cottage wash sometimes when it is hung out on the hedge. Well, among the swaddling clothes they found the baby; and they were so far from being disappointed that they felt quite loving, and they were licking it with their great rough tongues. I often think cows very kindly animals, but I never thought so more than then. Very likely the artist, with a kindly humour, wished to represent the homage of the creatures for the little Jesus. And he knew that they could not speak and praise with their tongues like men. So he made them worship in the only way their tongues could. I have seen your mothers smother you with kisses, and say they could eat you for affection. Thus their mouths would show forth your unspeakable praise.

So the second Christmas lesson I give you is to be kind to the dumb creatures. Christmas is not only all children's day, but all creatures' day. Some boys and girls who would not hurt children are very thoughtless, and even hard-hearted, about animals, and sometimes they are cruel. But these creatures are under Christ's care and affection. And the heart that would be cruel to a cat or a cow is like a boy with a cigarette—it is not a heart that manliness has much to do with. All the creatures in the world are, so to say, in the same stable with Jesus, and His blessing is over all. For He came with a very great salvation indeed.

17

THE PROBLEM OF FORGIVENESS IN THE LORD'S PRAYER, 1903

"Forgive us our trespasses as we forgive them that trespass against us."
—MATTHEW 6:12

Part I

THE LORD'S PRAYER IS less a prayer than a scheme of, prayer, a sketch. It is an outline, the notes of prayer, that we may learn the duty and power of praying with thought, intent, and cohesion, instead of uttering mere ejaculations.

It is not a prayer by Christ *with* His disciples, but one given to them. Luke says it was when He had *ceased* praying that He gave them this form. It was a prayer born in prayer. Its terse brevity represents the concentration in which true prayer leaves the mind and soul. Christ never led His disciples in prayer. He never says "Our Father" in a sense to include Him and them alike. His prayers were *for* them, not *with* them, and not even in their hearing, except to a small and accidental extent in the Garden. Public prayer is seldom purely extempore. Absolutely extempore prayer can only be between the soul and God. Prayer in public should be the fruit of careful preparation both in devotion and thought, as this most public of all prayers was.

The Lord's Prayer is liturgical in so far as this, that it prescribes the course which the prayer of a community should take in its main lines. Just as if I should take into the pulpit brief written memoranda of the course that our public prayer should follow—a thing I have always claimed the right to do, without anything surreptitious—though they are not always used. It seems absurd to prepare aids to thought in addressing men, while we are willing to be careless and slipshod, rambling and vapid, in speaking to God.

II: Published Sermons

The Lord's Prayer is not a simple prayer in one sense. It has at least two huge difficulties in it. It is possible to overdo the demand for simplicity both in prayer and preaching, till all effort on the part of spiritual intelligence ceases, and only certain easy sympathies have play, and religion becomes a spiritual luxury and sedative.

The two difficulties are:—

1. *Lead us not into temptation.*
2. *Forgive us as we forgive.*

Of these the most important is the latter. For Christ returns to it at the end of the prayer in verses 14 and 15. Or if the words were not used by Christ on this occasion (and Luke omits them), they were on another. They are in another context in Mark. And their addition to the Lord's Prayer by Matthew shows where its chief strain upon faith and life was felt to be by one part of the first Church at least.

This petition was never meant to encourage a side glance of satisfaction with our Christian facility in forgiving. I fear that that would be the result of making God's forgiveness depend on ours either as ground or as measure. But in the story of the Pharisee and the Publican, Christ has given its death-blow to that frame of mind, however subtle its form.

What is the exact difficulty?

Luke's version suggests it. There is a difference between Matthew and Luke. Matthew says *as* we forgive; Luke says *for*.

The meaning suggested is different. Which word did Christ use, and which meaning did He intend?

Possibly something has happened to the word in Luke. He seems to think that our forgiveness is the *ground* of God's. Forgive *for* we forgive—forgive *because* we forgive.

Now Matthew's suggestion is not that. Using *as*, he rather seems to suggest that our forgiveness is to be the *measure* of God's and not its ground.

But both these interpretations are wrong. They are not consistent, that is, with the central principles of Christ's work and teaching.

I. Christ Could Not Mean That Our Forgiveness is the *Ground* Or Reason of God's.

God does not forgive us *because* we forgive our enemies. The whole of Christianity comes to the ground if God's forgiveness did not come first, if it is not the type, if our forgiveness of others do not rise out of His forgiveness of us.

17: The Problem of Forgiveness in the Lord's Prayer, 1903

So the difficulty is this. We can only forgive in the moral strength of being forgiven; while here we seem to ask forgiveness because we have already merited it by forgiving. We seem told to earn it by doing what we cannot do till we have it.

Now that is impossible. Love and mercy to our neighbour is not the reason why God is gracious to us. But the grace of God is the main thing which enables man to love his neighbour.

Christ said of the sinful woman, "Much has been forgiven her, for she loved much."[1] And what loose, sentimental, mawkish morality has been based on a perversion of the words. Christ went on to say that to whom little was forgiven the same loveth little. Surely His meaning was clear enough. "*For*" does not explain the forgiveness, but the way He knew it. "For she hath loved much" was the ground for concluding she had been forgiven much. It was the outward and visible sign of forgiveness; it was not the reason why she was forgiven. It might, and should, soften our human judgment, but it could not be her absolution before the holiness of God. Those who say that forgiveness is easily given to erring love forget that the sin is against love, and is therefore more due to defect of love than to excess of it. It is against God's holy love, against love in its true divineness. If that had been felt, the sin would not have been done. Were forgiveness bestowed on love, how should we ever be forgiven by God, whom it is our great sin not to have loved? And if God forgive men because they love each other unwisely, some of the sins most deadly to society must be the lightest before God. Some sins most fatal to the soul would be most venial to its Saviour, which is both a moral and a religious absurdity.

We can never win the mercy of God by mercy of ours. If forgiveness be God's, not man's, it is just because it is undeserved, because it is grace toward the graceless, not love toward the amiable. Our real motive to forgive, and our power, lie in our forgiveness first by God. I speak of real forgiveness, what Christ calls *forgiveness from the heart*. And I mean forgiveness of a real wrong, of what we bitterly feel as a wrong, what it is past human nature to forgive. I do not speak of little offences and trifling insults, real or fancied, but of a great wrong embittering the soul at the centre, and the soul too of the strong, to forgive which we should at once confess was beyond our power. I speak of the forgiveness which is the greatest tax on our moral resource, and shows its weakness most. I mean the one triumph above all others for which the Grace of God is needed, and where it shows itself as really grace. To forgive in this way is a superhuman power. "You cannot," you say, and you go regretfully away. Of course *you* cannot. It can only be done by the forgiving God within you. It takes much forgiveness of you to raise

---

1. Luke 7:47.

you to that. It is no light matter, no case of good nature, or short memory, or generous contempt. It is a case of a new heart and a new will.

"I cannot forgive," you say, and you comfort yourself by the conclusion that there are things you are not called upon to forgive. But Christ will not allow that. You must part either with your rancour or your Redeemer. "I cannot forgive," you say and feel. Then your prayer, if you continue to pray, must be "Forgive me that I cannot forgive." This shows at least that you acknowledge the duty. It is glorifying the spirit of forgiveness which you confess you have not acquired. "Forgive me till I can forgive," you must pray." Make me daily so to feel the thousand pounds that Thou hast forgiven, that I may freely remit the hundred pence that are due to me. Make me realise where I should have been if Thou hadst claimed Thy rights, so that I may be ashamed to stand greedily for mine."

Paul has seized the true Christian principle, "forgiving one another, even as God for Christ's sake hath forgiven you."[2]

II. But it Would Be Wrong in Another Way to Think that Our Forgiveness is the *Measure* of God's.

This is an error that may find footing even on Matthew's *as*. You might admit that God was willing to forgive on other grounds than our forgiving, on the ground of His own; but you might also hold that He only gave out as much mercy as corresponded to ours. We do not earn it, it is of grace; but we only receive as much grace as we have shown.

"As much grace!" The words make a contradiction in terms. God loves us all or not at all. Grace would not be grace if it were not full, free, complete. Grace ceases to be grace if it is doled out as priests do. It throws open the Kingdom of Heaven. It does not palter at the gate. It does not haggle about terms, fitness, receptivity. If our forgiveness is to be like God's, it must not be the Pharisaic thrice, or Peter's seven times, but till seventy times seven.

> Give all thou canst; high Heaven rejects the lore
> Of nicely-calculated less or more.[3]

It is quite true that we cannot take God's grace in unless from the heart we forgive. That is psychologically, ethically true. But is not true theologically. It is another thing to say that God's grace does not go out to us except as we forgive. It is only because His grace goes out to us that we can treat in any

2. Eph 4:32.
3. From William Wordsworth's poem, "Inside of King's College Chapel, Cambridge" (1821).

17: The Problem of Forgiveness in the Lord's Prayer, 1903

gracious way those who have wronged us. We ask grace, not because we have reached the power of forgiving, but because we feel the chief work of grace is to supply that power. We must pursue it as a spiritual ideal. So long as we are incapable of it there is sin in us to be forgiven. We ask, trusting in a foregone forgiveness, and moved by it. We are afraid lest we make it of no effect, or bar its access to us. We ask, believing that God has broken sin in principle once for all. In grace He has forgiven the world. We ask that this may be carried home to us. We are in earnest about asking, because our moral effort is set on doing the like to men. How can we preach a gospel of forgiveness we do not practice? But our practice is not the measure of the gift we seek; it is a fruit of having it, and a sign of our earnestness in seeking more.

It is a great thing to realise that the forgiving grace of God is the deepest, mightiest, most permanent and persistent power in the moral world. Not that we may make it so, but that it *is* so. It *is* so. There is a universe of moral forces and soul powers about us, shaping us more really than our physical world does, and all its forces. All things work up into this moral order, this realm of the conscience, this passion which quells passion and teaches peace. And in this awful, certain realm, the mightiest power is grace, is Christ. I beg you to realise it, to arrest yourself, to compel yourself to stand still long enough in the hurry of interests, the press of pursuits, and the buzz of things, to take the fact and its meaning in. The greatest, subtlest, final power in the world, which will grow on you as life deepens and matures, is the grace of God. It has the promise and reversion of all things, and it will let nothing go. You have to do chiefly and lastly with a world in which this is the central principle, and everything which disowns this principle is destined to be broken.

Consider the rite of the Lord's Supper. It stands there simple but venerable. Almost the oldest institution in Europe is before your eyes. Through ages and ages of confusion, peril, perversion, and strife, the thing itself has endured, and is among us to this day, less likely than ever to be swept away by change, chill, or war. So, but much more so, the grace of God persists and works among all the inferior powers and preoccupations of the soul's world.

This is not a mere illustration. The rite lasts because it signifies the thing which lasts. It is among us because the grace of God is among us. It stands visibly for that grace. It is no creation of ours. It is not a mnemonic device of ours. It was not invented by man to keep the memory of a certain thing alive in a more or less artificial way. It is a historic gift to-man. It is there by God's providence as God's witness and Christ's presence. In the Lord's Supper God's forgiveness is not simply remembered by us, but offered us, carried home to us anew. The rite is the property of the whole Christian Church, and is its witness, its acted proclamation, of the gospel of forgiveness. God in the course of history offers Christ, the fount of history, anew. There is a long continuity in this historic act. Man repeats it, but it is a continuous act with God. And it stands, not as an artificial symbol or imported suggestion of God's persistent grace, but as that grace's own creation and expression. We did not place it on God's grace, as we might tie a knot to make us remember; but God's grace grew it, in the Church which His grace created. As this rite stands in the tumult of history, simple, peaceable, neglected, or abused, so the forgiveness of God stands amid the unseen powers that do most to shape us for weal or woe. But it is not simply one of them, it is the focus of them and their goal. It is the condition of our fellowship with the Eternal Life. We lay hold of that fellowship according as we lay hold of forgiveness, and show it forth. We enter the family of the eternal grace by becoming *blood relations of Jesus Christ*.

Part II

The key to the true interpretation is found by remembering that the prayer was given for use by men who had been forgiven. They were in the Messiah's Kingdom. And the initial gift which made the Kingdom the Kingdom, had been this of forgiveness.

I wish that many who urge the Kingdom on us in the Press and elsewhere, would remember that it is not founded on social righteousness, but on the forgiveness of sins; on which all social justice is founded. Social righteousness is the goal of the Kingdom—that is, of forgiveness. It is the *form* of the Kingdom. It is the order into which forgiven men fall as they realise and live up to what their forgiveness means. But it is not the soul of the Kingdom, nor its life; it is not the enthusiasm which moves the Kingdom, or moves men to it. It is beginning at the wrong end to start with it—that is, if it is the Christian Kingdom of God that is invoked and pressed. Of course mere Socialism does not profess to start from this root. It does not claim to be Christian; and if it be preached or criticised it must be in another way. But Christ's Kingdom of God does so start, and it is not fair to press the Kingdom of God by aid of the New Testament, while this first condition of sin and forgiveness is practically ignored, and its believers treated with condescension as very useful people socially, if they be not scared, and if they be treated with allowance and patience.

The disciples had been forgiven. That was the gift that made them members of the Kingdom. It was forgiven men, therefore, that were instructed to use this prayer, "Forgive us, as, forgiven, we forgive." It was a prayer for daily renewed forgiveness, then, not forgiveness in the sense of the great justification which changed the whole relation of God and man.

17: The Problem of Forgiveness in the Lord's Prayer, 1903

That was foregone. It was that great universal sense of forgiveness or justification that chiefly exercised Paul—the one universal, eternal act of grace, done once for all in Christ's person, and finished in His death. All daily forgiveness, all mutual forgiveness, is the detail of that, the working out of it. But it was not that great justification that Christ had in His mind here. He was speaking to a kingdom, already set up by that act latent in Himself. What He had in view, was the daily draft on this foregone and exhaustless grace, the periodic irrigation by the water of life once for all set free. "Give us this day our daily bread, *and* forgive us."[4] Observe how the two things are coupled and made parallel. The Lord's Prayer moves in these couplets or parallels, like a Hebrew poem or psalm. Thus:—

> Our Father, which art in Heaven,
> Hallowed be Thy name;
>
> Thy Kingdom come,
> Thy will be done on earth as it is in Heaven;
>
> Give us this day our daily bread,
> And forgive us our debts as we forgive our debtors;
>
> Lead us not into temptation,
> But deliver us from evil.

You observe that this prayer for forgiveness belongs to the couplet about daily provision, and expounds it to what is the true nature of heavenly food. It was for the daily bread of forgiveness that they were to pray; the daily sense of it, the habit and spirit of reconciliation; as with God, so with men; the realisation of it, not its creation at the first. "He that is bathed needeth not save to wash his feet."[5] The forgiven man is still soiled with daily dust, which must be daily removed. The sense is: "Renew Thy forgiveness, as we use Thy forgiveness to forgive." It is not repeat, but renew. Forgive us, as, forgiven, we forgive.

Now this *sense* of God's forgiveness does depend upon the use we make of it towards our neighbour. If we feel that we are forgiven and at peace with God, and if, at the same time, we do not let that change our bearing to those whom we find *trying*, the sense of divine forgiveness fades—we feel unforgiven. We cannot keep up the peace of forgiveness by God along with a *critical, exacting* spirit towards our neighbours. Our forgiveness of them is not the measure of God's forgiveness, but it does affect the extent to which we can take His forgiveness in.

There are three things we may distinguish:—

4. Matt 6:11–12a.
5. John 13:10.

II: Published Sermons

1. *The state of forgiveness.*
   The whole race is in that state before God through Jesus Christ.
2. *The sense of forgiveness*—when a soul realises that fact and is at peace with God.
3. *The spirit of forgiveness*—when the sense of it becomes the heart's habit, and works outward towards men.

It becomes a changed temper and settled frame of the soul, which cares far less for its rights than for its duties and sympathies. The form of the unforgiving spirit that mostly troubles *us*, is seldom implacable resentment; it is oftener the *exacting* spirit, or the *critical* spirit, when it gets the upper hand.

What this petition teaches us is, that if the *sense* of forgiveness do not continually pass into the *spirit* of forgiveness, that sense dies. We are as if we were not forgiven; we are hard and foreign masses in a forgiven world. We must pray for forgiveness, and chiefly for forgiveness for unforgivingness. We do not *have* forgiveness without forgiving, or at least we cannot keep it. Forgivingness is the condition for appropriating forgiveness, but not for moving God to forgive. Our forgivingness is really our practical thanksgiving for God's forgiveness. That is the force of St Matthew's "as."

You remember Zaccheus [sic]. Christ came to him, visited with him, treated him as a forgiven man. And you remember the result on Zaccheus. It roused the spirit of gratitude, of amends, of forgiveness. The spirit of praise for being visited and forgiven by God took this shape. Zaccheus was so moved that out of his fulness of heart he vowed what he did. This was not the *cause* of Christ's visit. It had not been Zaccheus's habit. It was the result of the visit. And it was an act of praise in the true sense, returning God's mercy *in the same kind*. It is much to feel "God has forgiven me, therefore I sing heartily and subscribe of my means." That is all of grace. But it is a still greater sign of grace to feel "God has forgiven me, therefore my heart is tender. I go out in pity, patience, and blessing to my brethren, black or white, seen or never seen, friend or foe."

Now read this petition in that way. "Forgive us our debts," you pray. Then there is a pause, as the forgiveness comes (never mind how long the pause is). It comes. We rejoice. We feel we must thank God somehow. We must offer a grateful sacrifice, and our true sacrifice of final thanks is returning our mercies in kind, and forgiving our debtors. We *pray*, we PRAISE, we promise.

It would be quite contrary, both to the spirit of this petition and to the whole Gospel, if we were to put off praying for forgiveness till we felt able to forgive all men. If we felt able for that we should not need much forgiveness. It is only the forgiveness we pray for that makes possible the forgiveness we show.

So the use of the Lord's Prayer in sincerity and earnestness is an ethical exercise—as prayer always should be.

It is the great school of the highest, finest morality. "Forgive as we forgive." That links theology and humanity in one ethical bond. Prayer is the school of humanity. What else is to teach it us? Does it come natural? Some of the common forms do, partly because they have been inbred in us by Christian tradition, partly because the divine has never quite left human nature. But when we come to the finer, rarer forms of it, what is to teach us humanity? Culture? Culture is more monastic in its tendencies than humane. And culture will not teach the highest, rarest, hardest accomplishment of humanity—to forgive. It stands on its refined dignity and its self-sufficient resource.

What is to keep up the glow of social enthusiasm? The love of man in some forms has already caught us. How is it to hold us? What is to make it more than a sentiment, a passing fashion of the heart, a tender fit, to be followed by a cruel, as so often happens? What is to make it an ingrained moral quality and spiritual habit? What is to create hearts large enough to bear with all men and restore them? What can make us love our enemies? If you can love your enemies you can love all men. That is love's last, greatest victory, the goal of love's culture. It is what makes love grace. But we can only love our enemies by one means—by prayer. It is not in human nature. It is a supernatural gift. It is only to be acquired by supernatural means—by prayer, by association with the greatest case of the kind ever known or possible—with God who loved us, and forgave us, and redeemed. "Herein is love, not that we loved God, but that He loved us,"[6] "While we were yet sinners, Christ died for us."[7] These are not texts, but truths.

Prayer, and prayer for forgiveness, is the condition, therefore, of the growth and permanence of social enthusiasm. It is the true, deep school of humanity. The evangelical foundation is the only social foundation, if what I have said be true. And it is true if the Lord's Prayer be true. You say, perhaps, that things are simpler than all that, and that we need not go so deep into theology for a practical sociology. But you have always said also that the ideal of simple religion was the Lord's Prayer. And yet here is the problem which stares you in the face from the centre of it. Besides, we have not been going into abstract theology, but practical, experimental theology, the theology which men should live in their souls and consciences, and which men try to evade by cant against theology and about

6. 1 John 4:10.
7. Rom 5:8.

simplicity. Your impatience of this theology is not, therefore, because it is obscure or abstract, but (forgive me) because it is hard, because it makes on you a moral demand which you resent. It is personal theology, but not individualist. It is a social theology. And you cannot really have any other kind of theology. A Christian theology must be social, because it is based on a social Godhead and the Kingdom of God. A Christian sociology must be theological, because the Kingdom of God rests entirely on forgiveness in Jesus Christ. When people tell you that the Gospel means a form of Christian Socialism, ask them what they mean. And if they seem practically indifferent to sin and its forgiveness as the foundation of socialism, follow them very critically and distrust them in the main. The foundations of the New Jerusalem are on Calvary. And the City of God is the Society of the Saved, and not merely of the just, nor even of the kind. The redeemed walk there. All social freedom rests at last on free grace. If society is to be remodelled, it must be on the principles of the Gospel, on the ethics of forgiveness; not on human heroism or sympathy, but on human helplessness and divine help. It stands at last on the faith that *there* is the bond of human brotherhood; there is the secret of social unity; there is the power which melts men to be members of each other; there is the power that keeps civilisation from slipping back to barbarism and disintegration through a selfishness, first refined, then gross. You demur to this elaborate idea of forgiveness, perhaps. You say love is enough. The Kingdom of God comes when men love each other. Yes; but, in the first place, the only love strong enough to overcome the breaking strain of human selfishness is our love of God. And, in the second place, that love is not mere affection; it is not our love answering His love in simple reciprocity, but it is the love that answers His grace. It is the grateful love, the worshipping love, the self-distrustful love of the forgiven. Mere affection does not forgive—at least beyond a certain limit. The affectionate are not always the forgiving. But grace is love with infinite power of forgiving. It is love prepared for the bitterness of human wrong, and more than equal to it. It is love which gets over not only lapses from love, but the neglect and contempt of a settled lovelessness and selfishness. We need all that grace for *the* effective bond of humanity, among the kind of men, women, and sin we have to deal with. We need the kind of love whose nature and property it is to forgive on a universal scale, love proof against all possible and future wrong, love that not only forgives man his wrong but assures God His holiness, love with infinite resources of forgiveness latent in it. The love of God forgave sin before *we* sinned, and slew the Lamb before the world was. We need for the Kingdom of God in humanity a love capable of doing the like— a love which forgives men before they wrong us, a heart so altered and

17: The Problem of Forgiveness in the Lord's Prayer, 1903

disposed towards men that wrong falling on it awakes forgiveness before resentment has time to grow. For surely that was the love of God in Christ Jesus our Lord. And His love is the only school of it. It is love, truly, which does not spare to inflict judgment. It has nothing fond, nothing foolish. Chastisement is our peace. Let none think forgiveness means mere amnesty, no judgment, no punishment. It carries in one hand peace, in the other a sword. But either hand is the hand of love, love holy, just, and wise.

This is divine love rising to a consecrated passion, to calm, solemn, inexhaustible, inflexible passion.

Some whom these words reach are young. You feel the stirring of early passion. Its eaglets are trying their wings in your soul's nest. For some time you will be much urged by passion, and much influenced by what comes in the form of passion either ignoble or noble, either for knowledge, or for power, or for each other. Let me bespeak your interest for the mightiest passion of all. The poets will teach you it is love. And your New Testament will speak in much the same words. But they will not mean the same thing. The love of human creatures for each other is, indeed, a great and divine thing. It is a great and godly thing, the dear, pure passion of one for another. It is great and godlike, too, that passion of pure, pitiful beneficence for men as brothers in their ignorance, care, pain, and grief, and of laying down life patiently and quietly for their comfort, healing, and elevation. But the greatest, godliest passion of all is connected neither with ties of affection nor works of well-doing (and we are blest in both). It is connected with sin and forgiveness, with guilt and grace. The greatest, last, humanest, passion is the passion to be forgiven. Do not withdraw your interest because I say so. It is not theological pre-occupation that says it. It is human and historic experience. The soul's history says it. It may not be so in every man, but it is so for the human soul, that soul whose face is all history. You will know one day, perhaps, when all other passions have been disappointed by loss, burnt out by time, or debased by abuse. This passion to be forgiven is the longest lived and most indestructible of all. For the present age it is in abeyance. It is more commonly known as the sense of sin. And the sense of sin seems in many religious quarters to be extinct. But it is not dead, it sleepeth. And one day, in the failure, perhaps, of many of the pungent schemes and interests whose taste now numbs the moral nerve, one day this passion will revive with a disillusioned and bitter cry. There is much to satisfy the hunger of the heart today, much at least that promises to do so; and the hunger of the conscience for righteousness, public or private, is urging many steps for a better state of things. But there are still, I suppose, as many hungry hearts as ever, and still a righteousness which social readjustments cannot meet, nor social elevation satisfy. There is another hunger than the heart's hunger for love and sympathy, and another than the conscience of wrongs crying out for redress. There is the hunger of the conscience for forgiveness, sin crying for mercy, for peace with God, for moral harmony within, and reconcilement with that Eternal Conscience with which we have for ever to do. That is the passion which out-lives all, and is greater than all passions beside—*except only one.*

For the greatest passion in Heaven or earth, time or eternity, is the passion of God to forgive, the passion in the passion and death of Christ to redeem.

That is the ruling passion in the moral and spiritual universe. Thus God's great passion meets ours.

When your hunger to be forgiven has found its bread of life in Christ as the forgiveness of God, there is one last height to climb in the strength of that food. You are invited to rise and share in the passion which makes God God, the passion to forgive, the movement of the Holy Ghost, the last moral victory of mankind over itself, where we are more than conquerors because we conquer ourselves, but do it in another, do it because we are redeemed. Thus the last enemy is destroyed.

But if this step be not taken, if the great refusal is made, then the forgiveness that came to you turns to a new condemnation; and your unforgiving becomes the one thing that has to be forgiven. For it is at the root of all your sin and failure beside.

18

CHRIST AT THE GATE, 1908

Principal of Hackney College

The Annual Sermon Preached to the National Free Church Council at Southport on Tuesday Evening, March 3, 1908.

"Come unto Me, all ye that labour and are heavy laden."
—MATTHEW 11:28

"Behold, I stand at the door and knock."
—REVELATION 3:20

ON THESE TEXTS I will venture, if I may, to speak of four things, which I will do with an alliteration for which I apologise, and yet it may aid the memory. First, as to Christ's Person—"Come unto Me." Secondly, as to Christ's public—the weary and heavy laden. Thirdly, as to Christ's promise—the "rest." Fourthly, as to Christ's pressure—the knocking at the gate.

Christ's Person

First, in respect of Christ's Person. Of all the great preachers and teachers that ever failed, the Lord Jesus Christ was the greatest. He failed at Capernaum and He failed at Jerusalem. He failed with the Pharisees, and He failed with

His own—"they all forsook him and fled."[1] It was the work of the cross alone that saved His word. It was the cross, with its voucher in the Resurrection, that made His word universal. It was the cross that revealed and crowned Him. Both His Person and His work were greater than His words could express: greater than any account He could give of either, except in the cross. Men turned from Him as His truth grew more great and inward. They complained they could not understand it; and still He mystified them with His parables, refused plain answers to plain questions, and declined a straight Yes or No.

But as men fell from Him it only deepened His intimacy with the Father and kindled His holy joy in the tremendous sense of what He was for God, and God for Him, and both for the world. This call, "Come unto Me," floats to us upon the flood-tide of His exalted experience; it is a sacred dithyramb, a lyric cry.

And yet it is said by some that the words, "Come unto Me," were no more than an invitation to come and be taught the secrets of Jesus: to take home His doctrine of God, to copy His religion, imitate His faith, and find in it the mystic peace of a communion like His own. But can you easily believe that that was all? that there was no more than that in His mind? A moment before He had spoken of the unique relation of His person to the Father, and declared that there was no access to the Father but as he gave it. Can you think that in this—the most exalted moment that we know in His life—He was but engrossed with religious precepts, and not flushed with endless spiritual resource in Himself, to whom He had just said all was delivered by the Father? Was there nothing in His consciousness that made Him avoid the teacher's common talk about "my word," "my law," "my truth," "my way," and made Him say "I will give you rest"? Is not the only true interpretation of such call that which Paul found—by the mediation of the cross—"Come into Me," rather than "Come into My way" and "Come into My wake"? Was John wrong when he translated "Follow Me" into "Abide in Me"?[2] Did the disciples who came at Christ's word not stay for Himself? Did they not at last find His word swamped in Himself? Through all His words, so poorly understood, He emerged upon them as the Christ, the Son of the living God. When should we find Christ's vast sense and sureness of Himself, if not in a moment so ecstatic as this? He was known by the Father when men were falling from Him every day and Capernaum sinking to hell—to a deeper hell than ungodly Sodom; and He knew in the Father more than a compensation for all that heart-breaking loss. Where but here should He emerge with the vast consciousness that in Himself was room for the laden

---

1. Mark 14:50.
2. John 15:4–7.

world and strength for its failing soul? Even if the cross were not in His thought, it was the Christ of the cross that spoke here. It was the consciousness at last consummated in the cross. It was the Christ with the cross *in* Him that here spoke what *on* the cross He did. The same Soul that redeemed offers here a stage, an instalment of the redemption, and He could speak this only by the selfsame moral power for all the world as enabled Him to die, and rise, and reign for it. The cross, which is for ever knocking solemnly at the world's gate, is here sounding sweetly in the world's ear.

Christ's Public

Secondly, His public. Jesus was growing unpopular. His first hope had been in the nation, and to the nation He made His first appeal. But the more He had to do with the national authorities and the upper classes, the more He failed. He became what we should call in another, disillusioned. From the influential Israel He turned to its lost sheep. From even them He had to turn to the little flock, to whom the Father had given the Kingdom. Like the old prophets, He was driven back upon a remnant, yea, the remnant of a remnant, an elect. But it was no proud elect; it was the *nepioi*—the blameless fools, the ripe in faith but babes in soul. He turned to the people, but it was to the pick of the people; it was not to Demos—not to the crowd—but to the godly in it, whose soul thirsted for Israel's salvation and found in Judaism no "water of life." He turned to those who pined for the Kingdom of God, but who found at Jerusalem only a canonical ring that gagged the Spirit, refused the Son, destroyed the Father, and made the hungry children orphans. He found at Jerusalem no more than the Catholic reformers and modernists have always found in the Curia round the Pope at Rome—a bureaucracy which stifles the Kingdom. Jesus found the way of God to be not through a national Church, but through a gathered Church sifted by His word. True, He blest the public, but it was to an elect that He appealed, and it is through a sympathetic elect that He still works. It was in an elect that He found Himself, and it is by an elect that He still comes to His own; it is a Church that saves the world. *Sine ecclesia nulla salus.*[3]

His Gospel's principle is a sifting principle. His fan is always in His hand. His is no uncritical action. He saves all men tomorrow by some men today. He brings the Kingdom by a Church, and the Church itself He winnows by deliberate rejections which are an irony upon much of our effusive, indiscriminate, impatient propaganda, our getting people in and our passion for voting power. Jesus found His hope to be not the people, but among the people. He

---

3. Without the church there is no salvation.

appealed not to the common man, but to the uncommon saint, to the few, the fit, the trustees of the future and of the whole.

And what does He here say? Permit some modern paraphrase. "All things are delivered to Me of the Father."[4] He did not here mean power but knowledge. The word is *panta paredothē*. I am attracted by the suggestion, a very new one, that the allusion is to a new and personal *paradosis*. *Paradosis*, as many of you know, is the usual word for the deposit of faith—transmitted knowledge, the tradition of the elders, paternal doctrine. What Jesus felt given to Him was a knowledge, a tradition direct from His Father. It was unique knowledge of God, but not legal, canonical, Talmudic knowledge. Nor was it Gnostic or Esoteric knowledge. It was not for professionals nor for *illuminati*.[5] It was the knowledge contained in humble, filial, experimental faith—truly religious knowledge—yet knowledge, not mere impression; knowledge given to the Son, and not merely to the saint, uniquely given by the only Father to the only Son.

"All is clear between Me and My Father. We perfectly understand each other. And I bow and I praise. Men fall from Me and misunderstand Me. I am alone but for the Father with me. None know Me but God: nay, none know God but I, and those kindred and humble souls to whom I open Mine. Even to them it is I that give the knowledge. I give it only to the humble and obscure like myself—the peasant saints. Come to Me, ye hungry sheep, that look up and are not fed. I, too, am of the still and godly strain. I will refresh you. Take the yoke that I will give you, as I take the yoke God gives Me. My own yoke you cannot take, but a yoke from Me you must take, for your soul's peace. It is light beside your law. Come and find the Kingdom in the Father and the Father in Me. Your yoke will be as easy as the Father's will to the Son, and your burden like love's whose lightest word is law." You see that what was filling Christ's mind at this moment was the revelation that it pleased the father to make through Himself to the godly few. He passed by those that had the public ear, the cultured, the capable, the eminent, and the astute, on the one hand, and the wrecks and rabble of life on the other. The Gospel is for these, but His call was not to these. The weary and laden were the hungry souls, the faithful, the godly, the holy and humble men of heart, the poor in spirit, sick for the Kingdom, but finding none of it in the Curialism of Jerusalem. It was a call to the prepared, not to the failures, the bankrupts and groundlings of life, not to the irresponsible, the casual, the sullen, the embittered, nor to the mere feckless populace of the time. It was to the holy stock: "I too, am of the simple saints, the gentle lives, the humbly good.

   4. Matt 11:27//Luke 10:22.
   5. The enlightened.

18: Christ at the Gate, 1908

I am at home among the God-hungry, the unworldly, the cottage saints." You are aware that exception has been taken to the self-consciousness of Christ's description of Himself as meek, because the truly humble are the last to know, and certainly to speak about it. But Jesus is not describing Himself here, he is classing Himself. He was not surrendering His humility by praising it, but He was confessing His affinities. It was not a subjective state; it was an objective stand. "My yoke is not lighter than the world's." How could the Man of the cross say it was? "But it is lighter than the scribes', the priests', the high eminences and Brahmins of the hour—lighter to the godly soul, if not to the natural heart." That is the sense of His words. I recall a saying of Comte: "We tire of thinking, and we tire of working, and we tire of playing, but we do not tire of loving."[6] What true lover of Christ ever tired of loving Him? If he cease to love he tires, but he does not tire of loving. Christ, therefore, is not contrasting His yoke with the world's yoke, but with the Church's. He is not appealing, He is not promising, to those who groan and sweat. The load was not that of the world and its worries, but the load of a false and exacting religion. His call was to the religious who were stifled by a wrong religion, not to the non-religious, crushed under a harsh world. It was a call by the elect to the elect.

Christianity was not born out of the misery of the proletariat, but out of the hunger and thirst for the Kingdom of the living, saving God; not from the impatience of wrong, but from the impatience of godlessness. It thought first not of man's poverty, but his lostness. Redemption was the one and ultimate condition of the race's weal. Christ was not a revolutionary, but a Redeemer. Christianity did not arise out of the poverty either of Judæa or of Rome. It was not a mass movement; that was the way of all the false Messiahs. It bore upon moral conditions, not economic, else it would have gone ahead like a fire in a forest, and then burned out. Whereas it went slowly, and burns still with unquenchable fire. The call was not to the submerged; it was to the emerged—it was to the half-emerged, at least. It was to them, but it was for the submerged. Christ speaks to the Church, but it is for the world. The elect were not monopolists, but first-fruits, as they are to this day. What they are chosen to be, all are called to be, all are destined to be. Christianity may or may not be directly for the masses at a given hour, but Christians are, and Christianity will not get to the masses till Christians take it. Christianity is a sacramental religion, and therefore it must have its holy elements. And the sacramental elements of Christianity are sacramental men. The true transubstantiation is that of the soul, what we call conversion. And the converted are still the few.

---

6. From Auguste Comte's *Discours sur l'ensemble du positivisme*: "We tire of thinking and even of acting; we never tire of loving," *A General View of Positivism*, 1.

II: Published Sermons

It pleases God to work by an elect in every age, and, therefore, Christianity must be as slow as the God who took that way. It must be slow if it is going to gather up all; it must be slow if it be the appeal of the cross to souls that live by something else than the *panem et circenses*[7]—soup and circuses, beer and bets. Christ has no word for those whose one idea of life is food and fun and a real good time, be they rich or poor, young or old—no word but judgment, though a judgment unto salvation. It was accordingly to a prepared and spiritual Church within the Church of Israel that Jesus said, "Come unto Me." He was more interested in the purity of His church than in its prestige. And I can hear these words at this moment spoken directly, not to the faithless, but to the faithful, and not to the Churches even, but to the true Church in them all—not to mere Christians, but to true confessors. And that earnest Church hears the call, and it moves in answer "back to Christ."

"Back to Christ"

"Back to Christ"—we have become familiar with the words. What do we mean by them? Back to what Christ? Back to the Christ of this call merely? To the lone, inviting voice which failed? To the exalted vision so soon to be submerged in His soul's night? Is it back to the religious Christ or to the teaching Christ, the healing Christ, the winsome Christ, to the moral personality which presents to an æsthetic piety a harmonious character and a calm repose? Nay, but it is no such balanced figure that we need or find. The Gospels present a choleric Christ as surely as they do a calm, and a Christ of passion more even than a Christ of peace. The Church must surely go back to the Christ that made the Church. And the Church was not made by the teaching, the healing, the beautiful Christ, but by the evangelical and the crucified Christ, and the risen Christ, the redeeming Christ *in* whom we possess our souls, and *to* whom we cannot call our souls our own. We must go back to the total Christ, and we must bind Him chiefly in the one act where His whole personality was condensed and straightened at that narrow gate that led to life in the cross. There was the crisis of Him who was the crisis of the world. It is in the cross alone that we have the whole Christ at His utmost. It is the cross that makes the call effectual. Let me ask you to watch a noble river pursuing its calm way through the uplands, where it gathers power from a thousand mazy rills. Follow it foaming in its farther course over fretting rocks, or brimming on many a silent reach, or winding through many populous scenes. And then at last, at its mouth, the banks rise and close, and the cliffs overhang and shut out heaven, and the beetling

7. Bread and circuses.

crags draw together (as Herod and Pilate shook hands) to bar its passage to the open sea. And there is but one outlet, paved with boulders, which is the gorge of the dismal night and deadly hate. And through this gulf of mist and torment the whole volume of the stream has to agonise, having on it all the weight of its depth, and all the power of its past. Only so can it emerge and expand into the ocean's space and peace and light. So through the gate and agony of death, straitened and darkened, poured the whole person of Christ in consummation upon the cross. And so He rose into the ample and eternal life. How can you part His death from all His life before?

Now, it is to such a Christ that we must return, to a Christ who culminated wholly in the cross. It was such a Christ that was latent in every miracle, every parable, every call. It was this Christ, radiant with the cross's victory, that emerged in the Resurrection. This is the Christ that now says, "Come unto Me." This is the call that, as we look back, sounds deepest in all His calls—the call from the cross. This is the call that not only invited the Church, but gathered it. It was this call that made the Church when the majesty and beauty of our text's appeal had been neglected and despised. It was this "Come" uttered in death that saved from futility the "Come" spoken in rapture. The call from His deepest humiliation did what was not done, and never could have been done, by the call from the gleaming height of His intuition. It was. Now to hear and know this is the victory that overcomes the world. But it is only the few that hear it, even in the Church. The Church's greatest triumphs are not gained over the world and outside the Church, but over the world within it. With these won the rest must follow. The world will come into the Church as the church comes into Christ. If we were thus missioned in ourselves we should not need to flog up missions to the heathen. Can the Church carry the power of the cross into the worldly and pagan parts of its own soul? then we shall soon carry it to the ends of the earth. The cross's conquest of all pagan souls means first its conquest of the whole Christian soul. The real cause of slack missions—and let us tell it with perfect and cruel frankness, if need be—is that we ourselves are but halfsubdued. The most fruitful contribution you can make to the conversion of the world is to take your place in the conversion of the Church.

The Promise of Rest

Thirdly, let me say something now about the rest promised to those who should come to meet the coming and call of Christ.

I would point out first that what Christ promises is really refreshment rather than repose. It is not quiescence, it is not calm. Calm is not all, though calm is well. It is power, power to go on; it is spiritual energy, knowledge, courage, and fortitude. The peace of believing is not the repose of gods who lie beside the nectar. The arch-believer Paul knew that when he said, "Being justified by faith we have peace with God."[8] He means confidence; he does not mean calm. Many of the greatest believers have known little of calm. Theirs were busy, even distracted lives; but in the midst of conflict and of affairs they had always the confidence of a victory already won for good and all, which at the very best could only follow up.

People complain sometimes that they have gone to Christ and have not found this rest—calm. I am not sure that they were promised calm at any special time; what they were promised was power, strength; and that is what we want. It is God's business to dispense calm. There is not much promise about calm, but there is about peace. But, if you did not get the rest and peace you sought, was it because you were more hungry for the rest than for Christ? Are there not some spiritual Epicureans whose quietism is not superhuman, but inhuman, unbrotherly and exasperating? There are many who seek in religion, in Christ, rest more than rescue, resignation more than obedience, and heart-happiness more than faith's perfection. I would say, Far better people than you—even true saints—have died and hardly known that peaceful and happy frame you complain Christ denies to your prayers. But if they had not religious rapture they had faith and confidence and power, and having done all they stood; and you knew where to have them in a crisis, and you don't always know where to have the quietist when the real crises arrive.

The Pressure of Christ

Fourthly, I want to speak about the pressure and the presence of Christ. If the call of Christ was to a prepared and select people, how can we go with it to the world? Did He, does He, invite the world? He does, surely, but have I not said that it is in something much greater than His invitation that we have to do with? It is the action of the cross where word becomes work; work which becomes decisive for the world. It is there that the call becomes a knock, an urgency and a solemn pressure; it is there that it goes to the world as its destiny. Only in the cross of Christ does the call become a power, only in the cross does Christianity become universal. Only in the cross does the love of the small, congenial group become love of mankind. Only in the preaching of the cross do we pass from the propaganda of a sect to a mission to the world. Only in the cross does the Christian group become a Christian Church, disciples

---

8. Rom 5:1.

18: Christ at the Gate, 1908

become apostles; the words of Jesus become the Word of Life, truth becomes power, invitations become pressures and judgments, and fraternal homilies rise to the true preaching of the mighty Gospel. The word of Christ would have failed without the cross and become but the illumination of a Jewish clan. But the work of Christ does not fail till it set judgment in the earth. It is in the cross that the winning call becomes the urgent pressure of another world upon the life and within the life—a new heaven and earth.

The pressure of the cross is either the world's supreme release or its supreme burden. It contains the world's last reality. One thing it cannot be, it cannot be evaded. It is life unto life or death unto death, and if it be not the world's life it is the world's misfortune. If Christ was wrong He was very wrong, and following Him we go further astray. But if He was so very wrong His effect on history is not only not salvation, it is something like stultification. What a poor thing human nature would be to have given in to Him as it has done if He was so wrong as wrongness upon His scale must be.

You may call this pressure of the cross immanence or transcendence, but Christ's action upon the world is now the mightiest matter in the world; you may call it the throb of an immanent Christ, bursting out of a world made in Him, or you may call it the knock of a transcendent Christ beating in upon us from the eternity which is His true home—the throb, it may be, of His swelling heart within, or the beating of His approaching wings from without. But it is instant in season and out.

That knocking at the gate! We think today on cosmic lines. Let us interpret it so. Have you considered the urgency, the importunity of the unseen world? We all know how great a fascination it has upon ourselves, and how perennial. Have we not buried our dearest dead there? Have we not sent them on there as hostages to wait our coming? Where our treasure is, how can it but be that our hearts should be also? And when people talk too scornfully about "other-worldliness," I sometimes wonder how they could if they had already deposited half their heart and life there to await the great reunion. Aye, and at our birth as with our death. Did we not issue from that unseen? And have we not a great homesickness? Do not our souls go out with our hearts and move to the great over-soul with a mighty passion? If that be so, can you think we should go out to that unseen with such curiosity and passion if we were not approached first by that unseen, if we were not sought by it, if it did not move to us more passionately than we to it? Do we seek our lost yonder more passionately than God seeks His lost here? That unseen world! How its waves beat upon us and solicit us; how it sets towards us and seeks us, sues us, and passionately claims us! In what way do you really think about that other world in which this world of ours is hung? How do you conceive of our spiritual environment? Do you picture Time poised in Eternity, like a glowing moon wading in a drifting mist? Do you imagine the world unseen around us to be an inert thing, dun, pale and ghostly, from which our eager life will shrink as from Sheol? Are we muffled and stifled in such cotton-wool? Nay, but the waves of that infinite sea are always making advances to our earthly shore. Its tides flow in upon us at every creek, and its currents sweep us and flood us with fullness from afar. It is not a lumpish world that is around us, but the seeking love of God. "The Father seeketh" us "to worship Him."[9] It is not a world of brooding cloud, of grey inertia and stifling calm, swift apathy and sheer oblivion, settling down on life like a final foe. Nay, that other world does not merely surround us. It makes for us, petitions us, clasps us, saves, fulfils, and completes us. Look you, this human life of ours, as we know it, is no placid, no sluggish thing, is it? There is a flush and thrill and fire and passion in it. It is a mighty matter; it is not flat, stale, and unprofitable. At its worst it is tragedy; at its best it is glory. So, only more so, is the spiritual world, the life eternal. Heaven is not pale. The gold of that land is good. Dante saw it as an infinite red rose. It is a vivid and eager world. It is a cloud of witnesses; the general assembly and church of the mighty firstborn, who live indeed in Christ redeeming in blood that speaketh.

Christ the Other World

Yes, for us that other world is Christ. There is mysticism for you, and there is no Christianity without it. Christ Himself our other world. And how He seeks us, not to be denied! Did He not bid us be importunate in our prayer? And did He bid us be in that what He was not? Was He, is He not importunate for us, besetting, beseeching us with all the urgency of eternity? "We pray you, as though Christ did beseech you by us, be reconciled."[10] Listen! What a note!—Christ praying to us. Christ is not simply there in case we should want Him, like a fire-escape. The world He inhabits is not there yawning like a grave to swallow us at last. His world is the resurrection and the life. He is there in incessant action upon us, striving with us, soliciting, importuning us. The whole atmosphere and providence of life is—must be, because He is life's destiny. We were made for Him and His salvation, and the true scheme of life is to live out that teleology of love. All things work together in time and in eternity that Christ should have His way with us. It is a tremendous pressure upon us that destiny of Redemption. It has all the weight of God, and all the sweep of the universe.

9. John 4:23.
10. 2 Cor 5:20.

18: Christ at the Gate, 1908

In all that comes and goes He only comes; comes to us as the fascination of the future, as the swelling of the present, as the impulse from the past. The future comes up like thunder upon us; posterity is at the gate; the new generation is knocking at the door—the new order summoning us to surrender. Unheard-of change fills the air. To the ear of faith it is the knocking of Christ. Again, the present!—the full heart of the present age swells with the sense of latent power, the confidence of immense victories, and the promise of imminent new discovery; it beats faster than the world's heart ever beat before, perhaps. It is Christ knocking at the gate. And the judgment that comes upon us from the past or the judgment we are piling up even in the future—it is still Christ at the gate of judgment, but it is a judgment unto salvation. Salvation is knocking ever louder at the gate in the long turmoil and judgment of history—the throbs of progress are the drums of the Kingdom of God. Judgment unto salvation—that is the principle of the cross. In Christ the march of history is the tramp of the millennium, the arrival of God's man. It is God's saving counsel that is the ground-plan of the world and the motive power of its course. The design that history hammers out is Redemption; that is what all the knocking of events spells out in a cipher. It is the Kingdom of God that is heaving under all the reeling ruin and rubbish of time. It is the immanent might and perpetual resurrection of Christ the Crucified that urges and orders all to the heavenly goal. The perpetual advent of Christ is the mightiest fact today, whether we feel it or not.

Is it not so? Who is to have the last word in human affairs at the great close? Do we not all believe that it is Jesus Christ, the King of saints, that shall judge the world? Well, if that faith be true it means more. If Christ is to have the last word then, does it not mean that He has the deepest, mightiest word now? What shall be at the end of history then is the thing at the bottom of history now. I hear the cynic laugh at my rhetoric as he looks at the society and politics of Europe. But I hear loud above that the laugh of Him, whose rhetoric is all the fine majestic ordinances of earth and sky, as He sits in heaven and laughs; and at the cynics He laughs most of all, with an irony that makes but rhetoric of theirs, with the eternal irony of the imperturbable redemption.

You tell the boy whose sand-castle has been covered and crumbled by the sea at noon that the moon has done it, and he mocks you—being well informed, for he is a Board school pupil, of course—for your silly attempt to amuse him. But it is his ignorance. You know the cause of the tides; he does not. Just such children are those who feel mocked to be told that it is the action of Christ, the Judge and King of all, that controls the great tides in the affairs of men, and brings civilisations to sand, or floats them to glory, according as they meet the conditions of God's eternal, holy righteousness in the cross.

II: Published Sermons

The Social Future

I will venture to put it differently. We think today not only on cosmic, but on social lines. Belief in the social future is the inspiration of all but the most incorrigible pessimists, and it means belief in progress, in development, in democracy. Ah! you say, now we are coming down from abstractions and coming to things real and actual. Progress, democracy—these things touch us. These things touch you! What theorists you are! What abstractions you pursue! When will you come to realities? Progress—was there ever a more abstract abstraction? Development—what better is that? The words stand at best for modes, not for things. They are methods, tendencies, which we believe we have observed, in which we persuade ourselves to believe. Democracy itself—what is it but an abstraction? At most a stage, the latest stage, of society; it is but man in a phase. Taken by itself it may easily enough fade into another phase. But mankind in its true self is the Kingdom of God. But these abstractions really and practically mean more. When we say we believe in progress, to any practical purpose, what we really believe in is not progress but something that progresses, something that progress realises, something it moves to, the goal of it eternally set in your heart. Our belief in development is belief in something that develops. If I believe in the growth of my child, I believe still more in the child that grows, in the life and the possibilities and purposes embedded in the life. If we trust democracy it is really Demos and its possibilities that we trust. And why should we trust the Demos? Is it for the men we see? Alas for the best of us! What is within and behind it all? Beneath all our ardours, enthusiasms, platforms, causes and sacrifices is there not this faith—that it is worth while, divinely worth while, worth God's while, and therefore alone worth man's while at last? The enthusiasm of humanity can only rest at last upon another and a deeper faith, upon the faith that the world and man are so built that salvation in some form is the plan of the universe; that it is cosmic. We believe, at bottom, that the victory of the holy conscience on a world-scale is sure and certain—give it time; that the triumph of the soul is in principle won; that the ethical man and the ethical state have the reversion of the future; that heart, reason, and conscience are destined to rule for ever over all. That incorrigible optimism—in a word, is it not the faith that, though the world lay in wickedness, God is holy, God is love, God is grace, God is endless power for the purposes of His grace; that the Lord God omnipotent reigneth; that the destiny of history is a foregone conclusion in Christ, and in the high spiritual places all is well? We have the faith that history in its movement is the working out of man's conquest by this God and this God's man, and God is steadily working this out by teleology—immanent and irresistible.

18: Christ at the Gate, 1908

I have been using the language of Christian faith, but have I not been describing the faith that underlies all sound, practical, and permanent optimism, all high and indomitable Idealism, even when Christian theology would be challenged or denied? When I speak about an immanent teleology in things I am only using an idea which has been a philosophical commonplace ever since the days of Kant. How is it possible to be a confirmed and practical optimist without the faith that your effort works in with a mightier drift of things which will not fail you, or mock you, and will not let you go? We must in our hearts believe in a world saturated with moral purpose, and not a brute or casual world—

> That blindly blundered on man's suffering soul.
> And leaves him blind about its final goal.

We have a goal for our world and that goal is Christ. It is this optimism that is the fundamental truth in democracy; it is the root of our wholesome conservatism and aristocracy. In moving to a future we are exploiting a past. We are unfolding a gift and not merely pressing to a goal. We are developing our estate and not merely fighting for the land. We are coming to a future which has already come to us in Christ. Democracy is but a half-truth. It must have a King. Aristocracy is just as true and as needful. It builds on an authority in things no less than democracy builds on an equality. The free personality of democracy is only possible under a free authority. The free soul is only possible in a free King. Do we not all believe in the rightful authority of a moral aristocracy? Do we not look forward to the conversion of the existing aristocracy to a real rule of the best? There must always be a House of Moral Lords. There must always be leaders and led, prophets and people, apostles and members, genius and its circle, an elect and a called. Ah! democratic and aristocratic principles are both deep in the foundations of our Christian faith.

But how are we to make people believe it? Can we go to a man like Tolstoi? For a man like him, here and there, perhaps, it may be so. But even then he is the victim of a very eccentric individualism, ending in anarchy, however noble. Can the mere insight of conscience, mere ethical genius, confirm the world in this mighty optimism, and assure you that the glorious end is so sure as to be already with us as our mighty creative centre, that the future kingdom is the most irresistible of present powers? How shall you know that the drums of the advancing future are the beating of the Eternal Heart? How shall you be sure that they are not the throbs of a human egotism swelled and inflamed? It is only by our faith that it is God in Christ that stands at our door and knocks. It is "Christ in you, the hope of glory."[11] He is with us and departs not.

Christ the One Apologetic

I know what you are ready to do—to confront me with the irony of existing Christendom. You may heap up the crimes of the past, and even of the Church. You may accumulate before my eyes the wrongs, anomalies, and miseries of the present. You may charge the civilisation of Europe after these two millenniums of Christianity with being little but a veneered paganism. It may all be too true. But it is not Christendom that is the religion of Christians. It is the Gospel. It is not Christians that make the evidence of Christianity, it is Christ. Christ is the one apologetic. Have we this Christ? We certainly have the Church—have we this Christ? Yea, we have this Christ, else we were no Church.

When all is said and done there is nothing upon earth outside the Church to cure the Church's anomalies, negligences, and ignorances. He alone can cure the Church whose forgiveness made the Church. It cannot be reformed from without. The worst errors of the saints are not to be set right by the critics and cynics of the world, nor by any who imitate them within the Church. It is only the Church of faith that can reform the Church of fact. It is only its own Master that can make it a true servant. Only its own truth can make its witness true. Let us by all means amend where we are vulnerable to the critics without. Let us take them as the prophet took pagan Cyrus, as servants of God for a purpose. But let us criticise them with their own vigour. We owe them little. They do not handle us as if they loved us. But the last critical word is with us. Say that, and take all the insults you may receive for saying it. Know ye not, or do you no more believe, that the saints shall judge the world? Is that but a first-century superstition, or the eternal principle of the final victory of holiness? Let us amend our procedure at due call. Let us be wise as serpents, and let us make our adversary our helper. But when it comes to reforming the Church, no outside criticism can do that; it can only correct. The severest criticism, and the most effectual, that the Church has to encounter is from within. It is sympathetic criticism. The Judge is at the door, and the Judge is on our side. He knocks that He may come in and sup. The Church's sharpest critic is its Creator and Redeemer. No critic from the world knows our really weak places and probes than like that Critic who never leaves nor forsakes us, because if He did the Church would cease to be a Church. We have no critic in the spirit of the world

11. Col 1:27.

18: Christ at the Gate, 1908

so searching as the Holy Spirit in the Church—only give Him orbits long enough to move in. We have none so subtle, so piercing, such a sword in our bones. Ask history. What is the greatest movement that ever arose in the Church since its foundation? Is it not the Reformation? And the Reformation was no product of the Renaissance. It was no purgation of the Church by culture from without, but a mighty effort of self-criticism from within. It was the Church reforming the Church and its faith. It was the reformation of faith, of religion, more even that of the Church. It was the Lord with His fan cleansing His floor. The criticism by the world is the merest gossip compared with the searching judgment in what the Spirit says to the Churches. Christ is always doing more for the Church than the Church is doing for Him—though it is our misfortune today to be more preoccupied with our work for Him than with His for us. Don't let us attach too much importance to the opinion of critics who are too disgusted with the Church to remain in it. What have we to learn, to any practical purpose, from a literary critic who protests with all the moral levity of the *littérateur*[12] against "the untruth that evangelical religion is a wholesome, or valuable, or desirable adjunct to human life"?[13] It is easy to find a plausible answer to life if you thin down the problem, but to deny the problem is too foppish an answer. The worst heresy is quackery. These people are symptoms we should heed, but they are not prophets we should hear. Remember that the Church is most open to the attack and hate of the world not in its weakness but in its strength. The absurdest thing about the Church is its cross. The offence of the cross is not ceased; it is still a scandal to the natural man and the bland humanist.

Amid all the errors, obscurantisms, perils, and confusions of the Church this Voice comes with no mere humanitarian appeal, yet with all humanity and its fortunes in its change. Amid all that grieves us in the Church we have a sure stronghold; and it is the real presence, the real call, the real knocking, the self-announcement of Christ in the Church's deep central experience of Him, and His control of its life. Oh, it is not the leaders of the Church that lead it, but its Lord. It is not its statesmen that steer it, but the Spirit. It is not the eminent Christians that preserve it, but the saints whose faith is more heavenly than it is lawful to utter, or whose prayers are too deep for their own tears or the public ears. It is they to whom Christ whispers. The rest may reason and welcome, but it is these fools that know. Over all the waves without, and all the broils within, there is one Voice with

---

12. A professional writer.

13. Gosse, *Father and Son*, 366–67: "After my long experience, after my patience and forbearance, I have surely the right to protest against the untruth (would that I could apply to it any other word!) that evangelical religion, or any religion in a violent form, is a wholesome or valuable or desirable adjunct to human life."

the rallying secret, the ruling spell, the piercing judgment, the saving grace and the calming power. "Come unto Me," "Turn ye to My stronghold, ye prisoners of hope." And to men long weary of political, dynastic, institutional Churches, Christ calls, "Come unto Me." And we follow the Voice. We learn to dissociate the imperial Churches, the curialist Churches, the State Churches, the worldly Churches, the merely sectarian Churches from the unworldly, superhuman Christ. We turn from those Churches whose officers invade the offices of Christ, whose machinery crushes the soul's life, and whose steam power quenches the Spirit's power. They may fade, but He endures. And He endures not to shatter them but to regenerate them. A Church He must have and will have, and a creed also; but they must be His own. He must rule in His own house, and He must put His own servants in their proper place, and their place is to make place for Him. It is to give free access to His great grace, His urgent coming, and His engaging call.

> Had I the grace to win the grace
> Of some old man complete in lore,
> My face would worship at his feet,
> Like childhood sitting on the floor.
>
> Had I the grace to win the grace
> Of childhood sitting shy, apart,
> The child should find a nearer place,
> And teach me resting in my heart.
>
> Had I the grace to win the grace
> Of maiden living all above,
> My soul would trample down the base,
> That she might have a man to love.
>
> A grace I have no grace to win
> Knocks now at my half-open door,
> O Lord of Glory, come Thou in,
> Thy grace divine is all and more.[14]

Come, Lord Jesus, oh, come quickly!

---

14. A slightly modified version of George MacDonald's poem, "The Grace of Grace" (1867).

19

Christ Our Sanctification, 1911

Christ, it is said by Paul, is made unto us righteousness and sanctification and redemption. And there are many, many still for whom the words are really and deeply true.

But on the other hand there are many, and they grow more, for whom they convey no real meaning, but only echoes of a meaning once real. Christ is our Master, Brother, Friend, Ideal, Sacrifice: but what do words like Paul's mean for much current religion? To many they are dried plants. They are technical religion, they are theology. They have no point of attachment in the circle of such people's experience. They are not only abstractions, but they seem abstractions foisted on a historical Person and a still living Person. The natural mind, even when religious, resents almost fiercely a phrase such as describes Christ to have been "made sin"; where, it is urged, in true and non-theological simplicity Christ would have said He bore sin's fruits or forgave it. Such obscurities, it is said, seem a part of the old conspiracy to smother personality in dogma. It is hard enough today to think of Christ as our Justifier; in what sense is He our Justification? How can a living person be described as anything that ends in -ation? In their impatience such critics forget that perhaps last night they heard a leader of the opposite party described as an abomination. And is Christ not still the Resurrection and the Life?

In so far as this frame of mind pervades the membership of the Church, it is a much more serious thing than a drop in numbers (of which, moreover, it is part cause). And it is a thing of which the Church's teachers should take what notice they can spare from the religious brattle and drudgery which destroy spiritual discernment.

Certainly there are forms of phrase and lines of thought in the New Testament which would not be used if the revelation were being conveyed for the first time today. And this clause may be one of them. But to recognize that does not entitle us to throw such words or thoughts overboard. That would be lightening the ship by getting rid of the stores; it would be increasing the speed by throwing over the coal. Rather let us use all effort to get power and pace out of them. Of course, the natural mind is impatient of what is not promptly intelligible, plainly clear, and directly straight. But then the very object of spiritual faith is to keep that kind of downrightness rightly down (if the phrase were let pass). It is to make us thrive habitually and inwardly on paradoxes, like "die to live," or, "I live, yet not I, but Christ liveth in me,"[1] which fly in the face of common sense but are the marrow of the soul. What might the Church not do were its ruling idea proficiency of soul instead of efficiency of sect? And the growth of our soul's proficiency, the efficiency of the kingdom, is just this, that we learn constantly to realize the great historic words, and to re-interpret them, and modernize their teeming truth. The hasty mind would away with all the language that does not come home to a public meeting. The spiritual expert, on the contrary (who abounds among our people), has the power to take honey from the carcase of the past, renew his strength, and refresh his comrades. Some have almost a genius in that way; and they may have so much of the apostolic experience that the apostolic phrases come rather as a relief than a trial; because they give expression to that which the language neither of literature, nor of business, nor of the affections, can utter.

And there are few harder tasks laid upon the Church's ministers in an age like this than to interpret the old phrases so that they neither drone nor drag, but come home to living men in the glow that begat them. We cannot merely repristinate. Sermons that at the Reformation shook half Europe, today not only read flat, but are intolerable. The "language of Canaan" comes to mean little to the present age, and the worthy pietism of a century ago must use another than its old dialect now. If we cannot restore, we can re-translate, reinterpret, and transform.

It has to be shown, for instance, how different it is to say "Christ redeemed" and "Christ is our Redemption"; to hear God say "I am your Saviour" and "I am your Salvation." He might save us, with His mighty resource, for something that was yet external to Himself. He could be the Grand Agent of a divine humanity by developing it into its own perfection out of what was a mere setback. But these things would not be the same as saving it from hostility and guilt into communion with His holy Self. That He should give us our perfection is not the same as that He should Himself be "our perfection and our life." He could even make us holy to a point and yet not be Himself our holiness; but we are called not to imitate but to partake of

---

1. Gal 2:20.

19: Christ our Sanctification, 1911

the divine sanctity, and to be holy with the holiness of God; just as we rise from the grave and death of sin by a divine exercise of the self-same power which raised Jesus from the dead. And we may recall here that the source of the great disputes which once gathered about a word like "justification" was this, that it was conceived more logically than organically, too legally and apart from living union with Christ as Himself our justification; it was conceived only as a status He gave us, detached from a life united with Him.

Many of our great religious words and ideas are undergoing a re-translation from thought to experience, and to modern experience. And to do it honestly is not easy. May we cherish a good supply of those experts and scholars of Christian experience—those initiates of the soul with the gift of its past tongues as well as its present, who are instructed, as the true scribes of the kingdom, to bring out things old and new. The work can be done by no amateur experience or private interpretation. To reform belief is to moralize it. It is to revive neither the old orthodoxy nor the old pietism. And that means converting an age and not a group; and converting the moral personality of our age, and not merely its thought or its sympathies. Conversion, after all, is the key to Christian truth; but it is the conversion of the Church's conscience no less than the worldling's soul. It is largely the re-birth of the regenerate, in a Church which is the general assembly of the twice-born.

To the modern cry for justice Christ must be shown to be not the Justifier only, but, more immanently, the whole historic righteousness of God. To the cry for social justice He must be shown to be Himself our public righteousness and social peace; and He must be shown to be this in a society of the united Churches first of all. It must be made clear that there can be no social justice at the long last but on the base of a conscience made just as God counts just—by faith understood as trust and communion. Sanctification must be given a closer organic connexion with social reform; but also social reform must not take the place of sanctification.

"Christ is made unto us wisdom and sanctification and redemption."[2] On the one hand, we rise to say, All the wisdom of the world is in reversion mine, for Christ is mine. All the public righteousness we ache for is already ours, for we have the world's Christ. We see not yet all things righteous, but we see Christ, to Whose holy "Yea" all righteous things are for ever sure. All the sanctity of an ideal world is ours, imperfect as we are, for He is ours, and we are organic with the Holiness of God. All the liberty of the world we expand and partake in, for we are "in Him" and He is its eternal Emancipation.

On the other hand, and conversely, my righteousness means all the justice of the world, involves it, and must work out to it; for my righteousness is

---

2. 1 Cor 1:30.

II: Published Sermons

Christ, and He is no private possession. My holiness is my hold of Him who is the holy destiny of the world. I cannot be right or holy in Christ if I am not waiting, praying, working in some way for social righteousness, reform, and brotherhood. Christian life is an integral part of Christian truth. My religion is but atomic, cellular, monastic, and doctrinaire, unless it move me to such action and sympathy. Consider the meaning of individual salvation by a world-Saviour; and then its converse truth of a world-salvation by an individual Saviour. When the Church grasps—really grasps—one of these in each hand, then its great hour will come. And when such a Christ and His salvation really take hold of the Church it will change its whole outlook and action upon life as passionately as a man is changed who sees coming his bride adorned for her husband.

20

THINGS NEW AND OLD, 1913

Preached at the Induction of Rev. W. H. Bennett, M.A., D.D., Litt.D., to the Principalship of Lancashire Independent College on October 9, 1913.

"Jesus saith unto them, Have ye understood all these things? They say unto Him, Yea, Lord. Then said He unto them, Therefore every scribe which is instructed unto the Kingdom of Heaven is like unto a man that is an householder, which bringeth forth out of his treasure things new and old."

—MATTHEW 13:51–52

THESE WORDS GIVE THE principle of the Christian teacher. He is a master, not an imitator, not an echo, a lackey of the great. He is a householder, a master of his subject, which is historic grace. Yet he is but a steward, not the owner. He is original but in part. His new is but getting deeper into the old; his old is capable of infinite novelty. The genius is more original in a way than the apostle; he invents, which the apostle cannot do; he can but elicit and expound. But the power of genius is less, because he is not so near the great Original; because he is but a lofty part of Nature rather than a new creation of grace. He does not sound the depths the Holy Spirit does. He does not dispense so rich a world. He moves heart and imagination, but he does not give the conscience peace with God, he does not regenerate.

II: Published Sermons

And the words should appeal to an age of transition like the present, so different from the Middle Ages, for instance. Christ Himself lived in just such a time. The old was ready to vanish away. A power was come into history which was to make all things new. It was a taxing time for those who had the work to carry out. It was easy to hang blindly by the old: it always is. It is as easy to rage furiously for the new. But the trial of spiritual power lies just in the faculty here credited to the true teacher. It is the power of things old and new. It is insight, and the insight of faith into grace. We need that more than criticism—insight, not fantastic but historic. The power of seeing the new pouring from the old, and of preserving the old creative in the new, the power of being struck with the old, always surprised by it, surprised not by the uncommon but the common, the power of wonder even at what we learn to expect, finding in precedent discoveries, and feeling (with all lovers) the old story happening to them for the first time, the old verb in the present tense.

The Past as a Prophecy

The case of Paul shows how truly a great spiritual teacher is marked by this quality. Nothing in Paul's revolutionary experience is more remarkable than his hold on the past and his power to reconstruct it, to discover in it the principle that had made a new world for him, the vital principle of the Eternal, glorifying the past, even in turning it upside down. And how valuable was that higher criticism of faith which taught Paul by a marvelous flash (in Galatians) what criticism has now reached in its own way—taught him to see that Gospel was before law, the prophetic before the levitical element in the Old Testament. To him the past was pregnant and prophetic. And that meant two things which must belong to a religion historic and alive. It meant that the past was not negligible; but it also meant that the past was not final. A prophecy is, in the nature of it, first living, second incomplete; deep in its present, hungry for its future. To treat the past as a prophecy, then, is to bring out of it things old and new; it is to give it life, but no monopoly of a life at the cost of the present. Living history is always Messianic—great with its Redeemer, its Realiser. If it were not, its contrast with its ideal would be only ironical. But it is prophetic. The ideal does not mock it; it fulfils itself through it.

History has been held to be prophetic—(1) as a type of the future, but the system of typology is now outgrown; (2) as prediction, but prediction is now secondary in prophecy; (3) as a symbol, or figure, or illustration, or allegory of the future, but history does not repeat itself thus. Eden is nothing that we can ever reproduce, or should wish to. So to restore, it has been said, is to "destroy." (4) As prelude or overture. Symbolic parable is one thing, actual prelude another. The past is not pictorial of the future, but pregnant with it. It is an integral part of the whole career of humanity. It is real action, forming the initial movements and stages of all we have come, and are coming, to be. The old has the new in its womb.

The Parable of History

This 13th chapter of Matthew is an account of a series of parables in which Christ explains the genius of the Kingdom of Heaven. They contain deep within them a philosophy of the soul, of society, and of history—all as Christian. The key of the soul is the master-key of history and society. The meaning and destiny of the world lie latent in these parables of the Kingdom, which seem so simple, but are so profound. The progress of nature and society is the Kingdom of God working up through civilisation and getting its head out to command it. The greatest of human interests is the Kingdom of God. And in that interest Christ's business was with the world—not with a soul here and there—with the world, and therefore in a striking way with the past, which is the portion of the world most intelligible to us. Yes, we know the present, but it is the past we understand; the present is too near to be understood. What past history had been moving to was of first moment for one whose work was to gather up history, and to fulfil the purpose of its God. To him, then, the past was one huge parable—a story with a meaning greater than the story. In this large sense I borrow the old word "parable" from a modern source and apply it to history.

The greatest poem since Milton's time is Goethe's "Faust." To understand "Faust" is to be put abreast (for better or for worse) of the spiritual temper and the mentality of the modern age. And this poem closes with a brief hymn uttered by the mystic choir of those who see the whole destiny of the soul in the light of love, and who sing their vision in words almost unspeakable and full of glory. "All that is passing is parable only."

Now that is part of the Christian view. It is not the whole, not the deepest view, I know. The past is more than a symbol with a lesson, more than a picture. It has reality within it. It is a sacrament, in which something spiritual is done and conveyed. It is part of the redemptive process. It does not simply represent it; it works it out. History is here as nature. The natural facts or incidents we use for illustrations are also Nature at work. They are acts and facts before we make symbols of them. They speak, but still more they do. The past is not a mere figure or forecast or type of the future; it is not its mirror; it is its prelude, nay, its mother. The prophets did not so much predict or depict the future; they did more to bring it about.

"Plain Men" and "Spiritual Aristocrats"

But still, to think of the past as a parable or symbol is true as far as it goes. The actual movement of history is a continual prophecy. It adumbrates. Prophecy and parable are but two forms of the same thing. The greatest prophecy is perhaps unconscious. It is history itself. So viewed prophecy is an historical painting on a large canvas, while the parables are genre pictures on a small scale; but the value of both lies in what is implied rather than expressed, and promised rather than possessed. Both appeal to faith rather than to sight, to a second sight, to penetration rather than observation; they are precious rather for what is not there at a first glance than for what is. History read with insight is a prophecy—its satisfaction is not in itself—as Nature round us read with insight is full of symbolic parables—it does much and suggests more. Both the past and the present, both the large life and the small, mean more than they say. They have a meaning beyond themselves or their sense of themselves. And one great power for dealing with life and history is the power that loves to deal with parables, with symbols, and to read one thing while seeing another. Yes, the divine power is the ironical power of saying one thing and meaning another in no ignoble sense. It is that fiction which is the truest truth. It is the power of seeing that such speech is the deepest of all. God is the great ironist. But God's irony on the present is a kind irony and an educative, a creative.

Let us by all means have great plainness of speech on due occasion. But if a man say that simple directness is the only mode or even the chief mode of spiritual expression, if the plain man is to set up as the measure of the spiritual world, he must be reminded, first, that no soul who grasps the cross is really a plain man, but a spiritual aristocrat who sees into the grand paradox of time and eternity; and, second, that both Nature and grace work more by hints and symbols than by blunt phrases. The mere unseen may be simple, but the spiritual world which the cross opened is a world of paradox. Plainness of speech is not worth the price if it costs squatness of thought and baldness of vision. God hideth Himself. He hid Himself in His revelation in Christ in such a way that everybody was deluded. The cross is the greatest irony in history. And Christ spoke constantly in parables which to most of his hearers were riddles. He always refused to answer point-blank questions. The cross which is the measure of the world is the supreme paradox in the world and the greatest irritant to common-sense. And, if there were no such obscurity of utterance on the part of God, where would be the need of insight as the grand faculty of the spiritual leader? "Be not as the horse or mule, which are guided by bit and bridle; I will guide thee by mine eye."[1] We will read each other's looks, whatever be our language. There would be no faith in dealing with a literal, obvious God. Inspiration is insight. Insight into Nature makes the poet; insight into grace and its history makes the saint and apostle. All would be sight, mere intellectualism, not faith, otherwise. And that this insight, this mutually interpretive power of the past and present, Nature and grace, is the gift of the Christian teacher—such is the meaning of Christ in this passage.

Christ's Habit of Parable

He has been setting forth, in symbol, the principles, the soul, of history, of eternity. He has been uttering Eternity in parables. As He himself spoke in Nature parables, so (He would suggest) God has kept speaking—nay, acting—in the long parable of history. As the Son made Nature speak of the Father so the Father made history speak of the Son, groan and travail with Him. But Christ had had to explain to the disciples some of the very parables by which he tried to interpret things. He had found that His allegories bewildered, His illustrations darkened; they were but explaining the unknown by the unintelligible. Did He thereupon change His style? Did he give up preaching in the manner natural to Him? No, probably He could not. At least, He did not. He preferred to wait and bring the intelligence of the disciples up to Him instead of going down to their level, so that there should be no obscurities offered and no effort needed any more. That would have been education made easy, grace trivialised, kindergarten theology. It would have absolved them from spiritual exertion. It would have released their strain, and so far it would have been agreeable to them. But it would have arrested their spiritual development. And He would exercise them to godliness. It is difficulty that educates in moral things. "Our adversary is our helper."[2] He explained a parable or two by way of sample, but they were exceptions. And, so long as He was a teacher, till near the very end and the greater works, He went on teaching in the same manner as before. The Last Supper was His last parable, an enacted parable which has become real history—nay, the centre of it. And the reason for this puzzling treatment was that what He aimed at was the culture of their insight. He would put them on their mettle. He would provoke their interpretive power. He measured their

---

1. Ps 32:8–9.
2. Burke, *Reflections on the Revolution in France*. A similar statement—"Our antagonist is our helper"—is also cited in Forsyth's sermon on Luke 11:9 (included in this volume).

spiritual progress by their interpretive power. "Do you not yet understand?"[3] For instance, He never told them He was Messiah; He made the discovery inevitable. Hence His great joy at Cæsarea in Peter's discovery of what He had been bearing in on his puzzled mind all along. Throughout Christ's reality was anything but matter of fact. His speech was not clear-cut and unambiguous. He set more store by an eloquent flexibility, a suggestiveness in language than by stiff accuracy. He cared more for the pliancy of forms than their correctness. It was more to Him that they should mean greatly than that they should speak exactly and lucidly. He was more ready to keep old formularies, and interpret them, than to found a sect on their rejection for bald new summaries. He was a great Nonconformist, but He was not a separatist, not a sectary. He was always craving to be understood as He Himself understood the past. And how amply, how generously, with what insight He understood the past! How tender He was with tradition, what feeling He had for it! I am sure some of our sectaries and iconoclasts would be loud and bitter were they themselves interpreted no more generously than they interpret the men, movements, and creeds that went before them. Intellectual generosity flowing out of spiritual insight is one of the great powers and sanctified virtues from the Holy Ghost.

The Preacher-Scholar

"Things new and old," then, are the eternal principles and powers which the pedant always misses, whether he be orthodox or rationalist. But the preacher-scholar lives on them. There is nothing like preaching the Bible to escape pedantry on the Bible. The great and genuine scholar cares for these principles and powers above all the particulars which encase them, or the cases which illustrate them. "Things new and old" does not mean the New Testament and the Old, nor the Gospel and the Law, nor any such dogmatic banality. It means the Eternal purpose and redeeming power which is ever there yet never there; ever doing, never done; ever perceived but never seen; ever open to the anointed vision, never apparent to the common eye. You yourself are a thing at once new and old. You are at this moment your own past, and yet you are at this moment what you never were before. The venerable world in an incessant series of new departures, conservative variation, ordered miracles. The old mercies of God are ever new. Our souls live by the incessant miracle on us of God's ancient mercy, His historic salvation, His Holy Ghost. The newest things are the oldest things freshly realised. The very fact of their novelty—what does it mean but that they have been lying there longer, waiting the hour that brings them to light. The modern

---

3. See Matt 15:17; 19:9; Mark 8:17.

20: Things New and Old, 1913

world, crackling with novelty, is, compared with the primitive, the world's old age; that was the youth of the world. The oldest things of all are the things whose discoveries make the great novelties of the future. "There is no new thing under the sun."[4] In one sense that is the utterance of weary satiety and premature decay. But in another sense it is as true as the eternal heavens, so fresh and strong. The greatest of all antiquities is the Creator God, the Ancient of Days who, sitting on His ageless throne, maketh all things new. Prophecy is old, fulfilment is new; but the fulfilment lay working in the heart of the prophecy, the new is the old only come to light. The prophecy brings itself to pass, not by suggestion but by its inner dynamic. The prophetic element in the past is the pressure of the future on it. It is the action of the present at its heart. The moral law is old, the law of love is new; but it is new only as a commandment. As a power and purpose it was always there. The new was always in the old; the new love is the fulfilling of the old law. The form of the parable, the imagery, is old; the thought beneath it is new; but the thought was from the beginning in the images, the things so used, else how could they reveal the thought? God is old, man is new; but God is ever in man, else how could man be a sacrament of God? How could our fathers and mothers convey to us the Fatherhood of God? Truth is old, but it teems into incessant novelty. No form of truth is final. Our creeds are at once old and new. It is not abolition they need but reinterpretation. It is the interpreter that should handle the creeds, not the iconoclast, not the scorner. And the new creed, if it is also a true creed, is one that carries us back deeper and deeper into the interior of the old, till it end in the Gospel of the Ancient of Days. Forms must be pliant to be of any spiritual use. Words must be flexible, else they become false as expressions of the subtlest and most vital thought. The world with its fixed laws is yet teeming with new revelation, not to say, new creation. The poet is always filling out science and keeping the flush on Nature's face and the light in its eye. Thought, with its close logic, is still bursting with new thought. The fixed law of nature and the severe processes of mind are melting every moment into larger reality. The more the world changes, the more it is the same; the more it comes to its true self, it becomes itself only more so. It passes into new meaning beneath the gaze of the inspired eye. The anointed soul, the householder of faith, is pouring—that is the word rather than merely "bringing forth"—out of his treasure his inheritance from the past, things new and old, truths and realities which are both at once. The Christian teacher, like his Master, is a reconciler. And I will here take occasion to say in the bygoing that it is the scholars and teachers that are at this moment doing most for the reunion

---

4. Eccl 1:9.

of the Churches. Sentiment will not do it; common work against social ills will not do it. What parts them is matters of fact and principle; and it is the adjustment of these that must move the obstacles away. We have the faith. Each Church is equally earnest to do the will of Christ and represent it. What is that will? Where is it found? In history. It is not each other we have chiefly to understand, but the historic revelation which is the foundation of us all. It is the calm, unprejudiced, scientific study of history by the scholars of soul and faith that is silently but surely removing the sources of division. Think what it means for such scholars to have removed from the first century both the monarchial episcopate and insulated independency. And that is but a sample.

Reconciling by Interpreting

The equipped and accomplished Christian teacher does not merely restore or repristinate, he reconciles. He lives in the interpreter's house. He reconciles by interpreting. He inherits the treasures of the past, and it is his business to appreciate them anew, to refashion them in his soul for the needs of the time, and fuse them with present truth and knowledge. How can he do that unless the heat of his own soul melt both present and past? How can there be any fusion in the ignorant soul that simply carries the hard present alongside the hard past, each grinding the face of the other? Collision, friction, not reconciliation, is the result. And collision is the result of most of the so-called efforts to reconcile the religion of the past with the science of the present, old theories and new faith. What we get is but some sort of accommodation, some *modus vivendi*,[5] some compromise, and no true reconciliation. The interpretation that reconciles must re-create. The only real and fundamental reconciliation is the new creation. It is the new creation that interprets the old. But we are prone to come to the task, not creatively but only critically, not with appreciation but with scrutiny, not with insight but with mere science, not as prophets but as pedants. We begin examining before we have appropriated enough to fit us to examine. Very few people, says Ernest Renan, have acquired the right to disbelieve in Christianity. And then we cling to the old and despise the new, or else we cleave to the new, and despise the old; but we do not go deep enough to get at things before they split into old and new, and so we do not find the interpretation of both. We do not rise to the great criticism which is appreciative, constructive, and part of the great reconciliation. The obscurantist and the iconoclast are equally mischievous. Their reaction is equal and opposite and sterile.

5. Way or mode of life.

20: Things New and Old, 1913

What better service can a teacher do you than to show you how significant the old things can be for the new world, how old and how stable are the best things that are new? It is the old Eternal God in Christ that turns the world upside down. And the changeless is the source of all change.

The Novelty of Eternity

How, again, can His teachers better serve you than by making you feel the eternity of these souls of your own which seem to you always so recent, so fresh, so full of engrossing interest? The novelty of eternity, the hoary antiquity of fresh vitality! If he unfold to you the truth of the Bible, he tells you of such paradoxes as that a revolutionary Christianity is as old as Creation. Without them, no Christianity. He handles truths and powers which saved souls ages ago as now. He is the exegete of the eternal. He is leading out of the Bible fold on fold of all that is in it. If he expound the Bible in its freshest light, what is he doing but drawing forth into the interest of our own day the faiths and truths that were already old in God when they first flashed upon the writers of the Book? If he rescue the Bible from the antiquarians, on the one hand, and the modernists on the other, from the mere literalist and from the mere mystic; if he show that the realities of Christianity are the ideals which science is rich in framing but powerless to ensure, that is the true apologetic. It is not polemic, it is consummation. Or if he show, for example, how the powers for which society is craving today are the social principles in prophet and Gospel; if he declare that, after all, the Bible historically read and competently preached is the best statesman's manual of our day, having the principle of the life that now is and of that which is to come—what is this but by the lore of the Kingdom of Heaven to bring forth from the great treasury of tradition things for ever new because so immortally old? When the heavens are stale, exhausted, then will the Bible become obsolete for the public. But it must be interpreted with the insight of the Kingdom of God the Saviour.

And, finally, if, with the vision which is learned in heavenly schools, he declares to you that the inexhaustible Jesus Christ is the same yesterday, today and for ever, that the old Jesus is still the new, immortal, royal Christ, that the old atonement is still the spring of all the great reconciliations, that Christ's Resurrection is the potency in all true renaissance, that the creeds of the past are immortally full of Him, but final none of them; if he tell you that any creed which deeply testifies of Him has a message and a truth in it which grows not old with its fading phrases, but broadens down from age to age, so that the very meaning of words suffers a regenerated change; if he go to these creeds neither to idolise them nor smash them, nor scrap

II: Published Sermons

them, but to inquire of them, to inquire as gently and respectfully as we should coax out of a grand old warrior in his honourable age the story of his combats, the meaning of his strife and the source of his power; if, learning and teaching these things, he send you back to the world to interpret with tongues the message which has been sounding mightily in the systems of age after age, and to declare the infinite variety of the Christ invariable and eternal; if he do these things, is he not bringing out of our Christian treasury things brightly new and things old and holy? Does he not teach us that the newest things are but the old things talking English, German, French? The greatest spiritual battles of today were settled in principle in the first few centuries, though not in form. The new things are the visible evolution of things already involved from before the foundation of the world. Even revolution may be compressed evolution. The very idea of creation is the pouring forth of things new and old. Creation is not making from nothing. For what was there in creation that was not first in God? All divine variety is but the action of divine unity, and all unity is the cohesion of divine variety. If the principle of development interprets the physical world, so on a higher plane the growth of the creeds is the interpretation of Christ. This is He of whom all the creeds bear witness, who goes on to produce new creeds that renovate the old.

Transformation Not Destruction

But this interpretation is slow and patient work. It is strange to the air of crude heresies, party cries, and rival camps. It ignores the narrow and the passionate on both sides. It is the way of the world either to swallow creeds whole or to denounce them wholesale. And such scribes have their quick success, their rapid reward. The divine scribe cannot win it. People say approvingly of the snap-action critics, "They do not bewilder us. We know in a moment which side they are on, we know where to have them." Well, it is easy to be clear if you are small enough, one-sided enough, shallow enough, if you deny enough, exclude and destroy enough. To show clearly the position of the Tower of London, you could proceed as the great fire did; you could burn down all round it, leaving it sharply exposed against the desolate sky. Or you could proceed as those do who know London through constant business in it. You could become so familiar with the bearings of the Tower to every street around it that you could at once call up in your mind the connection between Tower and City, and give a clear idea of the relation between the two. So with Christ and the creeds. Christ and the City of God. You will not understand Christ better by burning the creeds He inspired, but by understanding them;

20: Things New and Old, 1913

not by abolishing the Churches, but transforming them, interpreting them, and finding them the old witnesses of things indestructible and truths ever new. Christ has a great task to deliver us from that inelastic, rigid habit of mind, too prompt with notions and too poor in ideas, which offers us instead of the Christian reconciliation of old and new the pagan dilemma. Old or new hatred of old doctrine is chiefly due to poverty of religion, as the idolatry of it also may be. It is a confession of lack of insight to discern, interpret, and renovate. In the long run the narrow mind is the narrow soul on both sides; and from that may Christ deliver us ever more!

Holy love is Christian revelation. Love is the startling thing, the new. We never get tired of love as we do of everything else. But the holy is the old, the eternal. We cannot think of the holy but as the ancient of days, the hoary source of freshness without end. Holy love is the only love that, having loved the world from the beginning, loves it to the end in the kingdom of peace, power and joy.

21

Music and Worship, 1914

We cannot separate music and worship; the only question is how to combine them. And the chief justification for instrumental music in church is the help it gives to this end. If it separates music from worship, the instruments are better away. They are better away if they preoccupy the church with feelings or suggestions which are of the world (like the theatre or concert, etc.), or those which are aesthetic rather than spiritual. Concert pieces, or music in that style, may be foreign to the spirit of worship. It may be religious but not worshipful. One could but welcome the movement by Pope Leo XIII to chasten his church music, and eject the modern style which was destroying worship; though it seems going very far to use in the Sistine Chapel nothing later than Palestrina. Yet church music does not call for second-rate composers but for first-rate ones who keep art in the second place.

Music arose in Christian worship first, historically, from the custom of the Jewish Church; second, religiously, from Christian hymns, like the *Magnificat, Nunc dimittis,* or *Te Deum,* which sprang from the overflow of the Christian heart; and, thirdly and practically, it arose as a vehicle for the contagious expression of truth in the early Church. The creeds were sung. At a later date music gave wings to the Reformation in hymns like Luther's; and those of early Methodism from Wesley did the like. And it may be noticed here that much of what is foolish and offensive in the way of hymns is found in those which aim at attracting or impressing the public rather than expressing the Church and its truth. Church music is there to express the Church rather than draw the world. Praise is more essential to the Church than popularity.

21: Music and Worship, 1914

At first Christian worship was of the simplest kind, therefore its music was by the voice alone. This was caused also by the separation of the Church from Judaism and its protest against it. In respect of music there was both a legacy from Judaism and a reaction from it. The Jewish temple ritual was elaborate, antiphonal, and instrumental. It is a mistake to suppose that the Jews were Puritans in this regard, or in the matter of colours, as they were in images. But the synagogue worship was much quieter, and had more effect on the Christian Church. There was reaction from the temple but continuity with the synagogue. As Greek influence grew in the Church, its effect is seen not only in theology, but also in the abjuring of instrumental praise. Hellenism seems to have had no instrument in its ritual. The Christian praise was by voice almost entirely; as in the pagan world instruments were associated with wordly passion and frivolity; and the great soul-music was yet unborn. But the slow reception of the Apocalypse into the Church still did something to foster the ideal of instrumental, choral, and cosmic praise with trumpets, harps, and hosts.

This tendency was encouraged still more by the great influence of the Gregorian School of Music at Rome about 600 AD. And then came the invention of the organ, about the time of Charlemagne (say 800 AD). It was truly a providential gift. It made possible the development of harmony, the great feature of modern and western music; and it gave effect to the deep, complicated, yet reconciled and triumphant range of soul opened by Christianity.

Christianity has created music as a great art. But it has also developed a special and appropriate form of music for its own emotions of solemn cosmic power and peace. It created church music, with the same technical laws as all music, but a regenerate spirit. The organ arose to express this rich Christian soul. Most peoples have a national instrument; the organ is the instrument of the spiritual nation and people of God. It is the supreme instrument for worship.

For, in the first place, it is the instrument which draws the material world most fully to participate in the vast hymn of redeemed humanity. An orchestra would do this; but the organ abolishes the distractions and impertinences of a numerous orchestra, as Wagner hides his band under the stage.

In the next place, the organ is uncongenial to the music of passion, to what Meredith calls the "blood-emotions."[1] It is not exciting, but composing, solemnizing. It has not thrill but elation, not a cry but a peal. The violin trembles, the organ rolls. The one goes up to God for mercy, the other comes down with grace's majesty to man.

---

1. In George Meredith's *Diana of the Crossways* (1885).

Further, the symbolism of the organ is attractive for the community of the kingdom of God and its inspiration. The same wind among all the pipes is like the one Holy Spirit on the diversity of souls. The Spirit draws a different note from each, and makes harmony and reconciliation from all at the will of one. Of the many voices, not one is without signification.

We are, mankind is, an organ whose maker and builder is God. His Spirit draws from each soul its own note in a vast concert. Redeemed humanity is the final music and the perfect praise; and nothing but music, and orchestral music, can express at present anything so passing knowledge. One need not do more here than refer in the by-going to Milton's *At a Solemn Music*, and Browning's *Abt Vogler*.

Once more, liturgically, the Church felt the disorderliness and poverty of a mass of people taking part in worship on a spoken note. There was a loss of beauty, of solemnity, and especially of the unity, the decency, and order which worship implies. To express the soul of a mass of people calls for music, either as song or as oratory.

Art is not artificial. Our age and society become more musical. Music becomes a more common, and therefore a more natural, vehicle of expression. Hence worship becomes more musical without being less natural. We need simplicity, but there is one thing we need more, namely, naturalness, sincerity. An affected simplicity is false and unfit for worship. And it is very common. Now what is the form of worship natural to a crowd? Something musical. In private worship a sober simplicity may be natural, and a conversational note. But public worship is not simply private worship in public. It is not individual prayer overheard. So also with praise. It has the corporate note. Hence we do not sing lyrics but hymns—less poetic, perhaps, but more to the purpose. We should not pray or praise in public as we do in private. There is a volume, a compass, a reserve, a dignity, and even a stateliness, in public worship which cannot and need not be in private. And there is an intimacy in private worship which, in public, is undue. So to make public worship natural we need music, and even an instrument to give it an expression natural to its collective and congregational quality and dignity. People in church join in a musical tone where they are afraid of their own voices in a spoken note; and they go to worship where they get this vehicle. It is useless to complain of their not going to church if you refuse such means to make the service both congregational and beautiful—so long as it is earnest and sincere. What combines these public requirements is music—so long as the musicians do not take command. May I repeat that church music is there first for the church and its uses, and only next for the public; it is for praise, not enjoyment; it is spiritual, not aesthetic. The anthem is not a performance to conciliate a choir, but a sung sermon—a text with a musical commentary, where the comment should take its modest place, and where self-exhibition is sacrilege.

Life is made up of prose and poetry. The prose of Christian life is work, conduct, duty and even drudgery. The poetry of it is worship. And both high poetry and high worship run to song, to music. Music is the heart's release; so also is worship. The atmosphere of common worship therefore is music. The worship of the congregation takes musical expression in tune; the worship of the preacher takes it in eloquence. And both are escapes from baldness, both uplifted naturalness, speech born again. Poetry is home-sickness till it becomes Christian: then it is home-communion.

Worship is an expression of feeling, and feeling runs to music. Opera can be more true than drama, and that than narrative. It used to be said, "What is too poor to say, sing." So we have our dreadful, nauseous drawing-room songs, debasing both art and sentiment. But it is truer to put it thus, "What is too deep and fine to say, sing." Worship, as the Church's self-expression, runs to sacred art, which is the ample transfiguration of natural feeling; and, among the arts, it runs to music. And it does so first because that is the art of relief to the surcharged heart. The soul, smitten by the world, groans; but, smitten by God, it sings, as Memnon sang at the touch of light. Even creeds, I have said, were first sung, when belief was satisfying and joyful. Then worship runs to art, secondly, because music is the most spiritual and least material of all the arts. The sense medium is almost refined away. It is the soul itself in vibration.[2] Thirdly, because music is communal.

It is true, there is a worship too deep even for song, for music. We simply listen, and despair of expressing ourselves.

> Heard melodies are sweet, but those unheard
> Are sweeter.[3]

The deepest, heavenliest melodies are heard by the rapt soul. The truth of heaven strikes music from earth, but the music of heaven, when heard, strikes earth dumb. Hence the art in common worship must not be too high. It has a subdued, modest sense of its own inadequacy. One thinks of Raphael's St. Cecilia. At the singing of the angelic choir, heard through a rift in heaven, she forgets her instruments in rapture (even the small organ in her hand, which has outlived all the rest ere it breaks down). Magdalen forgets her sin and self. Paul forgets both book and sword, both theology

---

2. See my *Christ on Parnassus*, Chapter VIII. [This footnote appears in the original text.]

3. From John Keats' poem, "Ode on a Grecian Urn" (1819).

and warfare. John is in his element, and Augustine's passion is lost in sympathetic gaze at John.

But congregational worship is not of that mystic, rapt, and lonely sort. And musical worship should be congregational. It may be as elaborate as you like within that limit. If a picked chorus formed the whole congregation, the music might be highly artistic and yet natural and easy. But for most congregations it is responses, prayers, chants, hymns. Whatever it is, it should be congregational. To leave the singing to the choir or the praying to the minister is popish. It is strange that some should think it a rag and relic of Rome to have a congregational share by musical responses in prayer. It is just the opposite of Romish. Without abolishing anything so valuable as extempore prayer, the congregation should assert its place, and insist on participating publicly in the prayers—publicly and musically; since, as I have said, we get far more participation in a sung note than in a spoken.

In Romanism the minister is not simply a leader but a priest—he acts in place of the congregation, which he rules more than he represents. So the choir was at first composed of clergy. They did the singing. The congregation was excluded, as is still the case in Italy. The choir there does not lead, but monopolizes, as clericalism always does. But in Protestantism, in the Teutonic nature, in democratic conditions, the congregation is the choir, the anthem is quite subordinate to the hymn or chorale. The choir so-called is only a leader, for use and service. And in the same way, the minister in worship is no priest, no substitute, but a guide. It is a rag of popery to let the choir alone sing, and to let the minister alone pray. He is no leader, if he do not lead, if no voice and tone follow his voice, if he monopolize the speaking to God. And it is a burden which tends to injure him, as many could tell.

But, if praise be congregational, if it be worship and not exhibition, the music and the organ must also keep their proper place. The machine is the organ of the soul. The service of worship should never be a recital, or in any way preoccupied with instrument or artist. There are other occasions for that. The first place belongs to the intelligible word, the uttered word of truth and grace. The main thing of our Protestant worship is not our message to God, but God's to us. The people's tribute to God in worship is stirred by God's gift to his people. And that is the gospel word. Everything is created by God's gospel to us. Faith comes of hearing and grows into love. We must urge the supremacy and primacy of the word. God's living Word, Christ, is at the source of creation's praise. How truly the great musicians feel the need of the intelligible word to crown all the instruments can say! Wagner remedied by poetry music's defect. But the classic illustration of this is in Beethoven's Ninth Symphony, where the instruments of all the orchestra are unable to utter the joy of the universe, and the voice and the

21: Music and Worship, 1914

word must come in to help the players out, and to crown the praise with the poet's glorious strain.

May I quote from myself on this great work?

> The hunger of the heart is ever for fullness and satisfied joy. It is starved and vexed among the riddles, failures and tragedies of life. It remains empty and aching, after all the charm of nature and the spell of art. Not there do we find that solid fullness of reality which permanently fills and purifies the soul. And nowhere, perhaps, in all the soul's own art of music, has this hunger for joy and praise, this passion for fullness, appeasement and finality, been set forth as it is in this symphony set forth in its first collision with life's untowardness, its storm, pathos, and colossal despair, and in its final conquest of them all.

In the last movement, it has been said by a genius as great as Beethoven himself, the music becomes "of a speaking kind." The voice takes the place of the band. Poetry comes to the rescue of music. The passionate thought moves onward and upward, and instruments are found to be too weak and vague in what they convey. Something more positive, more explicit, more rational is demanded by the labouring idea than the emotional utterance of musical sound. Something more is wanted, to give the soul not only foothold but body, form, expression, and action. Inarticulate sound, however fine, mystical, and musical, is not enough to express the complete human spirit in its supreme effort to assert its final place in the universe of life. So the chorus of human voices breaks in on the summit of the instrumental struggle. The chorus enters with the living and corporate word, and carries the thought and feeling to its divine release and final height. It is no mere device, no feat of skill, no triumph of musical ingenuity, no invention of amazing cleverness and resource. Great inspiration does not work so. It is all forced on the artist by the spiritual necessity of his idea and the native movement of his mighty thought. His thought must pass beyond mere sound, and become a word. There descends a living, human, reasonable word on the crown of this great instrumental creation, to save it from inadequacy and collapse. The chorus breaks in with Schiller's sublime "Ode to Joy," a joy not in nature but in grace, in the promise and gift of universal love for all mankind.

> Be embraced in love, ye millions,
> Here is joy for every one.
> Far above yon sky pavilions
> Stands our common Father's throne.

II: Published Sermons

Above all the metallic orchestra of civilization there must emerge the human and corporate Word, Christ. Human concord, the joy of earth, the soul of the soul, and the grace of God can receive their consummation only in the enthronement of Him who is the living Son of God, God's intelligent and articulate word, the final, royal Christ. God, man, and nature can find the fullness of their utterance only in a human rational, loving, redeeming Word.

Even art feels, as faith knows, the fullness of completed being and its flush of perfect joy to be in that saving work of love which broke on the world in the cross to make men redeemed brothers in Jesus Christ to the glory of God the Father.

22

OUR EXPERIENCE OF A TRIUNE GOD, 1914

AS WE BEGIN LIFE, we rejoice in the world's harmony and rationality, its humanity and promise. The enthusiasm of humanity captures us. One man I know says, "I could take you to the field where it burst upon me at twenty." God is revealed as so natural in His love, as a magnified Father, as the consummation of all things fine and fair.

But sooner or later we come to a rude and raw contact with the muddles, babels, slums, bedlams, and, it may be, hells of life. The old gay harmony breaks up into collision. The fine fabric of our first world is shaken for many, shattered for some. "Die schöne Welt—sie stürzt, sie zerfällt."[1] And the very worst of it is that our own souls are in the collapse. Innocence is ruined there. "Weh! Weh! Du hast sie zerstört mit machtiger Faust."[2] Conscience is a steady guide no more. It is the accusing angel. The purist criticism of youth, by which we so freely and cruelly condemned others, we turn on ourselves.

The tender Father now becomes the solemn judge—even in the Son of His love. Christ's words, His ideal, His character, which we hailed as so noble, rise up to condemn us more than they cheer us. To the natural and benignant Father succeeds the historic and judging Son. The gentle and genial Jesus deepens into the high and holy, the austere and exigent Christ. And what a crisis comes then! We either turn and leave Him, or else we cleave to Him and turn to rend ourselves. Either we say (or we listen to those who say), "there are other and less humiliating ways of finding the real God

---

1. From Goethe's *Faust* (1808–1829): "The beautiful world—it collapses, it crumbles."

2. From Goethe's *Faust*: "Woe! Woe! Thou hast destroyed [the beautiful world] with a powerful fist."

than by forgiveness, by His justification of us." And we plunge for an opiate into philosophy, and find a God indeed but much more as a postulate than a certainty. Perhaps we take up with a "simple" piety, sometimes to end in a silly. Perhaps we turn to art, literature, social life, and even social well-doing. We take to a humanitarian religion, which tells us we are not so desperately bad at bottom after all, and which bids us take heart, let alone theology about Redemption by an ill-used God, and go to work for the amelioration of ill-used man. And we forget all the time that such optimism has only become possible to this age by the historic work of a Church and Gospel that preached a searching and judging forgiveness in the past. Either we take such lines, I say, or else we are made of sterner stuff, and we refuse those flattering unctions for our soul; and our eyes are opened, and we know we are poor, and wretched, and blind, and naked, and very guilty; and it is now "God be merciful." In the greatness of Christ, the ideals of Christ, we meet the unsparing holiness of God.

Then all our genial Christ goes up in the blaze of His Cross, so to say. We realise that the Father's holiness was most unsparing to the Son of His love. In the suffering of Christ, in the Cross, it is a Holy God we have, who spared not Himself in His own Son. The divine holiness, of which Christ said so little, becomes by His death the one revelation of His life. (The chief thing achieved by our life, and carried away from earth with us, may be something which we said very little about, and which few realised in us.) His love is the love of the holy for the guilty, the most wonderful kind of love (when we take time to think our faith) in a world where love is the marvel of it all. The love of God as the poets taught it, and the poet preachers, and the genial saints, the mere fatherhood Christianity—that is all too short to reach us. When we have come to the worst pass, such love from God does not get to us; it does not find the bottom and the bitterness of our perdition. We are not found for ever till we are plucked by the conscience from the fearful pit and the miry clay; not till we hunger for holiness as once we did for love and joy, and yet find holiness our dread; not till we thirst for peace with a judging God more than ever we craved for our young ideals in a splendid God.

> O only Source of all our light and life,
> Whom as our truth, our strength, we see and feel,
> But whom the hours of mortal moral strife
> Alone aright reveal.[3]

The Christ we once took in, almost gaily, as the soul's hero, breaks out upon us as a consuming fire; "As if a man should lean on a wall from

3. From Arthur Hugh Clough's poem, "Qui Laborat, Orat" (1862).

22: Our Experience of a Triune God, 1914

which a serpent bit him."[4] The Christ of our jubilant, and even jaunty, confession rounds on us suddenly, as He did upon Peter exalted with his revelations above measure; "Thou Satan!"[5] And the baptism which we lightly thought we could be baptized with like heroes descends to find us cowards or rebels, renegades or betrayers. And there is no spirit left in us before that Holy One, who burst forth as the village guest did, awful in the very breaking of bread.

Then the Revelation of the Holy comes home in our Redemption by the Holy and His Atonement, and by the Holy Ghost; and we never knew what revelation was till then. It was once an idyll for us, now it is a tragedy and a triumph. The old lights are gone. They failed because we were false. They ceased to be truth because we ceased to be true. Because we fell, our stars fell—to be will-o'-the-wisps. And there is but one way to replace them—another revelation, which now must be Redemption, replacing *us*. We discover that we must be redeemed into the power to believe to the end even in our old revelations. We need that holy love to enable as to believe in all love. The blood of Christ does something else than symbolise the divine sacrifice in us; it is the Sacrifice for us. It is not the classic case of all Sacrifice that kindles us; it is the one Sacrifice of God that humiliates us, but humiliates us into a new life in a new world. We are pulverised into a new creation. Then, we believe not only in the Father and in the Son but in the Holy Ghost and the love He sheds abroad in our hearts. We have found not only a truth but a certainty, a reality, a life that gives value to all truth. We have found not only life but eternity, not only a new world but the eternity of all worlds in Father, Son, and Holy Spirit. Whom it is poor religion to reduce to three phases either of God's manifestation or the soul's process. For that would leave us with but a variable God—an adaptable God rather than an eternal.

History and experience alike show that the destruction of interpersonal relations within God is reflected in the loss of personal energy and earnestness in religion, which is reduced to a religion of evolution rather than redemption, and of culture rather than faith.

That is what we need in a revelation, and have in Christ's—not fresh and startling light, but sure, final, and eternal reality; not truth but power; not something to see and know, but something that knows us and carries us. That is where real religion begins—when we cease to know anything except that we are known of God, and loved more than known. We try other ways. We pore, and brood, and ask egoistic questions about the meaning of life.

4. Amos 5:19.
5. Matt 16:23//Mark 8:33.

II: Published Sermons

There are thousands of the half-awake, the half-born, the soul-hungry, craving or fumbling for the meaning of life today, and peering to find it in life's interior, in flashes of genius, in spiritual arcana, in psychisms, occultisms, in profundities, among the wizards that peep and mutter, or the sages who search or soar. Or they turn to a mysticism which is either divorced from history or which forces a protesting history into its crystal moulds. Others think that work will be a narcotic, and from amid the luxuries of life they turn to seek Christian service. All these things may enrich us in their place. But the eternal meaning and last stay of life is not in its energies, and not in its interior. Genius, with its insight, has not what the saint has with his outlook of faith. We are never redeemed, however we are chastened, by sinking into ourselves. We do not receive our great revelation with closed eyes and introverted strain. Christ is not to be had by descending into subliminal deeps to bring Him up. Revelation is not in a process but in a crisis. And the crisis of all human life is at a point in human history. The meaning of life is only to be known from life's goal, not its career; and the goal of life is known but to God, Who achieved it in Christ, Who made us for Himself, in Christ and Who in Him sees the end from the beginning. It is known for certain but to God, and to those to whom He reveals it by His Son, His Cross, His Spirit. That is the meaning and truth of history. The truth of man is found not in his own recesses nor in historic currents, but in the destiny for which God made him and saved him. It is in His Cross God has not only revealed our destiny, but ensured it, brought it to pass, in the Holy Christ crucified, whose salvation is the source of our last moral certainty, and who is our Eternal Amen. God died for us in a sense which only a Trinitarian doctrine can convey. Certainty, finality for eternity, a Rock of Ages—that is what we want in the Revelation that secures all other revelations; that is the reality of which they are but metaphors. And that is what the Church finds by the Spirit in Jesus Christ and His Cross where God was present reconciling. The one Revelation that gives any revelation real meaning is the threefold revelation of the sure mercy of the Holy Father to our worst need in the Cross of His Son made certain and final in the Spirit.

The number is great at present of cultivated women who feel a heart hunger gnawing in the midst of every comfort. And, because life has been for them so sheltered and pure, they do not find themselves so readily when we speak of a Redemption from the tragic sin and guilt of the world. Their regards are perhaps more individual than general, more of the heart than the conscience, and their problems are more capable therefore of a mystic solution. And the like is true of many fine, high-minded, clean-minded youths. It should, therefore, be pointed out that such a central Redemption as I have spoken of as the foundation of a faith in a triune

22: Our Experience of a Triune God, 1914

God is the note rather of the collective Church facing the whole world and its sin; and it should not be pressed violently, prematurely, into the experience of every individual. To demand that every soul should run through the experience of a Luther or a Paul can only lead to the spiritual unreality which has been the bane of too much popular Evangelism. Doubtless such Redemption of the conscience by the Saviour is the central issue of the world and of the Church in it. But every soul is not the centre of a world or an age; nor is every soul equally near that central fire, though all live by its warmth. And there are outer circles in the great hierarchy of souls, where the central redemption from guilt acts rather as redemption from things unlovely or painful, from the base and from the sore, from the ignoble and from the bitter, from the gross and from the hard, from meanness and from care, from coarseness and from grief—from these things rather than from great, memorable, and world-tragic guilt. Christ redeemed us both from the burden of the conscience and from the burden on the heart, from being the slaves of sin and from being the slaves of calamity, from guilt and from death—by the Cross from ourselves and by the Resurrection from nature. And the message and task of the Church regards both. So we have within it diversities of operation. And the healers and helpers among women are as needful as the evangelists and prophets among men—as needful in their place and perspective, *i.e.*, so long as the amelioration does not say to the Redemption, "I have no need of thee."[6] It is incredible that Christ should have demanded from Mary of Bethany the agonies of repentance as a condition of true faith. Repentance may not be the female side of faith, as love, perhaps, is not the male. So long as Christ—the union of holiness and love—is the absolute victor and centre of the moral world for the whole Church, some of its members may be more directly called for the finer ministries and intuitions of tender sympathy, and others for the moral commands and committals of holy faith. If only we take the holy in an ethical sense and not merely in an æsthetic, if it be the white heat of righteousness and not the mere good form of piety, if it be moral worship, however rapt, and not mere reverence however fair. If only too the service in the name of sympathy be not a mere narcotic to ease the gnawings of an egoism still unbroken at the core; if only it be not taken up to dull the ache of souls that read Thomas Hardy (or, short of that great genius, his imitators) till they can trace behind all things but a sombre Fate instead of a loving God—a God most patient because Almighty, and slow because secure in a conclusive bliss.

---

6. 1 Cor 12:21.

II: Published Sermons

As I have named Mr. Hardy I will close with an expression of my surprise at the narrow culture of the later writers who now hold the reading public for the hour, who do not rise to discuss the moral destiny of a Humanity which is yet their working capital as *litterateurs*,[7] and who absolutely ignore the existence of the deepest passion and concern of human nature, its religion, which makes man man. It is neither their problem or their atmosphere; and is often their contempt. And contempt here is the trade mark and index of the dilettantist.

---

7. A professional writer.

23

THE MEANING OF A SINLESS CHRIST, 1923

IT IS VERY FREELY lamented in religious circles that no feature in the moral physiognomy of the day is more marked than the decay or absence of the sense of sin. And the remarkable thing is that it is a feature conspicuous in those circles most disposed to fall back on the teaching of Jesus in whom that sense was overwhelming. We are only putting the same thing in a more positive way when we observe the note of self-satisfaction, not only in the churches but in many of the pulpits of the day. Few seem to go beyond a general confession, with the strongest phrases pruned. They have erred and strayed but not rebelled. They hesitate to call themselves miserable offenders, or to say there is no health in them. Few seem to doubt that there is a vague fatherhood that will make all safe at last. Few seem really to doubt their final salvation somehow, or to regard the whole phase of Christ's teaching which contains such a word as "the door was shut."[1] Few consent to think of God the adversary with whom we must come to terms. Few seem afraid of being castaways. Few seem to feel but scarcely saved, or bought with an awful price. Few seem to realize a moral risk other than social discovery and disgrace. Few seem to have much idea of vigilance in connexion with their Christian life and destiny; they do not watch unto prayer, nor are they alert for the Eternal as for the humane. The old notion of spiritual conflict, of an agony at a strait gate, of a peril of perdition, seems to have died out of the Christian life. Many of the seniors, it is true, are exercised about the collisions of a business career with Christian ethic. And young people, to be sure, still struggle with certain temptations, and complain much of their need and of the little help they get. But that is not what I mean. I mean doubt or conflict about our mature or final position in God's sight in the great

1. Matt 25:10.

II: Published Sermons

trial, doubt about how we shall stand the great inquest of righteousness (when and wherever it comes—perhaps in a world-war) which meant so much for Jesus. People question everything now except their secure standing somehow with the God with whom they seldom have personal dealings or spiritual rest, and who is most valuable as an anodyne. They like to discuss questions about the existence of a God, His personality, His relation to Nature, and especially to Society, or even to Christ, about immanence, about immortality, about eternal punishment, and so on—only not about the state of their soul before Holy God where Jesus saw all things set and all souls judged. They are interested in religious problems, but not in the intimate problem of themselves and their spiritual destiny. Liberalism has narcotised them with a world-accepting ethic. Their concern is sprightly. They have some perplexity but no real misgiving. Science unsettles them in a pleasant sort of way, with a risky joy-like switchback ride; but the floor does not fall out of their moral world. They have never looked into the bottomless pit. Their spiritual safety is a genial matter of course. The love of God they can always depend on. The only doubt they know is interesting, intellectual doubt. Real religious doubt, concern about the soul of the race and goal of the world, belongs to a stage now outgrown. And so we speak of winning souls instead of converting them. We charm them wisely. We attract them kindly, and then when we get them in we do not always know what to do with them as souls. We cannot kindle them as the war has done. We try sometimes to answer intellectual doubt without providing the moral education that makes the answer intelligible. Whereas it might serve us better to aggravate and deepen it into religious doubt, fatal doubt of the kind that scares, and is really laid only by personal and evangelical faith. But it grows more and more hard for the preacher, as society grows in comfort and kindliness, to get through the tough soft rind of self-certainty, rising to self-satisfaction and even to self-complacency, which the general type of religion so often tends to breed. And it may be that there was nothing for it, even for God, but this huge calamity to shake us to our moral senses. He turns outward the judgment side of the salvation of the Cross.

When the Church makes this admission it makes more—it makes a confession. The Church has not only to admit that it does not bring the world to contrition, but it has to confess that it loses the power to impress upon its own members the meaning, the gravity of their sin, i.e., of the conscience of Jesus, whether put into His teaching or His conflict and Cross, or to make them realise the true moral inwardness both of His preaching and His passion. Even the war has not yet roused in the mass of good people the sense of moral awe. Our modern amiability smothers the flame of moral passion and profound thought, as the ash of our Christmas decorations puts the fire out

23: The Meaning of a Sinless Christ, 1923

when we crush them into the grate. Our religious growth, whatever direction it takes, does not include this. And it misses it, it does not take seriously enough the very words of Jesus, because it misses the authentic note of the Cross in the Gospel. The Church can stir people to compassionate kindness, to seemly worship, to much reverence for the name of Christ and the claim of religion. It can win from them large sums of money, and much practical sacrifice (however little it may *cost*). But it does not bring them to repentance, in any such searching sense of the word as it bore even in the discourses either of the Baptist or the Christ. Mystic piety is much more easy to produce, and more agreeable to feel, than penitent faith. Faith has been identified with love in an easy way that detaches it from the holiness that brought love to the Cross; and so it is severed from repentance. It is our treatment of the Cross that has reduced us below the penitential pitch with which Jesus began.

It is not that efforts are not made by preachers to redress this state of things, and to do so by a return to our Bible, and even to the Bible Christ.

1. We preach the wondrous, patient, endless love of God as the message of Christ. We say this preaching was the one thing He came to do. It was to hold up to us this love of God, shame us with our neglect of it, humble us with its ideal, and win us by its sacrifice. But it is doubtful if this produces more than a compunction far short of the repentance of faith at which Jesus aimed. And certainly it does not succeed in producing the effect that Christ in His conquering death had on His own. The remorse for our blindness to love can be dreadful enough, but it is not so humbling nor so hopeful as a repentance before the Holy One and our wound to Him. The dullness to sin, which I named has been concurrent with an unprecedented sensibility to the charming and the tender in God or man, with a Gospel and theology of the endless mercy and pity of God. But it may even be a case of cause and not more concurrence. The preaching of this tender, unwearied and universal love of God may be the cause of the deadening of the sense of sin. Pity ousts grace, and purity holiness. Sin is then reduced to a misconstruction by us of God's love, and a misunderstanding, which Christ came to put right. But the sense of sin, if we take its truly Christian form of humility, is due to something more than a charge against ourselves of misconstruction, or even fault. Humility is not a product of repentance alone, far less of chagrin. It is produced by a revelation not only of God's love but of the moral greatness and wonder of it; meaning thereby especially its qualitative greatness—not merely its amount or intensity, but its holiness. Life is not really "measured by intensity," any more than by duration, but at last by conscience, by sanctity. It is a blessed sense of the holy majesty of God's love that really kills our self-satisfaction and becomes the standing source of a habitual humility. "As

is thy majesty so is thy mercy."[2] A humility that rises but from a sense of guilt and repentance easily leads to self-scourging, and similar sterile forms of self-degradation. If we are told that Jesus set forth the love of God with little reference to His holiness let us recall His humility, both of word and life. His humility was not before the God of love but before the holy God (if we distinguish the inseparable). And His nearest explained it neither by the half-god of Arianism nor by the spiritual genius found in Jesus by modern thought, but only by a Son as holy in His eternal obedience as the Father in His eternity of sovereign sanctity. And so with us in our place and measure. The repentance not to be repented of comes with the exalted humility which at once faces and shares the holy majesty of God in the power of His new-creating Grace in Christ's Cross. Such at least is the apostolic witness. God *so* loved the world—not so intensely, nor so kindly, but so holily—that He gave His only Son—as a propitiation (says the same pen) to His holy name; that whosoever is united to Him should not perish in a mere repentance but should rise to the humility of Life holy and eternal. Was that a misunderstanding of the message of Jesus by those He did most to teach? Was it a perversion of His preaching by its most constant audience?

2. Or perhaps we preach the sinlessness of Christ as exhibited in the gospels of His word and deed, and try to make men measure themselves against that example or ideal. But sinlessness is after all a negative idea, and, in so far, incapable of producing a sense of sin. What is the positive bearing of Christ's sinlessness on *me* except as a positive revelation, as an energy, an act, of the holiness of God? No passive or negative purity, harmless and undefiled, can produce an effect so great and searching. Unworldliness cannot make us feel much more than unworthiness. We admire the figure of one so far above our weak will and our mixed motives; but the spectacle of a life so cloistered and remote does not humble or break us to the repentance of the saints as the holiness of the Cross does, which emerges in that final act of God at the passionate centre of man's tragic soul and history with a reality more active, positive, and masterful than our own worldly will of sin.

If we pass beyond the negative idea of sinlessness, and see in Christ's life one actively holy even unto death, the mere *spectacle* of holiness, even though it be beneficent and not merely unspotted, is after all but an æsthetic one—a piece of moral æsthetic like so much that deludes the conscience in a literary age. It is not dynamic for us, as the effect of Christ's death certainly was. It declares much but conveys little. It erects an ideal for admiration, but it does not go to the roots of the soul, tears up the matted weeds, and plant new life. The act of sin is not countered by an act in God. We do not rise beyond the

---

2. Sir 2:18. See Forsyth's sermon on this text published in this volume on pp. 332–33.

23: The Meaning of a Sinless Christ, 1923

best Hellenic range of morals, fertilised by Judaism. No mere worship of a most holy life can search, humble, confound and re-create us, as Christ has done to His classic own from His Cross. It does not carry us beyond saint-worship. Only the Cross has given Jesus the personal devotion His preaching claimed. The worship of the ideal Holy One could never have produced either the medieval Church or its Reformation. The Trisagion does not lift the Greek Church to the level of the Church of the West. It could not produce the Church which produced the Reformation. Besides, if the spectacle of a life of saintly beneficence or guidance were the main element in a divine revelation founding a religion, why was Christ's life and preaching so brief? Would it not have been more effective had it been prolonged to a ripe and mellow age, and had it proved and exhibited this sanctity in many more junctures and relations of life than we find in Him? He seemed to deprecate, also, we remember, an attitude to Him which simply called Him good, even in the highest degree. The records are too scanty to carry a picture of such holiness of life as both crushes and lifts us into the worship of the real presence of the Holiest God. From Christ's words and conduct we do gain the sense of the righteous Father of love, judgment, and salvation; but we do not even there gain that sense of holiness which destroys egoism and creates the most profound repentance, saving faith, and brotherly love.

The sinlessness reflected in the words as in the carriage of Jesus cannot be quite certain to us from the Gospel record of these. He did not so preach Himself to Israel, though He has so conveyed Himself to mankind. The story is not detailed enough in incident for that purpose, nor is it psychological enough in its insight. The belief cannot arise as the empirical impression from a life which we are allowed to see victorious in every phase of temptation, or whose suggestions we can trace pure to their inmost cell. For though He was tempted in all reality like us He was not tempted at every point; things that are deadly temptations to us were none to Him. We can believe the sinlessness of Jesus only in its positive form of complete holiness, i.e., in its perfect relation and satisfaction to a holy God. But how *we* to judge of that? We cannot see Him with God's eyes, nor weigh Him in God's scales. We must take God's word for it; and pre-eminently the great and crowning word of the Resurrection; wherein God, by a supreme act upon Him more powerful than any words, declared Himself perfectly well pleased with Him in that perfect work of the Cross where His whole life and person took effect in an act meant for God and fully understood by Him alone. We can realise His holiness with due gravity and certainty only from such an expression of Christ's final hallowing and complete delighting of holy God, His destruction of evil, and His re-creation of the race in a conflict not subliminal merely but truly moral, psychological, historic, and yet absolute. A victory in this region which were only relatively greater than ours, greater in degree but not in kind, corresponds neither to gospel nor epistle. It certainly destroys Christ's value as Saviour. It would not justify our worship of Him, nor entitle us to commit our sinful soul to Him for ever, without some flavour of idolatry.

The difficulties of course for systematic thought are here great, if not insuperable. It may be said that a temptation really like ours is incompatible with real unity with the God who is always above these stormy levels. And the only reply, here as often elsewhere, is that the two things cannot be reconciled by co-ordinating and adjusting, as if we were handling two empirical facts or truths. The fallacy of treating Revelation chiefly as truth and not experience becomes very mischievous here. And the reconciliation of the two things can only lie in our own—in the conviction and experience of the Church's faith that, in the work of Christ's person which makes us what we are with God, in the new life, we do have a supreme form of the paradox which is greatest in the greatest religions. We have His real unity with God riding, guiding, and ruling a real conflict, whose chief form was not in the wilderness with demons nor in the market place with Pharisees, but on the Cross. It was on the Cross as the crisis of all His crises, nay, as the node of the tragedy of existence, as the seal of every moral conquest besides, and the surety of every victory of ours— ours, who are more than fellow-conquerors, being loved and redeemed by His grace in which we stand. If His words touch us nearly and powerfully this work changes us for good and all, from glory to glory, in the Lord the Spirit.

The active holiness of Christ preached the holiness of a God who is the Act Eternal. And His preaching was not mere utterance, but revelation. It consisted in revealing the holiness of God, and not in enabling us to infer it. It enacted it, it did not simply reflect it. That is to say, it consisted in putting it into final and universal effect among men, as only a great and real act of God could do. It was not in exhibiting or exposing God's holiness in a spectacular, or æsthetic, or impressive way, but in conveying and establishing it. The cross set up the holy kingdom which the parables revealed. The Holy Father He preached Christ brought home to life by something that only the Holy Son of living God and actual man could do. His revelation was in the redemption, and not in something that led to it. It is a revelation and a redemption effected only by Atonement (unless the rest of the New Testament is a bathos upon the gospels); effected by a holy act that gives full justice and joy to the irrefragable holiness of God; by the satisfaction and delight given to that holiness of love by Him who alone knew it, and who could therefore meet it in the Cross and the judgment hallowed there. The historic obedience of the Cross, crowning the obedient holiness of Christ always, reveals, conveys and establishes for ever in the world the obeyed holiness of God. He perfected an obedience in which the Father found an entire satisfaction, or, in the language of the gospels, one in which He was well pleased. The miracle of Grace in Christ's death is the measure of that holiness—the Grace measures it and not the agony there, nor even the love. The supreme miracle is the union in Christ's God of holiness and grace. It is not simply the love of God that we have in the Cross, but His holy love dealing with sin in grace. Nowhere but in Christ's blood do we gain the due sense of God's holy love, or answer duly the revelation of which His words were full. It is the Cross that makes these truths revelation. The fulness of both Father and Son was about its true business in the Cross. Because, while other things might give us a sense of love's amount, this alone, I have been saying, gives us a due sense of its divine kind, its kind not simply as saintly, but as holy enough to be the perfect propitiation to holiness. It is the kind of the love that matters—holy, gracious and effectual on God and creative on man. God so loved, in such a way, that in Grace He gave for man a propitiation to His own holiness. Christ died because God required it; and God required it not simply as a lever to lift man but as a function of the self-respect of the Absolute, for His personal satisfaction and the hallowing of His eternal name. And who outside of His Godhead could do that? My point throughout is that the profounder reading of the gospels discovers this to be the latent mind of Jesus. It is the propitiatory element, the element that gives its due from among sinners to the personal holiness of God—that is the distinctive thing in the love of God as declared, preached, brought home by the whole Christ.

No human analogies or parables available in the discourse even of Jesus can indicate more than the intensity and persistency of God's love. They do not do justice to its nature. They do not open up the holiness of it, none of them being holy as the Son was holy. They do not give us that in it which makes the real gulf between God and man, and therefore not that which bridges it, that which relates His love at once to holiness and to sin. For the ideal of human love is reciprocity, mutuality, instinctive and without more ado; but the ideal of God's is reconciliation, redemption. In the one case we love those we find lovable or cannot help loving, in the other God loves those He finds hateful and malignant. The one loves with the instinctive unfreedom of nature, the other with the freedom which belongs only to choice, effort, and Grace. The divine quality is not the love but the holiness of it, and the miracle in it is its costly Grace, the standing miracle of a saving, instead of a consuming, contact between sanctity and sin. And this holiness of it means farther its nature, necessity, and power to establish itself in command everywhere, in the face of its antagonist and on the site of its negation—sin; to do so by abolishing the antagonism without abolishing the soul, but by subduing it to itself, and converting the quality and direction of its passion to holiness instead of annihilating it. Love in the face of sin can only assert itself as holy love; but that means as stung and wounded love. But assert itself it must, and not doctrinally only by the most urgent discourse, nor negatively in punishment merely, but positively in righteousness; so that judgment is not a terror but a hope, and the day of the Lord is not convulsion and catastrophe but creation, a new heaven and earth, wherein dwell the peace of righteousness and assurance for ever. Holy love must heal itself. The personality of God, being holy, must recover and assert itself in the sanctification of the whole universe, and by its own resources make itself good in its infinite harmony everywhere, in and between all souls. Its Apostle and its Gospel must treat its holiness seriously, as a first charge, as God's first concern. His one concern with man is to make him holy as He is holy. And this a holy love like Christ's could never do—it could never take its own holiness seriously—by just exhibiting a human ideal, type, or pattern, sacred in word and in action kind. That were too inert to be duly serious, serious adequately to the whole energy and action of God's person or man's crime; for lovelessness is too languid and negative as a description of the diabolism of human sin. The hallowing of God's name could be done only by really judging and subjugating once for all the unholy thing everywhere, killing it in its eye, and replacing Satan's kingdom by the kingdom of God. It could be done only by bringing to practical effect an answering and trusting holiness on a world scale amid the extremest conditions created by human sin, by bringing universal sin to the final light and fire of the eternal holiness it challenged, by showing both sin in its radical sinfulness and destroying it in the searching and consuming fire of holy heavenly love on earth. And this the death of Christ alone did; and, if He began and ended with the Father of holy love, He knew it did, even if He did not know it in theological categories but in personal. The death of Christ did it, as the active, and imperishable, and precious point, what we might call the diamond drill, of His whole life, person and energy. It was a piercing, a judgment, and a destruction in principle of the unholy power; and this by the enthronement of the Holy in the arena of human experience, under the conditions of a historic situation concrete with the soul of the race,[3] and on the infinite and eternal scale. It was a last judgment. More even the Almighty could not do. "O God, who showest Thine omnipotence most chiefly in having mercy and forgiving." Our salvation is only secure by that finality of judgment—only if there was now no more condemnation. The Redemption was objective thus, scathing all sin in this light by the same act which ransomed the sinner neither from God nor death but from godless death, and regenerated him with eternal life. The confession, the revelation, the establishment of holiness in Christ's Cross is the only means for the due revelation and destruction of sin, and for the

---

3. It was the man that Jesus found in the Jew. [This footnote appears in the original text.]

23: The Meaning of a Sinless Christ, 1923

erection of the holy kingdom by a hallowed King. It begets a conviction of sin and a repentance and confession of it, according to our living faith. No real confession of man's sin is possible which is not much more a confession of God's holiness. And this is the only sense in which Christ could confess our sin—by no such moral impossibility as a vicarious repentance, but by what is the divine thing in repentance, by the practical and atoning confession of God's sanctity. Sin is not a thing, it is a personal relation; and Atonement has meaning only as the adjustment of that relation in a way that must affect both sides and not man alone.

If the forced and final crisis of God's holy honour to His holiness in Christ's Cross was the supreme means of discovering sin in its sinfulness, then the chief reason why the sense of sin has fallen below the level of Christ's preaching is because this Atonement, to which the preaching rose, passes out of our message and leaves it without due moral force. The modification of our views about Eternal Punishment has led to the decay of the idea of judgment and hell altogether for the general mind, to its huge moral loss. And so the necessary modification of our views (more legal than moral) about an equivalent penalty in the Atonement has caused the whole matter to pass from our practical conscience and experimental concern; because atonement and equivalence were held to be convertible terms, and God's satisfaction in the Cross was made to seem His joy, not in His dear and holy Son, but in a *quid pro quo*.[4] And things have now gone so far that the Cross is regarded as a simple exhibition of God's love in sacrifice, and an exhibition more public in aim than powerful in effect. Sacrifice is honoured for its own sake, as in some of the most exasperating martyrdoms of life, which are simply ethical ritualism, equally gratuitous and epidemic. The eternal Guardian of the universal and immutable morality of holiness is made to regard and court nothing but man's love—as if we could divinely trust one whose passion to love and be loved overrode everything else; as if our conscience did not go behind such a God, and demand, in some form of justification, an understanding with the holiness we defiled. We could not respect, to say nothing of worship, a God who was love and nothing more, who smothered our conscience in it, and taught love at any cost. We could not honour a God owing nothing to Himself as the eternal and universal Righteousness beyond a grand prophet's message of mercy. That would not honour the God Christ preached. We could not treat as God a being too large in his build, too free and generous in his nature's lines, to be careful about anything in himself corresponding infinitely to our self-respect. The holiness of God is the self-respect of an absolute universal; and it is

---

4. One thing in return for another.

the death of Egoism, and the very stay and cohesion of social and cosmic existence. Could such a kindly God deal in love's saving way with creatures in whom He has placed conscience as an echo, or even a facet, of His own righteousness? Could such a God be capable of real regenerative forgiveness, or of anything beyond amnesty and benevolence? Is forgiveness worth anything which does not cost? If it do not cost can it create? And can it cost in any real sense if it is shown forth in a sacrifice which, however painful, is arbitrary merely, out of ethical relation to guilt, a piece of divine rhetoric without moral logic or urgency, merely impressionist and not regenerative, a sacred pose for sacred effect, and not a necessity which holiness makes? Even if such a God do not make light of sin He does not make enough of it. He does not make what the best conscience makes of it. He does not make *sin* of it, guilt of it, an eternal sin. He makes ignorance, weakness, waywardness imperfection of it—a child's faults—but not sin, not the sin of adult defiance, and deadly hate, and desperate wickedness. His holiness does not react against it with the whole passion of His eternal energy. The passion for His own holiness (which is the cohesion of the universe) is less than the passion for men's souls—meaning by that their affection. His desire to be loved, and to make men happy in that love, renders Him comparatively indifferent to the moral conditions on which love is great, and on which alone love can abide, and rule, and worship, and glorify Him. Nothing but the cross of Christ has power to glorify and bring to its own the holy God that Christ preached. His Cross preaches it with a success that failed His words, but it was the same gospel.

With such a cordial God as has taken the place of Christ's God need we ask why the moral influence of the pulpit decays in the very midst of its popularity; why preaching, as it grows interesting, and delightful, and humane, grows ineffective also upon moral life wherever the conflict is severe; why, especially, it is without effect on the ethic of international life, of public life, and of business life, where energy is tense and serious? As if any Gospel could affect more than the domestic side of life (that but for a time) which treated with so much ease the claim of universal righteousness in the holy nature of God. Nothing but holiness with the imperative of the Eternal is mighty enough to give the law to the conscience of the race and make love eternal. And such is the holiness that goes to action in Christ's cross alone. Some theories of justification are perverted enough. And it must be owned that these perversions contribute their own part to the debasement of our public ethic; for the public effect of our theology for good or ill is greater than we know at the time. But at least they do recognise the claim of a universal righteousness, a superhuman holiness. And they properly exhibit God's love for man as dealing with that holiness first of all—even for man's

23: The Meaning of a Sinless Christ, 1923

sake. They show, though often dimly and inconsistently, Godhead actually accepting for us the judgment of its own holiness. That is what really moves us to our moral centre, and so moves us as to leave us with no resisting power, so moves us as to change us, and so changes us as to make a new creation of our forfeit lives. The real justification is also regeneration. The other, the genial, Gospel is not a real dynamic, however moving the gifted and tender preacher be. And still more it is not a regeneration. It is not creative. And, however it may sustain an audience, or even a busy philanthropy on the scale of a congregation, it has not the range and depth of moral appeal that makes a Church of the Cross and captures society as a whole, because it does not grasp, and does not search, and does not satisfy the whole moral soul. There is something in a direct effort to impress us and capture our love which stiffens us to resist. The man who sits down deliberately and toils to move us and make us cry makes the people whose tears would be worth most to smile. Tears, moods, are but a tribute to real action, not its object. And the Gospel of a Saviour who even dies just to impress us with His love, instead of surprising us with joy as we discover Him going to the business of our case and really acting for us with God and against our enemy, captor, and accuser—the Gospel of such a Saviour must be ineffective on all but the weak. It is an æsthetic Gospel; sympathetic at best, and at worst sentimental; it is not action, it does not work; and it is part cause, part effect, of that green mould of sentimentalism which is sapping so much popular religion, and sinking adult men to read novels of mawkish piety that sell in tens of thousands and madden the manly mind to refuge in *Tom Jones*.[5] I confess if I regard but the moral result of the Cross, and seek to court its impressive action on me, I am far less moved by it than I wish to be, and I catch myself pursuing the mood I seem to lack rather than worshipping the Saviour. It is most impressive and fortifying to us when we regard that aspect of it which is not turned on us, but for us on God. It moves us most as the awful conflict and work for us sinners, caught amid spiritual powers that bemaze us, wherein God in Christ makes our bad cause His own, meets His own charge against us, Himself takes His own judgment of our sin, Himself for us faces our fierce accuser, meets and conquers the evil power that holds us, and saves us from a world riot of spiritual wickedness which He alone can measure and manage, not we. It is most impressive when we see Christ so engrossed in that objective task of subduing the reign of Satan to the kingdom of God in us that His desire for our love and trust is secondary, and, for the hour, may even be absent, in His thought. Only then have we the moral security which is so much more for the life of society or the soul

---

5. A reference to Henry Fielding's *The History of Tom Jones, a Foundling* (1749).

than a melting love. Our daily prayer should certainly be to flow down more at the presence of God's love. But only thus can we be so melted that we run permanently into a quite new moral mould, receive the regeneration, and are created anew into Eternal Life. Only thus is the new love also a new creation and a new life. We must have a God who *enacts* with us not only His love but His holiness no less. And holiness must go into action with sin as judgment, only not as judgment alone but, being holy love, also as grace. If love in the face of need or suffering can only be enacted and satisfied in sacrifice, in the face of sin holiness can only be enacted by its satisfaction in judgment, such judgment as God took for us in Christ's Cross, where He loved us much but honour, God's honour, more.

Were these thoughts, in whatever form, alien and absent from the mind of Jesus, His sonship to God, and His work for men? Is it really possible, for a criticism that settles from each extreme to its sober place, to deny that Jesus regarded it as the demand of a holy God that Messiah should go to death as a sacrifice for the sin of the world? There is no doubt about such a view being central to Paul's or Peter's or John's creed of the revelation of love. In this respect there is no real difference between the preaching of Jesus and the Gospel of Christ which made the preaching of the Apostles. And the attention we give to the latter is but a fuller exposition of the former, in a way required by the religious conscience of the race.

We shall never revive the sense of sin, regenerate the pagan conscience of Christendom, and set up the new ethic except by something that effectually revives for us the worship of holiness, something which is the energy not of love alone but of holy love—its real action, and not its mere manifestation. A real Atonement must come home and engage the conscience. We could not, and should not, listen to the Atonement sermons of fifty years ago. There has taken place a change of key. We are in process of a new orientation. And this is adjusted neither to the sinless character of Christ, nor to His profound teaching, nor to any exhibition, even by Him, of mere fatherhood. We have from the Father more than the Father; we have an Advocate with the Father. That is, we have a holy Father, whose holiness, and not His mere justice, both requires a propitiation and makes it. We have a God who in Christ is absolutely satisfied with His holy self. We have no power in history or in the soul that can reconstruct for us the truth of this matter but the Cross of Christ in its apostolic note of moral realism, mystic love, and racial redemption. God is Father only in Christ, and in the Christ whose holiness brought His love to the Cross. We must ethicise religion—so long as we do not reduce it to an ethic, or make the Kingdom of God but the organisation of society in love. But it cannot be done at the story of the Prodigal, but only at the Cross, as the glorifying of God's holiness by sin's judgment, at His own loving cost, for our

23: The Meaning of a Sinless Christ, 1923

moral recovery and Eternal Life. We shall not revive the sense of sin, and with it moral earnestness, we shall not heal religion of its moral slackness and its leprosy of non-moral sentimentalism, till we cease to regard man's need as the first charge upon the Gospel of Christ's Cross. We must come to recognise that first charge for what Christ Himself felt it to be - God's claim for the hallowing of His name as the real nature and the real establishment of the Kingdom. It is not the first condition precedent to the Kingdom; it is the veritable setting up of the Kingdom, the reconstitution among men of the Holy Throne, and the reign of its King.

I am as sure that the element of holiness in God's love was the ruling thing in the mind of the Jesus of action as I am at a loss to explain why it should be so far from explicit on the lips of Jesus the preacher, midway as He stood between the prominent holiness of the Old Testament and the New Testament place of the Holy Spirit. I do not feel that He avoided the word, or that the Evangelists did, because it was so engrained in the ceremonial Judaism which was the first Antichrist. For that would have prevented the use of words or ideas like sacrifice or blood. And I fear that one suggestion that offers itself to me here may be found more subtle than sound. But I will venture this. Love is a message and a gift that comes home to individuals and readily finds them; it fills the mouth of those who deal with individuals or groups of them; but holiness has a much less swift access, as may be proved upon any average congregation, whether of preachers or people. Its appeal is rather on the scale of the race, of the great conscience, whether of man or of God; and it supposes more maturity of moral concern than does an appeal to anything so prompt and general as love. A message of kindness is always more welcome than one of righteousness. Now Jesus did not begin His preaching with an appeal to the race, nor with the fate of the race, but with Israel. The bearing of His mission on the race was forced on Him as He went on to such ill success with His own people. And it is now almost a commonplace to say that it was the Cross that really universalised Christianity. There was therefore in the prophetic days and the preached appeals of Jesus less about the holiness and more about the mercy of the Father. For, on the one hand, He spoke as man had never spoken to the individual, and especially to the poor, with whom a heart appeal is more intelligible than a moral. And on the other hand, He spoke to the nation and its leaders, both familiar with the prophet's word of the righteous judge, and of the judgment day of the Lord in more or less apocalyptic form. He is as emphatic about the judgment to them as He is about the Father's love to the soul, sad or lost. And, as it is the holiness of God, applied as righteousness, that is the principle of all His judgments, there is no lack of the idea of holiness wherever judgment takes the prominent place it did in a soul like Christ's or its speech. And this is shown by the fact that, when the righteousness of God had been made honourable and universal in the Cross, there not only came speech of the holiness of the Father (especially in John) but that feature rose to be a factor in Godhead alongside Father and Son, in the experience and doctrine of the Holy Spirit; by whom Jesus both died and rose for the eternal salvation of the conscience of the race, in Whom, therefore, proceeding from Christ's perfect work, sacrifice becomes Atonement, ethic becomes religion, and goodness cannot stop short of entire sanctification.

We must not allow ourselves to be robbed of the apostolic height and depth within the Cross just because Jesus did not turn to explain Himself to men in the judgment hour of His engagement with a holy and elusive God, when He made His whole soul an offering to Him for sin. He explained by His Spirit, when it was all over and done. It is no part of divine greatness that it should be obvious and unmistakable. And if the dereliction was Christ's sense of the certainty but the elusiveness of the Holy Love, we must not let a like elusiveness in His own express words take from us the certainty which He gave us in a fulness of time, when, as the Holy Spirit, He spoke to us, by His apostles, of what was really accomplished in His death beyond all the insight of the best natural religion, or of a piety historic and homely but nothing more.

It may be more true to our theme to have pursued it as a principle than to have set it out in a systematic form, whose clear edges are apt to reduce the impressiveness of the vast spiritual contours. But after what has been said it may not be dangerous to condense into a few drops much that has saturated what has gone before; and to do it by touching some of the lines that prolong the preaching of Jesus into the Gospel of Paul and the Church.

For the one as for the other God was the God of Almighty and Holy Love; and it was the holiness of the love that perfected the Lover in His Cross. (It is perhaps hardly necessary at this stage to say that by the holiness of God is not meant anything merely transcendent and remote, but something intimate, concrete, ethical, social and historic, with all its mystic solemnity; so that righteousness is applied holiness.) Christ made offering in His death to the sovereign and imperative element in God's love rather than to the sympathetic, which in the sharp crisis of His great act He lost. That Cross was the greatest thing that Jesus did, it condensed His whole life and person; and, within that supreme act, the decisive moment reflected its chief aspect; it was therefore a sacrifice to the holy will of God before it was a blessing to the need of man. In Jesus as in Paul, though in different forms, we have the principles of sacrifice, expiation, and vicariousness; and for each they formed a divine requirement. The sacrifice satisfied the will, purpose, and heart of God. It founded a new covenant of atoned forgiveness. It was a vicarious act of the One for the many. And it was offered to the judgment inseparable from a holy God, but on that same God's initiative as the holy

Father. It is surely impossible to say that the Jesus of the Passion felt no strain between God's pitiful and His righteous holy Love. If the theoretical adjustment is hard for the theologian, how much harder the practical in the personal experience and act of the Redeemer. Reconciliation in a personality is always harder than adjustment in a system, because it is more religious. But the two forms of reconciliation, that of Jesus and that of Paul, are not only not incompatible they are inseparable. The minting is different, but the currency is the same. And for both Jesus and Paul the reconciling act was God's act of judgment-grace, holy mercy and righteous love.

For Jesus as for Paul the whole of mankind needs this Redemption. And it comes not by God's gift of a law whose keeping earns it, but by a pure gift of Grace. That, and not reward, is for both the principle of Salvation. It was the Father's good pleasure to give the kingdom. And to all the labourers alike He gives no wage, but what He thinks fit. Salvation is a matter not of right but of Grace. And therefore it is a matter of the Faith that answers Grace by its appropriation, not as an assent but as an experience. For both it is faith in the person of Christ; and in that person not as the ideal of spiritual excellence but as the active, dramatic Messiah, Judge, Quickener, and Regenerator of the soul of the race. For both it is a salvation as universal as the sin is—though for Jesus in the first stage of its process His address was to Israel. Yet it was the man He sought and found in the Jew. It is not Paul but Jesus that first teaches the blessing of His ransoming work upon the Cross to the many. And He does so as the Messiah, who embodies God's will with mankind, and with whom all must reckon at last.

For both Jesus and Paul the law was an ethical thing, of which Jesus took control as He was the living conscience of both God and man; so that He alters and amends it morally in such a matter as divorce. And He does such things in the name of the holy love whose law it was. The one might have said the greatest words of the other about love. (And indeed it is our faith that when Paul uttered such words it was Christ who said them.) Yet for neither could love ride over law, but it must deal with it.

For both the secret of the Son's person and cross was His holy obedience, His obedience therefore to the holy; and when we hear in Philippians ii. 8 that Jesus was exalted to a universal reign by His obedience to death and to the Cross, it is but the reflection of all that we find both in the doctrine and the movement of the Gospels.

It were better that everything should remain unsaid than that anything should be spoken that might tend to belittle the teaching of Christ or deflect His preaching of His salvation. If any way of putting things here should seem to suggest that, it would be a *bêtise*[6] quite foreign to my intent. There is not and cannot be any such truth in spoken word as there is in the word of Jesus. There is not, and never will be, truth coming from such a depth of inward life, and such a union of God and man. It is such truth, so great, deep and final, that it cannot be followed except in the power from whose depths it came without Christ's person behind it, and the Cross at the centre of that person and at the source of His Spirit. If we speak of the failure of Christ's preaching it was its failure with those who would have none of the Cross, and who therefore severed the truth of the Word from the power of the Deed. It was not the word of Christ that failed men, but men that failed His Word and Him. To treat Christ as a prophet without finding Him our priest, and to honour Him as our Master without calling Him our Absolute King, whose property we are by the purchase of His blood—that is to revere Him as He did not seek reverence, and to refuse Him the worship that is His own. Never man spake as this man because God never acted as He did in His Son. The truth of Jesus comes to itself and its own only in the Cross of Christ. The grace to the Prodigal Son becomes a certainty for the world only in the atoning work of the Son Eternal. The disciples who heard all the Lord said became apostles only at the grave of God's own Apostle—shall we say, of God as Apostle? And the group of His companions became the core of His Church only because of the founding of the kingdom in the mortal deed whose victory could not be holden of death, and whose truth, buried by old Israel, came to itself as power in the creation of a new Society to be the earnest of the New Humanity. In the work of Christ His words also rose again from the dead to an immortal life and power.

Finally, it may avert one misunderstanding, or parry one criticism, if I close with the remark that the necessary truth in such views as I have set out is a necessity for the Church more than for its individual members—affecting the simple soul as that must be affected by a standing or falling Church. It is not always quite relevant, therefore, if stray and lone voices, even in considerable numbers, plead that such a type of faith they do not feel to need for their own soul's peace or good.

---

6. Folly, foolishness.

Sources for Published Sermons

"An Allegory of the Resurrection." *The Christian World Pulpit* 61 (1902) 312–19. Published in a different form as "Holy Christian Empire," in *Missions in State and Church: Sermons and Addresses* (London: Hodder & Stoughton, 1908), 289–344.
"The Argument for Immortality Drawn from the Nature of Love: A Lecture on Lord Tennyson's 'Vastness.'" *Christian World Pulpit*, 2 December 1885, 360–64.
"'The Bible Doctrine of Hell and the Unseen': Sermon by the Rev. P. T. Forsyth, Preached in the Bradford Road Congregational Church, Shipley, Nov. 23rd." *Shipley and Saltaire Times*, 13 December 1879, 4.
"Christ at the Gate." *The Christian World Pulpit* 73 (1908) 177–82.
"Christ our Sanctification." *Wesleyan Methodist Magazine* 134 (1911) 732–34.
"Dumb Creatures and Christmas: A Little Sermon to Little Folk." *Christian World*, 24 December 1903, 13.
"Egypt: A Sermon for Young Men." *The Christian World Pulpit* 22 (1882) 275–78.
"The Empire for Christ." *The Christian World Pulpit* 57 (1900) 303–11.
Mercy the true and only Justice: A Sermon Preached in Shipley Congregational Church, on the Missionary Sunday, September 30, 1877. Bradford: Brear, nd.
"Music and Worship." *Homiletic Review* 67 (1914) 18–22.
"Mystics and Saints." *The Expository Times* 5 (1894) 401–4.
"Our Experience of a Triune God." *Cambridge Christian Life* 1 (1914) 240–46.
"Pessimism." *The Christian World Pulpit* 25 (1884) 42–44.
"Preaching and Poetry." *The Expository Times* 1 (1890) 269–72.
"The Preaching of Jesus and the Gospel of Christ. [VII:] The Meaning of a Sinless Christ." *The Expositor* 8th Series, 25 (1923) 288–312.
"The Problem of Forgiveness in the Lord's Prayer." In *The Sermon on the Mount: A Practical Exposition of the Lord's Prayer*, 181–207. Edited by E. Griffith-Jones et al. Manchester: Robinson, 1903.
The Pulpit and the Age. Manchester: Brook & Chrystal, 1885.
"The Slowness of God." *The Expository Times* 11 (1900) 218–22.
"The Strength of Weakness." *The Christian World Pulpit* 13 (1878) 85–87.
"Sunday Schools and Modern Theology." *The Christian World Pulpit* 31 (1887) 123–27.
"Things New and Old." *The Christian World Pulpit* 84 (1913) 273–76.
"The Turkish Atrocities: Sermon by the Rev. P. T. Forsyth." *Shipley and Saltaire Times*, 23 September 1876, 4.
"The Way of Life." *Wesleyan Methodist Magazine* 120 (1897) 83–88.

III

Unpublished Sermons

1

Sermon on Philippians 4:4

"Rejoice in the Lord alway[s]; again I will say, Rejoice."
—PHILIPPIANS 4:4[1]

THIS KIND OF JOY [i.e., the joy described in Philippians 4:4] can become a habit. It is something to be cultivated until it becomes the fixed tenor of our life. Joy is far too noble a thing to be confused with mere pleasure and happiness. It has lasting value: in the strength of this meat we go many days unto the next mount of God. Those who make merriment have a divine work to do in the world. It is a divine thing to lift the shadows from people's lives even for an hour. But we have to rise higher, into joy in the Holy Ghost. So much of our piety is spoiled because it is sepulchral—long faces are not indicative of real religion. We must learn how to be joyous in the Holy Spirit. The joy we find in a beautiful morning is due to the mingling of our full life with the life of the Universe, and it is a rare and uplifting thing. But it should be to us only a prophecy of the deeper joy of the Holy Spirit. In spite of the Cross prolonged through history, we must learn to speak of God's joy; but we can only do that if we have grasped the joy of Christ's finished work. The source of our deepest, holiest joy is the great deed God did once [and] for all on the Cross. We are often perplexed as to how we may escape from the pettiness of life. There is no way except in losing ourselves in much remembrance of the joy of God, His joy in Christ. Never be ashamed of joy; it is one of God's most blessed gifts to us. He will put it through the crucible in His

---

1. The text titles from the unpublished sermons, and which appear on the original manuscripts, are mostly taken from the English Revised Version.

own time, and in His own way. We must not force His hand like the monks did. Never make a parade of your sorrows when they come. "Appear not unto men to fast."[2] Cover your troubles up, consume your own smoke, never wear your heart on your sleeve. It is not hypocrisy to veil your sorrows. Gladness does not necessarily mean levity—"the smiling sea hath wondrous depths below." Is it not strange that the Religion of the Cross should have contributed so largely to the world's joy? This can only be because the Cross is the vanquisher of the world's last enemy. You will find that Paul links courage and joy; for him the only real joy was resurrection joy, that is, joy through victory. Health means joy, because health is the victory of life over disease. The Gospel is the soul's health, its victory over sin. Do not, however, be a slave to joy, as though you could not live without it. But praise God for the power to praise. It is a great thing to be able to be thankful. Remember above all that Christ is the secret source of all joy because He sets us free from self.

2. Matt 6:18.

2

SERMON ON MATTHEW 7:21

"Not every one that saith unto me, Lord, Lord, shall enter into the kingdom of heaven; but he that doeth the will of my Father which is in heaven."

—MATTHEW 7:21

CHRIST OFTEN USED His repulsive power in order to shed off those who did not like hard and rigorous sayings. If our churches did the same they might be smaller but stronger, like Gideon's army. Jesus was always sifting His followers, allowing many to go away who could not get into stride with Him. Only once does He appear to have been troubled about these continual losses, and that was when He feared He might lose those on whom He had expended such infinite pains.

These remarks of His [in Matthew 7:21] were not directed against palpable hypocrites but against people who deceive themselves first of all. Not works, but faith, was in His mind. It is easy to be sincere if you are shallow. It is easy to be consistent if you have a poor religion. Christian well-doing, like fruit, grows naturally out of faith. To be a prodigy in Church work is not necessarily to be a spiritual giant. It happens sometimes that those who do least accomplish most.

It is possible to be so active in the service of Christ as to forget to love Him. "Though I do all things but have not love I am nothing."[1] Many a man preaches Christ but gets in front of Him by the multiplicity of his own works. It will be your ruin if you do! Christ can do without your works—what He wants is you. Yet if He really has you He will have all your works.

---

1. 1 Corinthians 13.

III: Unpublished Sermons

God doth not need
Either man's work or his own gifts; who best
Bear his mild yoke, they serve him best. His state
Is kingly; thousands at his bidding speed,
And post o'er land and ocean without rest;
They also serve who only stand and wait.[2]

---

2. From John Milton's sonnet, "On His Blindness" (1652?).

3

Sermon on Hebrews 11:17–19

"By faith Abraham, being tried, offered up Isaac: yea, he that had gladly received the promises was offering up his only begotten son; even he to whom it was said, In Isaac shall thy seed be called: accounting that God is able to raise up, even from the dead; from whence he did also in a parable receive him back."

—HEBREWS 11:17–19

ABRAHAM'S FAITH WAS ALL in promises and the future. He had no great historic past, no Christ who is more a fulfilment than a promise.

Abraham's faith took the form of obedience. The actual form of his obedience here was wrong, judged by the ethics of a later age. The *form* of his obedience was wrong, but the *spirit* of it was right.

That in such an age Abraham should have exercised a faith of such a quality is evidence of the moral height which he had won.

He was called upon to trust a God who to all appearances went back on His own promises. It was not love against faith, but the faith of yesterday against the faith of today. Was it possible that God could forget His own promises?

He met the challenge with a threefold certainty. God had given him Isaac; therefore, God had the right to take him away. If God demanded him then it must be best for all, even for Isaac. And finally, the explanation could only be a greater fulfilment, perhaps even the raising of Isaac from the dead.

III: Unpublished Sermons

Isaac was really offered though he was never slain. As far as Abraham was concerned, the deed was already done. "Ripeness is all."[1] To be ready for anything is to have done it, no matter what the end. Abraham really gave back his son to God. The true sacrifice is the inner consecration of the will, whether it ever comes out or not.

More than that, Abraham surrendered to God even his own promises, and faith can reach no sublimer height.

So you have here a mighty victory of faith, a son of promise given back to God, and with him the promises of God and the hope of the future.

You have as well the final expression of God's mind against physical sacrifice, and the clear indication that what God wants is the sacrifice of the will, Shakespeare's "Ripeness," Paul's "Readiness," David's "willingness," "Because it was in thine heart."[2]

This too is the value of the Cross; the surrendered will that worked itself out in the life laid down.

---

1. From William Shakespeare's *King Lear*.
2. 1 Kgs 8:18; 2 Chr 6:8.

4

Sermon on 1 Peter 4:19

"A faithful Creator."
—1 PETER 4:19

FAITH ROLLS THE SOUL over onto God, and with the soul the world with its wonderful crooked aching past, its selfish unregenerate present, and its uncertain future. Faith realises that the very judgements of God show that He will never let us go. If God loves us enough to punish us, all may yet be well.

How could it be otherwise with a Creator? How we cleave to the work of our hands, the things on which we have spent our thought and time. No wonder God loves the world, since He has watched it grow through many ages, not just one soul but a world of souls. God and the world have lived long together.

Or think again of God's interest in making Jesus. He watched Him grow from babyhood to childhood, and from childhood to glorious manhood. Like a human father, but much more closely and with much greater understanding He watched Him as He went about doing good. He was with Him through all the pain and shame of the Cross, and afterwards in the Resurrection triumph. Is it any wonder that He called Him "My beloved Son"?

And then what about our remaking? God's greatest name is not "Creator," but "Re-Creator," "Redeemer." It is a tremendous thing to be able to say that the wreck and ruin of the world was as much within His power as the making of it at first from chaos.

III: Unpublished Sermons

God is faithful to the souls He made, and always will be. He is faithful to the souls He made and died for, and He remakes them by suffering, first His own suffering and then theirs.

Our very pain is a sign of God's remembrance of us, for it would be much worse if we were left in ghastly isolation. Be thankful that God cares enough for you to be angry with you.

5

SERMON ON PSALM 55:6 AND JEREMIAH 9:2

"Oh that I had wings like a dove! then would I fly away, and be at rest."
—PSALM 55:6

"Oh that I had in the wilderness a lodging place of wayfaring men; that I might leave my people, and go from them."
—JEREMIAH 9:2

JEREMIAH WAS BORN FOR the quiet way of life. The boldest men have moments like this, still more men of Jeremiah's mould. When it becomes a habitual frame of mind it is an evil, but so long as it remains an occasional experience it is a salutary reminder of how often our strength rests upon weakness.

God has given men feet not wings, and the order is fight not flight. We reach Heaven step by step, fighting all the way.

What we need most of all for this life is the courage of the prosaic. As someone has put it, "Above all, no heroics." If we get into the habit of indulging in heroics we too often end in a scream. Beware of the perorating spirit, the life that is all rhetoric. Heroism is a great thing, but fortitude is greater still.

You will have noted that the Psalmist speaks of the wings of a dove; that suggests a horizontal flight. It typifies longing for solitude. The Prophet Jeremiah speaks of eagle's wings, suggesting flight upward in the face of the

III: Unpublished Sermons

sun.[1] We very often crave for opiates when we should seek tonics, and yet the truest warrior is he whose heart often turns to peace.

As a rule, God is not found by waiting in the wilderness alone. He found Elijah there, but He sent him back into the world of men. We find ourselves amongst men, not sitting down, folding our hands, and waiting for miracles.

Rest is good so long as we recognise that the true end of life is not rest but victory. The rest of God is the power of God, the truest rest of all is an accession of strength.

The motto of the world is "Onward," the motto of the saint is "Upward," but the motto of the Cross is "Inward." You have acquired a real spiritual culture when you realise that you can only find the onward and the upward through the inward.

---

1. Possibly a reference to Jer 48:40 or 49:22.

6

SERMON ON LUKE 11:9

"Knock, and it shall be opened unto you."
—LUKE 11:9[1]

PRAYER IS NOT PRAYER unless it asks for something. It often means struggling for something. It is not bounded by nature but only by God.

Distinguish between a deep spiritual life and a quick spiritual sensibility. One of the dangers of our time is the feminising of Religion. One obstacle to the deepening of the spiritual life is prayer when it merely means submission.

It may be the will of God that we should struggle against His will. Christ sets more value upon importunity in prayer than He does upon submission.

Prayer may even change the will of God, or if it may not change His will, it may change His intention. Nothing can change His final purpose— He must save us.

If your importunity does nothing more, it may lift you into a position in which God may be able to grant you a gift [previously] withheld because of your unpreparedness.

In prayer you may often be called upon to resist the will of God. You can measure every Religion by the quality of its prayer. The Christianity of prayer lies in the spirit of it, especially when it expresses itself in resistance. The worst temptations that assail us often come from our Religion.

---

1. This theme is more fully attended to in the chapter, "The Insistency of Prayer," in Forsyth's *The Soul of Prayer*.

III: Unpublished Sermons

The element of will must always enter into prayer. We are to wrestle in prayer, and wrestling is in a sense resisting God's will. In love there is always a certain kind of resistance, but it is a resistance that enhances love.

> Two constant lovers joined in one,
> Yielding to each other yield to none.[2]

God, yielding to the resistance of prayer, yields to Himself; for He inspired the prayer.

In resisting God we may be doing His will, for He puts many things in our way to be resisted. There is a lower and a higher will of God, and the lower is there to be overcome. If you are born a labourer's son it is the will of God, but it need not be His will that you should become a labourer.

God ordained the resistance to His lower will, therefore it is true to say we are as right sometimes in resisting God's will as we are at other times in obeying it. Christ resisted His death, and only accepted it as a last resort. To the very end He hoped God would find another way. He went to the Cross freely but reluctantly.

Grace is the superior, and nature the inferior will of God. Redemption from the natural man involves resistance to God's will as nature. The obedience of faith is the chief end of all prayer, but that is not mere submission, it is often pressing our suit. How we love the grace that yields us a blessing! We conquer God, but in conquering we ourselves are conquered. As Edmund Burke once put it, "Our antagonist is our helper."[3]

We are entitled to bring anything before God that really troubles us, but the supreme Christian prayer rises above the personal sphere and prays, "Thy Kingdom come."

Too many people banish will and even thought from prayer. George Meredith is right when he says, "The curse of so much religion is that men cling to God with their weakness rather than their strength."[4]

It is a great thing to confess our sin, but it is a greater thing to confess our Saviour. Beware of the people who are always talking about the beauty of Religion, and the beauty of holiness. Sin is most vile, not because it is ugly, but because it is guilty.

Above all we were not made to talk, even to God, but to act, and all true prayer is acting upon God.

---

2. From Christopher Marlowe's poem, "Hero and Leander" (1598): "Two constant lovers being join'd in one, Yielding to one another, yield to none."

3. From Edmund Burke's *Reflections on the Revolution in France, and on the Proceedings of Certain Societies in London, Relative to that Event* (1790).

4. As noted above, this is a reference to words from George Meredith's *The Ordeal of Richard Feverel*, 2:117: "For this reason so many fall from God, who have attained to him; that they cling to him with their Weakness, not with their Strength."

7

SERMON ON PSALM 130:1

"Out of the depths have I cried unto thee, O LORD.
—PSALM 130:1

THIS [I.E., THESE WORDS from Psalm 130:1] is a cry of humility rather than despair. It is from a man who has been in the depths. Some have never been in the depths and have never been drawn to the heights. Real gratitude, humility and confidence, which lifts a man to the heights, is that which has been drawn from the depths.

This cry is alien to our age. Sometimes the Church is free from the sense of sin, but ever and again the sense of it sweeps over the world as it did at the Reformation.

It is strange, too, to a self-reliant race like ours. Yet, in our age and our race, there is a great sadness abroad—"the pessimism of the age."[1]

How very human the cry is! As yet there have been more depths than heights in history. With all our successes and progress there is mostly labour and sorrow. Most people spend the greater part of their days on the grey level, if not in the depths. It is dreadful to find how many people live quite alone—no friends, [and] no helps along the way. Even today, man is felt to be man by his superior capacity to suffer.

But the depth is simply the height inverted, as sin is the index of moral grandeur. "If the light that is in thee be darkness, how great is that darkness."[2]

---

1. This may be a reference to William Clark's sixth Baldwin Lecture (1887).
2. Matt 6:23.

III: Unpublished Sermons

The cry is not only truly human, but divine as well. God is deeper than the deepest depth in man. He is holier than our deepest sin is deep. There is no depth so deep to us as when God reveals His holiness in dealing with our sin. "Greater is He that is in you than he that is in the world."[3]

The New Testament does not think about limitations but about powers. It deals in ethical, not in philosophical categories.

The deepest depth of God's love is deeper than the deepest depth of man's hate. Man cannot hate infinitely, but God can love infinitely. As Wordsworth has put it,

> And consolations sorrows deeper are
> Than sorrow's deepest.[4]

The depth to which you cry is outside yourself. Think more of the depth of God than the depth of your cry. The worst thing that can happen to a man is to have no God to cry to out of the depth. The deepest depth of all, outside of God, is separation from God. You can often do more with wild sinners than with indifferent weaklings.

First then, we cry from the depth of our need, then from the depth of our sin and despair, and finally, deepest of all, we cry from the depth of our faith, which lifts up to the heights. We know then that if we fall, we fall deeper and deeper into the arms of God.

> If my bark sink,
> 'Tis but to another sea.[5]

For as our hell is deep so is our heaven deep. Our hell is so deep because we were made for so deep a heaven.

---

3. 1 John 4:4.

4. From William Wordsworth's poem, "The Excursion" (1814): "Fixed on the Cross, that consolation springs/From sources deeper far than deepest pain."

5. From William Ellery Channing's poem, "A Poet's Hope" (1843).

8

SERMON ON 1 TIMOTHY 4:7

"Exercise thyself unto godliness."

—1 TIMOTHY 4:7

THIS CHAPTER [I.E., 1 Timothy 4] was written against the Gnostics, who were guilty of an over-refinement of Christianity. There is often a tendency in this direction, which shows itself in many different forms. Asceticism is one, and asceticism tends to destroy sound judgement.

Christianity is much harder than any asceticism—"How hard it is to be a Christian." It is freedom, but true freedom is only possible under discipline, and the greater the aim, the more discipline is required. The simplicity of Greek sculpture is due to its utmost severity.

To have a real religious experience is a hard thing, and demands the severest discipline. Religion is cursed by hundreds of people who have never known it.

> Oh could I tell, ye surely would believe it!
> Oh could I only say what I have seen!
> How should I tell or how should ye receive it,
> How till He bringeth you where I have been?[1]

It means the greatest exertion to be godly, and still more to grow in godliness. The discipline we undertake is not to get rid of sin, but for godliness. We seek not to be saved but to be right.

---

1. From Frederick W. H. Myers' poem, "Saint Paul" (1867).

III: Unpublished Sermons

You have to exercise your own soul before you exercise the souls of others. The cure of souls must begin at home.

Again, you are to exercise yourself for the sake of godliness, not for your own sake. Mere self-culture is worth very little. For this reason, the best type of godliness is possible only in a society; that is, in the Church, or the Household of Faith.

Within the Church, the cultivation of the soul is best carried out by the cultivation of faith. But our faith should not be faith in faith, but faith in Christ. The height of faith is to lose sight of itself in Christ.

Trying to be good is a subtle temptation to many of us, but true goodness is unconscious of itself. It is like humility, which Luther calls "the eye that sees everything but itself." Such goodness is the natural product of faith in Christ.

Great is the mystery of godliness; indeed, it is the one orthodoxy.

9

SERMON ON 2 CORINTHIANS 4:17–18

"For our light affliction, which is for the moment, worketh for us more and more exceedingly an eternal weight of glory; while we look not at the things which are seen, but at the things which are not seen: for the things which are seen are temporal; but the things which are not seen are eternal."

—2 CORINTHIANS 4:17–18

THE PEOPLE WHO GO down under trouble are those who have made no preparation for it. We must face these questions and find some answer to them.

The fertilising of sorrow is under the Cross and Resurrection. In itself sorrow embitters, but there is something in the Cross which makes it educative. When we take it there, tribulation brings an eternal weight of glory.

No one ever saw all things working together for good; many believed it, and God knows it.

> The soul's dark cottage battered and decayed
> Lets in the light through chinks which time hath made.[1]

What we suffer simply helps us to get more and more in touch with the spirit. The body decays but the soul is made.

But God never leaves us helpless in our sorrows. When we are burdened He bids us escape into the great, the unseen, and the eternal.

Into the great. So much trouble is petty. If we are troubled by little things we may escape into great thoughts, great hopes, great certainties, or

---

1. From Edmund Waller's final poem, "Of the Last Verses in the Book" (1685).

III: Unpublished Sermons

a great future, but above all Paul would bid us escape into a great God, and a great Christ.

We are apt to be lost in the details of an earthly Christ and to forget that the most real Christ is the Royal and Eternal Christ.

Many people escape into cosmic emotions, contemplating the grandeurs of nature, but though this may enlarge the intelligence and calm the mind, it cannot satisfy the soul. If your soul is wrong, all nature cannot put it right.

Into the unseen. The truly great is always the unseen. All visible things are greatest when they are symbols of the invisible. The soul is the great unseen of the world, and over the unseen soul is the unseen God and the unseen Saviour.

There is no bigness in the unseen, but only greatness. Beware lest Christ become more for your imagination or for your admiration than for your salvation.

Into the Eternal. We escape into the region of the unchangeable and the sure. It is here our souls are healed.

Remember the answer to the question "What is God?" in the [Westminster] Shorter Catechism: "God is Spirit, infinite, eternal [and] unchangeable; in His Being, He is goodness and Truth." This is one of the greatest sentences in our language.

It is in such a God alone that a wounded and aching soul may find its wholeness.

10

SERMON ON LUKE 17:10

"Even so ye also, when ye shall have done all the things that are commanded you, say, We are unprofitable servants; we have done that which it was our duty to do."

—LUKE 17:10

JESUS DOES NOT USE the word "grace," but over and over again you find it implied, as for example in the parable of the vineyard, and here [in Luke 17] in the phrase "unprofitable servants."

Whenever you have done your duty, the only attitude for you is humility. Unlike the ordinary run of people, the Christian is more concerned with his duty than he is with his rights. It is a great advance in culture when that is so.

Note, first of all, that God does not think of us as unprofitable servants: that is how we are to think of ourselves. God did not think of the publican as the publican thought of himself. Real humility sets a man higher than integrity, and that is where Christianity clashes with the world's view of things. Epictetus once said, "I should like to say at death, 'God, I have never transgressed one of thy commandments.'"[1] That is lofty, but it is not Christian. "God be merciful to me a sinner,"[2] is far higher.

Note, in the second place, that "unprofitable" does not mean a bad servant; it only means a servant with whom there is no profit. If you execute every command of God, you only do your duty. God's demand is for all we

---

1. From Epictetus's *Discourses* 3.5.8: "Have I in any respect transgressed Thy [i.e., Zeus's] commands."
2. Luke 18:13.

III: Unpublished Sermons

have. There can be no work of supererogation. We can never come to the time when we can cry quits with God.

Our souls were made for the infinite love of God. To live by duty may be very high, but it is very cold. We were made for so much more than duty: we were made for Christ.

Our salvation is not by duty but by grace. Only the more we do our duty the more we shall be aware of the Grace of God.

Duty with Christ is inspired by love; duty without Christ strives after love in vain.

The grace of God is as great as our unworthiness. Indeed, it is far greater, so that our confession of unprofitableness becomes a hymn of praise to God. Nothing we ever do can save our souls, but only the grace of God.

11

SERMON ON ACTS 22:11

"I could not see for the glory of that light."

—ACTS 22:11

THERE IS A BLINDNESS which is due to a want of light. We need not dwell of that. There is also a blindness which comes from excess of light. The egoism of youth is such a blindness.

The true vision only comes when the Light of Life comes to us. When Christ becomes our source of vision, and our power of seeing, we get the right vision. It is part of His schooling in life to enable us to take the true measure of all things, of God first of all and then of ourselves. Christ places us at the centre of all things: the true view point.

Chalmers spoke of the "expulsive power of a great affection."[1] When Christ comes in, He turns out the worst part of a man's nature. By His light He hides certain things from us.

You will not see the meaner side of life, or if you see it you will rise above it, and live among the great mighty positive realities of God and the soul. Christ says, "Be of good cheer. I have overcome the world,"[2] and it is in that world where He has overcome [that] we are called upon to live.

---

1. Forsyth misquotes the title of Thomas Chalmers' famous sermon, "The Expulsive Power of a New Affection," a sermon preached at least four times (including in St George's Church in Edinburgh and in St. John's Church in Glasgow) between May 1822 and July 1823, and based on 1 John 2:15.

2. John 16:33.

III: Unpublished Sermons

Then you will not dwell too much on the faults of others, for you will be far too much taken up with the glorious perfection of Christ.

Again, Christ hides from us ourselves and our own subjectivity. There is a kind of piety which thinks more of self and its shortcomings than of Christ and His victory. Beware of fits of confession, they are generally morbid. Confession should generally be made only to God, and even then thanksgiving is the first thing, confession is secondary.

The most blessed thing of all is that, in Christ, our sins are hidden.

Beware of the small noisy lights, lest you miss the great light. As Emerson has told us, "When the half-gods go, the gods arrive."[3] Humanity often obscures Christ, but never forget He is the great light, and only in Him do we get the right vision.

---

3. The closing lines from Ralph Waldo Emerson's poem, "Give All to Love" (1846).

12

Sermon on 2 Timothy 4:7

"I have fought the good fight, I have finished the course, I have kept the faith."
—2 TIMOTHY 4:7

[THIS VERSE] IS A great retrospect: "I have finished the course." Life is made up of ends and of beginnings. Death is but the greatest crisis of many, and all crises are like Janus in the Roman Pantheon, two-faced. The end of one crisis is the beginning of another.

But with all the ebbs and flows of life there must be unity, some grand unity which constitutes life's reality. For us that unity is, in Paul's phrase, "For me to live is Christ,"[1] that is, Christ is my career.

The unity of our life is therefore objective, outside ourselves. It is not in the evolution of life but in its goal. When Wordsworth writes of a life whose "days are bound each to each by filial piety"[2] he is not truly Christian. When a man is truly Christian each day is bound to Christ, is devoted to Him, is lived in Him. Life is not realising a plan but fulfilling a mission. Thus a broken column in a Churchyard, symbolising a broken life, is an anachronism. There is no such thing as a broken life for the man of faith. All life is complete in Christ, and always complete. No matter when the end comes, the course is finished.

---

1. Phil 1:21.

2. Forsyth misquotes the line from William Wordsworth's poem, *Ode: Intimations of Immortality from Recollections of Early Childhood* (1802): "And I could wish my days to be/Bound each to each by natural piety."

III: Unpublished Sermons

The keeping of our souls is in the hand of Christ. Paul did not keep his soul; he kept the faith. No apostle starts out with Paracelsus' ambition, "I go to prove my soul."[3] That grand confidence is soon broken as it was with Paracelsus. An apostle has a charge, a trust. Paracelsus has an instinct he is going to follow with God's help, but the Christian is not working out anything that is within; instead, he is laying hold of eternal life.

Yet there is warfare to wage and something to prove. Paul's greatest triumph was not that he had worked out any instinct, still less that he had done any great works, but that he had kept the faith. The Christian man is fighting bigger battles than anything he has to face in business. It is a great warfare. All uncouth passions must be mastered; everything so natural to ordinary men must be carefully sifted and judged upon. He will know what it is to be forced down upon his knees again and again in the battle, even forced into the dust. It is a hard thing to be faithful in this calling but it is a terrible thing to fall. You have to cope, not only with ordinary things, but [also] you have to fight for your Gospel, for your faith. You have to war your way onward to a deeper grasp of that Gospel with which you began.

It is a great thing when a man, after facing the doubts and scepticism of the age, as well as those that are brought to him in his College course, is able to say, "I am trusting the same grace now that I did at the beginning."

The great thing is to keep our faith. Not being so full of love to Christ as to have confidence, but being so full of confidence in God's changeless, profound and most wonderful love in Jesus Christ. It is not the love that "I once felt" that saves us, but Christ's most wonderful love for us in the Cross.

Oh, what a fight it is, this fight for such a faith in such a Christ!

---

3. A reference to Robert Browning's poem, "Paracelsus" (1835).

13

SERMON ON PSALM 32:8

"I will guide thee with mine eye."
—PSALM 32:8

THIS [VERSE] MEANS THAT we are guided by intelligent sympathy. There are as many people who cannot see God as there are who refuse to follow Him. We are often at a loss to know what the will of God really is, but if God knows and feels for all souls, then He acts for and in all things, and all souls—and that is His Providence.

In our exalted moments and in luminous personalities we recognise God, but in periods of darkness in our experiences and in the world's history, God is working unseen. Even then, however, if we have a due sense of responsibility, we are being guided by Him. Paul was guided by the Spirit when he made judgements on the data before him.

Or again, if you pray, you are being guided by God. The very act of prayer, apart from the answer, is the guidance of God. The action of God upon us in prayer is just as real as our action upon Him.

The guidance of the godly is the guidance of God, but how are we to discern it? That is an art, and it comes late in life and not early. It needs much cultivation. To believe in God's guidance is one thing; to understand it is a very different thing. A man may be a mystic and yet not a saint; a saint is a man who can read the will of God, and whose judgment is therefore reliable. The great High School for this discernment is prayer. In prayer we must battle for discernment as we battle for our faith. Finally,

III: Unpublished Sermons

the source of all our belief in Providence is the Cross, in which God is always acting upon us for His kingdom.

14

SERMON ON 1 TIMOTHY 3:15

"The church of the living God."

—1 TIMOTHY 3:15

NOTE PARTICULARLY [HERE IN 1 Timothy 3:15] the phrase the "Living God." The living God is the basis of the living Church.

We must try and get home to people the idea of the Divine Personality. You know what an overmastering personality is, a magnetic man. He gives *you* a sense of power which dominates you. Such a power is Christ and the Living God.

We do not want people with views and sympathies, but men of conviction; men, that is, with an experience of God that grows with the years.

We must feel the grip of Christ, which we felt in that mighty business which made us Christians, and feel it forever; so that, when we lose our power to hold Christ, He shall stand over and hold us. Conversion may change its forms, but it must never lose its power.

We need the living God, for we need something as great as God over us, and we need something as mighty as human life is. How can we face the corporate life which is before us today? Only in the experience of a God who is mightier than life.

Then we need a God as near to us as life is. We must have a searching and a shaping God. This we have in the Son of the Living God.

The end of all our piety is to realise the Living God. Here we find how much more than historic was Christ, especially in His Cross.

The living God alone can make us living men; the mighty God alone can make us mighty men; the loving God alone can make us consecrated men.

15

SERMON ON PSALM 146:3

"Put not your trust in princes."

—PSALM 146:3

THE BIBLE IS NOT the book of kings but of the crowd; and yet it does not stand for mediocrity, for its motive is not one of levelling, but a higher kingship. The democracy of Christ is an aristocracy. The true court of the Kingdom consists of those nearest to the King.

The spirit of the Bible withstands kings and crowds alike when they come up against God. The question of today is, Will Christianity ever have to fight democracy for its life, as it has had to fight kings before now?

In spite of its democratic passion, the crowd is a great hero-worshipper, as Browning has reminded us in his Patriot.[1] The man of God must always be ready for praise or blame, and must take both alike.

The worship of Christ is the standing protest against hero worship, genius worship, [and] giant worship of whatever kind. The Bible is the Book of the little man, until he wants to rule for himself, when his rule becomes that of mere mediocrity. The Bible is against success worship, or the offence of the Cross has ceased. The hero may claim our gratitude and admiration, for he brings us many noble things, but we must never worship him.

Whatever else it is, the democratic principle of the Bible is not that of the rights of man. It begins by asserting that we have all sinned and come short of the glory of God. Whatever our labour, our pay is the same: one penny, and that penny is the grace of God. Ours is not the bond of equality but of service.

---

1. A reference to Robert Browning's poem, "The Patriot: An Old Story" (1855).

15: Sermon on Psalm 146:3

What an extraordinary reversal of the moral idea there will be at the Great Judgment! You can always judge the quality of moral greatness by the weakness that goes with it. The weakness of Christ was the Cross; that of Paul, in his own words, was that he was strong in weakness. In worldly greatness, the weakness is egoism, harshness, carelessness, and so on.

Trust not princes, but begin higher, with a Prince above all. Begin at the highest and make your descent from there. Earthly love aspires to heaven, seeking perfection there. Christian love comes down from Heaven, bringing its perfection with it.

In all this we see what a new world is opened to the little man, the poor man, the ordinary man. Christ discovered three things for us: the woman, the child, and the common man.

We all need the freedom the Bible creates for us. Our great danger is not the slavery spoken against on social and political platforms, but the slavery of complex daily life. If you work for human relations and circles, you become a slave to them; if you work for Christ, you are free to adventure in all directions. You must learn to descend upon your duties as Moses did from the mountain.

16

SERMON ON ECCLESIASTICUS 2:18

"As his majesty is, so also is his mercy."
—ECCLESIASTICUS 2:18[1]

(1) WHAT IS THE true nature of the divine majesty? It is not material vastness, nor the majesty of force, nor the majesty of mystery. It is not the majesty of thought, great as thought is. The true majesty of God is His mercy. That is the thing He did which a man would never have done—He had mercy on all flesh.

His greatness was not in His loftiness, but in His nearness. He was great, not because He was above feeling, but because He would feel as no man could. God's majesty is saturated through and through with His forgiving love, which comes out most of all in His treatment of sin.

Do we feel enough the moral majesty of the Cross? Have we ever really felt the majesty of God's mercy?

(2) What then, in the second place, is the nature of the divine mercy? God's mercy is not weak, for it belongs to the nature of His moral majesty. God does not save with a fragment of Himself. The whole God is in you and for you.

We pity misfortune with part of ourselves, but God pities us with His all. God saves to the uttermost, but it is with His uttermost, all He has. It

---

1. This sermon was preached at New Court Church, Tollington Park, London, on 30 April 1911. A version of this sermon was published as Forsyth, "The Majesty and the Mercy of God," 367, and then republished as Forsyth, "Majesty and Mercy," 305–7. See also Forsyth, *Revelation Old and New*, 86–89.

16: Sermon on Ecclesiasticus 2:18

took all His moral energy to save us. All the love and power in the universe are at work saving us. We are not saved by a mere turn of God's hand, but by the whole mighty power of the Cross. With us, mercy belongs to our spare time; with God, mercy is His business. Beneath us are the everlasting arms, and they are there to embrace, lift, hold and save us: not rocks, mark you, nor strong foundations, but arms.

The mercy of God is so near and so great that often we cannot see it. The Cross is a strange symbol of mercy. The pathos of life, and its terrible suffering, the ignorance of many, the dangers to which both young and old are exposed, the shattered hopes, and, over all this, nature's harsh cruel laws; all these things appal you? But turn and see the overwhelming mercy of God. "As his majesty is, so also is his mercy." We know something of the compassions of men, and feel them ourselves. What then must the compassions of God be? What, if they showed themselves in the Cross, with its extremity of suffering, its appalling shame, its utter abandonment of love?

If the Cross is not God's mercy, then it is His arraignment before the world.

17

Sermon on Romans 8:28

"All things work together for good to them that love God, and are called according to his purpose."

—ROMANS 8:28

ALL THINGS: THE FATE of your single soul is involved in the fate of the universe. That which saves your soul saves the universe.

Work together: The universe is active and mighty. We are surrounded by things that have a vital interest in us. All things work. We were made for and are called to action. The universe is not only operant, but co-operant. The whole universe not only speaks to us, but works out a mighty purpose with us.

For good: It is moral action. "Morality is the soul of things," says Matthew Arnold.[1] And it is the goal of things.

Keep this for your moments of despondency. The right that is in the world is far more, and far more certain, than the wrong. If you are right, everything works for you. You are in the wave that carries everything that is best to its goal.

Whose good is it? Yours? It depends upon whether you have made yourself one with that which is at the centre of the universe. It is good, first of all, for the Kingdom of God. The good is the holiness of God. What we

---

1. Here Forsyth misattributes these lines of Joseph Butler to Matthew Arnold. Arnold's words are, "Morality is the nature of things." Forsyth correctly attributes these words to Butler in Forsyth, *The Person and Place of Jesus Christ*, title page, 256. See also Forsyth, *Christ on Parnassus*, 274; Forsyth, *The Principle of Authority*, 179. Forsyth probably first read Butler's *Sermons* while at Aberdeen.

17: Sermon on Romans 8:28

call righteousness on earth, they call holiness in Heaven. Love is the outgoing of the holiness of God.

To them that love God: Affection is no pledge of success. There is no religious promise in humanity's love for humanity. True love is supernatural love. Everything can be turned by the loving mind into good. Deeper than this is Paul's meaning, the deep moving power of the love of God; the love God has for us.

Called according to his purpose. Lovers are called. They are made lovers, not by instinct, but by God.

Also, the called are lovers. Love is the badge and sign of the called. Having been forgiven much, we love much. But first it is not the love of men, but the love of God.

18

SERMON ON PHILIPPIANS 3:12

"Not that I have already obtained, or am already made perfect: but I press on, if so be that I may apprehend that for which also I was apprehended by Christ Jesus."

—PHILIPPIANS 3:12

ONE OF OUR PROBLEMS is that, while we have a perfect Word, we ourselves are imperfect. How can the Word and the man be made to coincide? In spirit, if not in compass, we may coincide—that is, we may move upon the same centre.

Note two things about Paul in this connection: first his modesty, and then his confidence.

His modesty: He is more satisfied with his goal than with his attainment. His modesty is not due to diffidence, but to the great conception he had of his Gospel. It is not due to the great problem he faced, but to the greatness of the power given [to] him to deal with it.

The minister of the Gospel is not a Man of problems first of all, but a man of power. He should know the greatness of the world within more thoroughly than the greatness of the problem about him. "Greater is He that is in you than he that is in the world."[1]

Paul was much more sure of the Gospel's grasp of him than of his grasp of the Gospel. In your ministry, you must trust not in what you bring with you from your books, but Him whom you bring with you to your books, and to everything else in life.

---

1. 1 John 4:4.

His confidence: There was nothing Paul was so sure of as the grace of Christ. He was not so much concerned about his own experience as about Him who brought that experience. His own experience was used by him to irradiate Christ.

Paul was the apostle of the Gospel which had broken him up, and would have ruined him, if it had not saved him.

To be able to say at any stage in life, "I have everything that God can give," is to have the victory that overcomes the world. But distinguish this from saying, "I have everything that [the] heart can wish." There are things you cannot have now because you are not ready for them, and because of the exigencies of the Kingdom of God.

19

SERMON ON MARK 14:3

"There came a woman having an alabaster cruse of ointment."

—MARK 14:3

[MARK 14] BEGINS THE history of the passion, and this story is like a star on the edge of the passion cloud.

1. The woman is not named. The work stands and the worker goes, as least as far as man is concerned. She belongs to the true aristocracy whose deeds outlive their names.

2. Mark the dumb eloquence of this woman. The eloquence of action is the greatest thing in the world.

3. What a delight this service was to Jesus. It was a fine devotion, finely and fitly expressed. It was a beautiful incident but it was more beautifully received. He turned to defend her from her critics. It was this which made an Elizabethan poet describe Him as the "first true gentleman that ever lived."[1] Look at the magnificent interpretation He put upon the act. It was far greater than she thought. She meant it finely, but it was taken more finely still. That is how God always takes our acts of worship.

4. Again, notice how sure Jesus was of his own power. He knew He could make her immortal. He was to make her immortal in history, but

---

1. Forsyth misquotes the line from Thomas Dekker's poem, "Patience," which appeared in Dekker's play *The Honest Whore* (1604–1635): "The best of men/That e'er wore earth about him, was a sufferer/A soft, meek, patient, humble, tranquil spirit/The first true gentleman that ever breath'd."

He had already ensured her immortality in Heaven. "Rejoice not in these things, but rather that your names are written in heaven."[2]

5. What is rewarded is not her loving nature but her love for Christ. The Gospel demands not love but faith, and piety only as it is created by faith. It is much more to love Christ than to love man; we love men most when we love them for Christ's sake.

Judas sold his Master for £3.10.0d, that was *his* estimate of his Master. *Hers* was this ointment which cost £10, and she would have given more had she possessed it.

Pedantry and economy need sometimes to be taught a lesson. There was a mathematician once who complained of [Milton's] *Paradise Lost* that it proved nothing! There are many who complain of Christian worship today on the same ground. The greatest work that any soul can do is to worship. We need to learn the utility of the useless. Even to think of the poor may sometimes be wrong—if it hinder us from remembering God and his Christ.

The saying "Work is worship" is not wholly true. It is untrue unless we also remember that worship is work.

---

2. Luke 10:20.

20

Sermon on Revelation 2:28

"I will give him the morning star."
—REVELATION 2:28

THE PECULIARITY OF THIS verse [i.e., Revelation 2:28] is that nobody knows exactly what it means, and we are therefore at liberty to let it suggest what it will.

(i) Let it stand for the morning star of our idealism. How magnificent is the credulity of youth as to the future! Does this mean that at the other end of life we shall still possess our young ideals, though they may be changed, sobered and ennobled by experience?

(ii) Or, again, the morning star might be the earnest of the Spirit. Christianity has its youth in us, when the earnest of the great time coming moves our spirits. This is the morning star of faith.

(iii) It is the benediction of those that overcome, and this suggests the flush and glory of moral victory. The insight which comes from moral victory reveals the future, and assures us of the coming day. More, every moral victory is a contribution to the victory of the whole moral world. The long future is with the moral victors.

(iv) But perhaps the morning star is prophecy, which is more than idealism. It is like Peter's lamp shining in a dark place until the day dawn. We must be sure of the "budding morrow at midnight."[1] Faith is the great morning star which is the life of prophecy.

---

1. The phrase, "There is a budding morrow in midnight," is from John Keats' poem, "To Homer" (1818), and was also later the title of a poem by Christina Georgina Rossetti.

20: *Sermon on Revelation 2:28*

God takes the morning star out of the sky of youthful idealism that He may give it back to us for a possession when we enter upon the full life of Christian faith.

21

Sermon on John 3:4

"How can a man be born when he is old?"

—JOHN 3:4

NICODEMUS WAS A PILLAR in his Church, yet he came to a young Rabbi, which suggests that his faith must have been seriously shaken, and he himself profoundly disturbed. The truth is that he had more passion for life than power to live. There are many people like that, some through physical weakness, and some from more deep rooted causes. But whatever the cause, it is a painful experience.

The meaning of his question is, How can I recover my soul's life and youth? It was full life, not long life, he wanted, but how can a man go back upon himself and begin again? Can we ever grow young again in soul? When ideals are disillusioned, does it mean there are no greater ideals beyond? "They that wait upon the Lord shall renew their strength"[1]—is that mere poetry?

New knowledge may fail to rejuvenate, but there remains a new experience—regeneration. Religious interest may be strong, moral puritanism intense, zeal for the Kingdom eager, without an experience of rebirth, regeneration. There are many religious people, both teachers and taught, who have never experienced eternal life through the new birth.

Eternal life is a far more searching thing than the Kingdom of God. We may live for the Kingdom and yet never have eternal life. John the Baptist was great, but not so great as the least in the Kingdom of those who are born again.

---

1. Isa 40:31.

We can never erase the line between the Church and the world, between the spirit and the flesh, between those who are born and those who are born again.

It is one thing to be influenced by the principles of the Kingdom and quite another to be in the Kingdom.

22

SERMON ON MARK 12:43–44

"Then he called unto him his disciples, and said unto them, Verily I say unto you, This poor widow cast in more than all they which are casting into the treasury: for they did cast in of their superfluity; but she of her want did cast in all that she had, even all her living."

—MARK 12:43–44

JESUS STOOD WATCHING. It is a minister's business to study his people. It was with the moral eye Jesus saw, and not with the eye of the artist.

It is quite possible that this poor woman had been robbed by those who cast in much. She cast in all her living, surely she might have kept back one coin!

1. Notice the kind of thing that took the eye of Jesus. He saw through all the sham and show of life. He not only sees but He sees through every act of our life. Jesus had nothing in common with the self-seeker, or the self-satisfied person.

He had deep vision rather than wide vision. Better be told you are deep in your religion that that you are broad-minded.

2. The judgment of Christ is the judgment of God. God loves the bowed and wholly obedient spirit. That is the whole lesson of the Cross.

3. God sees not as man sees. This means justification by faith or, in non-theological language, a man is accepted of God by that which only God can see and measure. We are judged not by ethic but by spirit, not by conduct but by faith.

22: Sermon on Mark 12:43–44

    You are giving God just what your gift costs you. The real contribution is the faith and love that only God sees. It is a subtle temptation to be pleased with ourselves because we love and serve God.

23

Sermon on Luke 10:41–42

"And the Lord answered and said unto her, Martha, Martha, thou art anxious and troubled about many things: but one thing is needful."

—LUKE 10:41–42

HERE [IN LUKE 10:41–42, we] have the counterpart of the Good Samaritan. That Parable told of service to man; this speaks of service to God. It is a commentary on that verse in the Psalms which reads, "It is good for me to draw near unto God."[1]

Matters of eating and drinking are not worthy to disturb the peace of the soul. Mary was attending to the Lord without distraction.

What did Christ really mean by this saying? First, that we do not need a multitude of things; simplicity is best, and then he glances off into spiritual things. "Few things, nay one!" He does not mean that the life of meditation is best, except on occasions, but there is really no need that Mary and Martha should be separate persons:

> A Mary in the Master's house,
> A Martha in her own.[2]

Notice, in the next place, the tremendous self-consciousness of Christ: His sense of His own value and His exclusive claim. Here is implied that there is something in life which is absolutely good, something in which the

---

1. Ps 73:28.
2. Attributed to an unnamed "recent poet" in Pitman, *Lady Missionaries in Foreign Lands*, 122.

23: Sermon on Luke 10:41-42

soul may eternally rest. But in order to find it, concentration is necessary. We must concentrate on eternal life, leaving all the petty nothings to be interested in few things, even in one, if we would make it our own. People everywhere are distracted and will not concentrate on Christ. We must allow a great many books to go unread, and a great many social visits unpaid, in order that we may concentrate on Christ.

One thing is needful—for God, for the Soul, and for Society:

1. For God

God concentrates Himself on Christ. The whole light of Eternity is poured forth upon us through the single soul of Christ.

The one thing needful for God was lost Man's salvation, and so He humbled Himself in the Cross. All the world belonged to Him, all stars, all powers, but not man. This one thing had to be done, and Christ alone, who was the Presence of God, could do it. What shall it profit God if He win the whole world and lose man?

2. For the Soul

Some people say that character is "the one thing needful," but what makes character?

What is the precious thing in life? "Love," says the poet; but love in the poet's sense is not enough—something else is needed to guide it and make it strong and wise. If you mean love in the right sense, it is true; but that is not love of wife or child, it is love of God. That is good because it is permanent.

We do not want rapturous experience; we want staying power. [The] love of God is good because it gives us power, poise, stability.

People sometimes lose their souls in Christian service; that is, they are swept off their feet. In a rough sea we need something to keep us stable.

We must rest on someone who does more than all we can do to reform society. We do a great thing when we interfere in social problems; they are so complicated. Because of this complication, good work is much at sea, and therefore it is imperative that the soul should be in port.

The one thing needful is the indwelling Christ, not mere religious exaltation, a touching of Christ from time to time, but living with Him. Too many people have to cry out, "Lord, if thou hadst been here my soul had not died."[3] Christ is the centre around whom true character is formed. Strong

---

3. John 11:21, 32.

characters always make you feel they have centres, and the strongest make you feel Christ is their centre.

3. For Society

The Kingdom of God? Yes, but do not stop there. Christ is necessary to society. You cannot have the Kingdom without the King, and you cannot have the true Kingdom without the Church. "*Transit amor multitudinis, et remanet caritas unitatis.*"[4] As A. B. [Alexander Balmain] Bruce says, Mary was the least in the household, but the greatest in the Kingdom of God.

Everything must revolve around our one centre, Christ. We do not live two lives, but put our whole personality into all our work. It is one thing to do everything for Christ, and quite another to do everything with Christ. Mary wished to be fed by Christ, Martha to feed Christ.

Mere work will often disappoint us, for we may thresh a cartload of corn for a bushel of wheat. Christ came not to be ministered to, but to minister, and our first duty therefore is to be ministered to by Him. Faith first, then works.

---

4. These words from St Augustine's *Sermo* 104.3 should read, "*Transit labor multitudinis, et remanet caritas unitatis*" [the multiplicity of toil passes away, the single unity of charity remains]. Forsyth was possibly drawing on the misreading in Meyer, *Kritisch exegetischer kommentar über das Neue Testament*, 346.

24

Sermon (Valedictory Address) on 1 Corinthians 4:1

"Stewards of the mysteries of God."

—1 CORINTHIANS 4:1[1]

I AM ABOUT TO speak to those, or more specifically to those, who are gathered here for the last time at an evening service.

You are about to go into the active ministry, and to become stewards of the mysteries of God, and I would have you realise how great is the work to which you have been called, and what will be expected of you by God.

My text divides itself into three parts—Stewards, Mysteries and God:

1. Stewards

You are first of all stewards, not owners. Men with a trust, not men with a property. You have to carry what many others have tried to carry—a Gospel, a Truth many times uttered. And so I would warn you not to strive to win notice by originality but only by the Gospel you preach. The truest things you will have to say are those that have been said many times, but they are still the most original. Grace is the most original thing in the world. However original sin may be, Grace is more original still. The Grace of God is so original as to be unexplainable.

---

1. Forsyth delivered this "Valedictory Address" in June 1909.

III: Unpublished Sermons

It is a great thing to have gifts to bring home to your hearers—truths, great truths, in a clever way. But remember always that the essential thing for a Minister is not gifts but faithfulness. Faithfulness not to your people but to God.

Where most Ministers fail is in forgetting themselves. You yourself are part of God's trust to you. Not only to subdue your passions, and purify your life, but also to look after the method of your work. Plan out every day as though you worked for an earthly master, and had to give an account of your time. Your time is not your own, and every moment of it must be used to some purpose. Your time is not your own; it is God's.

But a Minister's life is terribly difficult, and this is where the difficulty lies—every preacher has to be the greatest dogmatist and the humblest man in his Church. I have often told you that a man had better not be a preacher at all if he is not a dogmatist. It is not preaching to give utterance to a great sympathy, but to dogmatise about a definite Gospel. Nevertheless, the Minister must be the humblest man in his Church. He must realise the great responsibility and privilege of his position, and his own inadequacy.

So perhaps the art of living as a Minister is far more difficult than the art of preaching, and there is only one power that can help you, and that is communion with Christ. No amount of service to men can ever compensate you for neglecting communion with Christ. The Minister must know by personal contact the living Christ, and all his ministry will be spoiled unless he does.

And this leads me to my second point.

2. Mysteries

You are stewards in charge of a mystery. Now a mystery does not mean a Sacrament. It does not even mean something mysterious. The mysteries of God are to be preached upon the housetops. Mystery here means "type," "symbol," "parable." When Paul says, "I will shew [sic] you a mystery," he means "I will make clear to you by parable." The mysteries of God mean knowledge, not due to man's discovery, but to God's revealing grace.

The great mystery of God is found in the Gospel, and a great and wonderful mystery it is. In all our search into it, we must never cease to be awed and impressed by it.

Never make light of your vocation as a revealer of the mysteries of God. That never can be reverenced on Sunday which is made light of during the week.

But your duty as preachers is not to preach sermons, but to preach a Gospel. What you have to dispense to the people is not anything of yours but a revelation of God's mystery. The great storehouse of this mystery is the

Bible. The Bible is your source. If you learn from other people you will begin at once to imitate their bad points, for their good ones belong to their own personality, and were obtained through the Bible only. If you would be as the great men of the Church, you must obtain your personality where they obtained theirs. Christ alone can draw out the secret of your personality.

3. Now Lastly, These Mysteries Are God's:

We are in trust of the last and holiest reality of the world, the grace of God. Next to grace, the deepest thing in the world is sin. That which went deeper than sin and overcame it, is that of which we are in charge.

It is an insoluble mystery of an insoluble God. If we could solve God we could solve the world, but at the same time He would cease to be God. God is insoluble, yet nevertheless He has solved Himself by revelation. The great problem of life is solved by God Himself. Shakespeare puts the question supremely, God answers it finally.

See how great is the Gospel of which you are in charge. Rise to the dignity, the true dignity of the Cross! *Noblesse oblige!*[2] It will save you, let it save you!

Beware of your conduct. Be genial, be sociable! Oh yes, but never lose sight of your high calling, never lose sight of Christ, God's greatest mystery, your greatest power.

May He bless you and keep you. May He make His face to shine upon you. May He lift up the light of His countenance upon you and give you peace.

---

2. Nobility obliges.

25

SERMON (ORDINATION ADDRESS) ON JOHN 17:6

"I manifested thy name unto the men whom Thou gavest Me out of the world: thine they were, and Thou gavest them to Me."

—JOHN 17:6[1]

THREE THINGS—THE PROPERTY, THE Gift, the Use:

1. "Thine They Were."

These are God's people. Christ's people, not yours. You say they are "my people!" Yes, but only because they are the People of God.

To begin with, they cost Him more than they will ever cost you. If ever they are trying, and if ever they tax your patience, remember that. And if ever you feel unequal to your task, remember that they are more His than yours, because they cost Him more. Your Church is not in chief a Congregational Church, still less is it your Church—it is the Church of the living God, bought by Christ's most precious blood.

You will see then that the Church is composed of those who are His people in a very different sense than, for instance, "the earth is the Lord's."[2] The Spirit of the Lord fills and moves His creation, but what made the Church, and fills and moves it, is His Holy Spirit, something far more intimate to God than the power and order of creation, something dearer, something greater.

---

1. Forsyth delivered this "Ordination Address" on October 20, 1909.
2. Ps 24:1.

25: Sermon (Ordination Address) on John 17:6

All men are God's as part of His creation; they are His offspring. But there is something greater, diviner, than humanity; it is the Church of God. The Church of God is the finest product of humanity; it is the greatest thing in the universe. And this is so because it was produced by God in His Son and Holy Spirit. The Church is His own as no nation is, no society, no family. The Church is His as His Son is His—His in His Son. His not as a part of creation, but as a new creation in Jesus Christ. If in love He created the world, in much more love did He create the Church. It was in might and beauty He created the world; it was in Holy Love He created the Church. It is His as nothing else in the world is. It is the Church of His Son, and His Son is more to Him than all the world.

I speak of the Church, of course, as God sees it; God who sees the end from the beginning. You also must learn to see your Church like that; not as man sees it but as God redeemed it, and as God trusts it, and bears with it, and feeds it, and serves it, and waits for it while it grows to the mature man in Jesus Christ.

I have spoken of the property. I now come to speak of the gift. "Thine they were, Thou gavest them to me."

2. "Thou Gavest Them to Me."

Your ordination is an act and gift of God. He is putting His people into your hands.

He does not so much give you a position as a trust. He puts His Church in your care.

But it is also true that He entrusts this Church with you. If they treat you ill, it will affect your whole life, and just the same if they treat you well. A Minister is very much what his first Church makes him. But let them remember this, that to treat you well they must treat your Gospel better than you.

Therefore it is not popularity you must think about first. Do not crave morbidly for your people's love. Craving does not bring it, and often arrests it. Do not beg for sympathy.

Think of your Church from the other point of view, as a trust from God to whom you must be faithful in it. This Flock is committed to you by God. You do not simply take each other but, as in true marriage, God has given you to each other. This is really a marriage ceremony. You are being married to the Church.

This will comfort you when you are doubting if you should be at this work. Say to yourself, "Thou hast given them to me, the responsibility is

Thine." "*Da quod jubes et jube quod vis.*"³ I am not worthy. Yes that is true, but what is that to thee, follow thou Me!

Of course you are not worthy to preach the Gospel; none of us is worthy. But then your people are not worthy to hear it. If it depended on worth, there would be neither preachers nor listeners. The worth is where the power is, in Christ and God, who does not give us according to our deserts.

Lest you be overwhelmed with the greatness of your task, remember no Church is given to any man without the Saviour of the Church and of Him. After all, it is Christ's Church more than yours. He is the real Pastor of every real Church, and the Bishop of its Minister. You are but His curate.

Finally, the use of the gift:

3. "I Have Manifested Thy Name to Them."

What a charge—to be the living man on whom men depend for the living God! The people say to you as Minister, what Philip said to Jesus, "Show us the Father."⁴

"I have manifested Thy name." That means nature, and nature means presence and action—not truths about God but God Himself in action. It is not the Fatherhood of God you have to preach but God the Father. You have not to preach about God *to* people, you must preach God *into* people. So true preaching is not telling people, but acting on people, making people.

No amount of telling will ever convince people of the Father; it has to be lived into them. Therefore yours must be a personal ministry. When the personal God revealed Himself, it was in the person of His Son, Jesus Christ; and when Christ is to be preached it is by men, by a soul. You cannot reveal the Holy One by talking about holiness. "That is true," says someone, "You can only reveal the Holy One by being holy." But he knows little of himself who can say that. If we cannot preach the Holy God except by being holy, who can preach Him?

The holiness that fits you to preach about the Holy is not your personal sanctity and conduct, but your evident communion with the Holy Christ. It is a life faith you want more than a life conduct.

Why! Paul addressed such Churches as his by the name of Saints! Churches in which the grossest sins were evident. They were not saints by conduct but by faith.

---

3. "Give what you command, and command what you give." St Augustine, *Confessions* 10.29.40.

4. John 14:8.

25: Sermon (Ordination Address) on John 17:6

Your goodness is not equal to your task as a minister but your faith must be. You must realise that "My grace is sufficient for you."[5] So it is! Not even your faith is sufficient, but only His grace, for you have to reveal Christ as Christ revealed, in this sense, that in both cases it is the soul that tells. But there is this difference: He revealed God to us by the resources of His own soul, while you cannot do it from the resources of your soul but only from His. Nobody was for Him what He is for you with God.

The greatest thing you can give any man is your God and your Saviour. The reason why some ministers are valuable for other things than preaching, even valuable in spite of their preaching, is that they preach about God, and about Christ; they do not preach Christ. They are only messengers, not Sacraments.

A favourite type of preaching today is to analyse your soul; it is subjective, psychological preaching. It is weak, it is exhausting, it is dangerous. Analyse the Gospel in reference to the soul. You are a minister of the Word, not of the soul.

And that Word will be selective. There is real truth in the doctrine of election. You will not appeal to all alike. To try to do so is to make your Gospel colourless. There will be some whom you will not touch. On the other hand, there may be some given to you whom others have never touched.

If your Church were smaller, it might be more powerful. If you could shed off people as Christ did, you might be stronger, like Gideon's host. Christ alone has the promise and reversion of all men, and He only at the last. At first all forsook Him and fled.

You have but a corner of the vineyard, and cannot appeal to all men. Humility then is better equipment than ambition, even the ambition of doing much good. And remember as a last word: in the Christian ministry, all self-seeking is fatal.

---

5. 2 Cor 12:9.

Bibliography

Anderson, Marvin W. "P. T. Forsyth: Prophet of the Cross." *Evangelical Quarterly* 47 (1975) 146–61.
Andrews, Jessie F. "Memoir." In *The Work of Christ*, vii–xxviii. London: Independent, 1938.
Anonymous. *The Educational Record, with the Proceedings of the British and Foreign School Society*. Vol. 19. London: British & Foreign School Society, 1914.
Anonymous. "Our Photograph." *The Wyvern* 25 (1892) 67.
Arnold, Matthew. *Literature and Dogma: An Essay Towards a Better Apprehension of the Bible*. London: Nelson & Sons, 1873.
Barr, Browne. "P. T. Forsyth: The Preachers' Theologian: A Witness and Confession." In *P. T. Forsyth: The Man, the Preachers' Theologian, Prophet for the 20th Century: A Contemporary Assessment*, edited by Donald G. Miller et al., 31–42. Pittsburgh Theological Monograph Series 36. Pittsburgh: Pickwick Publications, 1981.
Barth, Karl. *Gespräche: 1963*. Edited by Eberhard Busch. Zürich: Theologischer, 2005.
———. "The Need and Promise of Christian Preaching." In *The Word of God and the Word of Man*, 97–135. New York: Harper & Brothers, 1957.
———. "Theologians: Barth in Retirement." *Time*, May 31, 1963. Online: http://www.time.com/time/magazine/article/0,9171,896838,00.html.
———. "A Theological Dialogue." *Theology Today* 19 (1962) 171–77.
———. "The Word of God and the Task of the Ministry." In *The Word of God and the Word of Man*, 183–217. New York: Harper & Brothers, 1957.
———. *The Word of God and the Word of Man*. Translated by Douglas Horton. New York: Harper & Brothers, 1957.
Barth, Karl, and Eduard Thurneysen. *God's Search for Man: Sermons*. Edinburgh: T. & T. Clark, 1935.
———. *Revolutionary Theology in the Making: Barth-Thurneysen Correspondence, 1914–1925*. Translated by James D. Smart. Richmond: John Knox, 1964.
Barth, Markus. "P. T. Forsyth: The Theologian for the Practical Man." *Congregational Quarterly* 17 (1939) 436–42.
Bebbington, David W. *Evangelicalism in Modern Britain: A History from the 1730s to the 1980s*. London: Routledge, 2005.
Bennett, William Henry, editor. *Faith and Criticism: Essays by Congregationalists*. London: Marston, 1893.
Binfield, Clyde. "The Significance of Baby Babble: P. T. Forsyth's *Pulpit Parables* and their Context." Unpublished paper. The Shergold Lecture, Narborough Congregational Church, Leicester, 2000.

Bishop, John. "P. T. Forsyth: 'Preaching and the Modern Mind.'" *Religion in Life* 48 (1979) 303–8.

Bonhoeffer, Dietrich. *Spiritual Care*. Translated by Jay C. Rochelle. Philadelphia: Fortress, 1985.

Bradley, William L. *P. T. Forsyth: The Man and His Work*. London: Independent, 1952.

Bray, Charles (Caroline "Cara"). *Elements of Morality in Easy Lessons, For Home and School Teaching*. London: Longmans, Green, 1882.

Brooke, Stopford Augustus. *Christ in Modern Life: Sermons Preached in St. James's Chapel, York Street, St. James's Square, London*. New York: Appleton, 1872.

Brown, James Baldwin. *The Doctrine of Annihilation in the Light of the Gospel of Love*. London: King, 1875.

Brown, Robert McAfee. *P. T. Forsyth: Prophet for Today*. Philadelphia: Westminster, 1952.

Burke, Edmund. *Reflections on the Revolution in France, and on the Proceedings of Certain Societies in London, Relative to that Event, in A Letter Intended to Have Been Sent to a Gentleman in Paris*. London: Revived Apollo, 1814.

Calvin, John. *Institutes of the Christian Religion*. Edited by John T. McNeill. Translated by Ford Lewis Battles. Library of Christian Classics 20. Philadelphia: Westminster, 1977.

Camfield, F. W. "Peter Taylor Forsyth." *The Presbyter* 6 (1948) 3–10.

Campbell, Reginald J. *The New Theology*. London: Chapman & Hall, 1907.

Carter, Dean. "Foreword." In *Marriage: Its Ethic and Religion*, by P. T. Forsyth, ix–xlx. Coromandel East, Australia: New Creation, 1999.

Child, R. L. "P T Forsyth: Some Aspects of his Thoughts." *Baptist Times*, May 20, 1948, 9.

Comte, Auguste. *A General View of Positivism*. Translated by John Henry Bridges. London: Trübner, 1865.

The Congregational Union of England and Wales. *The Congregational Year Book*. London: The Congregational Union of England & Wales, 1925.

Council of New College, London. "New College London: Extract from 386 Council Meeting at the College, 1 October 1874." Unpublished papers. Copies in Dr Williams's Library. London: 1874.

Cunliffe-Jones, Hubert. "P. T. Forsyth: Reactionary or Prophet?" *Congregational Quarterly* 27 (1950) 344–56.

Darlow, T. H. "Tributes to the Late Rev. Principal Forsyth, D.D." *The British Weekly*, 17 November 1921, 146.

Denney, James. *Letters of Principal James Denney to W. Robertson Nicoll, 1893–1917*. London: Hodder & Stoughton, 1920.

———. "Principal Forsyth on Preaching." *The British Weekly*, 24 October 1907, 57.

Eliot, T. S. *Four Quartets*. New York: Harcourt, Brace, & World, 1943.

Escott, Harry, editor. *P. T. Forsyth and the Cure of Souls: An Appraisement and Anthology of His Practical Writings*. London: Allen & Unwin, 1970.

———. *Peter Taylor Forsyth (1848–1921), Director of Souls: Selections from his Practical Writings*. London: Epworth, 1948.

Fairbairn, A. M. "Dale as a Theologian." In *The Life of R. W. Dale of Birmingham*, edited by Alfred William Winterslow Dale et al., 695–722. London: Hodder & Stoughton, 1899.

Forde, Gerhard O. *On Being a Theologian of the Cross: Reflections on Luther's Heidelberg Disputation, 1518*. Grand Rapids: Eerdmans, 1997.

Forsyth, P. T. "An Allegory of the Resurrection." *The Christian World Pulpit*, 14 May 1902, 312–19.

———. "The Argument for Immortality Drawn from the Nature of Love: A Lecture on Lord Tennyson's 'Vastness.'" *The Christian World Pulpit*, 2 December 1885, 360–64.

———. "As to the Causes of Decline." *Sunday School Chronicle*, 13 December 1900, 850.

———. "The Attitude of the Church to the Present Unrest." *The British Congregationalist* (1910) 214–15.

———. "Baldwin Brown: A Tribute, a Reminiscence, and a Study." In *In Memoriam: James Baldwin Brown*, edited by Elizabeth Baldwin Brown, 133–42. London: James Clarke, 1884.

———. *Christ on Parnassus: Lectures on Art, Ethic, and Theology*. London: Hodder & Stoughton, 1911.

———. *Christian Perfection*. Edited by W. Roberton Nicoll. Little Books on Religion. London: Hodder & Stoughton, 1899.

———. "The Church and Divorce: Principal Forsyth's Memorandum." *The British Congregationalist*, 30 November 1913, 885.

———. "The Church and the Children." *The British Weekly*, 15 May 1913, 169.

———. *The Church and the Sacraments*. London: Independent, 1947.

———. "Church, State, Dogma and Education." *Contemporary Review* 90 (1906) 827–36.

———. *The Church, the Gospel, and Society*. London: Independent, 1962.

———. "Churches, Sects and Wars." *Contemporary Review* 107 (1915) 618–26.

———. *Congregationalism and Reunion: Two Lectures*. London: Independent, 1952.

———. *Corruption and Bribery: A Sermon*. Bradford: Brear, 1882.

———. *The Cruciality of the Cross*. London: Hodder & Stoughton, 1910.

———. "The Decay of Brain Power: The Dangers of a Cheap and Scrappy Press." *Young Man* 14 (1900) 41–43.

———. "Dr. Martineau." *London Quarterly Review* 93 (1900) 217.

———. "The Efficiency and Sufficiency of the Bible." *Biblical Review* 2 (1917) 10–30.

———. "The Evangelical Churches and the Higher Criticism." In *The Gospel and Authority: A P. T. Forsyth Reader*, edited by Marvin W. Anderson, 15–52. Minneapolis: Augsburg, 1971.

———. "Faith and Experience." *Wesleyan Methodist Magazine* 123 (1900) 415–17.

———. *Faith, Freedom, and the Future*. London: Hodder & Stoughton, 1912.

———. "Faith, Timidity, and Superstition." *Evangelical Magazine* 108 (1900) 111–16.

———. "A Few Hints about Reading the Bible." *Biblical Review* 3 (1918) 530–44.

———. "The Foolishness of Preaching." *The Expository Times* 30 (1919) 153–54.

———. "The Fund and the Faith." *The British Weekly*, 29 May 1913, 219.

———. "Gain and Godliness." *Congregational Quarterly* 23 (1945) 356–8.

———. *God the Holy Father*. London: Independent, 1957.

———. "The Healing of the Paralytic." *The British Weekly*, 25 October 1894, 4.

———. *The Holy Father and the Living Christ*. London: Hodder & Stoughton, 1897.

———. "A Hymn to Christ." *The British Weekly*, 1 June 1899, 133.

———. "The Ideal Ministry of the Church." *Christian World*, 18 October 1906, 22.

———. "Intellectualism and Faith." *Hibbert Journal* 11 (1913) 311–28.

———. *"Maid, Arise": A Sermon to School Girls. Preached in Shipley Congregational Church, Sunday 28 July 1878*. Bradford: Brear, 1878.

———. "Majesty and Mercy." *The Christian World Pulpit*, 17 May 1911, 305–7.

———. "The Majesty and the Mercy of God." *The British Congregationalist*, 4 May 1911, 367.

———. *Mercy the true and only Justice: A Sermon Preached in Shipley Congregational Church, on the Missionary Sunday, September 30, 1877*. Bradford: Brear, nd.

———. "Ministerial Libraries: V. Principal Forsyth's Library at Hackney College." *The British Monthly* (1904).

———. *Missions in State and Church: Sermons and Addresses*. London: Hodder & Stoughton, 1908.

———. "Motherhood." *The British Congregationalist*, 26 September 1907, 255–56.

———. "The Newest Theology." *The British Weekly*, 7 March 1907, 581–82.

———. "Ordination Address, 20 October," Dr Williams's Library, London, 1909.

———. "Ordination Statement." *Shipley and Saltaire Times*, 25 November 1876, 4.

———. "Orthodoxy, Heterodoxy, Heresy, and Freedom." *Hibbert Journal* 8 (1910) 321–29.

———. *The Person and Place of Jesus Christ: The Congregational Union Lecture for 1909*. London: Hodder & Stoughton, 1910.

———. "The Pessimism of Mr. Thomas Hardy." *London Quarterly Review* 118 (1912) 193–219.

———. *Positive Preaching and [the] Modern Mind: The Lyman Beecher Lecture on Preaching, Yale University, 1907*. London: Hodder & Stoughton, 1907.

———. "Preaching and Poetry." *The Expository Times* 1 (1890) 269–72.

———. *The Preaching of Jesus and the Gospel of Christ*. Blackwood, Australia: New Creation, 1987.

———. "The Preaching of Jesus and the Gospel of Christ. [VII:] The Meaning of a Sinless Christ." *The Expositor* 8th Series, 25 (1923) 288–312.

———. *The Principle of Authority in Relation to Certainty, Sanctity, and Society: An Essay in the Philosophy of Experimental Religion*. London: Independent, 1952.

———. *The Pulpit and the Age*. Manchester: Brook & Chrystal, 1885.

———. *Religion in Recent Art: Being Expository Lectures on Rossetti, Burne Jones, Watts, Holman Hunt, and Wagner*. London: Hodder & Stoughton, 1889.

———. "The Rev. P. T. Forsyth, MA, on 'Robert Burns.'" *Shipley and Saltaire Times*, 23 March 1878, 4.

———. "The Rev. P. T. Forsyth, MA, on 'Robert Burns.'" *Shipley and Saltaire Times*, 8 November 1879, 4.

———. *Revelation Old and New: Sermons and Addresses*. Edited by John Huxtable. London: Independent, 1962.

———. *The Soul of Prayer*. London: Kelly, 1916.

———. *The Soul of Prayer*. London: Independent, 1951.

———. *Theology in Church and State*. London: Hodder & Stoughton, 1915.

———. "Things New and Old." *The Christian World Pulpit* 84 (1913) 273–76.

———. "The Turkish Atrocities: Sermon by the Rev. P. T. Forsyth." *Shipley and Saltaire Times*, 23 September 1876, 4.

———. "The Way of Life." *Wesleyan Methodist Magazine* 120 (1897) 83–88.

———. *The Weariness in Modern Life*. N.p., 1879.

———. "Why Am I a Liberal?" *Shipley and Saltaire Times*, 20 April 1878, 4.

———. *The Work of Christ*. London: Hodder & Stoughton, 1910.

Forsyth, P. T., and J. A. Hamilton. *Pulpit Parables for Young Hearers.* Manchester: Brook & Chrystal, 1886.

F. R. C. S. "A Medical Man's Tribute to Dr. Forsyth." *The British Weekly*, 1 December 1921, 203.

Gaunt, Alan. "P T Forsyth: The Preacher's Theologian." In *P T Forsyth: Theologian for a New Millennium*, edited by Alan P. F. Sell, 41–66. London: The United Reformed Church, 2000.

Gee, Maurice. *Plumb.* Wellington: Oxford University Press, 1980.

Giffen, Robert. "The Progress of the Working-Classes in the Last Half-Century." *Journal of the Statistical Society* 46 (1883) 593–622.

Goroncy, Jason A. "Bitter Tonic for Our Time—Why the Church Needs the World: Peter Taylor Forsyth on Henrik Ibsen." *European Journal of Theology* 15/2 (2006) 105–18.

———. "The Elusiveness, Loss, and Cruciality of Recovered Holiness: Some Biblical and Theological Observations." *International Journal of Systematic Theology* 10/2 (2008) 195–209.

———. "Fighting Troll-Demons in Vaults of the Mind and Heart—Art, Tragedy and Sacramentality: Some Observations from Ibsen, Forsyth, and Dostoevsky." *Princeton Theological Review* 13/1 (2007) 61–85.

———. "The Final Sanity is Complete Sanctity: Universal Holiness in the Soteriology of P. T. Forsyth (1848–1921)." In *"All Shall Be Well": Explorations in Universalism and Christian Theology, from Origen to Moltmann*, edited by Gregory MacDonald, 249–79. Eugene, OR: Cascade Books, 2011.

———. *Hallowed Be Thy Name: The Sanctification of All in the Soteriology of Peter Taylor Forsyth*, T. & T. Clark Studies in Systematic Theology. London: T. & T. Clark, 2013.

———. "John Calvin: Servant of the Word." In *Calvin, The Man and the Legacy*, edited by Murray Rae, Peter Matheson and Brett Knowles, 13–40. Hindmarsh: ATF Press, 2013.

———. "'Tha mi a' toirt fainear dur gearan': J. McLeod Campbell and P. T. Forsyth on the Extent of Christ's Vicarious Ministry." In *Evangelical Calvinism: Essays Resourcing the Continuing Reformation of the Church*, edited by Myk Habets and Bobby Grow, 253–286. Eugene, OR: Pickwick Publications, 2012.

Goroncy, Jason A., editor. *To Mend the World: A Confluence of Theology and the Arts.* Eugene, OR: Pickwick, 2014.

Gosse, Edmund W. *Father and Son: A Study of Two Temperaments.* London: Heinemann, 1907.

Grieve, A. J. "Congregationalism's Contribution to Theology: Some Material for a Bibliography." In *Essays Congregational and Catholic: Issued in Commemoration of the Centenary of the Congregational Union of England and Wales*, edited by Albert Peel. London: Congregational Union of England and Wales, 1931.

Griffith, Gwilym O. "Peter Taylor Forsyth." *The Christian World*, 13 May 1948, 1–2.

Gunton, Colin E. "The Nature of Systematic Theology: Anselm of Canterbury, Samuel Taylor Coleridge, and the Possibility of an English Systematic Theology." In *Theology through the Theologians: Selected Essays 1972-1995*, 1–18. Edinburgh: T. & T. Clark, 1999.

———. "The Real as the Redemptive: Forsyth on Authority and Freedom." In *Justice the True and Only Mercy: Essays on the Life and Theology of Peter Taylor Forsyth*, edited by Trevor A. Hart, 37–58. Edinburgh: T. & T. Clark, 1995.

Hamilton, J. A. *The Life of John Milton, Englishman, Partly in His Own Words*. London: The Congregational Union of England and Wales, 1870.

Häring, Theodor. *The Christian Faith: A System of Dogmatics*. Translated by John Dickie and George Ferries. Vol. 1. London: Hodder & Stoughton, 1915.

Hart, Trevor A. "Systematic—In What Sense?" In *Out of Egypt: Biblical Theology and Biblical Interpretation*, edited by Craig G. Bartholomew, Mary Healy, Karl Möller, and Robin Parry, 341–51. Grand Rapids: Zondervan, 2004.

Heine, Christian Johann Heinrich. *Pictures of Travel*. Translated by Charles Godfrey Leland. London: Trübner, 1855.

Heschel, Abraham Joshua. *The Prophets*. Vol. 1. New York: Harper & Row, 1962.

Higginson, R. E. "Peter Taylor Forsyth: Prophet and Pastor, 1848–1921." *English Churchman and St James' Chronicle*, 1 July 1955, 309, 315.

Hunter, Archibald M. "P. T. Forsyth Neutestamentler." *The Expository Times* 73 (1962) 100–106.

———. *P. T. Forsyth: Per Crucem ad Lucem*. London: SCM, 1974.

Huxtable, W. J. F. "P. T. Forsyth: 1848–1921." *Journal of the United Reformed Church History Society* 4 (1987) 72–78.

Jackson, George D. "The Biblical Basis of the Theology of P. T. Forsyth." ThD diss., Princeton Theological Seminary, 1952.

———. "The Interpreter at Work: XIV. P. T. Forsyth's Use of the Bible." *Interpretation* 7 (1953) 323–37.

Johnson, Mark D. *The Dissolution of Dissent, 1850–1918*. Edited by William H. McNeill. Modern European History: A Garland Series of Outstanding Dissertations. New York: Garland, 1987.

Jones, Edgar DeWitt. *The Royalty of the Pulpit*. New York: Harper & Brothers, 1951.

Jones, Frank F. "The Christological Thought of Peter Taylor Forsyth and Emil Brunner: A Comparative Study." PhD diss., University of St Andrews, 1970.

Larter, C. E. "Letter, St. Mary Church. 18 November 1921." *The British Weekly*, November 24, 1921, 196.

Lewis, C. S. *God in the Dock: Essays on Theology and Ethics*. Edited by Walter Hooper. Grand Rapids: Eerdmans, 1970.

———. "Introduction." In Athanasius, *On the Incarnation: The Treatise De incarnatione Verbi Dei*, 3–10. Crestwood, NY: St. Vladimir's Seminary Press, 1993.

———. *Reflections on the Psalms*. London: Fontana, 1967.

Lischer, Richard, editor. *The Company of Preachers: Wisdom on Preaching, Augustine to the Present*. Grand Rapids: Eerdmans, 2002.

Luther, Martin. "Heidelberg Disputation, 1518." In *Luther's Works*, Vol. 31: *Career of the Reformer I*, edited by Harold J. Grimm, 35–70. Philadelphia: Fortress, 1999.

MacKinnon, Donald M. "Aspects of Kant's Influence on British Theology." In *Kant and His Influence*, edited by G. M. Ross and T. McWalter, 348–66. Bristol: Thoemmes, 1990.

Manning, Bernard Lord. *This Latter House: The Life of Emmanuel Congregational Church, Cambridge, from 1874 to 1924*. Cambridge: Heffer & Sons, 1924.

Maurice, Frederick, editor. *The Life of Frederick Denison Maurice, Chiefly Told in His Own Letters*. 3rd ed. Vol. 1. London: Macmillan, 1884.

McKay, Clifford A., Jr. Review of *The Gospel and Authority: A P. T. Forsyth Reader*, by Marvin W. Anderson. *Journal of the American Academy of Religion* 40 (1972) 409–10.
Melville, Herman. *Moby Dick*. Oxford: Oxford University Press, 1998.
Meredith, George. *The Ordeal of Richard Feverel: A History of Father and Son*. London: Chapman & Hall, 1859.
Meyer, Heinrich August Wilhelm. *Kritisch exegetischer kommentar über das Neue Testament, Auch unter dem Titel: Kritisch exegetisches Handbuch über die Evangelien des Markus und Lukas*. Göttingen: Vandenhoeck & Ruprecht, 1855.
Miller, Donald G., Browne Barr, and Robert S. Paul. *P. T. Forsyth: The Man, the Preachers' Theologian, Prophet for the 20th Century: A Contemporary Assessment*. Pittsburgh Theological Monograph Series 36. Pittsburgh: Pickwick Publications, 1981.
Miłosz, Czesław. "I Sleep a Lot." In *The Collected Poems, 1931–1987*, 177–78. New York: Ecco, 1988.
Mozley, John Kenneth. *The Doctrine of the Atonement*. New York: Scribner, 1916.
———. *The Heart of the Gospel*. London: SPCK, 1925.
Nicoll, W. Robertson. "Principal Forsyth." *The British Weekly*, 17 November 1921, 145–46.
O'Siadhail, Micheal. "Out of the Blue." In *Poems 1975–1995: Hail! Madam Jazz and A Fragile City*, 124. Newcastle: Bloodaxe, 1999.
Owen, Wilfred. *The Collected Letters of Wilfred Owen*. Edited by Harold Owen and John Bell. Oxford: Oxford University Press, 1967.
Pascal, Blaise. *Pensées*. Translated by W. F. Trotter. London: Dent, 1908.
Peterson, Eugene H. "Foreword." In *The Soul of Prayer* by P. T. Forsyth, 2–5. Vancouver: Regent College, 2002.
Picton, J. Allanson. *Sir James A. Picton: A Biography*. London: Isbister, 1891.
———. *Spinoza: A Handbook to the Ethics*. London: Constable, 1907.
Pitman, Emma Raymond. *Lady Missionaries in Foreign Lands*. 3rd ed. London: Partridge, 1889.
Pitt, Clifford S. *Church, Ministry, and Sacraments: A Critical Evaluation of the Thought of Peter Taylor Forsyth*. Washington, DC: University Press of America, 1983.
Price, A. Whigham. "W. Robertson Nicoll and the Genesis of the Kailyard School." *Durham Journal* 86 (1994) 73–82.
Ritschl, Dietrich. *A Theology of Proclamation*. Richmond: John Knox, 1960.
Rodgers, John H. *The Theology of P. T. Forsyth: The Cross of Christ and the Revelation of God*. London: Independent, 1965.
Seeley, John Robert. *Natural Religion*. London: Macmillan, 1882.
Selbie, William Boothby. "Tributes to the Late Rev. Principal Forsyth, D.D." *The British Weekly*, 17 November 1921, 153.
Sell, Alan P. F. *Christ and Controversy: The Person of Christ in Nonconformist Thought and Ecclesial Experience, 1600–2000*. Eugene, OR: Pickwick Publications, 2012.
———. "P T Forsyth: Theologian for a New Millennium?" In *P T Forsyth: Theologian for a New Millennium*, edited by Alan P. F. Sell, 237–59. London: The United Reformed Church, 2000.
———. *Testimony and Tradition: Studies in Reformed and Dissenting Thought*. Aldershot, UK: Ashgate, 2005.
Shortt, Rupert. *Rowan Williams: An Introduction*. Harrisburg, PA: Morehouse, 2003.

Simpson, A. F. "P. T. Forsyth: The Prophet of Judgment." *Scottish Journal of Theology* 4 (1951) 148–56.

Stafford, Hugh. "Letter." *Baptist Times*, 3 June 1948, 8.

Stephenson, D. J. G. "Letter." *The British Weekly*, 31 January 1907, 22.

Sykes, Stephen W. "Theology through History." In *The Modern Theologians: An Introduction to Christian Theology in the Twentieth Century*, edited by David F. Ford, 229–51. Oxford: Blackwell, 1997.

Thielicke, Helmut. *Notes from a Wayfarer: The Autobiography of Helmut Thielicke*. Translated by David R. Law. New York: Paragon, 1995.

Thompson, David Michael. *Cambridge Theology in the Nineteenth Century: Enquiry, Controversy and Truth*. Aldershot, UK: Ashgate, 2008.

———. "Nonconformists at Cambridge Before the First World War." In *Modern Christianity and Cultural Aspirations*, edited by David Bebbington and Timothy Larsen, 176–200. London: Continuum, 2003.

Torrance, Thomas F. *The Christian Doctrine of God, One Being Three Persons*. Edinburgh: T. & T. Clark, 2001.

Updike, John. *Higher Gossip: Essays and Criticism*. Edited by Christopher Carduff. New York: Knopf, 2011.

Waddington, Norah. *The First Ninety Years*. Leicester, UK: Clarendon Park Congregational Church, Leicester, [1975].

Wiersbe, Warren. "Theologian for Pastors." *Moody Monthly*, May 1975, 97–101.

Williams, Rowan. *On Christian Theology*. Challenges in Contemporary Theology. Oxford: Blackwell, 2000.

———. *Resurrection: Interpreting the Easter Gospel*. London: Darton, Longman & Todd, 1982.

———. *The Wound of Knowledge: Christian Spirituality from the New Testament to St. John of the Cross*. 2nd ed. Cambridge: Cowley, 1991.

Williams, T. Charles. "A Tribute from Wales, by the Rev. T. Charles Williams, M.A." *The British Weekly*, 17 November 1921, 154.

Yeago, David S. "The New Testament and the Nicene Dogma: A Contribution to the Recovery of Theological Exegesis." In *The Theological Interpretation of Scripture: Classic and Contemporary Readings*, edited by Stephen E. Fowl, 87–100. Blackwell Readings in Modern Theology. Cambridge, MA: Blackwell, 1997.

Name Index

Abbott, Edwin A., 146
Abel, 190
Abiram, 95
Abraham, 87, 95, 97, 143, 185, 207, 307–8
Adeney, Walter Frederic, 164n1
Aeschylus, 84, 119
Ahaz, 197
Aitken, William Hay Macdowall Hunter, 149
Amos, Prophet, 32
Anderson, Marvin W., xiii, 33
Andrews, Herbert T., 32
Andrews, Jessie F., 8n26, 9–10, 17, 19–20, 32–33, 61n234, 64n245
Anselm of Canterbury, Saint, 50
Armitage, E., 164n1
Arnold, Matthew, 50, 77, 132, 159–60, 334
Athanasius, Saint, 36
Auden, W. H., 6n19, 65
Augustine, Saint, 23, 212, 274, 348n4, 354n3

Barr, Browne, 3–4, 33
Barth, Karl, 3, 5, 25, 28–29, 35, 41, 48
Barth, Markus, 27
Bates, William, 9
Beaumont, Margaret, 12n36
Bebbington, David W., 60n227
Beethoven, Ludwig van, 274–75
Bennett, William Howard, 164n1, 259
Berkeley, George, 105n1
Bernard of Clairvaux, Saint, 65
Besant, Walter, 162
Beth, Karl, 35–36

Binfield, Clyde, 11–12n36, 60n225
Bishop, John, 61n235
Black, John, 7
Blake, William, 10
Bonaparte, Napoleon, 187, 192, 219
Bonhoeffer, Dietrich, 3n9
Boniface, Saint, 212
Bowring, John, 18
Bradley, William L., 21
Bray, Caroline ("Cara"), 155
Brooke, Stopford Augustus, 159
Brooks, Phillips, 6n19
Brown, James Baldwin, 8–9, 100n4
Brown, Robert McAfee, 33
Browning, Robert, 50, 61, 82n5, 116n3, 119–20, 122, 128, 129n14, 159, 162, 173, 209n4, 272, 326n3, 330
Bruce, Alexander Balmain, 348
Buddha, Gautama, 77
Bultmann, Rudolf Karl, 48
Bunsen, Christian Karl Josias, 50
Burder, Henry Forster, 9
Burke, Edmund, 195n6, 263n2, 314
Burne-Jones, Edward, 14
Burns, Robert, 52
Butler, Joseph, 50, 334n1
Buttrick, George A., 6n19
Byron, Lord (George Gordon), 84, 125n8

Calvin, John, 33, 41, 64n246, 210
Camfield, F. W., 60n226
Campbell, J. Robertson, 8
Campbell, Reginald J., 11n35, 20
Carey, William, 221

365

Name Index

Carlyle, Thomas, 50, 132, 215n7
Carter, Dean, 19n60
Chalmers, Thomas, 323
Channing, William Ellery, 316n5
Charlemagne (Charles the Great), 271
Chaucer, Geoffrey, 102
Child, R. L., 63n239
Clark, William, 315n1
Cleopatra, 108
Clifford, John, 62
Clive, Robert, 221
Clough, Arthur Hugh, 278n3
Coleridge, Samuel Taylor, 225n1
Columba (Colum Cille), Saint, 212
Comte, Auguste, 243
Cranach, Lucas, 23
Cromwell, Oliver, 70–71, 219
Cunliffe-Jones, Hubert, 33n113

Dale, Robert W., 6n19, 27, 50, 62
Dante (Durante degli Alighieri), 65, 119, 162–63, 181, 248
Darlow, T. H., 59n215, 59nn218–19
Dathan, 95
David, King, 308
Davidson, Patrick, 7
Davison, William Theophilus, 18
Dekker, Thomas, 338n1
Demosthenes, 58
Denney, James, 26n86, 50, 59–60
Dibelius, Martin, 48
Dickens, Charles, 162
Disraeli, Benjamin, 69–70
Dodd, Charles Harold, 48
Doddridge, Philip, 21n69
Donne, John, 65
Dorner, Isaak August, 50
Dostoyevsky, Fyodor Mikhaylovich, 52
Due, Noel, xiv

Elijah, Prophet, 95, 312
Eliot, George, 50, 81n4
Eliot, T. S., 2, 65
Emerson, Ralph Waldo, 166, 324
Enoch, 95, 97
Epictetus, 321

Escott, Harry, 22n70, 33n113, 61n230, 63n241
Euripides, 119
Ezekiel, Prophet, 40, 50, 204, 210, 213

Fairbairn, Andrew M., 6n19, 18, 22n69, 27–28, 50
Farmer, Herbert Henry, 6n19
Fielding, Henry, 293n5
Forde, Gerhard O., 46n167
Forsyth, Isaac, 6
Franks, Robert S., 21n69

Garvie, Alfred E., 21n69
Gascoyne-Cecil, Robert A. T., 193
Gaunt, Alan, 26
Gee, Maurice, 5
Gideon, 305, 355
Giffen, Robert, 112n1
Glover, Richard, 17
Glover, T. R., 17–18
Goethe, Johann Wolfgang von, 50, 119, 121n3, 182n2, 261, 277nn1–2
Goodwin, Thomas, 21n69
Gore, Charles, 18
Goroncy, Jason A., 20n66, 28n104, 36n130, 50n183, 50n185, 51n187, 52n189, 53n194, 53n195
Gosse, Edmund W., 253n13
Grant, W., 6
Greenwell, Dora, 50
Gregory of Nyssa, Saint, 24
Grieve, A. J., 21
Griffith, Gwilym O., 22n72, 62
Grützmacher, Richard, 35–36
Gunton, Colin E., 23n74, 61

Hall, Robert, 137
Hamann, Johann Georg, 182n1
Hamilton, John Arthur, 8n25, 11
Handel, George Frideric, 12
Hardy, Thomas, 50, 52, 281–82
Häring, Theodor, 36n125
Harnack, Adolf von, 50
Hart, Trevor A., 26n84
Hastings, James, xiii
Hegel, Georg W. F., 7, 23, 50, 165

Name Index

Heine, Christian Johann Heinrich, 92n3
Henry, Matthew, 9
Herbert, George, 65
Herod, 245
Heschel, Abraham Joshua, 59
Hezekiah, King, 197–98
Higginson, R. E., 33n113
Holland, Henry Scott, 18
Homer, 119
Hopkins, Gerald Manley, 61
Horne, Silvester, 62
Horton, Douglas, 3
Horton, Robert Forman, 164n1
Houghton, W. S., 17
Hughes, Hugh Price, 62
Hunt, William Holman, 14
Hunter, Archibald M., 33n113, 47n172
Hunter, John, 7
Huxley, Aldous Leonard, 147
Huxtable, W. J. F., 6

Ibsen, Henrik, 50
Ihmels, Ludwig, 50
Isaac, 307–08
Isaiah, Prophet, 197–200
Ison, Bertha, 19

Jackson, George D., 47–48n172
Jacob, 61
Jeremiah, Prophet, 132, 311
John, Saint, 78–79, 99, 136, 240, 274, 294, 296
John of the Cross, Saint, 24
John the Baptist, 46, 285, 342
Johnson, Mark D., 8n27
Jones, Edgar DeWitt, 6n19, 60n224
Jones, Frank F., 19, 47
Judas Iscariot, 84, 339

Kaftan, Theodor, 35–36
Kähler, Martin, 35, 50
Kant, Immanuel, 7, 50, 88, 166, 251
Keats, John, 123n6, 273n3, 340n1
Keble, John, 91n2
Kempis, Thomas à, 137n2
Keynes, Neville, 17

Kierkegaard, Søren, 50, 61, 64
Korah, 95
Lang, Cosmo Gordon, 18
Larter, C. E., 9
Law, William, 50
Lawrence, Eric A., 164n1
Lessing, Gotthold Ephraim, 23, 50
Lewis, C. S., xvii, 2
Lischer, Richard, 48
Loofs, Friedrich Armin, 50
Luther, Martin, 23, 43, 46, 48, 50, 154, 210, 270, 281, 318

MacDonald, George, 254n14
MacKinnon, Donald M., 65
Mackintosh, Robert, 21n69
Maclaren, Alexander, 62
Magdalen, Mary, 273
Magness, Maria Hester (Minna), 8, 16–17
Manning, Bernard Lord, 20
Marlowe, Christopher, 314n2
Martha of Bethany, 346, 348
Martineau, James, 76n1
Mary of Bethany, 281, 346, 348
Mary, The Virgin, 166–68
Matthew, Saint, 228, 230, 234
Maurice, Frederick, 22
Maurice, Frederick Denison, 8, 22–23, 50, 76
McKay Jr., Clifford A., xiii
McPherson, Elspet, 6
Melville, Herman, 29
Meredith, George, 157, 158n1, 271, 314
Meyer, Heinrich August Wilhelm, 348n4
Mill, John Stuart, 186
Miller, Donald G., 33n113
Miłosz, Czesław, 5
Milton, John, 50, 65, 70–71, 119, 159n3, 162–63, 261, 272, 306n2, 339
Moberly, Robert Campbell, 18
Moses, 181, 331
Morgan, Campbell, 20
Mozley, John Kenneth, 24, 25n81, 33n113

Name Index

Muhammad (Mahomet), Prophet, 77
Myers, Frederick W. H., 317n1

Nero, Emperor, 84, 206
Newman, John Henry, 50, 76n1, 210
Newth, Samuel, 8
Nicodemus, 342
Nicoll, W. Robertson, 9, 45, 59
Niebuhr, Reinhold, 6n19
Nietzsche, Friedrich Wilhelm, 50, 221

O'Siadhail, Micheal, 40
Owen, John, 21n69
Owen, Susan, 39n138
Owen, Wilfred, 39n138

Palestrina, Giovanni Pierluigi da, 270
Palmer, Samuel, 9
Paracelsus, 326
Parker, Joseph, 62
Pascal, Blaise, 50, 126
Paul, Saint, 28, 32–33, 50, 55, 58, 63, 79, 87, 89, 98–99, 101, 131–32, 136, 139, 154, 173, 183–84, 209–10, 212, 230, 233, 240, 246, 255, 260, 273, 281, 294, 296–97, 304, 308, 320, 325–27, 331, 335–37, 350, 354
Paul, Robert S., 33n113
Payne, George, 22n69
Peter, Saint, 230, 264, 279, 294
Peterson, Eugene H., 61
Philip II of Macedon, 58
Picton, James Allanson, 9, 11–12n36
Picton, James Allanson, Sr., 11n36
Pilate, Pontius, 221, 245
Pitman, Emma Raymond, 346n2
Pitt, Clifford S., 24n76, 33n113
Plato, 88, 173
Leo XIII, Pope, 270
Price, A. Whigham, 59n216

Raleigh, Thomas, 164n1
Raphael (Raffaello Sanzio da Urbino), 273
Renan, Ernest, 266
Ritschl, Albrecht, xiv, 7, 50
Ritschl, Dietrich, 65

Rodgers, John H., 43n155
Rossetti, Dante Gabriel, 14
Rossetti, Christina Georgina, 340n1
Rothe, Richard, 35
Ruskin, John, 50

Salmond, Stewart D. F., 18
Sanday, William, 18
Schelling, Friedrich Wilhelm Joseph, 50
Schiller, Friedrich, 275
Schlatter, Adolf, 50
Schleiermacher, Friedrich D. E., 23, 50
Schopenhauer, Arthur, 50, 113–14
Schreiner, Olive, 162
Schubert, Franz Peter, 15
Seeberg, Reinhold, 35–36, 50
Seeley, John Robert, 126
Selbie, William Boothby, 38, 39n137, 62
Sell, Alan P. F., 21n69, 24n80, 64
Sennacherib, King, 198
Shakespeare, William, 119, 128, 308, 351
Shelley, Percy Bysshe, 84, 121n4
Shorter, Clement, 59n216
Shortt, Rupert, 65n251
Simon, David Worthington, 22n69
Simpson, A. F., 33n113
Smith, George Adam, 6n19
Smith, William Robertson, 7, 8n22
Southey, Robert, 127n11
Spencer, Herbert, 112, 162
Spinoza, Baruch de, 9
Spurgeon, Charles Haddon, 62
Stafford, Hugh, 62–63
Stafford, Mary Helen, 12n36
Stead, F. Herbert, 164n1
Stephenson, D. J. G., 59n221
Strauss, David Friedrich, 162
Stumpf, Carl, 7
Swinburne, Algernon Charles, 159
Sykes, Stephen W., 49n176

Taylor, Peter, 6
Tennyson, (Lord) Alfred, 10, 84n7, 88n1, 102, 119–23, 128, 159

Name Index

Thackeray, William Makepeace, 162n6
Thielicke, Helmut, 64
Thurneysen, Eduard, 29n105, 35
Thomas, H. Arnold, 164n1
Thomas, R. S., 65
Thompson, David Michael, 17n50, 17n54
Thompson, George, 6
Tolstoy (Tolstoi), Leo, 251
Torrance, Thomas F., 61
Troeltsch, Ernst, 50
Turner, Joseph Mallord William, 50

Updike, John, 10

Victoria, Queen, 192

Waddington, Norah, 12n40, 15–16,

Wagner, Wilhelm Richard, 10, 14, 116n4, 271, 274
Waller, Edmund, 319n1
Ward, Mary Augusta, 162
Watts, George Frederic, 14
Watts, Isaac, 21, 163
Wesley, John, 210, 270
Whittier, John Greenleaf, 85n8
Wiersbe, Warren, 28n102
Wilberforce, William, 71
Williams, Rowan, 2n4, 24
Williams, T. Charles, 32, 45, 61n234
Wolseley, Garnet Joseph, 193
Wordsworth, William, 114n2, 159–60, 162, 193n5, 230n3, 316, 325

Yeago, David S., 43n155

Zacchaeus, 234
Zahn, Theodor, 50

Scripture Index

OLD TESTAMENT

Genesis
1:31	109–18
25:8–9	95

Exodus
15	15

Deuteronomy
6:20–21	216n9

1 Kings
8:18	308n2

2 Chronicles
6:8	308n2

Job
3:18–19	96n2
7:10	96
10:22	96n1
17:6	96
26:6	96
30:24	96

Psalms
6:5	95
24:1	352n2
32:8	327–28
32:8–9	263n1
49:8	96
55:6	311–12
62:12	75–85
73:24	95–96
73:28	346n1
119:94	170
119:95–96	169–77
130:1	315–16
139:8	169n1
146:3	330–31

Ecclesiastes
1:9	265n4
1:14	109–18
9:10	95

Isaiah
5:19	199n1
11:6	156n6
14:9	96n3
19:24	106
28	198
28:23–26	197–203
28:28	203
40–66	197
40:31	342n1
54:7–8	83n6
60:22	178–96

Scripture Index

Jeremiah
9:2	311–12
48:40	312n1
49:22	312n1

Ezekiel
36:22	204n1

37:2	205n2
37:3–13	204–23
37:13	209n6, 216n8

Amos
5:19	279n4

APOCRYPHA

Wisdom of Solomon
3:2	97

Sirach (Ecclesiasticus)
2:18	286n2, 332–33

NEW TESTAMENT

Matthew
6:9–10	220n10
6:11–12	233n4
6:12	227–38
6:14–15	228
6:18	304n2
6:23	315n2
7:21	305–6
11:27	242n4
11:28	239–54
11:28–29	138n3
13	261–62
13:51–52	259–69
15:17	264n3
16:23	279n5
18:3	153n3
19:9	264n3
25:10	283n1

Mark
1–16	15, 228
8:17	264n3
8:33	279n5
12:43–44	344–45

14	338
14:3	338–39
14:50	240n1

Luke
1–24	228
2:7	224–26
7:47	229n1
10:20	339n2
10:22	242n4
10:41–42	346–48
11:2	220n10
11:4	228
11:9	263n2, 313–14
17:10	321–22
18:13	321n2
22:27	8

John
3:4	342–43
3:16	23
4:23	248n9
7:17	209n5
11:21	347n3

Scripture Index

11:32	347n3
13:10	233n5
14:8	354n4
15:4–7	240n2
16:33	323n2
17:6	352–55

Acts
12:19	18
22:11	323–24

Romans
1:16–17	23
5:1	246n8
5:8	235n7
8	18
8:28	334–35
8:38–39	177n4
10:1	99

1 Corinthians
1:30	255, 257
4:1	40, 349–51
12:21	209n3, 281n6
13	305n1

2 Corinthians
3:6	131
4:17–18	319–20
5:18–19	23
5:19	28
5:20	248n10
12:10	86–93

Galatians
2:20	256n1

Ephesians
4:32	230n2

Philippians
1:21	325n1

3:12	336–37
4:4	303–4

Colossians
1:27	252n11

1 Timothy
3:15	329
4	317
4:7	317–18

2 Timothy
4:7	325–26

Titus
3:14	140

Hebrews
10:10	158n2
11:17–19	307–8

1 Peter
2:17	69–74
4:19	309–10

2 Peter
3:4	199n2

1 John
1:1–3	65
2:15	323n1
4:4	316n3, 336n1
4:10	235n6

Revelation
2:28	41, 340–41
3:20	239–54

www.ingramcontent.com/pod-product-compliance
Lightning Source LLC
Chambersburg PA
CBHW071239300426
44116CB00008B/1095